m

FOURTH EDITION

Criminal Law
and the Canadian Criminal Code

Richard Barnhorst, B.A., LL.B.

Sherrie Barnhorst, B.A., LL.B.

McGraw-Hill
Ryerson

Toronto Montréal Boston Burr Ridge, IL Dubuque, IA Madison, WI
New York San Francisco St. Louis Bangkok Bogotá Caracas
Kuala Lumpur Lisbon London Madrid Mexico City Milan
New Delhi Santiago Seoul Singapore Sydney Taipei

McGraw-Hill
Ryerson

Criminal Law and the Canadian Criminal Code
Fourth Edition

ISBN: 0-07-090599-1

4 5 6 7 8 9 10 TCP 0 9 8 7 6

Printed and bound in Canada

Vice President, Editorial and Media Technology: Patrick Ferrier
Executive Sponsoring Editor: James Buchanan
Marketing Manager: Sharon Loeb
Developmental Editor: Sandra de Ruiter
Production Coordinators: Kelly Selleck/Mary Pepe
Supervising Editor: Anne Nellis
Copy Editor: James Gladstone
Cover Designer: Dianna Little
Cover Image Credit: © Garry Gay/The Image Bank
Formatter: Brian Lehen • Graphic Design Ltd.
Printer: Transcontinental Printing Group

National Library of Canada Cataloguing in Publication

Barnhorst, Richard, 1947-
    Criminal law and the Canadian criminal code / Richard Barnhorst, Sherrie
Barnhorst. — 4th ed.

Includes index.
ISBN 0-07-090599-1

    1. Criminal law—Canada. 2. Canada. Criminal Code. I. Barnhorst, Sherrie, 1948- II. Title.

KE8809.C57 2003   345.71   C2003-900732-4
KF9220.ZA2C57 2003

CONTENTS

Chapter Five: Pre–trial Criminal Procedure 97

PART TWO CRIMINAL CODE OFFENCES 141
Chapter Six: Jurisdiction and Public Order, Firearms, and Other Offences 143

4

4

Chapter Seven: Sexual Offences, Public Morals, and Disorderly Conduct 171

Chapter Eight: Soliciting and Procuring, Disorderly Houses, Betting, and Lotteries 193

Chapter Nine: The Offences of Murder, Manslaughter, and Infanticide 211

Chapter Ten: Criminal Negligence and Legal Duties 235

Chapter Eleven: Offences Involving Motor Vehicles 250

Chapter Twelve: Assaults and Related Offences Against the Person 272

Chapter Thirteen: Offences Against Property Rights 314

Appendix A: Narcotic and Drug Offences 376

Appendix B: Youth Criminal Justice Act 386

PREFACE TO THE FOURTH EDITION

The fourth edition of *Criminal Law and the Canadian Criminal Code*, like earlier editions, has been written for people who want to understand the principles of criminal law and the offences in the Criminal Code. This book will be useful to students in programs related to criminal justice, and to police officers, security personnel, probation officers, parole officers, criminologists, law clerks, and others involved in the criminal justice system.

This new edition is necessary to incorporate the changes that have been made to the criminal law since the publication of the third edition. The 546 cases and all sections of the Criminal Code that are in the third edition have been checked and updated. The changes include amendments to the Criminal Code as well as new statutes: the Controlled Drugs and Substances Act, which replaced the Narcotic Control Act, and the Youth Criminal Justice Act, which replaced the Young Offenders Act on April 1, 2003. The new edition includes cases that overrule caselaw found in the third edition as well as cases that rule on areas of criminal law that have not previously been addressed by the courts.

The format of the book is unchanged. Chapters One to Five cover basic principles of criminal law. The elements of offences and principles for establishing criminal liability are discussed. Pre-trial criminal procedure and general defences are discussed.

Chapters 6 to 15 are concerned with Criminal Code offences. Code sections are reproduced and elements of the offences are identified. Case decisions that interpret sections of the Code are provided to help in understanding how the sections have been applied to fact situations.

Additional features of the book are the two Appendices, the Glossary, and the Table of Cases. Appendix A deals with drug offences in the Controlled Drugs and Substances Act. Appendix B explains the major features of the new Youth Criminal Justice Act. The Glossary defines terms that have been boldfaced in the text. The Table of Cases provides an alphabetical listing of cases in the book for easy reference.

We would like to sincerely thank the reviewers of the manuscript whose comments and insights helped to ensure accuracy and quality of the text. They include:

Norm Bruce	*Algonquin College*
Paul Groarke	*St. Thomas University*
Randy Knapp	*Sir Sandford Fleming College*
Dianna McAleer	*Algonquin College*
Marie Murphy	*John Abbott College*
David Osborne	*Langara College*
Dave Patterson	*Grant MacEwan Community College*
Lynne Scott	*Durham College*
Brent Seaton	*Loyalist College*
Kwong-Leung Tang	*University of Northern British Columbia*
Larry White	*Mohawk College*

We would also like to thank Ann McNaughton, a lawyer who provided legal research assistance for the fourth edition. Ann's research work was excellent and was invaluable to us in preparing this new edition of the book.

Richard Barnhorst, B.A., LL.B., J.S.D.
Sherrie Barnhorst, B.A., LL.B., LL.M.

ABBREVIATIONS USED FOR CASE REPORT PUBLICATIONS

Note: In general, the report series Canadian Criminal Cases (C.C.C.) is used in this text. Cases are often reported in more than one series, so if C.C.C. is not available to you, check other case report series to find a case referred to in the text.

All E.R.	All England Reports (English)
Alta. L.R.	Alberta Law Reports
C.C.C.	Canadian Criminal Cases
Cox's C.C.	Cox's Criminal Cases (English)
C.R.	Criminal Reports
Cr.App.R.	Criminal Appeal Reports (English)
C.R.N.S.	Criminal Reports New Series
D.L.R.	Dominion Law Reports
E.R.	England Reports
M.P.R.	Maritime Provincial Reports
M.V.R.	Motor Vehicle Reports
N.S.R.	Nova Scotia Reports
O.R.	Ontario Reports
Sask.R.	Saskatchewan Reports
S.C.R.	Supreme Court Reports
W.C.B.	Weekly Criminal Bulletin

TABLE OF CASES

Part One
THE CRIMINAL LAW

Chapter One
AN INTRODUCTION TO LAW

A. THE NATURE OF LAW

Before looking at criminal law, we first consider the nature of the law in more general terms. Let us start with a definition: law is the body of rules that regulates the conduct of members of society and is recognized and enforced by the government. There are, of course, many rules regulating our conduct that are not part of the law. For example, the rules of a private club regarding the duties of club members are not part of the law. Likewise, the moral values that govern a person's conduct are not part of the law, although moral convictions and legal rules often overlap. These types of rules are not rules of law for two basic reasons: first, they are not officially recognized by the government as laws applying to all members of society; and second, their violation does not involve a penalty or other legal consequence imposed by the government.

1. Functions of Law

The above definition, although suitable for our purposes, does not indicate the wide range of functions served by the law. The law not only tells us what are our rights, privileges, and obligations, but also determines the structure of our government and assigns duties and powers to its various branches. The law even tells us how and by whom laws are to be made. An example of a law-making law is the Constitution Act, 1867 (formerly the B.N.A. Act, 1867). This statute creates our federal system of government. It divides the authority to make law on various subjects between the federal parliament and provincial legislatures. For example, certain areas, such as property and education, are given exclusively to the provinces. Therefore, a federal law on the topic of provincial schooling, for example, would be ***ultra vires,*** or beyond the scope of the federal government's authority. A statute that is *ultra* *vires* is not enforceable. In the same way, if a province enacts a law that touches an area given to the federal government by the Act, that law is also *ultra vires* and unenforceable.[1]

2. Classes of Law

There are two main classes of law: public and private. Public law consists of the rules that govern the relations among various branches of the government, and between the government and private citizens. The main types of public law are constitutional law, criminal law, and administrative law. Private law—or *civil law,* as it is also known—consists of the rules governing the relations between private persons or groups. Types of private law include contract law, which consists of the rules for making legally enforceable agreements; property law, which includes the rules for how to own or pass on property; and *tort law,* which is the law regarding *civil wrongs.*

3. Substantive and Procedural Law

Each class or type of law consists of substantive rules and procedural rules. Substantive rules of law describe our rights and duties; for example, the substantive part of the criminal law prohibits certain forms of conduct from which society has a right to be protected. Procedural law tells us how the substantive law can be enforced—that is, how our rights can be protected and our wrongs redressed. Thus, the rules that must be followed when an arrest is made are part of the law of *criminal procedure.* Whether an accused has a jury trial or not is also a matter of procedure. The following chapters are primarily concerned with substantive law; their focus is on defining and discussing specific criminal offences. However, they also cover some areas of criminal procedure. In the next chapter, procedural matters, such as the classification of offences and methods of trial are examined. Chapter Five discusses other topics of procedure, such as the powers of arrest and search.

B. SOURCES OF CANADIAN LAW

1. Common Law and Civil Law

There are two major systems of law in the Western world today—common law and civil law. Most English-speaking countries have a *common law* system. Notice that the term "civil law" has two meanings. It may refer to civil or private law, which was discussed earlier, or it may refer to the system of law that is used by many continental European countries. Except for Quebec provincial law, which operates under the civil law system, Canadian law is part of the common law tradition.

The civil law system is the older of the two. Its beginnings are traced back to the law of the Romans. In the sixth century, the emperor, Justinian, com-

---

1   Conversely, if a law is within the authority of the government that made it, it is *intra vires.*

piled a code or book of law that contained all of the great Roman laws. This code became the law in those parts of Europe under Roman control. After the Roman Empire collapsed, many of Europe's peoples continued to use Justinian's Code, or laws derived from it. In the early nineteenth century, Napoleon established a similar code, which was later adopted by many European countries. The Napoleonic Code also greatly influenced the authors of the Quebec Civil Code.

Between about 55 B.C. and A.D. 412, England was occupied by the Romans and, naturally, Roman law was used. In the fifth century, various Anglo-Saxon tribes invaded Britain, and the Romans were forced to withdraw. These invasions largely erased the influence of Roman law in England. For many centuries after the Romans left, diverse tribes and groups who had little contact with one another occupied England. Each community had its own law based on its own traditions and customs. There was no body of law that could be called English law.

It was not until William, the Duke of Normandy, conquered England in 1066 that a unified England started to evolve. One of William's first tasks was to establish a central government for the purpose of controlling his new land. Part of the strong central government developed by William and his successors consisted of a royal court system. Under this system, the king's judges travelled through the country holding court in large villages and trading centres. Each judge's route was called a circuit, and court sittings were known as assizes.

These early judges were in the difficult position of not having a set of rules or a code of law to guide them in their decisions. Sometimes Norman law was used, at other times local law. Often, neither was appropriate so the judges had to rely on their common sense and base their decisions on what seemed to them principles of justice and fairness. Eventually, the judges began discussing among themselves the cases they had heard and the decisions they had made. Gradually, it became a practice of the judges to follow decisions made in earlier cases if the same or similar facts were involved. In other words, rather than rely solely on their own judgment, judges thought back to previously decided cases. If they found one that matched (or was very similar to) the case presently being heard, they made the same decision as was made in the earlier case. Of course, the facts in one case were often not the same or even very similar to the facts in other cases, so the judges could not always find a case to follow. However, each time a decision was made in a particular situation, it created a *precedent,* or example, to be followed in future cases. The principle that was emerging was that like cases should be treated alike. Even today, we accept this principle as a basic rule of justice.

Once accurate written reports of cases became available to judges in the sixteenth and seventeenth centuries, it became much easier for judges to follow precedent. By the nineteenth century this practice had become a strict and binding rule called *stare decisis,* which means literally "to stand by." Today, judges in Canada still follow precedent. What this means, generally speaking, is that lower courts must follow the decisions of higher courts, and that courts of equal rank should try to follow one another's decisions, if at all possible.

By the process of making decisions in case after case, guided by the rule of precedent, the early English judges created a body of law that applied to all the people in England. This law was then common to all—hence, the "common law." Since the common law consists of the decisions of judges in particular cases, it is sometimes called *case law.*

Today, however, Canadian law also includes many statutes. So although Canada is called a "common law country," it has both case law and statute law as well as administrative law (discussed below).

2. Statute Law

Another way to make law is to pass a statute or an act that contains all the rules on a particular subject. As mentioned earlier, the Constitution Act, 1867, divides the authority to make *statute law*—which is also called legislative law—between the federal parliament and the provincial legislatures. Municipalities, which receive their law-making authority from the provinces, make a type of legislative law. Municipal laws are called by-laws.

In Canada, statute law always (with one exception) has priority over case law. This means that if there is a conflict between a court decision and a statute, the statute will overrule the court decision. In fact, judges are obligated to apply statute law where it exists, regardless of what the case law is on the same topic. This principle is called the *supremacy of parliament* rule. The exception to this rule (discussed later in this chapter) relates to cases where the Charter of Rights and Freedoms applies.

Statutes do not always conflict with case law. Sometimes statutes only codify the case law—that is, all the principles of law that are contained in a number of cases are put into one statute. Statutes may also clarify an area that is left unclear by case law. There are also statutes that are concerned with modern topics that have never been dealt with by case law. However, there are still large areas of law in the form of case law that have never been the subject of a statute and are still being developed by the courts. For example, much of the law of evidence, which consists of the rules for presenting evidence in court, is still in case law form.

An important point to mention is that the judges' law-making function does not end once an area is put into statute law. Statutes often need interpreting, and this task becomes the responsibility of the courts. The interpretations given to statutes in turn become part of the law. Why do statutes need interpreting? First, because they usually contain only general rules, there may be questions as to how the general rules apply to specific situations. Second, legislators, like all other people, do not always communicate clearly. Even when a statute seems quite straightforward, it may still be possible to read in more than one meaning. In either situation, the judge becomes the final interpreter and must decide what the legislators intended when they enacted the statute. Judges have several approaches available when interpreting a phrase (or word) in a statute. They look at the dictionary meaning of the words and at the context within which the words are used in the statute. They look for any interpretive aids in the statute itself, such as a preamble or headings. They may consider the French version of the statute, since the phrase in French may have a clearer meaning. They examine previous decisions to see how other courts have interpreted the phrase. They also try to determine the policy behind the law—to establish what the law is trying to achieve and what its practical applications are. An example of a case where a phrase had to be interpreted by the Supreme Court of Canada is *R. v. Lohnes*.[2] The accused was charged with causing a disturbance under s.175 of the Code. The section states:

175. (1) Every one who

(a) not being in a dwelling-house, causes a disturbance in or near a public place,

(i) by fighting, screaming, shouting, swearing, singing or using insulting or obscene language, . . .

is guilty of an offence . . .

The accused's neighbour complained that he had shouted obscenities at him, and a charge was laid. The case eventually reached the Supreme Court of Canada, which had to decide whether causing a disturbance meant causing emotional upset and annoyance, or whether it meant that the conduct interfered with the public's normal activities. In interpreting the phrase "causing a disturbance," the Court looked at the dictionary meaning of disturbance, which suggests that it is an interference with ordinary use or conduct. Within the context of the statute, the Court found that by referring to a public place, Parliament seemed to be saying that its objective was to protect the public, not from emotional upset, but from disorder calculated to interfere with normal activities. The Court also noted that s.175 appears under the heading Disorderly Conduct, which again indicates that Parliament had in mind not emotional upset but disorder that interferes with the ordinary use of a place. The Court looked at the French version of s.175, where the word used for disturbance is *tapage*, which connotes a disturbance involving violent noise or confusion disrupting the tranquillity of those in the area. In examining earlier cases, the Court found that the overwhelming majority of decisions stated that the conduct must cause an interference with the public's use of the place. In terms of policy, the Court stated that it would be unjust to expect persons to determine whether their conduct will be disturbing to the emotions of others. Fundamental justice requires that people know in advance whether their conduct is illegal. Also, the Court noted, there is a need to balance the right of persons to have peace with the right of others to express themselves, and this favours a definition of "disturbance" that requires more than emotional upset. The Court's conclusion was that, taking together all of these factors, a disturbance, under s.175, is conduct that caus-

---

2   *Lohnes v. The Queen* (1992), 69 C.C.C. (3d) 289 (S.C.C.).

es more than emotional upset. The accused was acquitted because there was no evidence that there was a disturbance in the use of the premises by the complainant.

3. Administrative Law

Administrative law is a growing source of law created by the executive branch of government. It consists largely of regulations made by members of federal and provincial cabinets and of the decisions made by administrative boards and tribunals. For example, the decisions of Ontario's Workers' Compensation Board in determining the eligibility of an injured worker for compensation form part of administrative case law. Administrative law is not generally concerned with criminal law.

C. THE CANADIAN CHARTER OF RIGHTS AND FREEDOMS

1. An Overview

In 1982, when the Constitution was repatriated, an important addition was made to it: the *Canadian Charter of Rights and Freedoms.* The Charter not only consolidated existing rights but also created new rights and freedoms for Canadians. Although this part of the Constitution applies generally to all areas of public law, it has special relevance to criminal law.

The Bill of Rights, which also sets out rights and freedoms, has been the law since 1960. However, because it is not a part of the Constitution, courts have hesitated to use it to overturn legally enacted legislation. The Constitution Act, 1982, makes it quite clear that courts are in certain situations no longer bound by the principle of supremacy of parliament. Section 52(1) states:

> **52. (1) The Constitution of Canada is the supreme law of Canada, and any law that is inconsistent with the provisions of the Constitution is, to the extent of the inconsistency with the provisions of the constitution, of no force or effect.**

The Charter of Rights and Freedoms sets out certain individual rights and freedoms that cannot be infringed upon by the government. Since the government acts through statute law, the Charter limits the legislative authority of the government. If a court finds that a statute violates a right or freedom protected by the Charter, the court will rule that the statute is unenforceable.

There are two important limitations to our rights and freedoms, however. The first is set out in s.1 of the Charter, which states:

1. The Canadian Charter of Rights and Freedoms guarantees the rights and freedoms set out in it subject only to such reasonable limits prescribed by law as can be demonstrably justified in a free and democratic society.

In other words, a court may find that although a statute violates the Charter, it is a *reasonable limitation* of our rights. For example, most provinces today have laws that allow the police to randomly stop cars to check for drunk drivers. These laws have been challenged as a violation of our right to be free from *arbitrary detention.* The Supreme Court of Canada has held that these laws do violate our right to be free from arbitrary detention, but that the laws are justified because they are attempting to control the social evil of drunk driving.[3] Another example relates to the law that prohibits the making and distribution of "obscene material." In *R. v. Butler,*[4] the Supreme Court of Canada held that this is a reasonable limitation on the right of freedom of expression. For such a limitation to be justifiable, (a) the objective of the law (e.g., controlling drunk driving or restricting the distribution of pornography) must be shown to be of sufficient importance to justify overriding a right or freedom, and (b) the law itself must be reasonable and demonstrably justifiable in a free and democratic society.[5]

The second limitation is in s.33, which allows a legislative body to pass a law that violates certain rights and freedoms if certain procedures are followed. It states:

33. (1) Parliament or the legislature of a province may expressly declare in an Act of Parliament or of the legislature, as the case may be, that the Act or a provision thereof shall operate notwithstanding a provision included in section 2 or sections 7 to 15 of this Charter.

This section is referred to as the *notwithstanding* or *override clause.* To override the Charter, the statute itself must state that the Charter does not apply. The statute will be valid for only five years. After that time, it must be reenacted. Also, the override clause can only be used for certain rights. Some rights and freedoms are absolutely protected—for example, our right to vote.

2. Rights and Freedoms Covered in the Charter

Examples of the rights and freedoms to which all Canadians are entitled are illustrated in the following table:

---

3   *R. v. Hufsky* (1988), 40 C.C.C. (3d) 129 (S.C.C.).
4   *R. v. Butler* (1992), 70 C.C.C. (3d) 129 (S.C.C.).
5   The test for determining whether a law is a reasonable limitation is discussed in more detail in Chapter Two at page 28.

Table 1–1
EXAMPLES OF RIGHTS AND FREEDOMS IN THE CHAPTER

TYPE OF RIGHT/FREEDOM	EXAMPLES
Fundamental freedoms	Freedom of conscience, religion, thought, belief, opinion, and expression; freedom of peaceful assembly and association.
Democratic rights	The right of Canadian citizens to vote or to run for office.
Mobility rights	The right of Canadian citizens to enter, remain in, and leave Canada, and the right of Canadian citizens and permanent residents to live and work in any province of Canada.
Equality rights	The right to be treated equally before and under the law; the right to the equal protection of the law and benefit of the law without discrimination—in particular, without discrimination based on race, national or ethnic origin, colour, religion, sex, age, or mental or physical disability.

The Charter also protects the two official languages of Canada: French and English.

The Charter has special importance to criminal law. To enforce the law, protect the public, and prosecute offenders, police and others in the criminal justice system are given certain powers to interfere with individual liberty. For example, the powers to search and make arrests are significant infringements of personal freedom. The Charter sets out the rules of procedure and the limitations on the authority given to law enforcement personnel.

The most important rights for criminal law are the legal rights set out in ss. 7 to 14.

Section 7 states:

> **7. Everyone has the right to life, liberty and security of the person and the right not to be deprived thereof except in accordance with the principles of fundamental justice.**

This is a general statement that a person cannot be denied life, liberty, or security of the person unless the principles of *fundamental justice* are followed. It applies to procedural as well as to substantive laws. The Supreme Court of Canada has said that the principles of fundamental justice are to be found in the basic tenets of our legal system and that it is up to the courts to develop the limits of these tenets.[6] In other words, the courts will decide on

---

6   Reference re Section 94(2) of the Motor Vehicle Act (1985), 23 C.C.C. (3d) 289 (S.C.C.).

a case-by-case basis whether a tenet of fundamental justice is being violated. For example, in *R. v. Hebert,*[7] the Supreme Court held that the right of the accused, once detained, to remain silent during the investigative stage of an offence is a principle of fundamental justice. This right was violated when the police placed an undercover agent in a cell with the accused, who then made incriminating statements to the agent. Also, the Supreme Court held recently that a provincial law that imposed a minimum seven-day sentence on a person who was driving with a suspended licence, even though the person had not been aware that his licence had been suspended, violated a principle of fundamental justice in that it imprisoned a person who had not really done anything wrong.[8] Another principle of fundamental justice is that people have a right to know in advance what conduct is prohibited. This means that a vague law that does not give fair notice to people of the conduct being prohibited is *void.*[9]

Sections 8 to 14 relate to specific situations involving the deprivation of life, liberty, or security of the person.

Sections 8, 9, and 10 concern pre-trial procedure and are discussed in Chapter Five.

Sections 11, 12, 13, and 14 are related to trial procedure and are discussed in Chapter Two.

D. FINDING THE LAW

1. Statute Law

The official government press publishes statutes. Usually, all the statutes (or Acts) passed in one legislative session are contained in one volume. Every 15 years or so, all the statutes are revised and consolidated into one set of volumes. Parliament then repeals the former statutes and enacts as law the newly revised ones. Revisions are necessary mainly to correct any errors in the original statutes and to incorporate any subsequent amendments. The last revision of the federal statutes was made in 1985. Thus, a law first passed in 1983 is found in the 1985 revised statutes. Each Act is given a separate chapter number and is listed alphabetically. A statute passed in 1986 is found in the sessional volume for that year. Statutes in the sessional volumes are usually listed in order of enactment. At the back of each sessional volume is a Table of Public Statutes that lists the Acts by title or subject matter. These tables are very useful for locating statutes and checking for amendments.

The titles of the volumes are often referred to in abbreviated form. Revised statutes are abbreviated R.S. followed by the initial(s) of the province, or by a C for Canada. If a sessional volume is referred to, the R is dropped. Next, the year of enactment is given. Thus, R.S.C. 1985 means "Revised Statutes of Canada enacted in 1985." If a particular statute is men-

7   *R. v. Hebert* (1990), 57 C.C.C. (3d) 1 (S.C.C.).
8   Supra, note 6.
9   Ref. Re ss. 193 and 195.1(2) of the Criminal Code (1990), 56 C.C.C. (3d) 65 (S.C.C.).

tioned, its chapter number is given after the year. Statutes are divided into sections. If a section is referred to, an "s." followed by the section number is written after the chapter number. For example, Criminal Code R.S.C. 1985, c. C-34, s.1.

Figure 1–1
READING A CASE CITATION

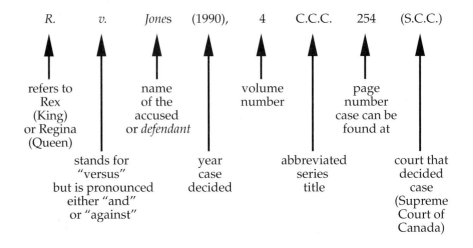

2. Case Law

There are many different series of case reports, including national, regional, and provincial series. Some case reports are official publications; others are printed by private publishing companies. Only the more important cases are contained in these reports. Most likely to be reported are cases that involve appeals, or set precedents, or concern unclear areas of law. Not everything that has occurred in a case is reported. Usually, only the judge's written decision—which often includes a recital of the facts and the reasons for the decision—is reported. If more than one judge has heard the case (an appeal court often has more than one judge sitting), and there is a ***dissenting opinion,*** this opinion is included in the report. A dissenting opinion results when the judges who have heard the case fail to reach a unanimous decision. In such a situation, the decision agreed to by a majority of the judges becomes the official decision of the court. The decision of the minority becomes the dissenting opinion. The court's decision is often referred to as the ***"holding" in the case.*** Similarly, a reference may be made to what the judge (or court) "held" in a case.

The case series most frequently referred to in the following pages are Canadian Criminal Cases, abbreviated C.C.C., and Criminal Reports, abbreviated C.R. At the beginning of this textbook is a table, "Abbreviations Used for Case Report Publications," that provides the names and the accepted abbreviations of all series mentioned.

To locate a case, you must be able to read case citations. Figure 1–1 on page 12 indicates the form used for citing cases and the meaning of each element of the citation.

Notice that the first name given in the case is Rex (King) or Regina (Queen), which indicates that the state or Crown is proceeding against (prosecuting) the accused. If the court's decision is appealed to a higher court, the name of the appellant (the party appealing) is given first, followed by the name of the respondent (the party responding).

Questions for Review and Discussion

1. Define the term "law."

2. **a.** Why are the rules of a private club not considered law?
   b. Describe other types of rules that govern our conduct, but are not laws.

3. What are some functions served by the law? Think of specific functions not mentioned in the chapter.

4. **a.** What are the two main classes of law?
   b. Define each class.

5. **a.** What is the difference between substantive law and procedural law?
   b. Indicate whether the following are procedural or substantive laws:
   (i) The legal definition of murder.
   (ii) The law that states how a search warrant is obtained.
   (iii) The law that requires the appeal of a court decision to be made within a certain time limit.

6. **a.** Explain the origins of the common law system.
   b. Why is this system called the common law system?

7. **a.** Explain the operation of the rule of stare decisis.
   b. What is a precedent?

8. Explain the two ways judges make laws:
   a. When a statute is involved.
   b. When there is no statute involved.

9. **a.** What does the rule "supremacy of parliament" mean?
   b. Explain how the Charter of Rights and Freedoms affects the principle of supremacy of parliament.

10. What are the two limitations on our Charter rights and freedoms?

11. Why does the Charter have special relevance to criminal law?

12. Discuss whether the Charter should include an override clause.

13. Discuss whether our rights and freedoms should be subject to reasonable limitations.

14. Write a paragraph explaining what s.7 of the Charter of Rights and Freedoms means. Include an example of a person being denied fundamental justice.

15. How should the following statutes be abbreviated?
    a. Criminal Law Amendment Act, 1990, Chapter 13, Statutes of Canada.
    b. Canada Evidence Act, Revised Statutes of Canada, 1985, Chapter C-5.

16. What should the citations be for the following cases?
    a. The Crown attorney prosecuted John Smith. The decision of the court was reported in Canadian Criminal Cases, the fifth volume, at page 305. The trial was held in 1984, in the province of New Brunswick before a provincial court judge.
    b. After being found guilty, Smith appealed the decision of the court to the province's Court of Appeal. The decision of the appeal court was reported in Volume 12 at page 305 of Canadian Criminal Cases. The appeal was heard in 1986.
    c. In 1988, the Crown prosecuted Sharon Brown in the Court of Queen's Bench in Manitoba. The decision of the court was reported in Volume 7 of Criminal Reports at page 46.

17. **a.** What is a "holding" in a case?
    b. What is a "dissenting opinion"?

Chapter Two
AN INTRODUCTION TO CRIMINAL LAW

A. THE NATURE OF CRIMINAL LAW

1. A Wrong Against Society

Most crimes have victims. However, crimes are also wrongs committed against society as a whole. When the crime rate goes up, everyone feels less secure and the whole community suffers. Individuals may actually change their activities if they believe that the streets are no longer safe. Therefore, the primary aims of the criminal law are to protect the public and to preserve the peace. Ensuring that our community is safe and secure is a duty carried out by the government through the police, the courts, and the correctional system.

2. The Distinction Between Criminal and Civil Wrongs

As mentioned previously, the civil law governs the interactions among private persons. For example, the law of contract sets out the rules that must be followed before an agreement between private parties will be enforced by the courts.

A breach of a civil rule of law is considered a civil wrong. Many civil wrongs are also criminal wrongs. For example, if Alex is accused of taking Yaman's car without her permission, Alex may have committed both the criminal offence of theft and the civil offence of trespass to goods. This civil wrong is a type of offence called a tort. Very briefly, torts are acts (or omissions) that all people have a duty to refrain from committing against other people. The usual remedy a victim of a tort may seek through a civil proceeding is compensation for the loss he or she has suffered. Thus, in the above example, Alex may be prosecuted (proceeded against) in a criminal court; and if convicted (found guilty), he may be sentenced to a suitable punishment. If Alex is found not guilty, he is ***acquitted*** and the criminal charge dismissed. If Yaman wishes to seek a civil remedy, she must sue (or proceed against) Alex in a civil court. If Yaman is successful against Alex, she is awarded compensation (usually money). If she is not successful, judgment is given in favour of Alex.

In the early days of the English law, little distinction was drawn between a civil wrong and a criminal wrong. If a person or the person's property was injured, either that person or the person's family sought revenge. Consequently, blood feuds between families were common, although the community might attempt to encourage the victim to accept compensation in the form of money.

At the same time, the idea of the king's peace was becoming established. The king could put certain people or property under his protection. Any-one who injured the persons or property being protected by the king had to pay the king a money fine. Some offences were so serious that a fine was inadequate. In such cases, the offender's "life and limbs" were at the king's mercy. Gradually, the king extended the area of his peace until it encompassed all the territory and persons under his rule. Since any wrong was an offence against the king, breaches of the peace came to be prosecuted by the king's agents in the name of the king.

Today, ***Crown attorneys*** (i.e., prosecutors), who are the agents of the federal or provincial Attorney General, undertake most prosecutions. A person appointed by the executive branch of the government occupies the Attorney General's office. This person's role is to act as the government's legal adviser and counsel. In a few situations, a private individual can prosecute a criminal offence. These private prosecutions are discussed in the section on the classification of offences.

Two important differences between civil and criminal wrongs should be emphasized. First, where a possibility of a civil action exists, the community has no interest in whether the victim decides to go to court. However, where a crime has occurred, it is usually the Crown attorney's decision whether or not to prosecute, even if the victim would rather not take any steps against the offender. Second, an important aim of the criminal law is to punish convicted offenders—typically, by fine or imprisonment. However, the civil law generally only permits a victim to be compensated for actual losses from the wrongdoer.

B. CRIMINAL LAW IN CANADA

1. Jurisdiction

The authority to enact criminal legislation is assigned to the federal government by the Constitution Act, 1867. This encompasses the authority over criminal offences and procedure. This means that the criminal law concerning what is a crime and how the criminal law is enforced is the same throughout Canada.

Other areas concerned with criminal law—that is, with the police, courts, and correctional facilities—are shared by the federal and provincial governments. For example, the RCMP is a federal police force; however, some provinces have their own police force (or have given municipalities the authority to set up municipal police forces). Also, the provinces are authorized by the Constitution to organize courts of criminal jurisdiction, but the federal government appoints and pays the salaries of superior court judges. As well, the federal government maintains the Supreme Court of Canada. The federal government runs federal penitentiaries for offenders who receive sentences of two years or more. The provinces are responsible for maintaining prisons and reformatories for federal offenders sentenced to less than two years, as well as for provincial offenders.

Although all crimes are federal offences, the provinces have the power to impose punishment by fine or imprisonment to enforce provincial laws æ- in other words, to create provincial offences. Provincial offences are similar to crimes, particularly because of the types of punishment possible. For example, a person may be imprisoned for violating a provincial law. Also, the court procedure can be similar, and even the same courtrooms may be used, with trials before provincial court judges. However, crimes are more serious than provincial offences. The offences we think of as crimes, such as assault, theft, and murder, are federal crimes. Provincial offences include violations under consumer protection legislation—for example, false advertising, violations of laws intended to protect the environment, and liquor control offences. There are areas where provincial and federal offences overlap—for example, driving offences. The provinces have the authority to regulate the use of streets and highways; therefore, every province has a statute that creates driving offences, such as speeding and illegal turns. The federal government created the more serious offences of impaired driving and dangerous driving, because of the serious harm that motor vehicles may cause. Provincial offences are sometimes referred to as quasi-criminal offences.

2. Sources of Canadian Criminal Law

The main source of both substantive and procedural criminal law in Canada is the Criminal Code. This federal statute was first enacted in 1869. At that time, it attempted to consolidate the English common law crimes applicable to Canada with the colonial laws. A significant addition was made in 1953 by what is now s.9, which states that no person can be convicted of an offence at common law, except for criminal contempt of court. This section was necessary to make it clear whether a person could be convicted of a common law offence that was not in the Code. However, s.8(3) of the Code preserves all common law defences. Thus, for example, the law regarding the defence of necessity has developed through case law.

Although the focus of this textbook is on the Criminal Code, there are many other federal statutes that create criminal offences. One of these, the Controlled Drugs and Substances Act is discussed in Appendix A.

C. THE CRIMINAL CODE

1. Structure

The Code contains both substantive and procedural rules. Substantively, it defines offences and sets out penalties for offences. Procedurally, it states the rules for making arrests, conducting searches, holding trials, and appealing court decisions.

The official Criminal Code is found in Chapter 34 of the 1985 Revised Statutes of Canada. Subsequent sessional volumes must be checked for amendments. Most people use one of the commercial versions of the Criminal Code that are published yearly. These versions incorporate all the amendments to the Code as of the date of publication. Generally, then, only one book is needed for finding the law. Most commercial publishers of the Code also send updates of new Code amendments to purchasers during the year. Of course, for the most up-to-date version of the criminal law, other resources would need to be consulted. The *Canada Gazette,* a weekly government publication, publishes new legislation as soon as it receives Royal Assent.

The Code is divided into 28 parts. Each part is divided into numbered sections, which may include subsections. Section 2 of the Code is very important, in that it defines certain words used in the Code. For example, the term "highway" is defined to include bridges (tunnels) that roads pass over (through). "Dwelling-house" is defined as any whole or part of a building or structure used as a permanent or temporary residence. Section 2 also gives the names of the courts in each province. For example, in Prince Edward Island the "court of appeal" is called the Appeal Division of the Supreme Court.

Part I starts with section 4 (or s.4) and covers general principles. For example, sections 8 and 9 (or ss. 8 and 9), which concern common law offences and defences, are in Part I. In s.19 is stated the important principle that ignorance of the law is not an excuse for committing a crime. Part I also contains the rules regarding parties to offences and attempted crimes.

Parts II through XIII define offences and penalties. Similar offences are placed in the same Part. For example, Part VIII contains offences against the person and reputation, such as murder, assault, dangerous driving, and defamatory libel. Parts XIV through XXIII deal with procedural matters, such as the rules for holding a *preliminary inquiry,* which is a hearing held before the trial for certain offences. Part XXIII contains rules governing the imposition of punishment—fines, imprisonment, probation, and so on. Part XXIV sets out the procedure for declaring a person a dangerous offender. Part XXV deals with *recognizances,* which are promises the accused makes to appear in court when being released to await trial. Part XXVI deals with the application of extraordinary remedies, such as habeas corpus, a hearing to decide if the detention of a person is legal. Part XXVII sets out the trial procedure for summary conviction offences. Part XXVIII contains various forms used in the criminal process, such as search warrants and indictments.

Commercial versions of the Code are often annotated. Codes that are annotated list and briefly describe important cases that interpret and apply each section. Annotated codes are useful, since the Code, like other statutes, is constantly being interpreted and applied by the courts.

2. Classification of Offences

The Code divides offences into three categories: *indictable offences;* offences punishable upon summary conviction; and *hybrid* or *dual-procedure offences.* Generally speaking, the difference between the first two is that indictable offences are more serious than summary conviction offences. Examples of indictable offences are murder, kidnapping, and robbery. Causing a disturbance in or near a public place and loitering on private property at night are summary conviction offences. A hybrid or dual procedure offence may be tried as either an indictable or a summary conviction offence. Examples of hybrid offences are theft of property valued at $5000 or less and mischief to property valued at more than $5000. The decision on how to treat a hybrid offence is made by the Crown attorney, usually at the time of the *arraignment* (which is when the judge reads the charge to the accused, who is then asked to enter a plea of guilty or not guilty). The Crown bases its decision on facts, such as whether the offender has a previous record of law breaking, and the circumstances surrounding the commission of the offence (e.g., whether violence was involved). Until a decision is made, a hybrid offence is treated like an indictable offence. If for some reason the Crown does not make a decision, the charge will be tried as a summary conviction offence if it reaches trial.

D. TRYING SUMMARY CONVICTION AND INDICTABLE OFFENCES

Summary conviction and indictable offences are treated differently before and during the trial. The penalties that can be imposed are also different. Differences in the trials of indictable and summary conviction offences are discussed below. Further comparisons are made in Chapter Five, where powers of arrest and search are discussed.

1. Summary Conviction Offence Trials

Part XXVII of the Code describes the procedure to be used for the trial of offences punishable upon summary conviction. Section 788 states that before a court proceeding (i.e., the trial) can begin, an information in Form 2 must be laid. This means that the informant must swear, under oath, in an affidavit, that he or she has either personal knowledge or *reasonable grounds* for believing that a certain person has committed an offence. The information is then signed by the informant and a justice of the peace. If the accused is not personally present and not represented by counsel or agent, the justice of the peace can issue an ***arrest warrant*** for the accused, or a ***summons*** that orders the accused to appear in court on a certain date. The accused does not have to appear personally; instead, an agent or lawyer can appear on his or her behalf.

Although informations are usually laid by police officers, any person may lay an information. A private person can prosecute a summary conviction offence if the Crown does not. A police officer can also be authorized to prosecute cases. However, Crown attorneys prosecute most offences.

Section 786 provides that the proceedings must begin (i.e., the information must be laid) no later than six months after the offence is alleged to have occurred unless the law provides otherwise. This means that there is a six-month limitation period on starting the prosecution of most summary conviction offences. In general, there is no limitation period for indictable offences.

Trials of summary conviction offences are held before "summary conviction courts" as defined in s.785. Usually, the trials are held before a provincial court judge or justice of the peace. Jury trials are not held in summary conviction proceedings. Similarly, preliminary inquiries are never held. A preliminary inquiry is a hearing that takes place before the trial to determine whether there is enough evidence to commit the accused to trial. This hearing is used only for certain indictable offences.

After the information is laid, and with both the accused (or the accused's agent or ***counsel***) and the ***prosecutor*** present, the accused is arraigned. The procedure used for arraignment is set out in s.801. It provides that the substance of the information must be stated to the accused, who is then asked to enter a plea of guilty or not guilty. If the accused pleads guilty, the court enters a conviction. If the accused pleads not guilty or refuses to plead, the court enters a not guilty plea and proceeds with the trial. At the trial, the prosecutor presents evidence; the accused may present evidence in defence. Both parties also have an opportunity to cross-examine each other's witnesses and to give summing-up statements to the court. Once the court has heard the evidence and statements presented by the prosecutor and the accused, it decides whether to convict the accused or dismiss the information.

Where the accused is convicted, the penalties that may be imposed are limited by s.787. This section provides that, unless the law states otherwise, a person who is convicted of a summary conviction offence is liable to a fine of up to $2,000 and/or imprisonment for not more than six months.

2. Indictable Offences

a. Origins of the Procedure

Starting in the twelfth century, the English method for bringing suspected criminals to justice was through the presenting of an indictment by a grand jury. The jury consisted of members of the local community whose duty it was to report all suspected crimes committed by their neighbours to the king or his agent. This report, which accused certain persons of specific crimes, was called an indictment. Originally, the jurors based their reports on their own personal knowledge. Gradually, as the jury system evolved, the grand jurors became persons without direct knowledge of the crime, who based their report upon the testimony of witnesses to the offence.

A grand jury system was used in some parts of Canada until recently. The *Attorney General,* or someone authorized by him or her, or by the court, would prefer (i.e., present) a bill of indictment before a grand jury. The jury then heard the testimony of witnesses called by the prosecutor. The accused and his or her counsel were not allowed to be present during the hearing—in fact, the proceedings were conducted in complete secrecy. One reason for the secrecy was to protect the reputations of innocent persons falsely accused of crimes.

After hearing the evidence presented by the prosecutor, the jurors decided whether there was enough evidence to send the accused to trial before a judge and jury. If a majority of the jurors decided that there was enough evidence for a trial, the foreman of the jury endorsed the indictment with the words "true bill." If a majority of the jurors decided that there was insufficient evidence for a trial, the indictment was endorsed "no bill."

Today, the Attorney General, or his or her agent, or someone with his or her consent, or with the consent of the court (e.g., a private person), prefers the written indictment before the court. This means, in effect, that the Attorney General or his or her agents are performing the functions previously performed by the grand jury.

b. Preliminary Inquiries

Grand juries were abandoned partly because preliminary inquiries serve the same function of disposing of weak cases without the time and expense of a full trial. Preliminary inquiries take place before the indictment is preferred and just after the accused is charged with an offence. Depending on the province, preliminary inquiries are usually held before a provincial court judge or justice of the peace. The main purpose of the hearing is to determine whether there is enough evidence to commit the accused to trial. During the hearing, the prosecutor presents evidence through the testimony of witnesses. The accused has a right to present evidence and to make a statement on his or her own behalf. Both parties can cross-examine each other's witnesses. After considering the evidence, the justice or provincial court judge decides whether to commit the accused to trial. That an accused is committed to trial does not mean the justice or judge has found him or her guilty. Being committed to trial after a preliminary inquiry simply means that there is "sufficient evidence" to hold a trial.

Preliminary inquiries permit the accused to hear the nature and judge the strength of the Crown's case. In this way, from the perspective of the accused, preliminary inquiries are preferable to the grand jury system.

The relevant Code sections on preliminary inquiries are ss. 535 to 551.

c. Methods of Trial

There are three methods of trial for indictable offences: by provincial court judge; by a judge without a jury; and by a judge and jury.

Some offences in the Code are within the absolute jurisdiction of the provincial court judges (i.e., judges appointed by the province; other judges who try criminal offences are appointed by the federal government). A judge and jury must try other offences. For most offences, however, the accused can elect the method of trial—that is, choose a provincial court judge, a judge alone, or a judge and jury. However, the accused may lose the right of election where the offence being charged is punishable by more than five years' imprisonment. In this situation, the Attorney General under s.568 may require the accused to be tried by judge and jury.

Section 553 lists the indictable offences that are within the absolute jurisdiction of the provincial court judges, in that the accused cannot choose another method of trial. Strictly speaking, other courts with criminal jurisdiction can try these offences (see s.468 and s.469). These are the less serious indictable offences, such as keeping a common gaming house, bookmaking, and betting; and hybrid offences, such as theft of subject matter that does not exceed $5,000 in value. These offences are tried in the same way as summary conviction offences, in that a formal indictment is not necessary and preliminary inquiries are not held.

Section 469 lists the indictable offences that must be tried in the province's superior court of criminal jurisdiction. This court is the province's highest-ranking trial court with criminal jurisdiction. Section 2 gives the name of the superior criminal court for each province. Generally, it is called the Supreme Court or the Court of Queen's Bench. In Quebec, it is called the Superior Court; in Ontario it is called the Superior Court of Justice. Generally, all trials of s.469 offences are before superior criminal courts and are by judge and jury. The one exception is that the accused and the Attorney General may jointly consent to the case being tried by a superior criminal court without a jury. This exception is set out in s.473.

The offences contained in s.469 are considered the most serious offences. They include treason, sedition, piracy, and murder.

All other indictable offences in the Code are electable except where (as mentioned above) the Attorney General can require a trial before judge and jury. An accused who elects trial by judge without a jury is tried by a judge as defined for each province in s.552. Until recently, some provinces had a middle level of court, called county or district court, which could try these electable offences. However, today, all of the provinces have only two levels of trial court—a court of criminal jurisdiction and a superior court of criminal jurisdiction. In general, the judges listed in s.552 are all superior or Supreme Court judges.

Part XIX of the Code, which starts with s.552, describes the procedure to be used where the trial is without a jury and before either a judge or a provincial court judge.

An accused who elects trial by judge and jury is tried by a superior court of criminal jurisdiction.

Unlike summary conviction offence proceedings, the accused must be personally present for the trial of an indictable offence (unless the court orders otherwise). In brief, during the trial each party calls its own witnesses, who give evidence under oath. Each party also has a right to cross-examine the other party's witnesses. After both the accused and the prosecutor finished presenting evidence, each has the right to sum up the evidence and make closing arguments to the jury (if there is one) or to the judge.

If the trial is before a jury, the judge sums up the case for the jurors. He or she instructs them on questions of law and may express an opinion regarding the credibility of witnesses or the importance of the evidence.

The jury, if there is one, returns a verdict of guilty or not guilty. If the trial is before a judge only, the judge makes the finding of guilty or not guilty. Depending on the verdict, the accused is either convicted or acquitted by the court. If the verdict is guilty, the judge sentences the accused to a punishment.

The possible penalties for indictable offences are much harsher than those for summary conviction offences. The Code sets out maximum terms of imprisonment for each offence, such as life, 14 years, 10 years, 5 years, or 2 years. In a few situations, the Code sets out a minimum punishment that must be imposed if the accused is convicted. For example, section 235 states that the minimum sentence for murder is life imprisonment. Usually, however, the judge can choose a sentence up to the maximum term set out in the Code. So, for example, a first offender is usually sentenced to far less than the maximum allowed. Section 734 allows the court to impose fines in addition to, or instead of, imprisonment if there is no minimum term of imprisonment required. If the offence is punishable by more than five years' imprisonment, the fine cannot be in lieu of, but only in addition to, a term of imprisonment.

E. THE CHARTER AND THE RIGHTS OF THE ACCUSED AT TRIAL

The Charter of Rights and Freedoms did not create all new rights. Some of our rights, such as the *presumption of innocence,* have a long history in English common law. The Charter has, however, given the courts new authority to examine legislation and to expand and further define our rights and freedoms. Section 11 of the Charter lists the rights and freedoms that apply to criminal trials. Below we look at each of the rights and at some of the more important decisions the courts have made in applying this section. Section 11 states:

11. Any person charged with an offence has the right

(a) to be informed without unreasonable delay of the specific offence;

The purpose of this paragraph is to ensure that the accused person knows the substance of the allegation so that a full defence can be made to it. It applies not only to criminal but also to quasi-criminal (e.g., provincial) offences, and whenever the accused is subject to penal consequences (i.e., a fine or imprisonment).[1]

(b) to be tried within a reasonable time;

The Supreme Court of Canada, in *R. v. Askov*,[2] made a decision that had far-reaching effects on the court system in Canada. In November 1983, the accused were charged with several offences, including conspiracy to commit extortion and assault with a weapon. One of the accused was released on a recognizance in December; the others were held until May, when they were released on recognizances. Although there were several court appearances for the accused, for various reasons the trial date was put off until September 1985, almost two years after the charges were laid. At that point the defence counsel asked that the proceedings be stayed because the delay breached the accused's right to a trial within a reasonable time. The Supreme Court of Canada agreed with the defence and ordered that the proceedings be stayed.[3] The Court found that most of the delay was a result of systemic problems in the particular court district. Courts were overburdened, with a backlog of cases. There was, as the trial judge noted, a chronic shortage of courtrooms and judges, with the result that long delays were common. The Court compared this court district to others in Canada and described it as one of the worst. For example, a comparable court district in Montreal had a median delay of 82.5 days compared with this district's median delay of 607 days. It concluded: "Justice so delayed is an affront to the individual, to the community, and to the very administration of justice. The lack of institutional facilities cannot in this case be accepted as a basis for justifying the delay."[4]

The Court set some general guidelines for determining whether a delay violates the Charter. It said that six to eight months should be the outside

---

1   *Wigglesworth v. The Queen* (1987), 37 C.C.C. (3d) 385 (S.C.C.).
2   *R. v. Askov* (1990), 59 C.C.C. (3d) 449 (S.C.C.).
3   When proceedings are stayed, the information that commences the proceedings is withdrawn. The Crown can stay proceedings under s.579 of the Code. Proceedings that are stayed are suspended. The Crown has one year from the time that the proceedings were stayed to recommence the proceedings. After that time, the proceedings are deemed to have never commenced and the Court will not allow the Crown to lay a new information. Courts also have the authority to direct a stay of proceedings to prevent an abuse of process where the Crown is acting oppressively. For example, proceedings were stayed in *Askov* because of the abuse of process caused by the lengthy delay in trying the accused.
4   *Supra*, note 2 at page 490.

limit in most cases from the time of committal for trial (after the preliminary inquiry) to the trial itself. Factors a court should take into account in deciding whether the delay is reasonable include:

- Length of the delay: The longer the delay, the more likely it is unreasonable.
- Reasons for the delay: This includes the inherent time requirement for preparing the case, actions of the Crown, actions of the accused, and delays caused by inadequate resources.
- Waiver: If the accused consents to a delay, it must be a fully informed and freely given consent.
- Prejudice to the accused: This includes the stress and loss of privacy during the delay, as well as factors, such as being subject to restrictive bail conditions or possible loss of evidence. There is an inference that a very long delay will unfairly prejudice the accused.

The immediate result of *Askov* was the staying of proceedings in up to 50,000 cases that were awaiting trial. The decision forced provincial governments to take steps to remedy problems caused by lack of resources.

Decisions since *Askov* have clarified and softened the effect of this case. In *R. v. Morin*,[5] the accused was charged with impaired driving on January 9, 1988. She first appeared in court on February 23, 1988. The trial date was set for March 28, 1989. On this date, her counsel asked that the charge be stayed because of the 14.5-month trial delay. The counsel's motion was dismissed and she was convicted. The Ontario Court of Appeal upheld her conviction. The Supreme Court of Canada dismissed her appeal, emphasizing that the *Askov* decision does not set out a mathematical formula to be followed when deciding whether a delay is unreasonable; rather, it requires a judicial balancing of the interests protected by s.11(b) against the causes of the delay. The Court also suggested that comparisons of court districts should be used cautiously, because the length of time that is reasonable is influenced by local conditions and practices. In this case, the Court suggested that an 8- to 12-month delay before the trial was appropriate. Therefore, a delay of 14.5 months raised the issue of reasonableness. However, when all the factors were considered, the delay was not unreasonable. A case of this type should take two months to prepare. Thus, the actual delay was 12 months. Given the significant growth in the area where the case was to be tried, a 10-month delay could be allowed. Since there was no evidence of prejudice to the accused, a two-month deviation was justified.

The Court also distinguished cases like *Askov*—that is, two-stage trials involving preliminary inquiries—from this case, in which the charge was a summary conviction offence. The Court stated that the *Askov* guideline for institutional delay after committal for trial should remain at six to eight months, while the guideline for cases tried in provincial court should be eight to ten months (the longer period being justified because of the greater caseload carried by provincial courts).

---

5   (1992), 71 C.C.C. (3d) 1 (S.C.C.).

In *R. v. Potvin,*[6] the Supreme Court of Canada clarified that s.11(b) does not apply to delay in hearing an appeal.

In *R. v. Collins,*[7] the Supreme Court of Canada dealt with a case where the delay was caused by Crown errors rather than by institutional delays. The Court ordered that murder charges be stayed where a two-year delay was caused by the Crown's indifference and tardiness in disclosing its case to the defence. The accused had pressed for an earlier trial date and had spent nearly two years in jail waiting for trial.

> **(c) not to be compelled to be a witness in proceedings against that person in respect of the offence;**

This paragraph can be considered with s.13:

> **13. A witness who testifies in any proceedings has the right not to have any incriminating evidence so given used to incriminate that witness in any other proceedings, except in a prosecution for perjury or for the giving of contradictory evidence.**

Section 11(c) ensures that an accused person has a *right to remain silent* and the right not to give self-incriminating evidence at his or her trial. Section 13 protects the accused at subsequent proceedings. For example, assume that Henry is convicted at trial and appeals the conviction and that the appeal court orders a new trial. The Crown cannot use Henry's testimony from the first trial to prove his guilt in the second trial.

> **(d) to be presumed innocent until proven guilty according to law in a fair and public hearing by an independent and impartial tribunal.**

This is one of our oldest and most important rights. It means that the accused does not have to prove that he or she is innocent; rather, the Crown has the burden of proving the accused's guilt. It is consistent with the right to remain silent. The fact that a person is charged with an offence does not mean that the person has committed the offence; all it means is that the police or Crown have reasonable grounds for believing that the accused committed the offence. The person is presumed innocent until the Crown proves otherwise in a court of law.

The prosecution's burden of proof is to establish the accused's guilt *beyond a reasonable doubt.* This means that, if at the end of the trial, the judge or jury has a reasonable doubt as to the guilt of the accused, the accused must be found not guilty. *Reasonable doubt* has been explained as follows: "real doubt . . . which an honest juror has after considering all the circumstances of the case and as a result of which [the juror] is unable to say: I am morally certain of his guilt. Moral certainty does not mean absolute certainty."[8]

The doubt must be based on the evidence given at the trial. It is not necessary for the Crown to disprove every possible defence to the charge; but if

---

6   (1993), 83 C.C.C. (3d) 97 (S.C.C.).
7   (1995), 99 C.C.C. (3d) 385 (S.C.C.).
8   *R. v. Sears* (1947), 90 C.C.C. (3d) 159 at 163 (Ont.C.A.).

the accused does raise a defence that is supported by some evidence, the Crown must disprove the defence beyond a reasonable doubt. Where the Crown must prove that the accused intentionally did an act, the Crown can rely on the presumption that he or she intended the natural consequences of the act. Thus, if Harriet fires a gun at John, a judge or jury may, but not must, presume that she intended to wound him.

The burden of proof in a criminal trial is much higher than in a civil trial. In a civil trial, the plaintiff must prove his or her case on a balance of probabilities—that is, prove that it is more likely than not that the *plaintiff's* claim is true. (The plaintiff is the person claiming an injury.) For example, Anne claims that Boris negligently drove a car and caused damage to her car. She sues Boris for the cost of repairing the car, as well as for any other expenses incurred because of the accident. She must prove that it was more likely than not that Boris drove his car in a negligent manner and caused damage to her car. It is not necessary for her to prove Boris's negligence beyond a reasonable doubt. However, if Boris is charged with dangerous driving, the prosecution must prove beyond a reasonable doubt that Boris committed each element of the offence. The different burdens of proof used in criminal and civil trials can have this interesting result: a person may be acquitted of the criminal charge, because the prosecutor fails to prove the case beyond a reasonable doubt, but found liable by a civil court, because the liability can be proved using the lower burden of proof.

Although the burden of proving that the accused committed the offence is on the prosecutor, some Criminal Code offences contain *"reverse onus clauses."* A reverse onus clause shifts part of the burden of proof to the accused. Similar to a reverse onus clause is a *mandatory presumption,* where a fact is presumed to exist unless the accused can prove otherwise. Since the enactment of the Charter, many of these clauses have been found to be violations of the Charter, and thus unenforceable. For example, in *R. v. Oakes,*[9] the accused was charged under the Narcotic Control Act with possession of narcotics for the purpose of trafficking (i.e., selling). Section 8 of the Act states that, once the Crown has proved possession, the burden shifts to the accused to prove on a balance of probabilities that he or she did not possess the drugs for the purpose of trafficking. The Supreme Court of Canada held that s.8 offends s.11(d) of the Charter because a judge could convict an accused of trafficking even if the judge had a reasonable doubt about whether the drugs were possessed for the purpose of trafficking. In other words, the accused, to avoid conviction, had to disprove on the balance of probabilities the existence of a presumed fact—that he or she had possession for the purpose of trafficking.

Although reverse onus provisions and mandatory presumptions offend the presumption of innocence, it is possible to uphold these provisions as reasonable limitations on a right under s.1 of the Charter. The Supreme Court in

---

9   (1986), 24 C.C.C. (3d) 321 (S.C.C.).

Oakes laid out the test for deciding whether a clause is a reasonable limitation. The first criterion the court must consider is whether the objective of the law is of sufficient importance to warrant overriding a right. At a minimum, the objective must relate to concerns that are pressing and substantial in a free and democratic society. For example, in *Oakes* the objective of the law was to control trafficking in narcotics. Second, the law in question must be reasonable and demonstrably justified. This second criterion involves a proportionality test: to decide whether the law is reasonable and demonstrably justified, the court should ask three questions. First, is the law carefully designed to achieve its objective? That is, is the law rationally connected to the objective and not unfair or arbitrary? Second, does the law impair the right as little as possible? And third, is the effect of the law on the right in proportion to the importance of the objective? In other words, the more serious the impairment of the right, the more important the objective must be.

The Supreme Court in *Oakes* held with regard to the first criterion that the objective of protecting society from the ills associated with drug trafficking is sufficiently important to override a Charter right. However, s.8 failed the proportionality test in that there is no rational connection between possession and the presumed fact of possession for the purpose of trafficking. In other words, it is not rational to presume that because a person has possession of a small amount of a narcotic, he or she intends to traffic in it.

In *R. v. Whyte*,[10] the Supreme Court upheld a law that infringes s.11(d). The accused was charged with having care and control of a car while impaired. For this offence, an accused can be charged even if he or she is not driving. For example, a person who is impaired and enters the driver's side of a car could be charged. In other words, the police do not have to wait for the accused to drive the vehicle before laying a charge. Section 258(1) of the Code sets out the presumption that a person in the driver's seat of a car is there for the purpose of driving the car. This presumption, in effect, shifts the burden of proof to the accused to show that his or her purpose for being in the seat was not to set the car in motion:

> **258. (1) . . .**
>
> **(a) where it is proved that the accused occupied a seat or position ordinarily occupied by a person who operates a motor vehicle . . . the accused shall be deemed to have had the care and control of the vehicle . . . unless the accused establishes that the accused did not occupy the seat . . . for the purpose of setting the vehicle . . . in motion . . .**

The Court allowed this infringement of s.1 because protecting the public from drunk driving is a matter of sufficient importance to override a constitutionally protected right. The presumption is a minimal interference, since the accused can avoid a conviction by giving a reason for being in the driver's seat. At the same time, it is impractical to require the Crown to prove an intent to drive.

---

10   (1988), 42 C.C.C. (3d) 123 (S.C.C.).

A situation that the Court has said is not a reverse onus clause, and that is allowable, is where a person must produce a certificate or permit to legally carry on a certain activity. For example, s.91 of the Code requires a person to have a permit to possess certain types of firearms. Section 117.11 [then s.106.7] of the Code states that where there is a question of whether a person has a permit, the onus is on the accused to prove that he or she has the permit. In *R. v. Schwartz*,[11] the Supreme Court of Canada held that s.117.11 (then 106.7) does not create a reverse onus provision (a minority of the Court dissented and said that it offends s.11(d) of the Charter). The Court said that s.117.11 creates a rule of evidence and does not require the accused to prove or disprove an element of the offence. In other words, all the accused must do is present the permit to show that he or she is exempt from the provision under which the charge was laid.

Section 11(d) of the Charter also provides that the accused has a right to a fair and public hearing by an impartial and independent tribunal. This right prevents "secret trials" and ensures fairness. As one court said: "Publicity is the hallmark of justice and trial in open court is the instrument through which publicity is effectively obtained."[12] However, in some circumstances the public can be excluded. For example, under s.486 of the Code, the judge or justice may exclude the public if he or she is of the opinion that "it is in the interests of public morals, the maintenance of order or the proper administration of justice to exclude all or any members of the public from the court room for all or part of the proceedings."

The Supreme Court of Canada has referred to impartiality as "a state of mind or attitude of the court in relation to . . . issues and parties . . . it connotes an absence of bias actual or perceived."[13] One of the reasons for appointing judges to the bench for life is to ensure their independence and impartiality. A judge can only be removed from the bench for a serious breach of duty. This means that judges can make decisions without being influenced by public opinion or by the governments that appointed them.

Section 11 continues:

(e) not to be denied reasonable bail without just cause;

This right means that a person who is arrested has a right to pre-trial release on reasonable bail unless reasonable grounds exist for not releasing the person. This right flows from the presumption of innocence: since a person is presumed innocent until proven guilty, it is unjustifiable to detain an accused until a finding is reached, unless there are reasonable grounds to detain the person. Pre-trial release is discussed in more detail in Chapter Five.

> **(f) except in the case of an offence under military law tried before a military tribunal, to the benefit of trial by jury where a maximum punishment for the offence is imprisonment for five years or a more severe punishment;**

---

11 (1988), 45 C.C.C. (3d) 97 (S.C.C.).
12 *F.P. Publications (Western) Ltd. v. R.* (1980), 51 C.C.C. (2d) 110 (Man.C.A.).
13 *Valente v. The Queen*, [1985] 2 S.C.R. 673.

The Supreme Court of Canada has said that s.11(f) confers a benefit on the accused that the accused may choose to waive. However, the waiver must be clear and unequivocal, and the accused must be aware of the consequences of the waiver.[14]

(g) not to be found guilty on account of any act or omission unless, at the time of the act or omission, it constituted an offence under Canadian or international law or was criminal according to the general principles of law recognized by the community of nations;

This section sets out the right not to be convicted of a retroactive offence. In other words, this section prevents the government from creating a new offence and applying it to previous conduct.

(h) if finally acquitted of the offence, not to be tried for it again and, if finally found guilty and punished for the offence, not to be tried or punished for it again;

This section states the protection against double jeopardy, or being tried twice for the same offence.

(i) if found guilty of the offence and if the punishment for the offence has been varied between the time of commission and the time of sentencing, to the benefit of the lesser punishment.

This section gives a convicted person the right to the lesser punishment where the penalties have been changed between the time of commission of the offence and the time of sentencing. In *R. v. Dunn*,[15] the Supreme Court of Canada held that an accused is entitled to the lesser punishment where the penalty has been lessened between the time of the conviction and the hearing of the appeal.

One other Charter right should be mentioned here:

12. Everyone has the right not to be subjected to any cruel and unusual treatment or punishment.

The Supreme Court of Canada stated in *R. v. Smith*[16] that the standard used for determining whether a punishment is cruel and unusual is whether it is so excessive as to outrage standards of decency. The guidelines set by the Court are:

• Whether the punishment is necessary to accomplish a valid penal objective.
• Whether the punishment is based on valid sentencing principles.
• Whether there are valid alternatives to the punishment.

These guidelines help courts determine whether the punishment is grossly disproportionate in relation to the offence.

---

14 *Turpin and Siddiqui v. The Queen* (1989), 48 C.C.C. (3d) 8 (S.C.C.); *Lee v. The Queen* (1989), 52 C.C.C. (3d) 289.
15 (1995), 95 C.C.C. (3d) 289 (S.C.C.).
16 (1987), 34 C.C.C. (3d) 97 (S.C.C.).

In *Smith*, the Supreme Court held that s.5 of the Narcotic Control Act, which imposes a minimum seven-year term of imprisonment for the offence of importing narcotics, violated s.12 of the Charter. The Court stated that a mandatory seven-year sentence was not justifiable when the amount of drugs imported could be small and only for personal use.

F. APPEALS

The procedure for appealing a court decision, where an appeal is possible, depends on a number of factors. The most important factor is whether the offence is indictable or is a summary conviction offence. Part XXI of the Code sets out the procedure for appealing indictable offences; Part XXVII includes the procedure for appealing summary conviction offences. The following is a general discussion of the appeal procedures that apply to both types of offences.

In every trial there are two main issues that must be determined: the facts of the case, and the law that applies to those facts. Grounds for appeal are based on questions of fact, questions of law, or questions of mixed fact and law. For example, Roberta is charged with murdering Jean by shooting her. Whether Roberta was the person who aimed and fired the gun at Jean is a question of fact. Once the facts of the case are decided, whether the offence of murder was committed is a question of law. That is, assuming that Roberta intentionally shot Jean, does this conduct constitute the offence of murder as defined by the Code? When a judge and jury try an accused, the jury's function is to determine the facts of the case, and the judge's function is to determine what law applies to the facts. If the trial is before a judge alone, he or she performs both of these functions (i.e., the judge acts as both the *trier of fact* and the *trier of law*).

Both the accused and the prosecutor have a right to appeal in certain situations. Sometimes the accused must obtain permission to appeal. The accused may be able to appeal either the conviction or the sentence; in other words, the appeal can be based on the decision of the court finding the accused guilty, or only on the punishment imposed by the court. Assume for example that Owen is convicted of assault under s.266 (the least serious type of assault) and sentenced to six years' imprisonment. Owen can appeal the sentence on a question of law because s.266 of the Code provides that the maximum term of imprisonment for this type of assault is five years.

The prosecutor can appeal a dismissal of the information, or the *acquittal* of the accused, or the sentence ordered by the court.

If the appeal court agrees that the trial court decision was wrong, it may allow the appeal. If the appeal court finds that the trial court decision was proper, it dismisses the appeal. Where the appeal is allowed, the appeal court may order a new trial, or direct an acquittal, or enter a verdict of guilty (except where there has been a jury trial), or change the sentence. Sometimes an appeal court decision is appealed to a higher court. The final and highest court of appeal in Canada is the Supreme Court of Canada.

G. HIERARCHY OF PERSONS AND COURTS WITH JURISDICTION OVER CRIMINAL MATTERS

One way of picturing the criminal court system is to imagine a pyramid. At the top of the pyramid is the Supreme Court of Canada, which only hears appeals. At the base of the pyramid are the justices of the peace. Trial courts occupy the lower levels of the pyramid. Appeal courts occupy the upper levels of the pyramid, which only review cases appealed from trial courts. At the middle of the pyramid are those courts in which both trials are held and appeals are heard. Generally, as offences become more serious or as they are appealed, they move up the pyramid.

Below are listed some of the main functions of the various levels of judicial authority in criminal matters, starting with the lowest level. Remember that each province is responsible for the administration of criminal law within its borders and that provincial variations are common.

Table 2–1
MAIN FUNCTIONS OF JUDICIAL AUTHORITY

TITLE	DUTIES
Justice of the Peace	— receives informations — issues summonses and warrants for search and arrest — holds bail and preliminary hearings — in some jurisdictions may try summary conviction offences
Provincial Court*	— functions of justice of the peace may be performed here — all but the most serious indictable offences may be tried here
Supreme or Superior Court	— the province's highest-level trial court — trials of the most serious indictable offences are held here, with or without a jury — hears some appeals involving summary conviction offences
Court of Appeal	— the province's highest appeal court — hears appeals from the trial court and lower-level appeal court
Supreme Court of Canada	— hears appeals from provincial courts of appeal

* In Ontario, this is the Ontario Court of Justice (Provincial Division).

Questions for Review and Discussion

1. Explain why crimes are wrongs against society.

2. Discuss the differences between civil wrongs and criminal wrongs.

3. Make a chart showing how federal and provincial governments share responsibilities for criminal law in Canada.

4. What is the main source of criminal law in Canada? Describe it.

5. **a.** Discuss some of the differences between indictable offences and summary conviction offences.
b. What is a hybrid offence?

6. What is the purpose of a preliminary inquiry?

7. Explain the three methods of trial for indictable offences.

8. What are the differences in trial procedure between a summary conviction offence and an indictable offence?

9. What is the difference between a question of fact and a question of law?

10. **a.** What did the case of *R. v. Askov* decide?
b. What was the immediate effect of this decision on the court system?
c. How have subsequent cases dealt with the issue of trial delay?

11. **a.** What does the presumption of innocence mean?
b. What other Charter rights are consistent with it?

12. **a.** What are reverse onus clauses?
b. What is the difference between a reverse onus clause and a mandatory presumption?
c. How have courts dealt with reverse onus clauses and mandatory presumptions?

Chapter Three

SOME GENERAL PRINCIPLES FOR DETERMINING CRIMINAL LIABILITY

A. THE ELEMENTS OF A CRIME

In general, every crime has a physical element, the *actus reus*, and a mental element, the *mens rea*. If either element is missing, then no crime has been committed.

1. The Physical Element of a Crime: *Actus Reus*

The physical element of a crime, the **actus reus,** is a Latin term that loosely translates as "guilty act" or "wrongful act." Although the term frequently refers to prohibited acts, it is more accurate to say that the *actus reus* includes all the parts of the crime other than the **mens rea,** which is the state of mind of the accused. In general, the *actus reus* of a crime consists of a certain type of conduct, a consequence of that conduct, and the circumstances surrounding the conduct.

In order to determine the *actus reus* of a particular offence, you must look at the definition of the offence. For example, consider s.265, which defines one way of committing the offence of assault:

> **265. (1) A person commits an assault when**
> **(a) without the consent of another person, he applies force intentionally to that other person, directly or indirectly . . .**

In this offence, the *actus reus* consists of (a) applying force to another person, and doing so (b) without the other person's consent. These parts of the crime do not refer to what was going on in the mind of the accused; rather, they refer to a physical occurrence (applying force) and a circumstance (without consent). The mental element, or *mens rea*, of the offence consists of the intention to apply force, indicated by the word "intentionally."

Below, each component of the *actus reus* is more closely examined: conduct, consequences, circumstances, and causation.

a. Conduct

The conduct involved in a crime may be an act, an omission, or a state of being.

Most crimes require that some act be committed. In criminal law, an act is a voluntary movement. For example, when Albert throws a punch at Bruce, Albert voluntarily moves his arm. In the same way, when Carol shoots a gun, she is committing an act if she pulls the trigger voluntarily.

An omission is the failure to act when there is a legal duty to act. As an example, s.215(l)(a) refers to such a duty:

215. (1) Every one is under a legal duty

(a) as a parent, foster parent, guardian or head of a family, to provide necessaries of life for a child under the age of sixteen years . . .

In brief, a parent has a legal duty to provide food, shelter and other necessaries for his or her children. If a parent omits or fails to perform this duty, without a reasonable excuse, then he or she has committed an offence.

Another example is the duty to assist a police officer when requested to do so:

129. Every one who . . .

(b) omits, without reasonable excuse, to assist a public officer or peace officer in the execution of his duty in arresting a person or in preserving the peace, after having reasonable notice that he is required to do so . . . is guilty of . . .

(e) an offence . . .

This section is clearly not prohibiting an act; rather, it is creating a duty to act, and a person who omits or fails to perform this duty has committed an offence, unless there is a reasonable excuse for failing to act.

Some offences require neither an act nor an omission. Instead, they simply require a state of being or "status." For example, s.354 prohibits a person from "having in his possession" anything that was obtained by crime:

354. (1) Every one commits an offence who has in his possession any property or thing . . . knowing that . . . [it] was obtained by . . .

(a) the commission in Canada of an offence punishable by indictment . . .

For example, if Bill is wearing a stolen watch, then he has it in his possession—simply having it is enough. There need not be some act or omission for the *actus reus* of this offence.

Another example of a state of being is found in s.201:

201 . . . (2) Every one who

(a) is found, without lawful excuse, in a common gaming house or common betting house . . .

is guilty of an offence . . .

Again, no act or omission is necessary. Simply being "found in" a common gaming house or common betting house is sufficient.

(I) VOLUNTARINESS

It is a general principle of criminal law that a person's act or omission must be voluntary if he or she is to be held responsible for it. An act was defined earlier as a voluntary movement. If a movement is involuntary, then under the criminal law, there is no act, and therefore no criminal responsibility.

An example of an involuntary (or automatic) movement is the beating of a heart. Other examples are the bodily movements of a person undergoing an epileptic seizure, and actions committed while sleepwalking. The general point is this: if a person has no control over his or her physical actions, then he or she will not be held criminally responsible.

If the conduct that forms part of the *actus reus* of a crime is not voluntary, then the accused can use the defence of automatism. Automatism and other defences are discussed in Chapter Four.

(II) INNOCENT AGENT

A person will not escape criminal responsibility by using the innocent actions of someone else to achieve an unlawful purpose. For example, Allen might try to sell drugs to Brigit by sending his 12-year-old son to deliver the package containing the drugs and to collect the payment. If the son had no idea that he was delivering drugs, he would be innocent of any wrongdoing. However, Allen would be guilty of trafficking even though he was not involved in the actual sale. Under the criminal law, the acts of Allen's son, in this situation, are considered to be the acts of Allen; thus, Allen is held responsible for the *actus reus* of the crime.

b. Consequences

Some crimes require a consequence as part of the *actus reus*. The consequence involved in a crime is the result of an act or an omission. For example, the consequence or result in homicide is the death of a human being:

222. (1) A person commits homicide when, directly or indirectly, by any means, he causes the death of a human being.

Another example is mischief, in which the "consequence" part of the offence is damage to property:

430. (1) Every one commits mischief who wilfully
(a) destroys or damages property . . .

In both these examples, the Code section does not mention any particular conduct that must cause the consequence to occur. In other words, a person may cause the death of a human being by shooting or stabbing the person, by planting a bomb in the person's car, or by some other act. Regardless of which act is done, a homicide has been committed if the act caused a person to die. Similarly, a person commits mischief if he or she causes damage to property—for example, by throwing rocks through the windows of a house, by breaking down its front door, or by some other destructive act.

The point here is that the definitions of many crimes mention a consequence without mentioning any particular act or omission. In most situations, it is not necessary to distinguish between conduct and consequence. For example, it is usually precise enough to say that Joan killed Maria or that Joan damaged Maria's property. However, the distinction is very helpful when it comes to understanding the concepts of causation, intention, and recklessness, which is discussed later in this chapter.

Another point about consequences is that more serious offences are sometimes distinguished from less serious offences by the consequences of the act or omission. For example, criminal negligence causing bodily harm is punishable by a maximum of ten years' imprisonment, while criminal negligence causing death is punishable by a maximum of life imprisonment.

c. Circumstances

Usually, conduct is not criminal unless it is committed in certain circumstances that form part of the *actus reus* of a crime. For example, s.280 includes many circumstances:

> **280. (1) Every one who, without lawful authority, takes . . . an unmarried person under the age of sixteen years out of the possession of and against the will of the parent or guardian of that person . . . is guilty of an indictable offence . . .**

The circumstances that must be present for this offence to be committed are: (a) the taker must not have lawful authority (an example of a taker with lawful authority might be a social worker acting under a court order); (b) the taken person must be unmarried; (c) he or she must be under the age of 16; (d) at the time of the taking, the taken person must have been in the possession of his or her parent or guardian; and (e) the taking must have been against the will of the parent or guardian of the person. If any one of these circumstances is not present, the *actus reus* is not complete, and thus the offence has not been committed.

Another example is found in s.177, trespassing at night:

> **177. Every one who, without lawful excuse . . . loiters or prowls at night upon the property of another person near a dwelling-house situated on that property is guilty of an offence . . . .**

Here, the circumstances that form part of the *actus reus* are: (a) the loitering or prowling must occur at night; (b) it must occur on another person's property; (c) it must occur near a dwelling-house; (d) the house must be situated on that property; and (e) the loitering must be without lawful excuse. All of these circumstances must be present for the offence to be committed. For example, if the loitering or prowling occurs during the day, or if there is no dwelling-house on the property, then there is no *actus reus,* and thus no offence under s.177.

d. Causation

When the *actus reus* of a crime includes certain consequences, the crime is committed only if the conduct of the accused caused the consequences to occur. So, if Frank is charged with murdering Paul, then it must be shown that Frank's conduct caused the death of Paul. In most criminal cases, there is no problem in establishing a causal link between the conduct of the accused and the consequence. For example, Irma punches Noreen, breaking Noreen's nose. It is clear that there is a direct cause-and-effect relationship between Irma's act and Noreen's broken nose.

In some cases, however, it may not be clear whether there is a causal link that supports criminal responsibility. Problems may arise when there is more than one accused involved, or when intervening events occur. For example, in an English case, a person was stabbed and taken to hospital. At the hospital, he was given an antibiotic to which he was allergic, and was improperly given intravenous fluids. The direct cause of his death was the improper medical treatment he received; in fact, the original wound had almost completely healed by the time the victim died. The Court held that the accused was not legally responsible for causing the death of the victim.[1]

The rule at common law is that the act must be at least a contributing cause outside the de minimis (trivial) range. For example, *R. v. Smithers*[2] involved two teenage hockey players. Smithers and another boy argued after a hockey game in which Smithers had been subjected to racial taunts. The argument escalated, with Smithers kicking the victim in the chest. The victim vomited and died from suffocation. It was determined that the victim had a rare physical condition that caused him to aspirate his vomit, leading to suffocation. The Supreme Court of Canada held Smithers liable for manslaughter for causing the death, even though the kick would not have ordinarily led to the death of a person. The Court held that the acts of Smithers were a contributing cause outside the *de minimis* range. The Court also recognized that the "thin skull" rule applies in criminal cases. That is, the perpetrator of the crime takes the victim as he or she is. In other words, even if the consequences of the wrongful conduct are greater than expected because of the victim's condition (e.g., a thin skull), the perpetrator is still responsible for the consequences.

Recently, the Ontario Court of Appeal upheld the *de minimis* test in *R. v. Cribben.*[3] The accused was involved in a robbery. He had punched the deceased hard in the face and kicked him. The co-accused then began to

1   *R. v. Jordon* (1956), 40 Cr.App. R. 152 (C.C.A.); see also s.225 for a similar rule, discussed in Chapter Nine.
2   [1978] 1 S.C.R. 506.
3   (1994), 89 C.C.C. (3d) 67 (Ont.C.A.).

punch and kick the deceased while beating him with a beer bottle. The deceased was left by the side of the road, where he drowned in his own blood. The court held that it did not matter whether it was the co-accused's acts or the accused's acts that caused the death. The judge had correctly instructed the jury that the accused could be found guilty of manslaughter if the assault by the accused contributed to the death of the victim. The assault did not have to be a substantial cause of death.

In a recent case, however, the Supreme Court of Canada held that where the charge is first-degree murder under s.231(5) (where death is caused in the commission of certain offences including sexual assault), a higher standard of causation is required. In *R. v. Harbottle*,[4] the Crown had to show (a) that the act or series of acts was a substantial and integral cause of death, and (b) that there was no intervening act of another person that resulted in the accused's act no longer being a substantial cause of death. The Court added that, in most cases, the accused must play a very active role—usually a physical role—in the killing, and that the underlying offence must be part of the same transaction as the murder. The accused was a party to the brutal sexual assault of a young girl. He had held her down while another man strangled her, causing her death. The Supreme Court found that the accused's actions were a substantial and integral cause of the victim's death, and dismissed his appeal of a conviction for first-degree murder.

The Supreme Court in *Harbottle* did not overrule the *de minimis* test in *Smithers*; rather, it said that it is a proper test in a manslaughter charge. However, where the charge is first-degree murder under s.231(5), a "substantial and high degree of blameworthiness" is required to reflect the seriousness of the crime and severity of the penalty.[5]

To summarize, the Supreme Court of Canada now recognizes two tests for causation: the contributing cause outside the *de minimis* range test, and the substantial cause test. It will be up to the courts in future cases to determine which offences, other than first-degree murder, under s.231(5) are sufficiently "blameworthy" to use the substantial cause test.

2. The Mental Element of a Crime: *Mens Rea*

For a crime to occur, the *actus reus* must be accompanied by a certain guilty state of mind, the *mens rea*. The *mens rea* of a crime is the element that makes the crime "blameworthy" or morally wrong. The courts recognize several types of *mens rea:* intention, knowledge, recklessness, wilful blindness, penal negligence, *mens rea* and the Charter, and absolute liability offences.

a. Intention

In some crimes, it must be shown that the accused person intended or "meant to" cause a certain wrongful consequence. For example, if Alfred hits

---

4   (1993), 84 C.C.C. (3d) 1 (S.C.C.).
5   Ibid., at page 13.

Bryce without Bryce's consent, then he is guilty of assault, but only if he intended to hit Bryce. If Alfred *accidentally* hits Bryce—for example, while practising his baseball swing—then he did not act intentionally, so no assault was committed.

Many Code sections clearly require intention by using such words as "intentionally," "wilfully," or "means to." One example is the offence of obstructing a peace officer in the execution of his or her duty:

> **129. Every one who**
>
> **(a) resists or wilfully obstructs a public officer or peace officer in the execution of his duty or any person lawfully acting in aid of such an officer . . .**
>
> **is guilty of . . .**
>
> **(e) an offence . . .**

In the offence of obstructing a peace officer, a person is guilty only if he or she intends or means to wrongfully obstruct or interfere with the officer.

In a Supreme Court of Canada case, it was stated that where intent is required, it is enough to prove that the accused foresaw the consequence as a "substantial certainty."[6]

(I) SPECIFIC INTENT

Some offences require a special or ulterior intent. These are called *specific intent offences.* In general, such offences are indicated by the words "with intent" or similar words (e.g., "for the purpose of").[7] As an example, consider s.348:

> **348. (1) Every one who**
>
> **(a) breaks and enters a place with intent to commit an indictable offence therein . . .**
>
> **is guilty of an indictable offence . . .**

In this offence, it must be shown not only that the accused intended to break and enter but also that he or she did so with the specific intent to commit an indictable offence, such as theft. If it is shown, for example, that the person broke into a place in order to obtain shelter from a storm, then the offence in s.348(l)(a) has not been committed. On the other hand, it is not necessary to show that the person actually committed an indictable offence. It is enough to show that the person broke and entered with the intent to commit an indictable offence.

Another example of a specific intent offence is a form of robbery found in s.343(c):

---

6   *R. v. Chartrand* (1994), 91 C.C.C. (3d) 396 (S.C.C.).
7   However, this is not always the case. A notable exception is murder (s.229).

343. Every one commits robbery who . . .

(c) assaults any person with intent to steal from him . . .

To commit this crime, a person must not only assault someone but also must do the assaulting with the intent to steal from the victim. If it is shown that Marla assaulted Blake, but it is not shown that the assault was done with the specific intent to steal, then Marla is guilty of assault, but not robbery. The assault here is a ***lesser-included offence***—that is, an offence contained within the major offence. A lesser included offence has some but not all of the elements of the major offence.[8]

Offences, such as assault, that do not require a specific intent are called ***general intent offences.*** The Supreme Court of Canada explains the distinction between a general intent offence and a specific intent offence in the following way:

> *In considering the question of mens rea, a distinction is to be drawn between "intention" as applied to acts done to achieve an immediate end on the one hand and acts done with the specific and ulterior motive and intention of furthering or achieving an illegal object on the other hand. Illegal acts of the former kind are done intentionally in the sense that they are not done by accident or through honest mistakes, but acts of the latter kind are the product of preconception and are deliberate steps taken toward an illegal goal. The former acts may be purely physical products of momentary passion, whereas the latter involve the mental process of forming a specific intent.[9]*

One of the significant differences between specific intent offences and general intent offences has to do with the availability of the defence of intoxication. Generally speaking, intoxication is a defence to specific intent crimes but not to general intent crimes. Important exceptions to this rule have been established as a result of Supreme Court of Canada decisions and amendments to the Code. The defence of intoxication is discussed fully in Chapter Four.

(II) INTENTION AND MOTIVE

Intention is different from motive. Motive refers to some reason for committing the crime; it is what explains why the person acted as he or she did. In general, it is not part of the *mens rea* of a crime. A person may commit a crime for a good motive and still be found guilty. For example, a man may want to free his father from the pain of cancer. So he gives his father a poisonous drug, and his father dies as a result. Here the *actus reus* (killing the father) and the *mens rea* (intending to kill the father) of murder are both present, and thus a crime has been committed. The motive—the son's desire to put his father out of his misery—is irrelevant to the issue of criminal responsibility; the son will be found guilty of murder.

---

8   Section 662 of the Code allows that an accused can be convicted of an included offence if it is proved and the major offence is not proved.
9   *R. v. George* (1960), 128 C.C.C. 289 (S.C.C.) at page 306.

The important point to remember is that the motive is usually not part of the actual crime. This means that if the *actus reus* and the *mens rea* of a crime are present, the accused is criminally responsible regardless of the motive.

However, motive can be relevant in at least two ways. First, the prosecution can offer a motive as evidence of the intentions of the accused. For example, if Betty stood to inherit $100,000 on Greta's death, then clearly Betty had a motive for killing Greta.

A second way that motive is relevant relates to sentencing. An accused who has been found guilty of a crime may receive a lighter sentence from the judge if he or she acted with a good motive rather than a bad one. For example, Betty might receive a lighter sentence for murdering Greta if it was an act of mercy (e.g., "mercy killing") rather than greed (e.g., to inherit money).

(III) INTENTION AND VOLUNTARINESS

It is sometimes difficult to distinguish the intention of the *mens rea* from the voluntary conduct of the *actus reus*. Although *mens rea* is referred to as the mental element of the crime, strictly speaking, the *actus reus* also has a mental element in that the act must be voluntary. In general, voluntariness refers to control over bodily movements, whereas intention refers to the state of mind regarding the consequences or results of those bodily movements. For example, a person may voluntarily shoot a gun but the person may not be intending to kill anyone. The act of shooting is under the person's control and, therefore, is voluntary. But if the person did not intend human death or serious bodily harm as a consequence of the act, then the person did not have the *mens rea* or criminal intent for the offence of murder. As the Supreme Court said in a case: "Mens rea . . . refers to the guilty mind, the wrongful intention of the accused. Its function in criminal law is to prevent the conviction of the morally innocent—those who do not understand or intend the consequences of their acts."[10]

b. Knowledge

In many crimes, it is necessary that the accused have knowledge or awareness of certain circumstances. This is sometimes indicated by the word "knowing" or "knowingly" in the definition of the crime. For example, s.131 states:

> **131. (1) Subject to subsection (3), every one commits perjury who, with intent to mislead, makes before a person who is authorized by law to permit it to be made before him, a false statement under oath . . . knowing that the statement is false.**

If a person gives false evidence at a trial but does not realize that the evidence is false, then the crime of perjury has not been committed. Without knowledge of this circumstance, there is no *mens rea* and, thus no offence is committed.

---

10 *Theroux v. The Queen* (1993), 79 C.C.C. (3d) 449 (S.C.C.).

The general rule is that the word "knowingly" in the definition of an offence applies to all the elements of the *actus reus.* Even when "knowing" or "knowingly" is absent from the definition of the offence, knowledge of relevant circumstances is usually required. For example, in *R. v. McLeod,*[11] the accused was charged with assaulting a police officer, contrary to what is now s.270(1)(a):

270. (1) Every one commits an offence who

(a) assaults a public officer or peace officer engaged in the execution of his duty or a person acting in aid of such an officer . . .

The police officer, dressed in plain clothes, tried to stop a fight between two youths. The accused was one of the many bystanders watching the fight. When the officer tried to stop the fight, the accused, not knowing that he was a police officer, pushed the officer and told him to mind his own business. The court held that the accused was not guilty because he lacked the necessary knowledge to commit the offence. Without the knowledge that the person interfering was a police officer, the accused had no *mens rea.*

c. Recklessness

Recklessness is a third type of *mens rea.* In some offences, it is not necessary that the accused actually intended to commit the wrongful consequence. Instead, it may be enough for criminal responsibility that the person was reckless.

In general, a person is reckless when he or she is extremely or grossly careless. Although the law has not always been clear on this point, it is now settled that recklessness requires ***subjective foresight*** of harm—that is, that the accused actually foresaw the potential harmful consequence of his or her actions. There are court decisions that have said that a person could be reckless even though he or she did not foresee the possibility of a harmful consequence. These decisions state that the question is not whether the accused actually foresaw the consequence; rather, it is whether a reasonable person, in the position of the accused, would have foreseen the consequences, and whether the conduct of the accused represents a gross departure from the conduct of a reasonable person.[12] This is called ***"objective foresight."***

The Supreme Court of Canada has come down in favour of a subjective standard for recklessness. The Court in *Sansregret v. The Queen* stated that "recklessness, to form part of the criminal *mens rea,* must have an element of the subjective. It is found in the attitude of one who, aware that there is a danger that his conduct could bring about the result prohibited by the criminal law, nevertheless persists, despite the risk."[13]

In other words, a person is reckless when he or she foresees the possibility of a harmful consequence and then takes the risk that the harm will not

11 (1954), 111 C.C.C. 106 (B.C.C.A.).
12 *R. v. Nelson* (1990), 54 C.C.C. (3d) 285 (Ont.C.A.).
13 (1985), 18 C.C.C. (3d) 223 (S.C.C.) at page 233.

result. The person must be aware of the danger involved. A person who does not have this subjective awareness or foresight, is not reckless. For example, Alice wants to practise her target shooting, so she attaches a target to a tree in a public park. She sees that the tree is in front of a children's play area in which children are playing. Alice's first shot misses the target and wounds one of the children. Alice has clearly been reckless because she foresaw the possibility of injury even though she had no intention of causing injury. She did not intend the harmful consequence, but she foresaw the possibility of it and took the risk.

Under this definition, to be reckless, the risk that is taken must be unjustifiable. Some risks are justifiable. For example, the doctor who performs heart surgery foresees the possibility of causing the death of the patient, but the doctor is not being reckless by operating. The risk is reasonable, or justifiable. On the other hand, in the target-shooting example, it is neither reasonable nor justifiable for Alice to take the risk.

Some Code sections clearly require recklessness by using the words "reckless" or "recklessly." An example is one type of the offence of arson:

> **434.1 Every person who intentionally or recklessly causes damage by fire or explosion to property that is owned, in whole or part, by that person is guilty of an indictable offence . . . where the fire or explosion seriously threatens the health, safety or property of another person.**

Even if the offence does not include the word "reckless," courts have held that recklessness is sufficient where the mens rea is knowledge of certain circumstances. For example, for the offence of possession of stolen property, a person must have knowledge that the property was obtained through the commission of a crime. Recklessness as to whether the property was obtained through the commission of a crime is a sufficient *mens rea* for the offence.

d. Wilful Blindness

A concept that is closely related to recklessness is **wilful blindness.** The Supreme Court in *Sansregret* defined wilful blindness as, "where a person who has become aware of the need for some inquiry declines to make the inquiry because he does not wish to know the truth. He would prefer to remain ignorant."[14]

An example of the application of wilful blindness is *R. v. Blondin*,[15] a decision of the British Columbia Court of Appeal. The accused was charged with importing narcotics contrary to s.5 of the Narcotic Control Act. Almost 1.5 kilograms of hashish were found inside a scuba-diving tank that the accused was trying to bring into Canada. The accused admitted knowing that there was something illegal in the tank but stated that he did not know it was a

---

14 Ibid., at page 235.
15 (1970), 2 C.C.C. (2d) 118 (B.C.C.A.).

narcotic. Knowledge that the substance being imported is a narcotic is an essential ingredient of the offence of importing narcotics. The court held that this requirement was satisfied if it was proven that the accused had been reckless about what the substance was or had wilfully shut his eyes as to what it was.

e. Penal Negligence

The debate over subjective versus objective liability was not finally settled with *Sansregret.* The Supreme Court of Canada recently recognized a fourth type of *mens rea:* penal negligence, which is based on an objective standard. Penal negligence requires that the Crown establish (a) the *actus reus*—that the conduct was either a marked departure from that of a reasonable person or a dangerous and unlawful act, and (b) the *mens rea*—that a reasonable person would have foreseen the risk of harm. The central case that established this principle was *R. v. Creighton,*[16] where the accused was charged with manslaughter for causing death by means of an unlawful act. The accused and the victim were drug users. The accused had injected the victim with cocaine, with her consent. She eventually died from a drug overdose. The unlawful act on which the charge of manslaughter was based was the injection of the cocaine (legally defined as trafficking under the Narcotic Control Act). Creighton was convicted and eventually appealed to the Supreme Court. His appeal was dismissed. The Court held that the test for *mens rea* of unlawful act manslaughter is, in addition to the *mens rea*, required for the underlying offence (injecting the cocaine), objective foreseeability of the risk of bodily harm that is neither trivial nor transitory in the context of a dangerous act. In other words, a reasonable person in Creighton's place would realize that injecting the victim with cocaine is an unlawful and dangerous act that involves a risk of causing serious bodily harm.

The Supreme Court, in *R. v. Gossett,*[17] which was released with Creighton, applied this same test to another case of unlawful act manslaughter. This time the unlawful act was the careless handling of a firearm under s.86(2). A police officer had yelled at a fleeing suspect, "Stop or I'll shoot." He then pointed the gun in the direction of the suspect and the gun went off, killing the suspect. The jury acquitted the officer, but the court of appeal ordered a new trial. The Supreme Court dismissed the accused's appeal, holding that the proper test to be applied to the accused was whether, in carelessly handling a firearm, his behaviour was a marked departure from the standard of care of a reasonably prudent person. Similarly, in *R. v. Finlay,*[18] a case involving the careless storage of firearms, also under s.86(2), the Court held that the objective test for penal negligence applies.

In *R. v. Naglik,*[19] the offence charged was a failure to provide necessaries to a child. The Supreme Court held that the responsibility under s.215, which sets out the duty of parents to provide necessaries for their children, is objec-

---

16 (1993), 83 C.C.C. (3d) 346 (S.C.C.).
17 (1993), 83 C.C.C. (3d) 494 (S.C.C.).
18 (1993), 83 C.C.C. (3d) 513 (S.C.C.).
19 (1993), 83 C.C.C. (3d) 526 (S.C.C.).

tive. The question is whether the parent's conduct in not providing necessaries was a marked departure from the conduct of a reasonable parent in the circumstances where it was reasonably foreseeable that the failure to provide necessaries would lead to danger to the life or health of the victim.

f. Mens Rea *and the Charter*

Section 7 of the Charter of Rights and Freedoms contains the guarantee that a person will not be deprived of life, liberty, or the security of the person except in accordance with the principles of fundamental justice. One of the principles of fundamental justice is that there must be evidence of "moral blameworthiness" before a person is held criminally responsible and subject to possible imprisonment. In other words, the criminal law should not punish those who are without fault. The question for the Supreme Court in the above cases was this: "What is the minimum requirement of fault *(mens rea)* under the Constitution?" The Court answered this question by setting different standards of fault for different offences:

(I) OFFENCES THAT REQUIRE SUBJECTIVE MENS REA

The principles of fundamental justice require that the *mens rea* of an offence reflect the stigma and penalty attached to the offence. Certain crimes are connected with such severe social stigma and penalty that subjective foresight of harm is required for the *mens rea*. At the moment, these offences are murder, attempted murder, theft, and crimes against humanity.[20] So, for example, the offence of murder requires that the accused either intended to cause a person's death or intended to cause bodily harm that the accused knew was likely to cause death.[21]

(II) OFFENCES OF PENAL NEGLIGENCE

Those Criminal Code offences that do not have a severe social stigma or penalty attached allow an objective foresight of harm for the *mens rea*. The *actus reus* must be either conduct that is a marked departure from that of a reasonable person, or a dangerous and unlawful act. As you may see from the cases discussed above, the Supreme Court has been deciding case by case the type of *mens rea* required for particular offences. This is an area of law that is still evolving. We will have to wait and see how the Court interprets various offences. Remember that the Court is setting minimum standards. It is entirely possible for Parliament to create crimes that require a higher level of fault.

There are two other categories of offences that the Supreme Court has discussed in terms of liability requirements. These are regulatory offences (or ***strict liability offences***) and absolute liability offences.

---

20 See, for example, *R. v. Vaillancourt* (1987), 39 C.C.C. (3d) 118 (S.C.C.), and *R. v. Finta* (1994), 88 C.C.C. (3d) 417 (S.C.C.).
21 See, for example, *R. v. Logan and Johnson* (1990), 58 C.C.C. (3d) 391 (S.C.C.).

g. Regulatory Offences and the Defence of Due Diligence

The general rule is that *mens rea* is an essential element of an offence; however, some offences do not require *mens rea*. These are not true criminal offences in the sense of there being a moral blameworthiness attached to them. They are regulatory in nature; that is, their purpose is to regulate some aspect of human conduct, often to protect vulnerable members of society. These are known as regulatory or strict liability offences. For these, the Crown only needs to prove the *actus reus* of the offence. An accused person will be convicted unless he or she uses the defence of due diligence. This defence has two parts: the accused will be found not guilty on proving on balance of probabilities that he or she (a) acted as a reasonable person in the circumstances, or (b) had an honest but mistaken belief in facts that, if they had been true, would have rendered the act innocent. Note that one of the differences between offences of penal negligence and those of strict liability is that offences of penal negligence require conduct that is a marked departure from that of a reasonable person, or a dangerous and unlawful act, whereas strict liability offences only require a departure from the conduct of a reasonable person.

Strict liability offences are often created by statutes dealing with health, safety, and the general welfare of the public (e.g., the Food and Drugs Act). These offences are contained in provincial legislation and federal statutes other than the Criminal Code. For example, the Supreme Court of Canada, in *R. v. Sault Ste. Marie*,[22] held that the offence created by the Ontario Water Resources Act, which made it an offence to discharge materials into the lake that might impair the quality of the water, is one of strict liability.

The decision of the Supreme Court, in *R. v. Wholesale Travel Group*,[23] held that regulatory offences which are based on strict liability do not offend s.7 of the Charter as long as the due diligence defence is available. This case involved a charge under the Federal Competition Act, which protects consumers from false advertising.

h. Absolute Liability Offences

There is one other possible category of offences: **absolute liability.** For these offences, the Crown only has to prove the *actus reus* of the offence to gain a conviction. The accused cannot use the defence of due diligence. This means that a person who acts with no fault at all can be convicted of committing an offence. In general, these offences have been found to violate s.7 of the Charter because they deny liberty without following the principles of fundamental justice.[24] However, a recent decision of the Supreme Court of Canada establishes that absolute liability offences are valid where there is no possibility of imprisonment as a penalty. In *R. v. Pontes*,[25] the accused was charged under a provincial law with driving while prohibited. The British

---

22   (1978), 40 C.C.C. (2d) 353 (S.C.C.).
23   (1991), 67 C.C.C. (3d) 193 (S.C.C.).
24   Ref. Re s.94(2) of the Motor Vehicle Act (1985), 23 C.C.C. (3d) 289 (S.C.C.).
25   (1995), 100 C.C.C. (3d) 353 (S.C.C.).

Columbia Motor Vehicle Act provided that a person convicted of certain serious provincial and Criminal Code driving offences automatically and without notice would be prohibited from driving from the date of sentencing. The penalty for a first conviction for driving while prohibited was a fine of not less than $300 and not more than $2,000 and imprisonment for not less than seven days and not more than six months. Another statute, the British Columbia Offences Act, provided that notwithstanding the provisions of any other act, no person would be liable to imprisonment for committing an absolute liability offence, and that no person would be imprisoned for failure to pay a fine. The case eventually reached the Supreme Court of Canada on the issue of whether the offence was a strict liability or an absolute liability offence. The Court held that the effect of the provisions of the Motor Vehicle Act was to create an absolute liability offence to which the defence of due diligence did not apply. However, because of the Offences Act, which stated that its provisions overrode any other act, no person could be imprisoned for an absolute liability offence. The Court concluded that the s.7 guarantee of fundamental justice does not apply where a person is not at risk of imprisonment; therefore, the offence was valid.

3. Concurrence of *Mens Rea* and *Actus Reus*

It is a general principle of criminal law that for an offence to occur, both the *mens rea* and the *actus reus* must be present at the same time. In most cases, this principle does not present any problems. For example, in the case of theft, the act of stealing and the intent to steal usually occur at the same time. However, sometimes it is not so clear. For example, Al picks up a coat in a restaurant thinking that it belongs to him. When he gets home, he realizes that the coat is not his, but he decides to keep it. Here the *actus reus*, the taking of the coat, occurred at the restaurant; the *mens rea*, the intention of depriving the owner, did not arise until later. The question is whether Al should be found not guilty because the *actus reus* and *mens rea* did not occur at the same time. In answering this question, the criminal law relies on the fiction that the act of taking the coat continued until the point at which Al formed the *mens rea* to commit the crime. Thus, Al is guilty of theft.[26]

Another situation where the courts have had to decide whether the *actus reus* and *mens rea* are concurrent is where there is a series of acts and the *mens rea* is present for only part of the time the acts are occurring. For example, in *Meli v. The Queen*,[27] the accused appealed his conviction for murder. At his trial, it was established that he intended to kill the victim, and beat him until he thought he was dead. He then threw the victim over a cliff. It was shown that the victim died from exposure and not from the beating. The accused's defence argued that the *mens rea* and *actus reus* were not concurrent; when

---

26 See, for example, *Fagan v. Metropolitan Police Commission*, [1969] 1 Q.B. 439. The accused accidentally drove his car on to a police officer's foot. When he realized what he had done, he refused to move the car. He was convicted of assault based on the fiction that the *actus reus* continued until the intention to assault formed.
27 [1954] 1 All E.R. 373 (P.C.).

there was intent, there was no death (during the beating), and when the death occurred, there was no intent. The appeal court upheld the accused's conviction, stating that the beating and the throwing of the victim over the cliff represented one continuing transaction. At some point, the *mens rea* coincided with the series of wrongful acts that made up the transaction.

This case was cited with approval by the Supreme Court of Canada in *R. v. Cooper.*[28] One of the issues on appeal was whether the *mens rea* and *actus reus* were concurrent. The accused and his ex-girlfriend had been drinking together. They went for a ride in his car and stopped at a secluded parking lot. The accused testified that they argued. During the argument, the deceased hit him, at which point, he became angry and grabbed her by the throat. He then said that he recalled nothing until he woke up and found the body beside him. Expert witnesses testified that the deceased probably died after about two minutes of pressure on her throat. The defence argued that the accused was so drunk that he blacked out shortly after he started shaking her, and thus did not have the intent to kill her at the time she died. The Court held that it is not necessary that the *mens rea* continue throughout the commission of the wrongful act—that is, the entire act of strangulation. It rejected the decision of the appeal court that if the intent disappeared before the point when death became likely, then the accused could not be found guilty. The Court stated that if death results from a series of wrongful acts that are part of a single transaction, it is only necessary to establish that the requisite intent coincided at some point with the wrongful acts. When the accused seized the victim by the neck, it was open to the jury to infer either that he intended to cause her death or that he meant to cause her bodily harm that he knew was likely to cause her death.

B. PARTIES TO AN OFFENCE

In general, parties are persons who are criminally responsible for the commission of the offence. In most situations, all persons who are *parties to a crime* are liable to the same punishment. Their involvement may take place either before or during the commission of the offence. The relevant Code sections on parties are ss. 21 and 22, which define parties as those who actually commit the crime, or who aid and abet or counsel the commission of a crime.

1. Aiding and Abetting

21. (1) Every one is a party to an offence who

(a) actually commits it;

(b) does or omits to do anything for the purpose of aiding any person to commit it; or

---

28 (1993), 78 C C C (3d) 289 (S C C)

(c) abets any person in committing it.

The person who actually commits the offence is referred to as the principal or the perpetrator. A person who acts through an innocent agent is considered to actually commit the offence, and thus is a principal.

Paragraphs (b) and (c) of s.21(1) mean that anyone who helps or encourages another person to commit an offence is a party, and is thus responsible for its commission. More specifically, "aid" means to help or give assistance and "abet" means to encourage another to commit a crime.

In order to find a person guilty of *aiding or abetting,* it is only necessary to show that the person understood what was taking place and encouraged or assisted the principal in committing the offence. The encouragement or the assistance given by the person must be intentional. If the conduct of a person has the effect of helping the principal to commit a crime, but the person did not intend to help the principal, then it is not aiding or abetting. For example, Albert lends his tools to Bernice because he thinks Bernice needs them for house repairs. Instead, Bernice uses them to break into a shop. Albert would not be guilty of aiding or abetting the commission of the offence. Another example: Alice, a bank security officer, forgets to lock the door to the bank. This omission helps Bill rob the bank. Alice would not be guilty of aiding or abetting because she did not intend to help in the commission of the crime. In *R. v. Hibbert,*[29] the Supreme Court of Canada held that the meaning of the term "for the purpose of" in s.21(1)(b) refers to intention, not desire. The accused was charged as a party to the offence of attempted murder. The principal offender had threatened to shoot him if he did not help him lure the victim into meeting them in the victim's apartment lobby by calling him on the apartment's intercom. The Court stated that, even though the accused did not desire the victim, who was his friend, to come to the lobby, he still intended for him to come to the lobby when he called him on the intercom. The accused could raise the defence of duress (discussed in Chapter Four), but he could not argue that he did not act for the purpose (the intention) of aiding the commission of the offence.

In general, a person who is merely present at the commission of an offence will not be guilty of aiding and abetting. There must be some active assistance or encouragement. Simply being present and not objecting to the offence is not aiding and abetting. For example, in *Dunlop and Sylvester v. The Queen,*[30] the accused were present during a sexual assault involving several men. It was established that they did not know the assault was going to take place and had only brought cases of beer to the place where the assault was occurring. Although they observed the assault, they did not participate. They were not held liable for the crime. However, a "look-out man" is an aider and abettor. In *R. v. Cunningham,*[31] the accused was stationed at the entrance of a common betting house for the purpose of signalling to the keepers of the house if the police approached. The court held that the

---

29 (1995), 99 C.C.C. (3d) 193 (S.C.C.).
30 (1979), 47 C.C.C. (2d) 93 (S.C.C.).
31 (1937), 68 C.C.C. 176 (Ont.C.A.).

accused was assisting in the continued operation of the house by preventing the police from obtaining evidence.

Merely being present at the scene of a crime may lead to criminal responsibility where there is a duty to act. In *R. v. Nixon*,[32] the accused was a police officer in charge of the lock-up for the night at a Vancouver jail. Police had picked up a man for being drunk in public. He was severely beaten at the station when he gave a false name. Nixon was present at the beating, but did not participate. The trial court judge held that, under the B.C. Police Act and ss. 27 and 28 of the Criminal Code, the accused had a duty to protect the victim, which he failed to discharge. Therefore, he was guilty of aggravated assault. The B.C. Court of Appeal upheld his conviction.

In some cases, it is difficult to determine whether there is active assistance or encouragement. For example, in *R. v. Kulbacki*,[33] the accused, a 20-year-old man, allowed a 16-year-old girl to drive his car. While he sat beside her, she drove the car over 140 kilometres an hour, and the accused did not do or say anything to stop her. He was charged with aiding and abetting the commission of the offence of dangerous driving. His defence was that he did nothing to encourage the commission of the offence, but was merely a passive observer, and therefore should not be liable for aiding and abetting. The court held that the failure of the accused to try to stop or prevent the girl from committing the offence, when he was in a position to do so, and when he had the authority to do so, amounted to encouragement; thus, he was aiding and abetting. The court also pointed out that every passenger in an unlawfully driven car is not necessarily an aider and abettor because he or she might not have any authority over the car or any right to control the driver.

An aider and abettor may be charged with aiding and abetting in the commission of a particular offence or may simply be charged with the offence.[34] If the offence is one which requires subjective intent, it is possible for the party who is not the principal offender to be found guilty of a lesser included offence—for example, in the case of murder, with manslaughter. In *R. v. Kirkness*,[35] the accused and another man, the co-accused, broke into a house for the purpose of robbery. During the break-in, the co-accused strangled and suffocated a woman they found in the house. Both men were charged with first-degree murder. The trial judge acquitted the accused of first-degree murder. The court of appeal ordered a new trial on the grounds that the trial judge erred in not leaving to the jury a possible conviction for manslaughter. The Supreme Court of Canada upheld the accused's acquittal. The Court stated that where a person is charged with aiding or abetting in the commission of a murder, to be found guilty of murder the accused must have the same intent that the principal needs—that is, an intention to cause death, or bodily harm of a kind likely to cause death. Here it was not proved

---

32 (1990), 57 C.C.C. (3d) 97 (B.C.C.A.); leave to appeal to S.C.C. refused.
33 (1966), 1 C.C.C. 167 (Man.C.A.).
34 *R. v. Harder* (1956), 114 C.C.C. 129 (S.C.C.).
35 (1990), 60 C.C.C. (3d) 97 (S.C.C.).

that the accused knew before entering the house that the other man would kill the victim. There was no evidence that he was party to the suffocation. In fact, there was evidence that he told the co-accused not to strangle the victim. Although the Court confirmed that a conviction for manslaughter is possible where there is not sufficient proof of intent, in this case, the accused was not liable for manslaughter, since there was no evidence that the accused aided or abetted in an unlawful act that would cause bodily harm short of death.

2. Common Intention

A person is also a party if his or her conduct falls within s.21(2):

> **21. (2) Where two or more persons form an intention in common to carry out an unlawful purpose and to assist each other therein and any one of them, in carrying out the common purpose, commits an offence, each of them who knew or ought to have known that the commission of the offence would be a probable consequence of carrying out the common purpose is a party to that offence.**

To be convicted under this section, (a) the accused, and at least one other person, must form a common intention to carry out an unlawful purpose, and to help each other in doing so; (b) one of them in carrying out the unlawful purpose must commit an offence different than the unlawful purpose; and (c) the offence must be one that they knew or should have known would probably result from carrying out the common purpose.

The difference between s.21(1) and s.21(2) was summed up by the Ontario Court of Appeal in R. *v. Jackson*:

> *[Section 21] is aimed at those who participate in the actual offence for which liability is imposed. Section 21(2) widens the circle of criminal culpability to include those who do not participate in the alleged crime but who do engage in a different criminal purpose and foresee the commission of the alleged offence by a party . . . as probable consequence [of the criminal purpose].*[36]

The decision in *Hibbert*,[37] discussed above, also referred to s.21(2). Consistent with its interpretation of s.21(1), the Court stated that it is not necessary that a party desire the unlawful purpose that the party and the other person carry out, but only that the party and other person formed an intention in common to commit the unlawful purpose.

The Supreme Court of Canada recently considered this section, specifically requirement (c) and the words "ought to have known," along with the issue of the *mens rea* required for murder. In a series of decisions, the Court held that because of the stigma and penalties attached to murder and

---

36   (1991), 68 C.C.C. (3d) 385, at page 421.
37   *Hibbert*, see note 29.

attempted murder, these offences require a subjective intent,[38] —— that is, the accused must actually intend to cause death or intend to cause bodily harm that he or she knows will likely cause death. One of these cases also considered s.21(2). Since the words "ought to have known" are included in s.21(2), it was possible for someone to be convicted of murder who did not have the subjective intent that the offence of murder requires. In other words, a person is not the principal could be convicted of murder with a lesser degree of fault than was required for the principal. This was the situation in *R. v. Logan and Johnson*.[39] The accused were parties to a robbery of a convenience store. They had entered the store wearing masks and armed with revolvers. One of the other parties shot the clerk, who was severely injured. They were convicted of attempted murder based on s.21(2); in other words, it was found that they had formed a common intention with the other party to commit an unlawful purpose, the robbery, and that they either knew or ought to have known that it was probable the other party would shoot and that a death would result. The Supreme Court ruled that where a party is charged with murder, the section cannot be used to convict the party if he or she did not have the intent required for the offence of murder. To apply the section in this situation would be a denial of fundamental justice under s.7 of the Charter. More generally, the Court also held that in order to convict a person under s.21(2), for any offence, the accused must have the necessary intent for the actual offence. In other words, if the offence requires subjective intent, then the accused must have that intent.

As mentioned earlier in this chapter, the offences that at present require subjective intent are murder, attempted murder, theft, and crimes against humanity. Just as with aiding and abetting under s.21(1), even though the party cannot be found guilty of murder, it is still possible for the person to be found guilty of manslaughter, if the intent needed for that crime is proved.[40]

3. Counselling an Offence

22. (1) Where a person counsels another person to be a party to an offence and that other person is afterwards a party to that offence, the person who counselled is a party to that offence, notwithstanding that the offence was committed in a way different from that which was counselled.

(2) Every one who counsels another person to be a party to an offence is a party to every other offence that the other commits in consequence of the counselling that the person who counselled knew or ought to have known was likely to be committed in consequence of the counselling.

---

38   *R. Martineau* (1990), 58 C.C.C. (3d) 353 (S.C.C.); *R. v. Luxton* (1990), 58 C.C.C. (3d) 449 (S.C.C.); *R. v. Arkell* (1990), 59 C.C.C. (3d) 65 (S.C.C.); and *R. v. Logan and Johnson* (1990), 58 C.C.C. (3d) 391 (S.C.C.).
39   Ibid., *R. v. Logan and Johnson*.
40   *R. v. Davy* (1993), (indexed as *R. v. Jackson*), 86 C.C.C. (3d) 385 (S.C.C.).

To counsel means to advise or recommend. *Counselling* also includes procuring (instigating or persuading), soliciting, and inciting.

The general idea in s.22 is that a person is a party to an offence if the person advises or gets another person to commit an offence, even if the crime is committed in a way different from what was suggested.

In *R. v. Soloway*,[41] the victim met a woman in a bar and offered to take her home. She invited him in when they reached her home. Inside were several other people, including the accused, Soloway. The victim fell asleep on the couch. He woke up when he felt the woman taking his wallet out of his back pocket. He pretended to be asleep to avoid a fight. There was no money in the wallet, and she started to put it back. Soloway then told her to keep the identification papers because they could be sold. Soloway was convicted of theft because of his role in counselling the theft of the victim's wallet.

Under s.22(2), a person is a party to any other crime that is committed if the person knew or ought to have known that it is likely to be committed as a result of the counselling. Section 22(2) raises the same issue as s.21(2) concerning objective and subjective foreseeability. As yet, this section has not been challenged in court.

Counselling is an offence in itself. Therefore, an offence is committed even if the counselled offence is not committed. For the offence of counselling, it does not matter whether the person counselled was persuaded or ever had the intent to commit the crime. An accused who is convicted of the offence of counselling instead of as a party to the offence will be punished under s.464:

> **464. Except where otherwise expressly provided by law, the following provisions apply in respect of persons who counsel other persons to commit offences, namely,**
>
> **(a) every one who counsels another person to commit an indictable offence is, if the offence is not committed, guilty of an indictable offence and liable to the same punishment to which a person who attempts to commit that offence is liable; and**
>
> **(b) every one who counsels another person to commit an offence punishable on summary conviction is, if the offence is not committed, guilty of an offence punishable on summary conviction.**

C. ACCESSORY AFTER THE FACT

Section 23 creates a separate offence of helping someone who has committed an offence. The person who provides such assistance is not a party to the offence but may be convicted of being an *accessory after the fact* (i.e., of helping after the offence has been committed) if his or her actions fall within s.23:

---

41 (1975), 28 C.C.C. (2d) 212 (Alta.C.A.).

23. (1) An accessory after the fact to an offence is one who, knowing that a person has been a party to the offence, receives, comforts or assists that person for the purpose of enabling that person to escape.

There are three main requirements for this offence. First, there must be knowledge that the other person has been a party to an offence. In *R. v. Vinette*,[42] the accused did not deny having assisted another person in disposing of a corpse by throwing it to the bottom of a flooded quarry in a weighted trunk. The court decided that this was enough evidence in itself to indicate that the accused had knowledge that the other party had been a party to the crime of homicide. The accused need only have knowledge of the person's participation, not an awareness of the legal classification of the offence.

Second, the accused must help the party to the offence escape. A person who does not disclose that an offence has been committed in his or her presence, or who does not assist in apprehending the party, is not an accessory. In general, assistance is anything that goes beyond a mere omission to aid in the capture of the offender. In *Young v. R.*,[43] the accused told two murderers that their names were known to the police and that the police had the licence plate number of their car. The court held that this was assistance because it went beyond a mere omission to aid in their capture and actually helped them escape apprehension.

Third, the assistance must be given with the intention of helping the criminal to escape. For example, in *R. v. McVay*,[44] the accused was charged with murder. A witness at the trial had, at the accused's request, disposed of a pair of jeans that, it was alleged, the accused wore at the time of the offence. The question raised was whether the witness was an accessory, since by disposing of the jeans he had helped the accused escape. The Ontario Court of Appeal stated that the jury, after weighing the evidence, was required to decide whether the witness knew that the accused had committed a murder at the time he disposed of the jeans. Only if he knew of the murder would he be an accessory after the fact.

If the principal is acquitted of the offence, then the accessory is acquitted. However, it is possible for an accessory to be indicted even if the principal is not indicted or convicted. Section 592 provides:

592. Any one who is charged with being an accessory after the fact to an offence may be indicted, whether or not the principal or any other party to the offence has been indicted or convicted or is or is not amenable to justice.

Section 23.1 sets out a similar rule for an accused charged with aiding, abetting, counselling or procuring, or being an accessory with regard to being convicted:

---

42 (1974), 19 C.C.C. (2d) 1 (S.C.C.).
43 (1950), 98 C.C.C. 195 (Que.C.A.).
44 (1982), 66 C.C.C. (2d) 512 (Ont.C.A.).

23.1 For greater certainty, sections 21 to 23 apply in respect of an accused notwithstanding the fact that the person whom the accused aids or abets, counsels or procures or receives, comforts or assists cannot be convicted of the offence.

Section 23.1 was added to the Code in 1985 to make it clear that a person can be convicted as a party or accessory even if the other party cannot be convicted—for example, if the principal party is a child or cannot be found.

In *R. v. McAvoy*,[45] the accused, a taxi driver, gave an unknown person a ride to a department store. The person entered the store, stole some items, and ran out while being pursued by two store employees. The accused drove off with the thief while the pursuit was still on. The person who actually committed the theft was never found, but the accused was charged with being an accessory. The Ontario Court of Appeal upheld his conviction.

However, if the principal has not previously been convicted, before an accessory can be convicted, the Crown must still prove that the principal committed the offence.[46]

D. ATTEMPTS

A person can commit an offence by merely trying to commit an offence. The offence of attempting a crime is defined in s.24:

24. (1) Every one who, having an intent to commit an offence, does or omits to do anything for the purpose of carrying out his intention is guilty of an attempt to commit the offence whether or not it was possible under the circumstances to commit the offence.

There are three essential elements to an attempt: the intent to commit the offence; some act or omission toward committing the offence; and non-completion of the offence.

The intent required in an attempt is the same as the intent required in the completed offence. For example, in an attempted theft, there must be the intent to steal; and in an attempted murder, there must be an intent to cause a death. Thus, if Angela shoots at Pierre intending to kill him, but misses, this is an attempted murder.

In addition to intent, there must be some act or omission done for the purpose of carrying out the intent. The rule is that the act or omission must involve more than mere preparation to commit the crime—it must be immediately, not remotely, connected with the commission of the crime. In other words, a person who is only preparing to commit a crime is not committing an offence. However, a person who commits some act or omission that amounts to more than mere preparation may be guilty of an attempt.

At what point a person's conduct goes beyond preparation and becomes an attempt depends on the circumstances of the case. However, the conduct must go forward to the stage where, if there had not been some intervention

45 (1981), 60 C.C.C. (2d) 95 (Ont.C.A.).
46 For example, see *R. v. Anderson* (1980), 57 C.C.C. (2d) 255 (Alta.C.A.).

or interruption, the offence would have been committed. In R. v. Deutsch,[47] the accused was charged under s.212(1)(a) with attempting to procure a woman to have illicit sex with another person. He had advertised for a secretary/sales assistant. During each job interview he told the applicant that she would be expected to have sex with prospective clients and would earn substantial bonuses for completed contracts. Each applicant ended the interview when she was told what was expected, before being offered the job. The Supreme Court of Canada held that the accused had gone beyond mere preparation and that the attempt was complete. In its ruling, the Court said that there is no general rule for drawing a line between an attempt and mere preparation: "The application of the distinction must be left to common-sense judgment." The Court went on to state that consideration must be given to (a) the nature and quality of the act compared to the nature and quality of the offence, and (b) the relative proximity of the act in terms of time, location, and acts required to complete the offence.

Here are some other instances where the courts have found attempted crimes:

In *Henderson v. R*,[48] the accused and two others planned to rob a bank. They obtained the necessary equipment, which included guns and ammunition. On their way to commit the robbery, they saw a police car parked in front of the bank. They drove away in another direction and were later apprehended by the police. The Supreme Court of Canada ruled that their conduct amounted to an attempt to commit robbery.

In *R. v. Cline*,[49] the accused disguised himself in large, dark sunglasses and approached a 12-year-old boy in a dark area of a street and asked him if he would carry his suitcases. The accused had no suitcases with him. The boy refused and ran away. The accused chased the boy and caught up with him, and then let him go after telling him not to tell anyone of the incident. Evidence at trial showed that the accused had previously tried to lure boys into alleys by asking them to carry his suitcases. On some occasions, the accused succeeded and committed indecent assaults. The appeal court held that no indecent assault was committed but that the accused was guilty of an attempted indecent assault. The court distinguished the acts of preparation from the actual attempt in the following way: the accused chose a time and place where he might obtain a victim; he went to that place at the chosen time; and he disguised himself and waited for an opportunity. These were all acts of preparation, and he was ready to embark on the course of committing the crime. When the accused approached the boy and tried to lure him away, he was going beyond mere preparation, and thus these actions amounted to an attempt to commit the offence.

Section 24(1) makes it clear that it is no defence to an attempt charge if it was impossible in the circumstances to commit the offence. In *R. v. Detering*,[50] the accused was charged with fraud under what is now s.380.

---

47 (1986), 27 C.C.C. (3d) 385 (S.C.C.).
48 (1948), 5 C.R. 112 (S.C.C.).
49 (1956), 115 C.C.C. 18 (Ont.C.A.).
50 (1982), 142 D.L.R. (3d) 87 (S.C.C.).

380. (1) Every one who, by deceit, falsehood or other fraudulent means, whether or not it is a false pretence within the meaning of this Act, defrauds the public or any person, whether ascertained or not, of any property, money or valuable security . . .

(b) is guilty of . . .

(ii) an offence . . .

Detering operated a car repair business. The Ministry of Consumer and Commercial Affairs was investigating car repair businesses suspected of cheating the public. Harris, an inspector from the ministry, brought a car to Detering's garage. The transmission had been slightly damaged so that it could be easily repaired. Detering told her that the transmission needed rebuilding. Harris had the work done and paid the bill, which stated that the transmission had been rebuilt. When the car was examined, it was found that the transmission had not been rebuilt.

Detering was found not guilty of fraud because Harris was not actually deceived. However, the Supreme Court of Canada held that he could still be found guilty of attempted fraud, even though it was impossible for the offence to be committed, since the investigator could not be deceived.

Section 24(2) states that the issue of whether the act of the accused is an attempt or mere preparation is a question of law. This means that it is the judge's function to decide whether the actions of the accused, as found by the jury, amount to an attempt.

E. PENALTIES FOR ACCESSORIES AND ATTEMPTS

Unless there is a section that sets out a penalty for being an accessory to or attempting a specific offence, the penalties for being an accessory or attempting an offence are set out in s.463:

463. Except where otherwise expressly provided by law . . .

(a) every one who attempts to commit or is an accessory after the fact to the commission of an indictable offence for which, on conviction, an accused is liable to . . . imprisonment for life is guilty of an indictable offence and liable to imprisonment for a term not exceeding fourteen years;

(b) every one who attempts to commit or is an accessory after the fact to the commission of an indictable offence for which, on conviction, an accused is liable to imprisonment for fourteen years or less is guilty of an indictable offence and liable to imprisonment for a term that is one-half of the longest term to which a person who is guilty of that offence is liable;

(c) every one who attempts to commit or is an accessory after the fact to the commission of an offence punishable on summary conviction is guilty of an offence punishable on summary conviction; [i.e., six months' imprisonment and/or a fine of up to $2,000]

(d) every one who attempts to commit or is an accessory after the fact to the commission of [a hybrid offence] . . .

(i) is guilty of an indictable offence and liable to imprisonment for a term not exceeding a term that is one-half of the longest term to which a person who is guilty of that offence is liable, or

(ii) is guilty of an offence punishable on summary conviction.

Exceptions to the penalties in this section are for the offences of attempted murder and accessory after the fact to murder:

239. Every one who attempts by any means to commit murder is guilty of an indictable offence and liable to imprisonment for life.

240. Every one who is an accessory after the fact to murder is guilty of an indictable offence and liable to imprisonment for life.

F. CONSPIRACY

In general, a *conspiracy* is an agreement (or "common design") by two or more persons to do an unlawful act or to do a lawful act by unlawful means. It is immaterial whether the unlawful act is committed or not. Even when the conspirators change their minds, or do not get the opportunity to perform the unlawful act, they have committed the offence of conspiracy once they have reached their agreement. So, if Bibi and Irene plan to kidnap Michelle and they are arrested before they can carry out the kidnapping, both of them will be guilty of conspiracy.

Assume that Bibi and Irene made the same agreement as above, but Irene only pretended to agree—that is, Irene agreed but had no intention of carrying out the agreement. This was the situation in *R. v. O'Brien*,[51] where the accused was charged with conspiracy to commit kidnapping. O'Brien asked Tulley to help him kidnap a woman named Pritchard. He offered to pay him for his help. Tulley agreed and received several payments. When O'Brien started pressuring him to actually carry out the kidnapping, Tulley went to the police and to Pritchard's husband and told them the plan. At O'Brien's trial, Tulley testified that he never intended to carry out the kidnapping but was just going along with O'Brien. On appeal, the Supreme Court of Canada ruled that O'Brien could not be convicted of conspiracy because there was no true agreement between Tulley and O'Brien. For the agreement to exist, there would have had to be a common intention to carry out the unlawful plan, and Tulley had only been pretending to have the intention to commit the kidnapping. On the other hand, the Court in O'Brien also said that the offence of conspiracy is committed even if one party later withdraws from the plan, since the offence is already complete.

---

51 (1954), 110 C.C.C. 1 (S.C.C.).

The Supreme Court has said that a husband and wife cannot be found guilty of conspiring together because in law they are considered one. However, if a third party is involved, they can all be convicted.[52]

The main section dealing with conspiracy is s.465:

465. (1) Except where otherwise expressly provided by law, the following provisions apply in respect of conspiracy:

(a) every one who conspires with any one to commit murder or to cause another person to be murdered, whether in Canada or not, is guilty of an indictable offence and liable to a maximum term of imprisonment for life;

(b) every one who conspires with any one to prosecute a person for an alleged offence, knowing that he did not commit that offence, is guilty of an indictable offence and liable

(i) to imprisonment for a term not exceeding ten years, if the alleged offence is one for which, on conviction, that person would be liable to . . . imprisonment for life or for a term not exceeding fourteen years, or

(ii) to imprisonment for a term not exceeding five years, if the alleged offence is one for which, on conviction, that person would be liable to imprisonment for less than fourteen years; and

(c) every one who conspires with any one to commit an indictable offence not provided for in paragraph (a) or (b) is guilty of an indictable offence and liable to the same punishment as that to which an accused who is guilty of that offence would, on conviction, be liable; and

(d) every one who conspires with any one to commit an offence punishable on summary conviction is guilty of an offence punishable on summary conviction.

Sections 465(1)(a) and (b) provide for specific conspiracy offences—that is, conspiracy to commit a murder and conspiracy to unlawfully prosecute a person.

Section 465(1)(c) makes it an offence to conspire to commit any other indictable offence.

Section 465(1)(d) makes it an offence punishable on summary conviction to conspire to commit a summary conviction offence.

It is also the offence of conspiracy to conspire while in Canada to do something outside Canada if it is a crime by the laws of the other place. Similarly, it is conspiracy to agree outside Canada to commit a crime inside Canada. In this regard, see s.465(3) and (4).

---

52 *Kowbel v. The Queen* (1954), 110 C.C.C. 47 (S.C.C.).

Questions for Review and Discussion

1. Define *actus reus* and *mens rea*.
2. What are the components of the *actus reus* of a crime?
3. Explain the two rules concerning causation.
4. List the types of *mens rea* discussed in this chapter.
5. What is the difference between a general intent offence and a specific intent offence? Give an example of each.
6. Why is the difference between general intent and specific intent offences important?
7. Explain the difference between intention to commit an offence and the motive for committing an offence. Make up an example illustrating the difference between motive and intention.
8. Explain the difference between a voluntary act and an intentional act.
9. What is the position of the Supreme Court on the *mens rea* for recklessness?
10. What is penal negligence?
11. How are strict liability offences different from other offences?
12. When are absolute liability offences valid?
13. What are the essential elements of aiding and abetting? Give an example of each.
14. What does it mean to counsel an offence? When can counselling itself be an offence?
15. What are the essential elements of being an accessory after the fact?
16. What are the essential elements of attempting an offence?
17. What is the difference between conspiracy and aiding and abetting?
18. Marion asked Sarah to take care of her infant boy for a few days. Marion also asked Sarah to give the infant a teaspoonful of "medicine" every night. In fact, the medicine was poison. Sarah did not think that the infant needed medicine, so she did not give it to him. She put the medicine on a shelf in her living room. Later, Sarah's five-year-old son gave the infant a large dose of the "medicine," and the infant died. Marion was charged with murder. Should she be convicted? What else, if anything, do you need to know?
19. Ava, Benny, and Claudia are walking through the park. They see their enemy, Donny, who is walking with a friend. They decide to "have some fun." So Benny and Claudia hold back Donny's friend while Ava punches and kicks him. Benny and Claudia laugh and yell their support to Ava. Meanwhile, Efrum, who is walking his dog, stops for a moment to see what is going on. Efrum decides not to get involved and walks on. Ava is convicted of assault causing bodily harm. Should Benny or Claudia be convicted of anything? What about Efrum? Explain.
20. Murray, Josie (Murray's wife), and Rosa agree to steal some money from

Pete's clothing store. They also agree that Pete will not be harmed and that no weapons will be used. Murray enters the store and gets Pete's attention by asking him questions about an article of clothing. Then Josie enters the store and walks toward the cash register while Rosa acts as a lookout near the store entrance. Pete notices Josie reaching into the drawer of the cash register and yells loudly. Rosa panics, pulls a gun and shoots Pete, severely wounding him. Murray, Josie, and Rosa run from the store and go to Dan's apartment around the corner. They tell Dan what has happened. Dan agrees to let them use his car, and Murray, Josie, and Rosa drive to a hiding place. Pete later dies from the wound he received. Explain the responsibility of Murray, Josie, Rosa, and Dan in this case.

Chapter Four
DEFENCES

A. INTRODUCTION

There are many types of *defences* that an accused can raise. An accused who says, "You have the wrong person, I was at work when the crime occurred," is using an *alibi* defence. A person who raises an alibi defence is saying that he or she was somewhere else when the alleged crime took place, and that it was therefore impossible that he or she committed the crime. Some defences are justifications for conduct that would otherwise be criminal. For example, a police officer who shoots a fleeing suspect may have a justification for his or her actions. Other defences are excuses. For example, a person who commits a crime because of a threat may raise the defence of duress to excuse his conduct. The difference between a justification and an excuse is that where conduct is justified, it is not wrong in the context in which it occurs. Conduct that is excused is wrong but because certain circumstances exist, the actor is excused from criminal liability. Another type of defence is that an essential element of the offence is missing. For example, the defence of mental disorder is based on the premise that the person was incapable of having the *mens rea* for the offence. The Criminal Code and the common law contain defences to criminal charges. Section 8(3) of the Code states that all common law defences apply to criminal charges, except as they are changed by Parliament:

> **8. . . (3) Every rule and principle of the common law that renders any circumstance a justification or excuse for an act or a defence to a charge continues in force and applies in respect of proceedings for an offence under this Act or any other Act of Parliament except in so far as they are altered by or are inconsistent with this Act or any other Act of Parliament.**

This section should be read with s.9, which abolishes common law criminal offences. In other words, there are no longer any common law crimes

65

(except for contempt of court). However, common law defences are still available unless altered by or inconsistent with an Act of Parliament (i.e., legislation).

The general rule is that an accused does not have to prove his or her defence: it is enough merely to produce some evidence that raises a reasonable doubt in the mind of the jury. Before a judge allows a jury to consider a defence, that defence must have "an air of reality." In other words, an accused person cannot just assert a defence without any evidence. If a judge finds that the defence does meet this minimal threshold, it is then up to the jury to decide whether the defence raises a reasonable doubt as to the accused's guilt.

B. INCAPACITY OF CHILDREN

Section 13 of the Criminal Code states:

> **13. No person shall be convicted of an offence in respect of an act or omission on his part while that person was under the age of twelve years.**

The law presumes that children under the age of 12 do not have the mental capacity to understand the nature and consequences of their acts and to distinguish between right and wrong. Without this mental capacity, there can be no *mens rea* or "guilty mind" and, thus there can be no offence.

Children under the age of 12 who commit crimes are handled under provincial legislation, usually in the form of child welfare or protection laws. Children over 12 and under 18 at the time of the alleged offence are held responsible for their criminal acts. However, they are treated differently and separately from adults. The Young Offenders Act governs the treatment of young people who break the law. An overview of this statute is given in Appendix B.

C. MENTAL DISORDER

The defence of mental disorder is that the accused did not have the *mens rea* for the offence. In general, when a person is found not guilty, that person is given a full acquittal and is free to resume his or her life. This is not the situation when the defence of mental disorder is used. As explained in more detail below, a person who successfully uses this defence is not released until a hearing is held to determine whether he or she is a danger to the public.

Section 16 sets out the defence:

> **16. (1) No person is criminally responsible for an act committed or an omission made while suffering from a mental disorder that rendered the person incapable of appreciating the nature and quality of the act or omission or of knowing that it was wrong.**

1. Meaning of Mental Disorder

Section 2 of the Code defines "mental disorder" as a disease of the mind. Whether a specific condition is a disease of the mind is a question of law for the judge to decide. Medical evidence is very relevant in deciding whether the accused suffers from a disease of the mind, but it is not the determining factor, since medical opinion may well differ. The Supreme Court of Canada has stated that part of the consideration is a policy component concerning public safety. For example, one factor to consider is whether the accused suffers from a recurring condition that is a continuing danger to the public. This suggests that the accused's condition should be treated as a mental disorder.[1]

Courts have recognized a number of mental disorders, such as schizophrenia, senile dementia, paranoia, melancholia, and certain types of epilepsy, as diseases of the mind. Excluded, however, are self-induced states caused by alcohol or drugs, and temporary conditions, such as hysteria and concussion. Delirium tremens caused by alcohol abuse is considered a disease of the mind. Once the court decides that the condition is a disease of the mind, it is up to the jury to decide whether the accused suffered from the disease at the time the offence was committed.

2. Appreciating the Nature and Quality of the Act

Appreciating the nature and quality of the act refers to the physical act and its consequences. It means more than knowing what is happening. The Supreme Court considered the meaning of the term "appreciates" in *Cooper v. The Queen*.[2] The accused had killed the victim by choking her to death. The psychiatric evidence was that the accused, because of the state of his mind, would not have been able (a) to form the intent to kill, or even (b) be aware enough to have the capacity to take a life. However, the accused did have the capacity to form the intent to choke the victim. The Court, in considering the meaning of "appreciates," stated:

[A]ppreciates imports [more than] mere knowledge of the physical quality of the act. The requirement . . . is that of perception, an ability to perceive the consequences, impact and results of the physical act. An accused may be aware of the physical character of his actions (i.e., choking) without necessarily having the capacity to appreciate that, in nature and quality, that act will result in the death of a human being.[3]

3. Knowing That the Act Is Wrong

A person may appreciate the nature and quality of his or her act; but if not capable of knowing that the act is wrong, that person still may be found insane.

1   *R. v. Parks* (1992), 75 C.C.C. (3d) 287 (S.C.C.).
2   (1980), 51 C.C.C. (2d) 129.
3   Ibid., at page 147.

The Supreme Court has held that "wrong" means the person knows the act is morally wrong, not just legally wrong. *R. v. Chaulk*[4] involved two teenage boys who had broken into a home in Winnipeg. They stabbed and bludgeoned the sole occupant to death. The evidence was that they both suffered from paranoid psychosis, and this made them believe that they had the power to rule the world and that killing was a necessary means to that end. Although they knew that killing was against the law in Canada, they believed that they were above the law. They were tried in adult court and found guilty. The judge did not allow the jury to consider the defence of insanity, because the accused knew the acts were against the law. (The term "insanity" was used until the law was amended in 1992, when the term "mental disorder" was substituted.) Their appeal to the Manitoba Court of Appeal was dismissed. On appeal to the Supreme Court, it was held that the meaning of knowing something is wrong is broader than just knowing it is illegal. The question is whether the accused was unable, because of a disease of the mind, to understand that he ought not to have committed the act and that the act was morally wrong in the circumstances. A more recent decision of the Supreme Court emphasizes that the focus is not on whether the accused had a general capacity to know right from wrong but on whether the accused lacked the capacity of an ordinary person to rationally decide whether the particular act was wrong.[5]

4. Presumption of Sanity

Section 16 of the Code states:

> **16. . . . (2) Every person is presumed not to suffer from a mental disorder so as to be exempt from criminal responsibility by virtue of subsection (1), until the contrary is proved on the balance of probabilities.**
>
> **(3) The burden of proof that an accused was suffering from a mental disorder so as to be exempt from criminal responsibility is on the party that raises the issue.**

The effect of the presumption in s.16(2) is that, unless the issue is raised, an accused is presumed not to be suffering from a mental disorder. This presumption has been challenged under the Charter of Rights and Freedoms as violating the right to be presumed innocent. The Supreme Court, in *Chaulk*,[6] held that the presumption of sanity does violate the constitutional right to be presumed innocent, but that the violation is justified in a free and democratic society. The Court stated that it would be an "onerous burden" for the Crown to have to disprove insanity in every case (i.e., to prove that the accused is sane). In other words, if it could not be presumed that an accused

---

4   (1990), 62 C.C.C. (3d) 193 (S.C.C.).
5   (1994), 91 C.C.C. (3d) 8 (S.C.C.) was cited at 30 C.R. (4th) 195 (S.C.C.).
6   Supra, note 4.

is sane in every case, the prosecution would have to prove beyond a reasonable doubt that the accused was sane—a heavy burden indeed. The burden of proof where mental disorder is raised is a balance of probabilities. In other words, it must be proved that it was more likely than not the accused was suffering from a mental disorder when the act was committed.

5. Who Can Raise the Issue of Mental Disorder?

Until recently, a common law rule stated that the prosecution could raise the issue of mental disorder over the objections of the accused. The trial judge had to give permission for the Crown to do this. Permission would only be given if it were shown that there was substantial evidence of mental disorder and that there was convincing evidence that the accused committed the offence. A Crown might raise mental disorder where, for example, the Crown believed that the accused was a danger to the public and that the likely term of imprisonment the accused would receive if found guilty of the offence would not be sufficient to protect the public.

The Supreme Court, in *R. v. Swain*,[7] held that the common law rule that allows the Crown to raise insanity in certain situations violates the accused's Charter right under s.7. The Court stated that it is a rule of fundamental justice that the accused is entitled to control his or her defence—that is, choose which defences to use. Since this was a common law (i.e., judge-made) rule, not a statutory rule, the Supreme Court stated that it could reformulate it so that it did not offend the Charter. To safeguard the accused's right, the rule should be that the Crown can only raise insanity if the accused has already put his or her mental capacity into issue or if the accused has been found otherwise guilty. In the latter case, the trial would have two parts: the first part to determine whether the accused was guilty of the offence, and the second to determine whether the accused was not guilty because of insanity. Since *Swain*, the Code has been amended to incorporate this court decision. Section 672.12 allows the court, on its own motion or on application of the accused or prosecutor, to order the assessment of the accused's mental condition. Under s.672.11 the court can order an assessment whenever it has reasonable grounds to believe that such evidence is necessary to determine whether the accused was suffering from a mental disorder so as to be exempt from criminal responsibility. When the assessment is requested by the Crown, the court cannot order the assessment unless (a) the accused has put his or her mental capacity for criminal intent into issue, or (b) the prosecutor satisfies the court that there are reasonable grounds to doubt that the accused is criminally responsible, because of mental disorder.

Section 672.34 preserves the two-part trial required by Swain by requiring a finding that the accused committed the offence but is not responsible because of a mental disorder:

---

7   (1991), 63 C.C.C. (3d) 481 (S.C.C.).

**672.34 Where the jury, or the judge . . . finds that an accused commit-
ted the act or made the omission that formed the basis of the offence
charged, but was at the time suffering from a mental disorder so as
to be exempt from criminal responsibility . . . the judge or jury shall
render a verdict that the accused committed the act or made the omission but is not criminally responsible on account of mental disorder.**

6. Disposition on the Finding of Not Criminally Responsible Because of Mental Disorder

Until the decision in *Swain,* when an accused was found not guilty by reason of insanity, the court had to order that the accused be kept in "strict custody . . . until the pleasure of the lieutenant governor of the province is
known" (s.614(2), now repealed). In other words, the trial judge had no
choice regarding the disposition of the case. This practice was called automatic detention. The decision of the Supreme Court of Canada, in *Swain,*
rejected the practice of automatic detention. The facts in *Swain* were: The
accused was charged with assaulting his wife and two children. The evidence was that he had swung his children around his head and splashed
them with water and then carved an X on his wife's chest. He explained that
he was ridding them of devils. While on bail awaiting trial, he received drug
therapy for seven weeks as an in-patient. He was then released and lived
with his family for 18 months until his trial. The Crown raised the issue of
insanity over the accused's objections, and he was found not guilty by reason of insanity. The court ordered his detention. The case eventually reached
the Supreme Court of Canada, which held that the practice of automatic
detention violated Swain's Charter rights under s.7 and s.9 (the right to be
free from arbitrary detention), and that it was not a justifiable limitation
under s.1 of the Charter. There were two reasons why not:

First, there was no requirement that a hearing be held before detention
was ordered to determine whether the accused was a present danger to the
community. This was a denial of fundamental justice under s.7.

Second, even if a hearing were required, there were no criteria or standards set out in the law for a judge to apply in deciding whether the accused
should be detained or released. For example, the judge was not directed to
consider whether it was likely that the accused would commit a violent
crime in the future. The lack of criteria made the detention arbitrary, and this
violated s.9 of the Charter.

The Court wrote: "The duty of the trial judge to detain is unqualified by
any standards whatsoever. I cannot imagine a detention being ordered on a
more arbitrary basis."[8]

The particular facts in *Swain* made this arbitrariness especially obvious. It
appeared that he had been successfully treated before his trial and was no
longer a danger to the community, yet the trial judge had no choice but to
order his detention.

---

8   Ibid., at page 535.

The Court stated that it would give the federal government a six-month transition period to change the law. During this period, anyone found not guilty by reason of insanity could be confined, but the accused's case would have to be reviewed within 30 to 60 days to determine whether the accused was still insane.

In 1992, the government enacted Bill C-30, which set out the new procedure for dealing with an accused person found not guilty because of mental disorder. This legislation also replaced the term "insanity" with the term "mental disorder." The new procedure provides that where a finding of not criminally responsible because of mental disorder is made, the court can either hold a disposition hearing or send the case to a provincial review board, which must review the case within 45 days. If a court holds the hearing and makes an order other than an absolute discharge, the review board must review the case within 90 days.

Section 672.54 states:

> **672.54 Where a court or Review Board makes a disposition . . . it shall, taking into consideration the need to protect the public from dangerous persons, the mental condition of the accused, the reintegration of the accused into society and the other needs of the accused, make one of the following dispositions that is the least onerous and least restrictive to the accused:**
>
> **(a) where a verdict of not criminally responsible on account of mental disorder has been rendered in respect of the accused and, in the opinion of the court or Review Board, the accused is not a significant threat to the safety of the public, by order, direct that the accused be discharged absolutely;**
>
> **(b) by order, direct that the accused be discharged subject to such conditions as the court or Review Board considers appropriate; or**
>
> **(c) by order, direct that the accused be detained in custody in a hospital, subject to such conditions as the court or Review Board considers appropriate.**

7. Capping Dispositions

A criticism of the earlier law was that a person who was found not guilty because of insanity could be detained longer than a person found guilty. For this reason, the insanity defence was used cautiously and usually only for serious offences.

Sections 672.64 and 672.65 were intended to deal with this problem. Section 672.64 provides that a person found not criminally responsible because of a mental disorder cannot be detained longer than the maximum period of detention for a person who is found guilty. Section 672.65 applies to persons who may be dangerous to the public if released. It provides a procedure for declaring a person a dangerous mentally disordered person where the offence involved is a serious personal injury offence. When this finding is made, the cap on the person's detention can be increased to life. Although the House and Senate have passed these sections, neither has been proclaimed into force. This is to allow the provinces time to amend related legislation.

D. AUTOMATISM

A person whose conduct is involuntary may raise the defence of automatism. Automatism refers to a state in which a person has no conscious control over bodily movements. In other words, the person's behaviour is "automatic." Examples of involuntary, unconscious behaviour are acts done while sleepwalking and during an epileptic seizure. In effect, the accused is saying that he or she did not have the *actus reus* of the crime.

For automatism to be a defence, the cause of the automatism must be something other than a disease of the mind or voluntary intoxication by alcohol or drugs. If a disease of the mind causes an involuntary, unconscious act, the defence is mental disorder, not automatism. This is sometimes called "insane" automatism; the defence of automatism is called "non-insane" automatism. Similarly, if intoxication causes the involuntary, unconscious act, the defence is usually intoxication, not automatism.

Automatism caused by a physical injury was a successful defence in *R. v. Bleta.*[9] The accused was charged with murder. Several witnesses testified that they watched a fight between G and the accused that culminated in the accused stabbing G fatally in the neck. Although the stories of the eyewitnesses differed as to the details of the fight, it is clear that blows were exchanged between the two men. The accused either fell down or was knocked down, and struck his head forcibly on the pavement. G started to walk away; the accused, having regained his feet, followed him and pulled out a knife, with which he delivered the fatal blow. Two of the onlookers observed that when the accused got up, he staggered and appeared to be dazed. One police officer also commented on his apparently dazed condition.

The accused contended that the blow to his head when it struck the sidewalk deprived him of all voluntary control over his actions. In other words, the accused was saying he was in a state of automatism when he stabbed G.

A psychologist gave evidence that supported the accused's defence. The trial judge summarized the psychologist's evidence: "The doctor says that the actions of the accused when he stabbed the deceased were purely automatic and without any volition on the part of the accused. He was, in fact, in the condition of a sleepwalker or an epileptic, and since he had been in a fight, he automatically continued it."[10]

The jury believed that the accused was in a state of automatism when he stabbed G, and acquitted him on the charge of murder. The Supreme Court of Canada upheld the decision of the trial court.

---

9 [1965] 1 C.C.C. 1 (S.C.C.).
10 Ibid., at page 8.

Automatism may also be used as a defence when the accused's involuntary, unconscious act results from taking a drug without knowing its effect. For example, in *R. v. King*,[11] the accused was charged with impaired driving. His dentist had injected him with a drug. The accused did not know the drug's effects, nor was he made aware of the effects. Shortly after he drove away from the dentist's office, the drug caused the accused to lose consciousness, and he drove into a parked car. His act of driving while impaired was considered an involuntary act, and he was found not guilty. The result would have been different if the accused had known that the drug would produce unconsciousness.

If the accused is aware of being subject to states of unconsciousness, automatism will not be a successful defence. For example, in *R. v. Shaw*,[12] the accused suffered from a physical disability, which the court concluded was probably epilepsy. Although the accused knew he was subject to attacks that caused unconsciousness, he continued to drive his car. On one occasion he suffered an attack while driving. He slumped or fell, and this caused the car to accelerate. The car went off the highway and collided with a tree. Two passengers were killed and three others were injured. Because the accused was aware that he could become unconscious while driving, the court held that he could be found criminally responsible for his conduct.

A person who is sleepwalking is considered to be in a state of automatism. For example, in *R. v. Parks*,[13] the accused was charged with murdering his mother-in-law and attempting to murder his father-in-law. The evidence was that he drove 20 kilometres from his home to his in-laws' home and attacked his in-laws in their bed. His defence was that he was sleepwalking at the time. He had recently been under great stress because of a gambling addiction that led him to steal from his employer. The jury accepted psychiatric evidence that Parks was sleepwalking, even though the crime involved very complex behaviour. He was acquitted of both charges. Both the Ontario Court of Appeal and the Supreme Court of Canada rejected appeals by the Crown that the defence should have been insanity, not automatism.

The possibility of automatism being caused by a severe psychological blow was recognized by a court in *R. v. K.*[14] The accused killed his wife and was charged with manslaughter. The trial judge summarized the testimony of the accused:

He gave evidence concerning his depression in the months before this tragedy and following the sale of his farm. He described the affection he had for his wife . . . He described his worry over his own depression and the problem that he was facing, whether he was going to leave with his family to go to Vancouver or not. He also described his actions on the day of the tragedy: the telephone call from Mrs. S. saying repeatedly, "your wife is leaving, your wife is leaving," how he went outside looking for the girls [his daughters], met his wife on the street, returning home, going upstairs and

---

11 (1962), 133 C.C.C. 1 (S.C.C.).
12 (1938), 30 C.C.C. 159 (Ont.C.A.).
13 (1992), 75 C.C.C. (3d) 287 (S.C.C.).
14 (1970), 3 C.C.C. (2d) 84 (Ont.H.Ct.).

then coming down again, and then seeing his wife and putting his arms around his wife, saying to her, "please don't leave." To the accused, in his evidence, the rest is like a dream. He remembers falling and getting up, his wife being on the floor calling for help.[15]

People who saw the accused after the incident agreed that he appeared to be in shock. His eyes were glazed and he repeatedly answered questions by saying that he did not know what had happened.

A psychiatrist supported the accused's evidence by stating that in the days before the incident, the accused had become extremely depressed about having sold his farm and the possibility of his wife leaving him. The psychiatrist felt that he had entered a state of automatism as a result of the severe psychological blow of learning that his wife was leaving him. This psychological blow produced a state in which "the mind registered little, and from then on the accused did not know what was happening, his mind no longer being in control of his actions."

The judge instructed the jury that if they accepted the above evidence, they should find the accused not guilty. However, if they believed that a disease of the mind caused the state of automatism, they should find the accused not guilty by reason of insanity. The jury returned a verdict of not guilty.

Note, however, that the ordinary stresses and disappointments of life are not sufficient to be considered psychological blows to induce automatism. This was the decision of the Ontario Court of Appeal (affirmed on appeal to the Supreme Court) in *R. v. Rabey*.[16] Rabey, a male student, learned that a female classmate he had a crush on had written a note making fun of him. He took a rock and attacked her. His defence of automatism failed.

An important difference between the defences of automatism and mental disorder is that an accused who is found not guilty because he or she was in a state of automatism at the time of committing the offence, is immediately released from custody. Recall, this is not the situation with the defence of insanity.

Automatism is a defence to a charge of committing a strict liability offence. Remember from Chapter Three that a strict liability offence involves an *actus reus* (physical element) but no *mens rea* (mental element). Since the acts of a person in a state of automatism are not voluntary, no *actus reus* exists.

E. INTOXICATION

1. Introduction

The law regarding intoxication as a defence has undergone significant changes recently. Until the Supreme Court of Canada decision in *R. v. Daviault*,[17] intoxication by alcohol or drugs was not a defence to a criminal charge.

---

15 Ibid., at page 85.
16 (1977), 37 C.C.C. (2d) 461 (Ont.C.A.); affd. 54 C.C.C. (2d) 1 (S.C.C.).
17 (1994), 93 C.C.C. (3d) 21 (S.C.C.).

However, it could be a partial defence to a charge of committing a specific intent offence. That is, if it could be shown that the accused was too intoxicated to form the specific intent required, then the accused would not be guilty of the offence. However, the accused could still be found guilty of any included offence if it only required general intent. The decision in *Daviault*, and subsequent legislation, have changed the situations where this defence can be used. In *Daviault*, the accused was charged with the sexual assault (a general intent offence) of an 85-year-old woman. The accused was a chronic alcoholic and on the day of the assault had consumed a large amount of alcohol—so much, in fact, that it would have caused death or a coma for an ordinary person. Expert evidence was that he may have been in a blackout state in which he lost contact with reality. The trial judge acquitted the accused on the grounds that, because of the accused's intoxication, there was reasonable doubt as to whether the accused had the minimal intent necessary for the assault. The court of appeal held that the trial judge erred in allowing the defence, and substituted a conviction. The Supreme Court of Canada allowed the appeal and ordered a new trial. The Court stated that not allowing the defence of intoxication to general intent offences violates s.7 of the Charter. The principles of fundamental justice require that criminal offences have *mens rea*. The intention to become drunk cannot be substituted for the intention to commit an assault. It is also a violation of the presumption of innocence under s.11(d) of the Charter to convict someone when there is reasonable doubt regarding the existence of *mens rea*. The Court fashioned a new rule to deal with intoxication as a defence. It states that the accused can use the defence of intoxication when it is established that the accused was in a state of intoxication akin to automatism or insanity.[18] Also, as with the defence of mental disorder, the accused has the burden of proving on a balance of probabilities that he or she was in an extreme state of intoxication.

This decision was roundly criticized, especially by women's groups, who felt that allowing drunkenness as a defence—to sexual assault in particular—would allow men to unfairly escape criminal responsibility. The federal government responded by enacting s.33.1, which came into force in September 1995. It states:

> **33.1 (1) It is not a defence to an offence referred to in subsection (3) that the accused, by reason of self-induced intoxication, lacked the general intent or the voluntariness required to commit the offence, where the accused departed markedly from the standard of care as described in subsection (2).**
>
> **(2) For the purposes of this section, a person departs markedly from the standard of reasonable care generally recognized in Canadian society and is thereby criminally at fault where the person, while in**

---

18 A previous Supreme Court of Canada case, *R. v. Bernard* (1988), 45 C.C.C. (3d) 11, suggested that such a rule might apply in a proper case. It was not until *Daviault* that the Court clearly developed the rule and made it part of the law.

a state of self-induced intoxication that renders the person unaware of, or incapable of consciously controlling, their behaviour, voluntarily or involuntarily interferes with or threatens to interfere with the bodily integrity of another person.

(3) This section applies in respect of an offence under this Act or any other Act of Parliament that includes as an element an assault or any other interference or threat of interference by a person with the bodily integrity of another person.

Section 33.1 was enacted in response to *Daviault*.[19] Section 31.1 places a limit on the self-induced intoxication defence. The defence recognized in Daviault will not be available for any of the offences referred in s. 31.1(3) if the accused departed markedly from the standard of care described in s.31.1(2). The effect of s.31.1(2) is to deem a certain level of fault in an accused who departs markedly from the standard of care set out in that subsection. Section 31.1(3) would likely include most of the personal injury offences since even a threat of interference with the complainant's bodily integrity would be sufficient to trigger the limits set down in s.31.1(3).

Note that this section applies only to crimes of violence. The rule in *Daviault* still applies to general intent offences that do not involve personal violence—for example, mischief (wilfully destroying property). Also, since this law applies to general intent offences, intoxication could still be a defence to a specific intent offence, such as robbery (assault with intent to steal). Presumably, the accused would still be able to raise the defence to the crime of robbery, but could not use it for the included offence of assault.

2. When the Defence of Intoxication Can Be Used— A Summary

With the decision in *Daviault* and the enactment of section 31.1, how and whether intoxication is used as a defence will depend on the type of offence involved.

The rule in *Daviault* allowing the defence of intoxication applies to general intent crimes that do not involve personal violence. The intoxication must be so extreme that the accused is in a state of unawareness similar to automatism or insanity. The court pointed out in *Daviault* that expert evidence will ordinarily be necessary to show that the accused was in such a state.

Section 31.1(1) does not apply where the Crown fails to prove that the intoxication was self-induced, in the sense that the accused intended to become intoxicated either by voluntarily ingesting a substance knowing, or having reasonable grounds to know, that it might be dangerous, or by recklessly ingesting a substance, such as prescription medication.[20] While section 31.1 violates sections 7 and 11 (d) of the Charter, the court held in *Vickberg*, that it was a reasonable limit within the meaning of s. 1, and therefore valid.

19 Supra, note 17.
20 See *R. v. Vickberg* (1998), 16 C.R. (5th) 164 (B.C.S.C.).

The defence cannot be used for general intent offences involving personal violence.

If the defence is used for specific intent offences, then evidence of intoxication can be considered to determine whether the accused was so impaired by drugs or alcohol that he or she could not have formed the specific intent necessary for the offence. Recall from Chapter Three that specific intent crimes require an extra or ulterior intent. The accused does one illegal act for the purpose of achieving another illegal act. *R. v. George* is the classic case on using intoxication as a defence to a specific intent crime.[21] The accused was charged with robbery and the included offence of assault, having violently manhandled an 84-year-old man until the victim agreed to give him his money. The accused raised the defence of intoxication. He was found not guilty of robbery, which requires an assault with intent to steal, but guilty of the included offence of assault. In other words, the Court held that the accused was too drunk to form the specific intent to steal but could form the intent to apply force to another person.

F. DURESS AND COMPULSION

The defence of duress operates as an excuse for criminal conduct. The defence is that the accused had no realistic alternative course of action available where he or she was subjected to an intentional threat from another person. There are two defences of duress. One, referred to as compulsion, is in the Criminal Code, and the other is a common law defence. The two defences apply in different situations.

1. Compulsion Under the Code

The Criminal Code defence states:

> **17. A person who commits an offence under compulsion by threats of immediate death or [the word grievous has been removed from the Code] bodily harm from a person who is present when the offence is committed is excused for committing the offence if the person believes that the threats will be carried out and if the person is not a party to a conspiracy or association whereby the person is subject to compulsion, but this section does not apply where the offence that is committed is high treason or treason, murder, piracy, attempted murder, sexual assault, sexual assault with a weapon, threats to a third party, or causing bodily harm, aggravated sexual assault, forcible abduction, hostage taking, robbery, assault with a weapon or causing bodily harm, aggravated assault, unlawfully causing bodily harm, arson or an offence under sections 280 to 283 (abduction and detention of young persons).**

---

21 (1960), 128 C.C.C. 289 (S.C.C.).

Before an accused can rely on the defence of compulsion as outlined in s.17, the following must first be established:

- The accused committed an offence not listed in s.17.
- The accused committed the offence because he or she believed the threats of immediate death or immediate grievous bodily harm would be carried out.
- The threats were delivered by a person who was present at the time the accused committed the offence.
- The accused was not a member of a group planning to commit the offence.

A 1993 decision of the Quebec Court of Appeal, *R. v. Langlois,*[22] held that s.17 violates s.7 of the Charter in that it allows a person who is morally innocent to be convicted of an offence. This is because (a) the defence is not available for all offences, (b) the accused must face threats of immediate death or bodily harm by a person who was present when the crime was committed, and (c) the defence does not apply when the threats are made against a member of the accused's family. In *Langlois,* the accused was a recreation officer at a penitentiary in Quebec who was caught trying to smuggle drugs into the prison. His defence was that threats had been made against the safety of his wife and children. He did not feel that he had time to contact the police or that they would be able to adequately protect his family. A jury acquitted him. The Crown appealed on the grounds that the judge should not have left the defence of duress with the jury. The court of appeal dismissed the appeal, holding that s.17 violates the Charter, and is therefore unenforceable. Without s.17 operating, the accused was able to use the common law defence of duress. This decision appears to be contrary to the Supreme Court of Canada decision in *R. v. Carker.*[23] The accused was charged with having unlawfully and wilfully damaged public property-plumbing fixtures in the accused's prison cell. The accused testified that he committed the offence during a disturbance, in the course of which, a substantial body of prisoners, shouting in unison from their separate cells, threatened the accused (who did not join in the disturbance) saying that if he did not break the plumbing fixture in his cell he would be kicked in the head, his arms would be broken, and he would get a knife in the back at the first opportunity. The Court decided that although there was little doubt that the accused committed the offence under the compulsion of threats of death and grievous bodily harm, these were not threats of "immediate death" or "immediate grievous bodily harm." After all, the persons who were uttering the threats were locked up in separate cells.

Previous interpretations of s.17 required the threatener be present at both the time and place of the committed offence. The requirement of immediacy (threat of immediate death or bodily harm) and presence (threat from a per-

22 (1993), 19 C.R. (4th) 87 (Que.C.A.).
23 (1967), 2 C.C.C. 190 (S.C.C.).

son who is present when the offence is committed) infringe the Charter of Rights and Freedoms and is not saved by s. 1.

The case of *R. v. Ruzic*,[24] struck down the presence and immediacy requirement of s. 17. The court in *Ruzic* stated ". . . a threat will seldom meet the immediacy criterion if the threatener is not physically present at or near the scene. The immediacy and present requirements, taken together, clearly preclude threats of harm. . . . Thus, by the strictness of its conditions s.17 breaches s. 7 of the Charter because it allows individuals who acted involuntarily to be declared criminally liable." [25]

2. The Common Law Defence of Duress

The Supreme Court, in *R. v. Paquette*,[26] held that the common law defence of duress, which existed before s.17 was enacted, can be used in situations not covered by s.17—that is, where the accused is not the principal actor. The accused drove the getaway car from a robbery where an innocent bystander had been killed. He claimed that the principal actors had forced him to do so at gunpoint. Since the charge was murder, Pacquette could not use the s.17 defence. However, the Court held that the common law defence was still available where the accused was not the person who actually committed the offence.

The common law defence of duress does not exclude any offences. An objective test is used to determine whether it is available to the accused: What would a reasonable person have done in the circumstances? Also, it does not require that the threat be of immediate death or bodily harm—that is, the threat could be for the future. Finally, under the common law, the presence of the threatening person is not required when the crime is committed.

The Supreme Court of Canada recently considered the defence of duress in *R. v. Hibbert*.[27] The accused was charged with the attempted murder of his friend, Cohen. Hibbert ran into Bailey in the lobby of an apartment building. Bailey, who was a drug dealer, and who the accused believed was armed with a gun, ordered Hibbert to take him to Cohen's apartment. When Hibbert refused, Bailey forced him into the basement and punched him in the face. Bailey and the accused then went to Bailey's car, where two women were waiting. Hibbert sat in the back while Bailey drove. Bailey dropped the women off and then ordered Hibbert to sit in the front seat. Bailey drove Hibbert to a phone booth and told him to phone Cohen to ask him to meet him (i.e., Hibbert) in Cohen's lobby. They went to Cohen's building, where Hibbert buzzed Cohen on the intercom. When Cohen arrived in the lobby, Bailey shot him. Bailey was never found, but Hibbert turned himself in to the police the next day. One of the issues that reached the Supreme Court of Canada was whether, to use the defence of duress, the accused must show that he did not have a "safe avenue of escape." The Court held that a person

24 (2001), 153 C.C.C. (3d) 1 (S.C.C.).
25 Ibid., at pages 28-29.
26 (1976), 30 C.C.C. (2d) 417 (S.C.C.).
27 (1995), 99 C.C.C. (3d) 193 (S.C.C.).

cannot rely on the defence of duress if he or she had an opportunity to safely remove himself or herself from the situation of duress. Furthermore, whether a safe avenue of escape existed is determined on an objective standard: Would a reasonable person see an avenue of escape? However, when considering the perceptions of a reasonable person, the personal circumstances of the accused are relevant and important and should be taken into account.

G. NECESSITY

The defence of necessity is a type of excuse. It is related to the defence of duress in that duress is a particular type of necessity. In *Hibbert*,[28] the Court explained that the difference between duress and necessity is that, in a case of duress, the danger is caused by intentional threats of bodily harm, while in a case of necessity, the danger is caused by forces of nature or human conduct other than intentional threats of bodily harm. The defence of necessity, which has developed through the common law, is rarely used. The Supreme Court of Canada has said that in situations of emergency, where normal human instincts compel a person to break the law (i.e., where there is "no legal way out"), the defence may be used. The emergency must present a threat to the self, or the accused must be acting for altruistic reasons.

The case that confirmed the existence of this defence is *Perka et al. v. The Queen*.[29] The accused were smuggling drugs from Columbia to Alaska. The drugs were delivered to the accused's ship by plane in international waters off Columbia. The drugs were to be dropped in international waters off Alaska. The ship encountered poor weather conditions and developed mechanical problems. For the safety of the crew, the ship entered a Canadian bay to make repairs. The ship then became grounded. The next day, the police investigated and found the drugs. The accused were charged with importing drugs into Canada. Their defence was that they never intended to enter Canada but acted out of necessity to save themselves. The Supreme Court of Canada held that the accused could raise this defence. It would be up to a jury to decide whether the facts were as the accused claimed. If the facts were as claimed, compliance with the law was impossible, since the situation was such that failure to act would have endangered the lives and safety of the accused. The Court also noted that the accused were not doing anything illegal in Canada until they brought the boat ashore.

H. CONSENT

In limited circumstances an accused may use as a defence the fact that the victim consented to the accused's act. For example, if the accused engaged in

---

28 Ibid.
29 (1984), 14 C.C.C. (3d) 385 (S.C.C.). See also *R. v. Latimer* (2001), 150 C.C.C. (3d) 129, where the court outlined three essential elements which must be considered in assessing the defence of necessity.

a fight with another individual, and as a result of the fight was charged with assault, he may be able to argue that the other person consented to the fight. If it can be established that both parties consented to the fight, the accused may be entitled to an acquittal.[30]

1. Offences for Which Consent Is Not a Defence

There are several offences for which consent is specifically mentioned as not being a defence. For example, the victim's consent to be killed is no defence to a murder charge. Section 14 states:

> **14. No person is entitled to consent to have death inflicted on him, and such consent does not affect the criminal responsibility of any person by whom death may be inflicted on the person by whom consent is given.**

There are several sexual offences against children where consent may not be a defence unless certain circumstances exist. These offences include sexual interference (s.151), invitation to sexual touching (s.152), sexual exploitation (s.153), and the offences of sexual assault (ss. 271 to 273). These offences are discussed in Chapters Seven and Twelve.

2. Consent by Fraud or Threats of Bodily Harm

When consent is available as a defence, the victim's consent must be a real or valid consent. If the consent is obtained by fraud, it is not considered real, and therefore cannot constitute a defence. For example, if a physician tells a female patient that her treatment requires her to have sexual intercourse with him, her consent is not valid. Similarly, consent obtained through threats of bodily harm is not valid.

3. Consent and Sexual Assault

Sections 273.1 and 273.2 of the Code are special provisions regarding consent and the offences of sexual assault. These 1992 amendments to the Code were referred to in the media as the "no means no" provisions. They are discussed in more detail in Chapter Twelve. Briefly, however, s.273.1 sets out certain situations where "no consent is obtained"—for example, where the accused induces consent by abusing a position of trust, or where the complainant initially agrees to engage in sexual activity and then expresses a lack of agreement to continue. Section 273.2 concerns situations where the accused cannot rely on the defence of mistaken belief in consent—for example, where the accused's mistaken belief arose from self-induced intoxication or wilful blindness.

---

30 The Supreme Court in *Jobidon* (1991), 66 C.C.C. (3d) 454 held that a person cannot consent to a fist fight that causes serious hurt or nontrivial bodily harm. Therefore, consent can only be valid where minor hurt results from a fistfight. This issue is discussed further in Chapter Twelve.

I. THE PERMISSIBLE USE OF FORCE: SELF-DEFENCE, THE DEFENCE OF OTHERS, AND DEFENCE OF PROPERTY

1. Responsibility for Excessive Force

In some situations a person is justified in using force. Self-defence, defence of others, and the defence of property are justifications for using force against another person. The general rule is that only as much force as necessary in the circumstances can be used. A person who uses an excessive amount of force is held criminally and civilly responsible. In other words, the person could be sued in a civil action or charged with a crime. Section 26 sets out a person's criminal responsibility:

> **26. Every one who is authorized by law to use force is criminally responsible for any excess thereof according to the nature and quality of the act that constitutes the excess.**

So, for example, a person who uses excessive force for self-defence could be charged with assault or even murder depending on the circumstances.

2. Use of Force to Prevent Commission of an Offence

Anyone can use as much force as reasonably necessary to prevent the commission of certain offences. This defence is set out in s.27:

> **27. Every one is justified in using as much force as is reasonably necessary**
>
> **(a) to prevent the commission of an offence**
>
> **(i) for which, if it were committed, the person who committed it might be arrested without warrant, and**
>
> **(ii) that would be likely to cause immediate and serious injury to the persons or property of anyone, or**
>
> **(b) to prevent anything being done that, on reasonable grounds, he believes would, if it were done, be an offence mentioned in paragraph (a).**

The offences to which paragraph (a) refers are discussed in Chapter Five under arrest without warrant. However, in general, any offence that is likely to cause serious harm to a person or property falls within this section.

3. Self-defence

a. Against an Unprovoked Assault

Section 34(1) provides that a person may use force in order to protect himself or herself against an unprovoked assault:

34. (1) Every one who is unlawfully assaulted without having provoked the assault is justified in repelling force by force if the force he uses is not intended to cause death or grievous bodily harm and is no more than is necessary to enable him to defend himself.

The offence of assault includes threats and attempts to apply force to another person. This means that the person need not wait to be physically assaulted before acting in self-defence.

An accused can rely on s.34(1) as a defence only if he or she did not provoke the other person to commit the assault. If the accused did provoke the other person to commit the assault, then the accused may be able to rely on s.34(2) or s.35, discussed below. For the purposes of s.34 and s.35, provocation includes provocation by blows, words, or gestures (s.36).

Section 34(1) applies to situations where the accused did not intend to cause death or grievous bodily harm. The important point is the accused's intention and whether the force used was no more than necessary; it is not whether death or grievous bodily harm resulted. For example, in *R. v. Kandola*,[31] the accused was charged with manslaughter after he and the deceased had been involved in a long and escalating argument. The death occurred when the deceased and his friends appeared at the accused's home after telephoning threats to sexually assault all the women in the house. The police were called after the phone call, but no car was dispatched. They were called again when the deceased and his friends arrived at the house. Again no car was sent to the house. The deceased banged on the door while his friends surrounded the house armed with hockey sticks and possibly a rifle. The police were called for a third time. The tape from this phone call indicated sounds of hysterical fear and bedlam as the house, which contained 16 people—including four or five women and two children—was clearly under attack. The accused took out a handgun, crawled to a window on the top floor, put his arm out the window, and fired blindly. He did this, he testified, in order to scare off the attackers. One of the bullets killed the deceased. The accused was convicted of manslaughter at his trial. The judge held that the accused had taken an unjustified risk in firing the gun as he did. The appeal court disagreed. The court held that all of the elements for using the defence were present: the accused was unlawfully assaulted; he did not provoke the assault; he was justified in repelling force by force; he had a reasonable doubt whether the appellant intended to cause death or grievous bodily harm; and the force used by the accused—firing a warning shot without aiming at the assailant—was no more than was necessary to enable him to defend himself. The court stated that, in this case, the consequences of shooting the gun were not intended. Once the trial judge found that the accused was justified in using the amount of force that he did use, the defence was made out. Also, the appeal court noted that courts are tolerant in measuring the necessary amount of force needed in genuine cases of self-defence.

---

31 (1993), 80 C.C.C. (3d) 481 (B.C.C.A.).

b. Section 34(2) and Self-defence

(2) Every one who is unlawfully assaulted and who causes death or grievous bodily harm in repelling the assault is justified if

(a) he causes it under reasonable apprehension of death or grievous bodily harm from the violence with which the assault was originally made or with which the assailant pursues his purposes, and

(b) he believes, on reasonable grounds, that he cannot otherwise preserve himself from death or grievous bodily harm.

Section 34(2) applies in situations where the accused did intend to cause bodily harm or death. Under s.34(2), there are three requirements that a person who causes grievous bodily harm, or who kills another in self-defence, must meet:

- There must have been an unlawful assault.
- The accused must have been under a reasonable fear of death or serious bodily harm.
- The accused must have believed on reasonable grounds that there was no other way to save himself or herself.

The requirements have subjective and objective elements. Regarding the first, the Supreme Court of Canada, in *R. v. Pétel*,[32] said that the question is not whether the accused was being unlawfully assaulted, but rather, did the accused reasonably believe that she was being unlawfully assaulted? Thus, an honest but reasonable mistake as to the existence of the assault is possible.

Regarding the second element, the issue is whether a person in the situation of the accused would have been under a reasonable fear of death or serious injury. For example, the case discussed on the next page, *R. v. Lavallée*, involved a woman who had been repeatedly battered by her husband over a four-year period. The question for the Supreme Court was whether a woman in the accused's position and with her experience would have a reasonable apprehension of death or serious physical harm. Although s.34(2) does not specifically require the accused to have been in "imminent" (immediate) peril when he or she acted in self-defence, courts have "read" this requirement into the defence as a way of ensuring that the self-defence really was necessary. However, recent court decisions, discussed below, have ruled that imminent peril is not always necessary for the defence.

Regarding the third element, although the accused's belief that there is no other way to save himself or herself must be based on reasonable grounds, it is not necessary to consider whether an ordinary person would have held the same belief. Rather, the important questions are: Did the accused actually believe that there was no other way to save himself or herself? And was the belief based on reasonable grounds?

---

32 (1994), 87 C.C.C. (3d) 97 (S.C.C.).

The Supreme Court of Canada has recently ruled that s.34(2) applies even though the accused may have provoked the assault, because the words, "without having provoked the assault" are not used, as they are in s.34(1). The Court acknowledged that this is a somewhat illogical result, because s.35, which specifically deals with provoked assaults, requires a person to "retreat" before he or she is justified in using force for self-defence, while s.34(2) does not have such a requirement. The Court suggested that the law of self-defence needs to be "cleared up" by legislative action.[33]

Recently, the Supreme Court, in *R. v. Lavallee*,[34] expanded self-defence by accepting evidence of "the battered woman syndrome." In this case, experts testified that the accused felt "trapped, vulnerable, worthless" and unable to leave the relationship despite being repeatedly abused by her husband over a four-year period. On the day of the killing, he found her hiding in a closet. He handed her a gun and dared her to shoot him. He said that if she did not shoot, he would kill her later. When he turned to leave the room, she shot him in the head. The Court held that where the battered woman syndrome applies, the accused does not need to prove imminent peril; a well-founded anticipation of peril is enough. The Supreme Court, in *Pétel*,[35] clarified the place of imminent danger in self-defence cases. The Court stated that, when self-defence is claimed, there is no need for imminent danger. This is only one factor that juries must consider in deciding whether "the accused had a reasonable apprehension of danger and a reasonable belief that she could not extricate herself otherwise than by killing her attacker."[36]

c. Section 35 and Provoked Assault

Section 35 specifically deals with situations where a person provokes an assault on him or herself by another person (e.g., by insulting the other person or by assaulting him):

> **35. Every one who has without justification assaulted another but did not commence the assault with intent to cause death or grievous bodily harm, or has without justification provoked an assault upon himself by another, may justify the use of force subsequent to the assault if**
>
> **(a) he uses the force**
>
> **(i) under reasonable apprehension of death or grievous bodily harm from the violence of the person whom he has assaulted or provoked, and**
>
> **(ii) in the belief, on reasonable ["and probable" not in Code] grounds, that it is necessary in order to preserve himself from death or grievous bodily harm;**

---

33 *R. v. McIntosh* (1995), 95 C.C.C. (3d) 481 (S.C.C.).
34 (1990), 55 C.C.C. (3d) 97 (S.C.C.).
35 Supra, note 32.
36 Ibid., at page 104.

(b) he did not, at any time before the necessity of preserving himself from death or grievous bodily harm arose, endeavour to cause death or grievous bodily harm; and

(c) he declined further conflict and quitted or retreated from it as far as it was feasible to do so before the necessity of preserving himself from death or grievous bodily harm arose.

In other words, to justify the use of force under s.35, the accused must satisfy all of the following criteria:

- The accused must have assaulted another or in some other way provoked an assault on himself or herself.
- The accused must at no time have intended to cause death or grievous bodily harm.
- After being assaulted, the accused must have been in reasonable danger of death or bodily harm.
- The accused must have believed on reasonable and probable grounds that the force used was necessary to prevent death or grievous bodily harm occurring to himself or herself.
- The accused, before using force, must have exhausted all other ways (such as retreat) of avoiding the use of force.

4. Preventing Assault and the Defence of Others

Sections 34 and 35 deal with situations where an assault actually occurred. Section 37 is concerned with situations where force is used to prevent an assault from occurring.

37. (1) Every one is justified in using force to defend himself or any one under his protection from assault, if he uses no more force

than is necessary to prevent the assault or the repetition of it.

(2) Nothing in this section shall be deemed to justify the wilful infliction of any hurt or mischief that is excessive, having regard to the nature of the assault that the force used was intended to prevent.

Sections 34, 35, and 37 overlap to some extent; however, s.37 does specifically allow a person to defend anyone under his or her protection from assault. The category of persons under protection is not defined, but presumably it includes members of a person's immediate family and any others with whom the person has a close relationship. In *R. v. Wiggs*,[37] the accused was charged with assaulting a boy who, with several other boys, attacked his son. The boys threw his son to the ground, sat on him, and punched and kicked him. The father rushed to the defence of his son; in stopping the attack, he struck one of the boys, causing injury to his face. The court found the father not guilty because, in defending his son, he had used no more force than was necessary in the circumstances.

---

37 [1931] 3 W.W.R. 52 (B.C.C.A.).

5. Defence of Property

The defence of property involves real property or personal property. *Real property* refers to land and to structures attached to the land. *Personal property* refers to movable things, such as a car, a television set, a chair, and so on.

Besides the specific sections discussed below, recall s.27, discussed earlier, which provides a general defence to anyone who uses force to prevent the commission of an offence "that would be likely to cause immediate and serious injury to the person or property of anyone . . ."

a. Personal Property

Sections 38 and 39 deal with a person's right to defend movable property that is in his or her possession:

> **38. (1) Every one who is in peaceable possession of personal property, and every one lawfully assisting him, is justified**
>
> **(a) in preventing a trespasser from taking it, or**
>
> **(b) in taking it from a trespasser who has taken it,**
>
> **if he does not strike or cause bodily harm to the trespasser.**
>
> **(2) Where a person who is in peaceable possession of personal property lays hands on it, a trespasser who persists in attempting to keep it or take it from him or from any one lawfully assisting him shall be deemed to commit an assault without justification or provocation.**
>
> **39. (1) Every one who is in peaceable possession of personal property under a claim of right, and every one acting under his authority, is protected from criminal responsibility for defending that possession, even against a person entitled by law to possession of it, if he uses no more force than is necessary.**

Both these sections apply to persons in possession of personal property. This does not necessarily mean that they own the property. For example, Gina may be renting furniture from Janice. Even though Gina does not own the furniture, if she is in peaceable possession of it, she has a right to defend it.

Under s.38(1), force involving striking or causing bodily harm to the trespasser may not be used to prevent a trespasser from taking the movable property. Under s.39(1), force may be used, even against the lawful owner, but only if the person in peaceable possession has possession under a *claim of right*. In other words, the person must honestly believe, on reasonable grounds, that he or she has a right to possess the property. Thus, a possessor under a claim of right is in a much stronger position than a possessor who does not have some basis for claiming that he or she has a lawful right of possession.

Under s.38(2), a trespasser commits an assault if he or she tries to take movable property from a person in peaceable possession, and if the possessor puts his or her hands on the property. In *R. v. Doucette*,[38] C. had failed to make his payments on a television set that he was purchasing under a conditional sales agreement. Three bailiffs, acting for the seller of the television, entered C.'s house to repossess the set. They were not acting under the authority of a court order, and C. told them to leave. While C. was leaning on the television set, the bailiffs grabbed it and began carrying it away. C. followed "in a threatening manner," and the bailiff, Doucette, believing that C. was about to strike him, hit him in the mouth, knocking him to the floor. Doucette was charged with assault. The court found the accused guilty and made the following points:

- It was illegal for the bailiffs to repossess the television set by the use of force.
- As a peaceable possessor of movable property under a claim of right, C. was protected from criminal responsibility for resisting the taking of the property.
- The bailiffs were trespassers, at least from the point at which C. protested against their being in his house.
- Apart from the actual force applied to C., the bailiffs could be charged with committing an assault under s.38(2) because they persisted in taking the property after C. had leaned on it.

b. Dwelling-house and Real Property

Sections 40 and 41 apply to a person who is in peaceable possession of a dwelling-house or real property and uses force to defend it:

> **40. Every one who is in peaceable possession of a dwelling-house, and every one lawfully assisting him or acting under his authority, is justified in using as much force as is necessary to prevent any person from forcibly breaking into or forcibly entering the dwelling-house without lawful authority.**

> **41. (1) Every one who is in peaceable possession of a dwelling-house or real property, and every one lawfully assisting him or acting under his authority, is justified in using force to prevent any person from trespassing on the dwelling-house or real property, or to remove a trespasser therefrom, if he uses no more force than is necessary.**

> **(2) A trespasser who resists an attempt by a person who is in peaceable possession of a dwelling-house or real property, or a person lawfully assisting him or acting under his authority, to prevent his entry or to remove him, shall be deemed to commit an assault without justification or provocation.**

---

38   (1960), 129 C.C.C. 102 (Ont.C.A.).

Section 40 allows a person to use as much force as is necessary to prevent a person from forcibly entering his or her home without lawful authority. "Dwelling-house" is defined in s.2 as:

> . . . **the whole or any part of a building or structure that is kept or occupied as a permanent or temporary residence, and includes**
>
> **(a) a building within the curtilage of a dwelling-house that is connected to it by a doorway or by a covered and enclosed passage-way, and**
>
> **(b) a unit that is designed to be mobile and to be used as a permanent or temporary residence and that is being used as such a residence.**

In *R. v. Kephart*,[39] the accused used this defence to the charge that he had obstructed a police officer in the execution of his duty. The accused had attempted to prevent a police officer from entering his home. It was established that the officer did not have a lawful right to enter the home; therefore, the accused could use this defence.

Section 41(1) is broader, in that it allows a person to use force to remove trespassers not only from his or her home but from any part of his or her real property. For example, a person may forcibly remove a trespasser from the front lawn. The elements of the defence were discussed in *R. v. Born with a Tooth*.[40] The court said that the defence has four elements: the accused must be in possession of land (possession requires some control over the land); the possession must be peaceable (peaceable does not mean peacefully—it refers to a possession not seriously challenged by others before the incident in question); the victim of the assault must be a trespasser; and the force used to eject the trespasser must be reasonable in the circumstances.

This section also applies to commercial property—for example, to shopping malls. In *R. v. Keating*,[41] the owner of a mall grabbed and threatened a boy he found skateboarding in the parking lot of the mall. Signs were posted that prohibited skateboarding. The trial judge found the accused guilty of assault and uttering a death threat. On appeal, the court held that the judge erred in finding that a defence under s.41 was not available to the accused. The court also held that although the complainant was initially an invitee to the mall, once he began skateboarding it was open to the court to find that he was a trespasser, since he had been invited to the mall to shop, not to skateboard.

In *R. v. Montague*,[42] the issue was whether the accused had used more force than was necessary in removing a person from his property. Atkinson came to the door of the accused's home and asked him if he would be interested in a discussion of the Bible. The accused said he was not interested and told him to leave. Atkinson agreed to leave. At this point in the case, there was a conflict in the evidence; however, the accused admitted that he pushed

39 (1988), 44 C.C.C. (3d) 97 (Alta.C.A.).
40 (1992), 76 C.C.C. (3d) 169 (Alta.C.A.).
41 (1992), 76 C.C.C. (3d) 371 (N.S.C.A.).
42 (1949), 97 C.C.C. 29 (Ont.Cty.Ct.).

Atkinson to get him to leave. He then followed Atkinson to a point on his property about seven metres from the house and pushed him down in a snowbank. Atkinson got up and ran to the road, with the accused chasing after him. The court concluded that, even if Atkinson was a trespasser, the accused had used more force than was necessary. The court found that Atkinson was actually leaving as requested when the accused proceeded to follow him out. There was nothing to suggest that Atkinson would not have continued leaving if the accused had simply closed the door and stayed in his house. His attack on Atkinson at the snowbank was an assault and was clearly not necessary for the defence of his property.

Under s.41(2), a trespasser who resists an attempt by the possessor of the property to remove him from that property is guilty of an assault. However, in order to be guilty, the trespasser must perform some overt act of resistance. Passive resistance is not sufficient to justify a conviction. In *R. v. Kellington*,[43] about 25 persons came to the offices of the Social Services Department of the city of Vancouver at about 5 p.m. They were there to get information about the department's policy regarding funerals for indigent persons. The director of the department discussed the policy with them for about 30 minutes. Then disagreements arose between the director and the group, and he asked them to leave the building. They refused, and the police were called to remove them. One member of the group simply remained seated in a chair until arrested. She was charged with assault under s.41(2). The court found her not guilty because she had done no overt act to resist her removal from the property.

J. MISTAKE OF FACT

A person who commits a prohibited act while believing that certain circumstances exist, that do not actually exist, may be able to rely on the defence of mistake of fact. A *mistake of fact* is an error as to some circumstance. For example, if Albert takes Brian's book believing it to be his own, he is acting under a mistake of fact. A mistake of fact will be a defence to a criminal charge if (a) the mistake was an honest one, and (b) no offence would have been committed if the circumstances had been as the accused believed them to be.

So, in the example above, Albert will not be guilty of theft if he had an honest belief that the book belonged to him, since, if the book had belonged to him, no offence would have been committed. Mistake of fact is a defence to most charges under the Code, because a person who is acting under a mistaken belief in the facts does not have the *mens rea* or guilty mind required to commit the offence. In the example above, Albert did not have the *mens rea* to commit theft (i.e., the intent to deprive the owner).

---

43 (1972), 7 C.C.C. (2d) 564 (B.C.S.C.).

The Supreme Court of Canada dealt with the defence of mistake of fact in *Beaver v. R.*[44] The accused was charged with illegal possession of a narcotic drug. He had sold heroin to an undercover RCMP officer. His defence was that he honestly believed that he was selling sugar, not heroin, even though he had told the officer he was selling a narcotic. The Court found the accused not guilty because "[t]he essence of the crime is the possession of the forbidden substance and in a criminal case there is in law no possession without knowledge of the character of the forbidden substance." In short, to be guilty of illegal possession of a narcotic, the accused must know that he or she has a narcotic. A person who has an honest but mistaken belief that the substance is sugar does not have the knowledge required for possession. The mistaken belief must be honest; it does not have to be reasonable. Whether a reasonable person would have believed that the heroin was sugar is merely one factor to be considered by the jury in determining whether the accused's mistake was an honest mistake.

Now consider the following situation: Alice is charged with possession of narcotics. She says that she thought she was in possession of counterfeit money.[45] Mistake of fact is not a possible defence here, because, if the facts had been as Alice believed them to be, an offence would still have been committed.

Several sections in the Code limit the defence of mistake of fact for sexual offences involving young people. For example, under s.150.1 an accused cannot use this defence to a charge of touching a person under 14 years of age for a sexual purpose unless the accused took all reasonable steps to ascertain the age of the young person. These rules are discussed in Chapter Seven under sexual offences. As mentioned earlier, there are also special rules regarding mistaken belief of consent when the charge is sexual assault. These rules are discussed in Chapter Twelve with the offences of sexual assault.

K. MISTAKE OF LAW

The general rule that "ignorance of the law is no excuse" is contained in s.19:

19. Ignorance of the law by a person who commits an offence is not an excuse for committing that offence.

In other words, everyone is presumed to know the criminal law. A mistake of fact is an error as to some circumstance or fact. A mistake of law is an error as to the legal status of the circumstance or fact. For example, in *Beaver* the accused was found not guilty of possession of heroin because he honestly believed that the heroin was sugar. This was a mistake of fact. However, if Beaver had known that he had heroin, but honestly believed that it was legal to possess heroin, he would have been making a *mistake of law*, and thus would have been guilty.

---

44 (1957), 118 C.C.C. 129 (S.C.C.).
45 See, for example, *R. v. Kundeus* (1975), 24 C.C.C. (2d) 276 (S.C.C.).

1. Mistake of Civil Law

In some situations, a mistake of civil law may be a defence. A mistake of civil law occurs when a person has an honest belief that he or she has a legal right under the civil law, but in fact does not have the right. In *R. v. Howson*,[46] the accused, the operator of a car-towing service, was charged with theft. Haines had parked his car on private property. There were signs on the property stating that unauthorized cars would be towed away at the owner's expense. The owner of the private property asked the accused to remove the car. The accused towed it to a yard surrounded by a high fence and guarded by an attendant and a dog. When Haines arrived at the yard, the attendant told him he could not have his car unless he paid $12.00 for the towing and storage. Haines did not get his car back until the next evening, when he paid the towing and storage charges.

The offence of theft is committed if a person deprives a property owner of the property "without colour of right." The term *colour of right* refers to an honest mistake of fact or law that leads a person to believe that he or she has a legal justification for the actions performed. In *Howson*, the accused had no legal right to refuse to release the car, but he honestly believed that he had the legal right to refuse until the money was paid. The court found the accused not guilty because he acted with colour of right. He had made a mistake of law, and thus was acting without the *mens rea* required in the offence of theft. However, the court warned the accused that now that he was aware of his legal position, he could not rely on the same mistake of law as a defence to any similar charges in the future.

2. Officially Induced Error

The defence of *officially induced error* is a recently recognized defence by some provincial courts of appeal. Its existence reflects the fact that we live in an extremely complex society and that we need to be able to rely on the advice of government officials regarding the law. The defence may be used for breaches of regulatory laws (not true crimes) where the accused was aware of a possible illegality and sought the advice of the government official in charge of enforcing the law. The Ontario Court of Appeal[47] has said that to use this defence, the accused must show that he or she relied on an erroneous legal opinion and that the reliance was reasonable. Whether the reliance was reasonable will depend on factors such as the efforts the accused made to ascertain the law; the complexity or obscurity of the law; and the position of the official who gave the advice. For example, in *R. v. Bauman and Bauman*,[48] the two accused, a husband and wife, were charged under a municipal by-law with operating a business in a family dwelling. Ms. Bauman was a denture therapist. Before opening the office,

---

46 (1966), 3 C.C.C. 348 (Ont.C.A.).
47 *R. v. Cancoil Thermal Corp. and Parkinson* (1986), 27 C.C.C. (3d) 295 (Ont.C.A.).
48 (1994), 32 C.R. (4th) 176 (Ont.C.J.Prov.Div.); see also 18 O.R. (3d) 772.

her husband purchased a copy of the by-law and asked a city planner if they could open a business in their home. The planner assured him that they could. The accused were acquitted at their trial and the Crown's appeal was dismissed because both the trial and appeal courts accepted the defence of officially induced error. In this case, the law was complex, the official had a significant position, and the advice was definitive and reasonable.

There is some indication that the Supreme Court of Canada will, once an appropriate case comes before it, recognize the defence of officially induced error as an excuse to regulatory offences or crimes. In *R. v. Jorgenson*,[49] the accused was the owner of a video store that carried "adult videos." He was charged with selling obscene material under s.163(2). Although he was acquitted on other grounds, one of the nine Supreme Court judges who heard the case, Chief Justice Antonio Lamer, argued that the defence of officially induced error should be available to Jorgenson because the videos in the case had been approved by the Ontario Film Review Board (note, criminal courts are not bound by the decisions of provincial review boards regarding whether a film is obscene). Since it was not necessary to consider this defence because the Crown failed to prove the *mens rea* of the offence, the other judges expressly refrained from commenting on the availability of this defence. However, Lamer pointed out that there are an "astounding number" of laws for which a person in Canada can incur criminal liability. Although people are expected to know the law, "it is certainly reasonable for someone to have assumed he knows the law after consulting a representative of the state acting in a capacity which makes him an expert on that particular subject."[50]

L. ENTRAPMENT

In a 1988 decision, *R. v. Mack*,[51] the Supreme Court of Canada held that the defence of entrapment exists as part of the doctrine of abuse of process. The defence of entrapment may be allowed when someone has been "set up" or trapped into committing a crime by the police or police informants. These situations often arise in drug investigations. The facts in *Mack* were these: Over a six-month period, a police informer repeatedly asked the accused to sell him drugs. The accused refused to do so until the informer threatened him, at which point he agreed to find him some drugs. The accused testified that although he had once been involved with drugs, he had since given up his drug-related lifestyle. The Court held that the police conduct was unacceptable in this case and that the charges against the accused should be stayed. The Court set out guidelines for deciding whether police conduct amounts to an abuse of process. First, the police cannot provide opportunities for people to commit crimes unless they are acting on reasonable suspi-

---

49 (1995), 102 C.C.C. (3d) 97 (S.C.C.).
50 Ibid., at page 104.
51 (1988), 44 C.C.C. (3d) 513 (S.C.C.).

cions that the people are already engaged in crime, or unless they are carrying on a bona fide investigation. As one judge said, the police cannot randomly test the virtue of people. Second, even when the police do have reasonable suspicions or are carrying on a bona fide investigation, they cannot go beyond providing opportunities—that is, they cannot actually induce a person to commit a crime. A more recent decision, *R. v. Barnes*, dealt with the issue of what a bona fide investigation is. Here, a police officer approached the accused in a Vancouver shopping mall and asked him if he had any "weed." At first the accused said no. The officer asked several more times. Finally, the accused agreed to sell the officer a small amount of hash. The trial judge allowed the defence of entrapment because the police had been engaged in "random virtue testing." The Supreme Court of Canada upheld the decision of the B.C. Court of Appeal, overturning the trial court decision, holding that the defence did not apply in this case. The accused had been approached in an area known for drug trafficking, and the police were conducting a bona fide investigation. It did not matter that the police did not have reasonable grounds to suspect that the accused was involved in crime. His physical presence in an area where a particular criminal activity was occurring was enough.

Questions for Review and Discussion

1. Make a list of different types of defences.
2. Does the accused have to "prove" his or her defence? Explain.
3. Where are defences found?
4. What is the age at which the law presumes children do not have the capacity to commit crimes?
5. What must be established on behalf of the accused if he or she is to be found not criminally responsible because of mental disorder?
6. What is the meaning of the word "wrong" as it is used in the defence of mental disorder?
7. What happens to an accused who is found not criminally responsible because of a mental disorder?
8. **a.** Define the defence of automatism.
   b. What is the difference between insane and non-insane automatism?
9. How is the defence of automatism different from the defence of mental disorder?
10. **a.** What are the rules regarding the defence of intoxication for general intent crimes and for specific intent crimes?
    b. How did the decision in *Daviault* change the law? How did the government respond to this decision?
11. Explain the differences between the Code defence of compulsion and the defence of duress at common law.
12. When can the defence of necessity be used?

13. What did the Supreme Court decide in the case of *R. v. Lavallee?*

14. Discuss situations where consent may not be a defence.

15. What is the general rule concerning the use of force in self-defence, the defence of others, and the defence of property?

16. What does mistake of fact mean when it is used as a defence?

17. In what circumstances might mistake of law be a defence to a crime?

18. How is mistake of fact different from mistake of law?

19. **a.** What is the defence of entrapment?
    b. What guidelines must the police follow to avoid this defence being raised?

20. H.'s boat was destroyed in a fire, and he made an insurance claim for his loss. A short while later, a former employee told the police that H. had paid him to destroy the boat. H. was charged with arson, insurance fraud, and perjury. The employee claimed that on a certain date, he and H. had a conversation during which H. asked him to burn the boat. H. testified at his trial that at the time that conversation supposedly took place, he was elsewhere. Is H. raising an alibi defence? Explain. See *R. v. Hill* (1995), 25 O.R. 97 (Ont.C.A.).

21. Henrik owes $500 to Borje, a well-known underworld figure. Borje threatens Henrik by saying, "If you don't pay me by 10 p.m. tonight, you'll be dead tomorrow morning." Henrik knows that Borje is serious and will carry out the threat if necessary. So Henrik breaks into a store, steals $500, and makes the payment to Borje. Henrik is charged with break, enter, and theft. He raises the defence of compulsion. Will his defence be successful? Explain.

22. Sam had been drinking large amounts of alcohol and had taken Valium pills when he broke into his son's school. He broke a lock on the principal's office door, forced open a file drawer, and stole a cash box containing $140. He buried the cash box under a pile of brush. He claimed to have no memory of these events. The police questioned him a few days after the break-in because the police had found his fingerprints at the school. Realizing what he might have done, he searched for the metal box with a metal detector. He found the box and contacted the police. He also arranged to return the box to the principal and to pay for the damage caused by the break-in. Can Sam use the defence of intoxication? Explain. See *R. v. Shea* (1981), 24 C.R. (3d) 189 (P.E.I.S.C.).

23. M. was charged with speeding on the Trans-Canada Highway. She admitted to speeding but claimed that she was doing so because a pickup truck had approached her rapidly from behind. She said that to avoid an accident, she had increased her speed and then changed lanes to let the truck pass. Does she have a defence to the charge? Explain. See *R. v. Morris* (1994), 32 C.R. (4th) 191 (B.C.S.C.).

Chapter Five
PRE-TRIAL CRIMINAL PROCEDURE

A. INTRODUCTION

Generally, criminal procedure can be separated into three distinct phases: pre-trial procedure, trial procedure, and post-trial procedure. This chapter considers only the more important aspects of pre-trial procedure, including the powers of arrest and search, pre-trial release, and rights of the accused before and after arrest.

B. BRINGING THE ACCUSED BEFORE THE COURT

1. Beginning the Process

Once the police have reasonable grounds for believing that someone has committed a crime and have decided to lay a charge, their next step is to decide how to begin the process that will eventually bring the suspect before a court where criminal liability can be determined. Initially, the police have three choices, not all of which are available in all situations. They can (a) issue an appearance notice, (b) go before a justice to ask for a summons to be issued, or (c) make an arrest, with or without a warrant. Generally speaking, arrests are only made when an appearance notice or summons is inadequate—for example, if there are reasonable grounds to believe that the accused will not show up in court. As you will learn later in this chapter, even when the accused is arrested there are many points along the way to trial where he or she may be released and an appearance notice or summons issued.

Part XVI of the Code, starting with s.493, sets out the procedures for bringing the accused before a justice, who is defined in s.2 of the Code as a justice of the peace or provincial court judge, and for the pre-trial release of the accused where the accused has been arrested. The forms referred to in this chapter are contained in Part XXVIII of the Code.

2. Appearance Notice (Form 9)

Section 496 provides that where a peace officer does not make an arrest (see page 108 for when an arrest cannot be made), the officer may issue an appearance notice if the offence is one of the following:

- An indictable offence mentioned in s.553 (these are the least serious indictable offences).
- A hybrid offence.
- An offence punishable on summary conviction.

An appearance notice is a written form given to a person, usually at the scene of the crime by the police. It contains the accused's name, the substance of the charge, and the time and place the accused must attend court to answer the charge (s.501). If the person is being charged with an indictable offence, the appearance notice may state a time and place that the accused is to go for fingerprinting and photographing, as required by the Identification of Criminals Act.[1] The appearance notice also contains the text of s.145(5) and (6), stating that it is an offence to fail to appear in court, or for the purposes of identification, without lawful excuse. Section 502 is also contained in the appearance notice; it states that a judge may issue a warrant for the arrest of an accused who fails to appear in court or for identification.

The accused signs the form in duplicate and receives a copy, and is then free to go.

Once an appearance notice is issued, an information must be laid before a justice as soon as practicable, or at least before the time stated in the appearance notice for the accused to appear in court. Section 506 provides that the information may be in Form 2. Recall from Chapter Two, that an information is a sworn affidavit that the informant has personal knowledge or reasonable grounds for believing that the named person has committed an offence. If the informant makes out a case against the accused, the appearance notice is confirmed (s.508).

3. Summons (Form 6)

The police may go before a justice and ask that a summons be issued.

A summons is a court order commanding the accused to appear in court on a certain day and time. To obtain a summons, the officer must lay an information before the justice of the peace. If the officer makes out a case against the accused and an arrest warrant is not necessary, a summons is issued. Section 509 sets out the requirements for a summons:

> **509. (1) A summons issued under this part shall**
>
> **(a) be directed to the accused;**
>
> **(b) set out briefly the offence in respect of which the accused is charged; and**

---

1   R.S.C. 1985, c.I-1.

(c) require the accused to attend court at a time and place to be stated therein and to attend thereafter as required by the court in order to be dealt with according to law.

(2) A summons shall be served by a peace officer who shall deliver it personally to the person to whom it is directed or, if that person cannot conveniently be found, shall leave it for him at his last or usual place of abode with an inmate thereof who appears to be at least sixteen years of age.

As with an appearance notice, the summons may require the accused to attend a certain place for the purposes of the Identification of Criminals Act, and will contain a notice that failure to appear at court or for identification is an offence and that the judge may issue an arrest warrant (s.145(4), s.510).

4. Arrests

a. Introduction

An arrest can consist of the actual seizure of the accused's body. It is sufficient for the arresting person to merely touch the accused and to announce that the person is under arrest.

An arrest can also be made by words alone.[2] The arresting person must use words such that the person being arrested is made aware that his or her freedom is being restricted and that he or she is compelled to follow the instructions of the arresting person.

b. Use of Force

A peace officer may, if necessary, use force in making an arrest. This power is granted by s.25:

25. (1) Every one who is required or authorized by law to do anything in the administration or enforcement of the law . . . is, if he acts on reasonable grounds, justified . . . in using as much force as necessary for that purpose.

This section applies not only to the police but also to anyone required or authorized by law to do anything in the administration or enforcement of law. For example, a private person who is assisting an officer is justified in using reasonable force.

Section 25(3) limits s.25(1). It deals with force that is intended or is likely to cause death or grievous bodily harm. It states that no one is justified in using such force unless the person believes on reasonable grounds that it is necessary for the self-preservation of the person or the preservation of anyone under that person's protection.

Subsections (4) and (5) are exceptions to subs.(3) and set out other circumstances where the police can use force intended to cause serious harm or death. Section 25(4) states:

---

2 *R. v. Whitfield*, [1970] 1 C.C.C. 129 (S.C.C.).

25 . . . (4) A peace officer, and every person lawfully assisting the peace officer, is justified in using force that is intended or is likely to cause death or grievous bodily harm to a person to be arrested, if

(a) the person is proceeding lawfully to arrest, with or without warrant, the person to be arrested;

(b) the offence for which the person is to be arrested is one for which that person may be arrested without warrant;

(c) the person to be arrested takes flight to avoid arrest;

(d) the peace officer or other person using the force believes on reasonable grounds that the force is necessary for the purpose of protecting the peace officer, the person lawfully assisting the peace officer or any other person from imminent or future death or grievous bodily harm; and

(e) the flight cannot be prevented by reasonable means in a less violent manner.

Section 25(4) was amended in 1994. Until the 1994 amendment under this section, police could use "as much force as necessary" to prevent the escape of a suspect, unless the escape could be prevented by reasonable means in a less violent manner. In effect, the police could use deadly force to prevent the escape of a person for a relatively minor crime. The amendment requires that when a suspect takes flight, before a peace officer or anyone lawfully assisting that officer can use force likely to cause death or serious bodily harm, these circumstances must exist:

- The peace officer or other person must believe on reasonable grounds that the force is necessary to protect the officer or other persons from imminent or future death or grievous bodily harm.
- The arrest must be lawful.
- The offence must be one for which a person can be arrested without a warrant.
- The flight must not be preventable by reasonable means in a less violent manner.

Presumably, the amendments will prevent situations such as in *Priestman v. Colangelo*,[3] where a police officer used the former s.25(4) to justify his actions. Constables P. and A. were on patrol duty when they received a message on their radio telephone reporting the theft of a car. Almost immediately they saw a motor vehicle that they believed to be—and that later turned out to be—the stolen vehicle. The police car pulled up alongside the stolen car, and P. ordered the driver, S., to stop. Both officers were in uniform, and S. no doubt realized that they were police officers. Instead of stopping, he pulled around the corner and drove away at a high rate of speed. The police car followed and tried three times to pass the stolen car in order to cut it off,

---

3   (1959), 124 C.C.C. 1; 19 D.L.R. (2d) 1 (S.C.C.).

but each time S. pulled to the south side of the road and cut off the police car. On the third occasion, the police car was forced over the south curb onto a boulevard and was compelled to slow down in order to avoid colliding with a hydro pole. Following this third attempt, and as the police car went back onto the road, P. fired a warning shot into the air from his .38 calibre revolver. The stolen car increased its speed. When the police car was one-and-a-half to two car lengths from the stolen car, P. aimed at the left rear tire of the stolen car and fired. The bullet hit the bottom of the frame of the rear window, shattered the glass, ricocheted, and struck S. in the back of the neck, causing him to lose consciousness immediately. The stolen car went over the curb on the south side of the road, grazed a hydro pole, crossed a street, and, in coming to a stop, struck the veranda of a house. Before hitting the house the car ran into and killed two people waiting for a bus.

Constable P. took the position that S.'s escape could not have been prevented by reasonable means in a less violent manner. In other words, P. believed that he was justified in firing his revolver. The court agreed with P., finding that his actions were justified by s.25(4). He had used no more force than was reasonably necessary to prevent S.'s escape.

Section 25(5) allows a peace officer to use force intended or likely to cause death or grievous bodily harm against an inmate who is escaping from a federal penitentiary. The peace officer must believe on reasonable grounds that the inmates of the penitentiary pose a threat of death or grievous bodily harm to the peace officer or another person, and that the escape cannot be prevented by other reasonable means in a less violent manner.

c. Liability for Excessive Use of Force

If more force than necessary is used to arrest the accused, the arresting person may be sued in a civil court for assault and be required to pay damages. In addition, the arresting person can be prosecuted in a criminal court for the offence of assault or one of the more serious criminal offences involving bodily harm. Section 26 of the Code provides:

> **26. Every one who is authorized by law to use force is criminally responsible for any excess thereof according to the nature and quality of the act that constitutes the excess.**

d. The Right to Enter Private Property to Make an Arrest

Whether the arrest is made with or without a warrant, the police have the authority in some situations to enter private premises to make an arrest. The authority to enter private premises for a warrantless arrest for an indictable offence was decided by the Supreme Court of Canada in *R. v. Landry.*[4] Landry was charged with assaulting a peace officer in the execution of his duty contrary to s.270 of the Code. A public transit inspector observed two youths trying to open car doors in a parking lot at the back of a shopping

---

4   (1986), 25 C.C.C. (3d) 1 (S.C.C.).

centre. The inspector called the police. When the police arrived, the inspector gave them a description of the youths and told them that he had seen the youths enter an apartment building. One of the officers approached the building and looked through a basement window, and saw two males who matched the description given by the inspector. The officer then went to the door of the apartment. There was conflicting evidence on whether the door to the apartment was opened by the accused or already open when the officer arrived. However, it was agreed that the officer stood in the doorway of the apartment and asked the accused if he lived there. The officer then told the two youths they were under arrest. Landry indicated that he did not want to go anywhere. The officer then entered the room and took physical control of Landry. A fight broke out that resulted in Landry being charged with assaulting a peace officer in the execution of his duty. The issue for the court was whether the arrest was legal or not—that is, whether the officer had the authority to enter a private premises without permission and without a warrant for arrest. If the arrest was not legal, then the charge against Landry could not stand.

Landry was acquitted at his trial on the grounds that the officer was not in the execution of his duty because he had no power to enter a private premises to make a warrantless arrest. An appeal by the Crown to the Ontario Court of Appeal was dismissed. The Supreme Court of Canada allowed the Crown's appeal and ordered a new trial. The Supreme Court held that the Criminal Code is silent on the spatial limits of arrest without warrant (i.e., on whether an arrest without a warrant is lawful on private premises). Therefore, the Court considered the common law on the point. The Court held that at common law, the police have the authority to make a forcible entry to private premises to effect an arrest. Thus, where the police have the authority to make an arrest without a warrant under s.495(1)(a)— that is, for indictable offences—in proper circumstances, the police may enter a private premises to make an arrest. The policy underlying this law, the Court said is that "there should be no place which gives an offender sanctuary from arrest." The circumstances that must exist are as follows:

- The officers must have reasonable and probable grounds for believing that the person is on the premises.
- The officers must give notice of their presence (e.g., by knocking or ringing the doorbell).
- The officers must give notice of their authority (i.e., announce who they are).
- The officers must give notice of their purpose.

Landry was limited to situations where the accused was being arrested for an indictable offence under s.495(a). Another decision has dealt with police authority to enter where a provincial offence is involved.[5] In this case, the

---

5   *R. v. Macooh* (1993), 82 C.C.C. (3d) 480 (S.C.C.).

police observed the accused motorist running a stop sign. When the police attempted to pull the accused over, he accelerated and went through two more stop signs. He then pulled into an apartment parking lot, exited his car, and ran to an apartment. The officer went to the apartment, identified himself, and called to the accused. The accused did not answer. The officer entered the apartment and told the accused he was being arrested. The accused refused to leave, and an altercation broke out. The accused was charged with impaired driving, failing to stop for an officer, failing to submit to a breathalyzer test, and assaulting an officer. The trial judge found that the police did not have the right to enter the apartment and excluded the evidence gathered after the entry. The accused was acquitted. The case eventually reached the Supreme Court of Canada on the issue of whether the police had a right to enter the apartment. The Court held that under the common law there is a right to enter private premises to make a warrantless arrest when the officer is in "hot pursuit" of a suspect. To be in "hot pursuit" or "fresh pursuit," the accused must be followed in a manner that is continuous and conducted with reasonable effort so that the pursuit and capture and the commission of the crime form a single transaction. The Court, using similar reasoning as in *Landry*, stated that it is unacceptable that a person about to be arrested should be able to take refuge in his home or the home of another person. Practically, the Court noted, offenders should not be encouraged to seek refuge, since it may create situations of danger. The police authority applies to all offences, provincial or federal, as long as the police have the authority to make the arrest. The Court specifically stated that this decision is limited to cases of hot pursuit; it does not cover situations where there is no hot pursuit and police want to make a warrantless arrest for an offence that is not indictable.

In the subsequent case of *R. v. Feeney*,[6] the accused was charged with murder after a man was found dead at his home. Blood was splattered everywhere and Sportsman brand cigarettes were found at the scene. A local resident suggested police speak with Feeney. The officer arrived and knocked at the door and said "Police." There was no response so he entered with his gun drawn. He found Feeney asleep, and when he woke him he noticed blood splattered all over the front of Feeney's shirt and Sportsman brand cigarettes on the table. Feeney was arrested and eventually convicted of second-degree murder. He appealed to the Supreme Court of Canada.

The Supreme Court of Canada in Feeney made new law, overruling its prior decision in *Landry*.[7] The Court held in *Feeney* that, as a general rule, a warrant is required to enter and arrest a person in a dwelling-house. Further, in *Feeney*, the Court upheld an individual's privacy interest in a dwelling-house by finding that police violate section 8 of the Charter by forcible entry to make a warrantless arrest absent circumstances of "hot pursuit" of a fleeing suspect. Sopinka J., noted that the common law has always placed a high

---

6   (1997), 115 C.C.C. (3d) 129 (S.C.C.).
7   Supra, note 4.

value on the security and privacy of a dwelling, and citing *Hunter and Southam*,[8] noted the shift in emphasis from trespass and property rights to the reasonableness of the search and the increase, under the Charter, of the legal status of the privacy of a dwelling.[9] Sopinka J., stated that ". . . the additional burden on the police to obtain a warrant before forcibly entering a private dwelling to arrest, while not justified in a case of hot pursuit is, in general, well worth the additional protection to the privacy interest in dwelling-houses that it brings.[10]

The Court stated that the test in *Landry* no longer applied to warrantless arrests, and found that the requirements for a warrantless arrest under section 495 of the Criminal Code were not met.

Sections 529.1 to 529.5 were enacted in response to *Feeney*. Section 529.1 provides for judicial authorization of entry into a dwelling-house to make an arrest, while section 529.3 provides statutory authority for a warrantless entry in exigent circumstances. To assist the police officer, section 529.5 provides that the officer may now obtain a "telewarrant" rather than appearing before a justice of the peace to make an application to obtain the warrant.

5. Arrest Without Warrant

a. Arrest by Any Person

In England, under the common law, every person had a duty to apprehend persons who broke the "king's peace." The persons who had been arrested would then be turned over to the king's agents for trial. Canadian law continues this practice in the Criminal Code by providing that in certain situations a private person can make an arrest. Section 494 spells out three such situations:

> **494. (1) Any one may arrest without warrant**
>
> **(a) a person whom he finds committing an indictable offence; or**
>
> **(b) a person who, on reasonable grounds, he believes**
>
> **(i) has committed a criminal offence, and**
>
> **(ii) is escaping from and freshly pursued by persons who have lawful authority to arrest that person.**
>
> **(2) Any one who is**
>
> **(a) the owner or a person in lawful possession of property, or**
>
> **(b) a person authorized by the owner or by a person in lawful possession of property**
>
> **may arrest without warrant a person whom he finds committing a criminal offence on or in relation to that property.**

---

8 (1984), 14 C.C.C. (3d) 97 (S.C.C.), note 52.
9 Supra, note 6 at page 154-5.
10 Ibid., at page 156.

The first situation arises when the arresting person finds the accused in the act of committing an indictable offence. Indictable offences include hybrid offences, since a hybrid offence is treated as indictable until the Crown chooses to have it tried as a summary conviction offence. This decision is usually made at the time the accused is arraigned (see Chapter Two).

The second situation, described in s.494, arises when a person believes on reasonable grounds that the accused has committed a criminal offence and is escaping from and being freshly pursued by persons having lawful authority to make an arrest. "Criminal offence" includes summary conviction offences as well as those that are indictable. It does not include provincial offences.

A person who has "lawful authority" includes, of course, a peace officer. It also includes any person who is granted the power to make an arrest by the Criminal Code. Thus, a private person who finds someone committing an indictable offence has a lawful authority to arrest the accused.

The third situation under s.494 in which anyone may make an arrest arises when an owner of property (either real or personal property), or a person (such as a tenant) lawfully in possession of property, finds an accused committing a criminal offence on or in relation to that property. Thus, if Alex is renting a house, Alex may arrest Brian if he sees Brian deliberately break a window in the house.

Section 494(3) states that whenever an arrest is made by a person who is not a peace officer, that person must deliver the arrested person to a peace officer "forthwith." One court has said that forthwith does not mean "instantly" but "as soon as reasonably practicable under the circumstances."[11]

Section 30 provides an additional power of detention to the private person. Anyone who sees a breach of the peace is justified in interfering to prevent the continuation or renewal of the breach and may detain any person involved in or about to join in the breach. Thus, if a person is in a bar and a brawl starts, the person may grab and hold back anyone who wants to join in, or who has already joined in, until the police arrive.

The criminal law also places a duty, in certain circumstances, on persons to assist the police in making an arrest when requested. Section 129(b) states:

129. Every one who . . .

(b) omits, without reasonable excuse, to assist a public officer or peace officer in the execution of his duty in arresting a person or in preserving the peace, after having reasonable notice that he is required to do so . . .

is guilty of . . .

an offence . . .

---

11 *R. v. Cunningham and Ritchie* (1979), 49 C.C.C. (2d) 390 (Man.Co.Ct.).

b. Arrest by Peace Officer

Peace officers have the authority of any person to make an arrest and, in addition, to other powers.

Section 495 of the Code defines the situations where a peace officer may make an arrest without a warrant. Subsection (1) lists the general rules for making an arrest without a warrant. These general rules are limited by the exceptions in subs.(2). In other words, to decide whether an officer can make an arrest without a warrant, you must first look at the general rules in subs.(1) and then check the limitations in subs.(2). This two-step scheme is a result of the bail reform legislation that was passed in the 1970s. The philosophy of the legislation was that people should be held before trial only if there is a clear reason for holding them. It was felt by those responsible for law reform that too many people were being arrested, and/or detained while awaiting trial. Thus, one purpose of the legislation was to limit the authority of the police to make arrests when other methods, such as appearance notices and summonses, would do just as well for ensuring attendance at trial.

Section 495(1) provides:

> **495. (1) A peace officer may arrest without warrant**
>
> **(a) a person who has committed an indictable offence or who, on reasonable grounds, he believes has committed or is about to commit an indictable offence,**
>
> **(b) a person whom he finds committing a criminal offence, or**
>
> **(c) a person in respect of whom he has reasonable grounds to believe that a warrant of arrest or committal, in any form set out in Part XXVIII in relation thereto, is in force within the territorial jurisdiction in which the person is found.**

The term "peace officer" is defined in s.2 of the Code. It includes a mayor, a warden, a sheriff, a prison guard, certain customs officials, a pilot in command of an aircraft while the aircraft is in flight, certain military personnel, and, of course, police officers. Note that private security officers employed by department stores or businesses are not peace officers. These people have only the power of arrest that other ordinary persons possess, as discussed earlier.

Section 495(1) sets out five situations where a police officer may make an arrest without a warrant.

1. Where the arresting officer knows that the person has committed an indictable offence.
2. Where the arresting officer believes on reasonable grounds that the accused has committed an indictable offence. This situation demands that a "reasonable grounds" test be used to determine whether an arrest can be made. It is not necessary that an indictable offence has actually been committed. It is enough if the arresting officer personally believes that there are reasonable grounds to make the arrest (i.e., to believe that an

indictable offence has been committed). However, it must be objectively established that the reasonable grounds existed.

Generally, "reasonable grounds" are grounds that would lead any ordinary, prudent, and cautious person to have a strong and honest belief that the person to be arrested has committed the offence. If the accused is later acquitted of the charge, the arrest may still be lawful. The important questions are: whether a reasonable person standing in the shoes of the peace officer would have believed that reasonable grounds existed for making the arrest; and whether the officer personally believed that the reasonable grounds existed.

For example, in *Koechlin v. Waugh and Hamilton*,[12] the neighbourhood in which the accused was arrested had been subject to a number of break-ins a few nights earlier. The accused and a friend were stopped by the police at approximately 11 p.m. The accused was observed to be wearing shoes that matched the shoes worn by the suspect. The accused explained that he was returning home from a show. The police decided to arrest him on the suspicion of having committed the break-ins. The court held that these facts did not amount to reasonable and probable grounds for believing that the accused committed the break-ins.

3. Where the arresting officer has reasonable grounds to believe that an indictable offence is about to be committed. This situation also involves a reasonable grounds test. If a police officer has an honest belief based on reasonable grounds that an individual is about to commit an indictable offence, then he or she may make the arrest, even though that person has not yet made an attempt to commit the offence. Under s.503(4), where a person about to commit an offence has been arrested, the police must release the person unconditionally as soon as practicable after they are satisfied that detaining the person is no longer necessary to prevent the commission of an indictable offence.

4. Where the arresting officer finds the accused committing any criminal offence. The Supreme Court of Canada has held that this situation applies where the officer finds the accused "apparently" committing an indictable offence. This interpretation protects the officer from being sued for false imprisonment if the accused is later found not guilty of the offence.[13] "Any criminal offence" includes summary conviction offences as well as those that are indictable. It does not include provincial offences. Arrest powers for provincial offences are contained in provincial statutes.

Note that the only powers a police officer has to arrest for a summary conviction offence, without a warrant, are those granted by situation 4 and by the right that everybody has under s.494 (i.e., to arrest anyone where there are reasonable grounds to believe that the person has committed a criminal offence and is being freshly pursued by persons with lawful authority to make an arrest).

---

12 (1957), 118 C.C.C. 24 (Ont.C.A.).
13 *R. v. Biron* (1975), 23 C.C.C. (2d) 513 (S.C.C.).

5. Where the arresting officer believes on reasonable grounds that the accused is the subject of a warrant. The warrant must be in force in the territorial jurisdiction in which the accused is found at the time of arrest. In other words, if it is in force in only one county or district of a province, then it cannot be used to arrest an accused who is found in a different county or district.

c. Section 495(2) Limitations on Power to Arrest Without a Warrant

A police officer's right to arrest without a warrant is limited by subs.(2) of s.495, which states that unless certain circumstances exist, an arrest cannot be made without a warrant for indictable offences listed in s.553 (these are primarily offences involving gambling, keeping a common bawdy house, and fraud in relation to fares), for hybrid offences, or for summary conviction offences. A police officer cannot make an arrest without a warrant unless he or she considers, on reasonable grounds, that it is in the public interest to do so. "In the public interest" is a general term which means that the safety and well-being of the public is to be given priority.

An example of when an arrest could be made under s.495(2) is if a person refuses to give his or her name to an officer who has reasonable grounds to believe an offence has been committed by that person. In such a situation, an arrest is in the public interest.

In determining whether the public interest is served by an arrest, the police officer must consider all the circumstances of the offence, including:

- The need to establish the identity of the person.
- The need to protect and/or keep evidence.
- The need to prevent the continuation or repetition of the offence or the commission of another offence.

The arresting officer must also decide whether there are any good reasons for believing that the accused, if not arrested, will fail to show up on the court appearance date.

A peace officer who decides that an arrest is not needed may issue the accused with an appearance notice or obtain a summons. Recall that an officer who issues an appearance notice must also lay an information before a justice.

d. Summary of Power of Arrest Without Warrant Under s.494 and s.495

The following briefly summarizes a police officer's powers to arrest without a warrant:

- The officer must be presented with one of the five situations outlined in s.495(1), or in that part of s.494 which entitles any person to make an arrest.
- The officer who is presented with such a situation must then consider whether the offence in question falls within the three categories of offences in s.495(2). If it does not, an arrest can be made.

- If the offence does fall within one of the three categories, then the officer must decide whether an arrest should be made, on the basis of the public interest. If an arrest should not be made, the officer can give an appearance notice to the accused or go before a justice to have a summons issued.

e. Additional Powers of Arrest Without Warrant

The Criminal Code provides three additional police powers of arrest without a warrant. Section 31(1) reads:

> **31. (1) Every peace officer who witnesses a breach of the peace and every one who lawfully assists the peace officer is justified in arresting any person whom he finds committing the breach of the peace or who, on reasonable grounds, he believes is about to join in or renew the breach of the peace.**

Breach of the peace is not defined in the Code. Generally, situations that may amount to a breach of peace involve threats of violence, such as when a group of people are loitering and becoming unruly. The British Columbia Court of Appeal[14] said that this section only applies to breaches of the peace that have actually happened. It went on to say, however, that under the common law a police officer can arrest without warrant where the officer honestly and on reasonable grounds believes that a breach of the peace is about to occur. Since there is no offence of committing a breach of the peace, this is a similar situation to where an officer arrests a person about to commit an offence—that is, the person cannot be charged with an offence. However, it is possible for the arrested person to be taken before a justice and required to enter a peace bond at common law. This procedure is discussed in more detail in Chapter Twelve.

The second situation that includes the power to arrest without a warrant is related to the keeping of gaming houses. Section 199(2) allows a police officer to take into custody any person whom he or she finds in a gaming house.

The third situation where an officer can arrest without warrant is under s.524(2)(a). An officer can arrest where he or she believes on reasonable grounds that (a) an accused has contravened or is about to contravene any summons, appearance notice, promise to appear, undertaking, or recognizance that was given or entered into or (b) an accused has committed an indictable offence after any summons, appearance notice, or similar has been issued or given.

6. Pre-trial Release When Arrest Is Without a Warrant

The general principle of the law is that a person should not be held before trial unless there is a reason. If the offence is not one listed in s.469—which includes the most serious offences (e.g., murder, treason)—the Code sets out

---

14 *Hayes v. Thompson et al.* (1985), 18 C.C.C. (3d) 254 (B.C.C.A.).

several points where the reasons for the arrest are reviewed and the person who has been detained can be released.

If the accused has been arrested without a warrant and the offence for which he or she has been arrested is one of the following:

- an indictable offence listed in s.553
- a hybrid offence
- a summary conviction offence

s.497 provides that the peace officer must release the accused as soon as is practicable once there is no longer a reason for the arrest, and either obtain a summons or issue an appearance notice. So, for example, where a police officer arrests an accused in order to confirm the accused's identity, once the person's identity is confirmed, if no other reason for holding the accused exists, the accused must be released.

If the accused is not released, then under s.498 the officer in charge of the lockup must review the arrest. The "officer in charge" is the person responsible for the place where the accused has been taken. The officer in charge has the same obligation as the arresting officer to release the accused if the offence is one of those listed earlier and there is no longer a reason for the arrest. The officer in charge has an additional duty to release a person if the offence is one punishable by imprisonment for five years or less and if the reason for the arrest no longer exists. If the officer in charge releases the accused, that officer can have a summons issued or have the accused give a promise to appear (Form 10), or have the accused enter a recognizance not exceeding $500. A recognizance is an agreement made by the accused that he or she will pay a certain amount of money on failing to appear in court as required (Form 11). If the accused is not ordinarily resident in the province or lives more than 200 kilometres from the place of custody, but the offence occurred in the province in which he or she is being held, the officer in charge must release the person on a recognizance not exceeding $500. The officer can also require the person to deposit money or other valuable security up to the value of $500. If the offence is alleged to have been committed in Canada but outside the province in which the person is being held, the officer in charge cannot release the person.

7. Arrest with a Warrant (Form 7)

When the police lay an information alleging that a named person has committed an offence, if the accused has not been arrested or issued with an appearance notice, and has not given a promise to appear or entered a recognizance, the justice will issue either a summons or a warrant for arrest. A warrant for arrest is a document issued by a justice that commands the police to arrest a named person and to bring the person before the court. A justice may issue a warrant pursuant to s.507 for the arrest of a person where there are reasonable grounds to believe that the person has committed a criminal offence. Before issuing the warrant, the justice must also believe that an arrest is in the public interest. A justice must issue a summons unless there are reasonable grounds for believing that it is necessary, for the public interest, to issue an arrest warrant. An arrest warrant may also be issued if the accused disobeys an appearance notice or a summons.

Under s.29(1), anyone who executes a warrant has a duty to have the warrant in hand where this is feasible, and to produce it for the inspection of the accused if requested.

8. Pre-trial Release When Arrested with a Warrant

Unless the offence is one listed in s.469, a justice may endorse the arrest warrant so that it authorizes the release of the accused by the officer in charge. If the justice endorses the warrant, the officer in charge pursuant to s.499 can release the accused on a promise to appear, or on entering a recognizance for an amount not exceeding $500. If the person being released is not a resident of the province or does not ordinarily reside within 200 kilometres of where he or she is being held in custody, the officer in charge must require the accused to enter a recognizance not exceeding $500.

In addition, the officer in charge can require the person who is being released on a recognizance or promise to appear to enter an undertaking in Form 11.1. Thereby, the person undertakes to do one or more of the following:

- Report at a certain time to a named police officer or other person.
- Remain within a certain territorial jurisdiction.
- Notify the police or other designated person of any change of address or employment.
- Abstain from communicating with a witness or other person or going to a place except in accordance with certain conditions.
- Deposit his or her passport.

9. Pre-trial Release With or Without an Arrest Warrant

Under s.503(2) an officer in charge can release any person charged with any offence except for those listed in s.469, whether the person is arrested with or without a warrant. This release power is discretionary, unlike the other situations discussed earlier, where the officer must release the accused if the reasons for making the arrest no longer exist. The officer can release the accused on the person giving a promise to appear or entering a recognizance not exceeding $500, with or without further undertakings.

10. Pre-trial Release by Justice or Superior Court Judge

An accused who is still in custody must be taken before a justice within 24 hours or as soon as possible (s.503, s.515). Unless the accused pleads guilty or is charged with an offence under s.469, the justice will determine whether the accused will be (a) kept in custody or (b) released on giving an undertaking to appear in court on a certain day. The undertaking may contain conditions, such as to remain within a certain territorial jurisdiction or to notify the police of any change in address or occupation (Form 12). The accused may be required to enter a recognizance, (Form 32), with or without sureties. A *surety* is a person who agrees to pay the money set out in the recognizance if the accused does not appear for his or her court date. In effect, the surety is responsible for ensuring that the accused appears for his or her court date.

For most offences it is up to the Crown to "show cause" why the accused should not be released. For example, the Crown might establish that the accused has failed on previous occasions to appear for court and that therefore detention is necessary to ensure attendance.

Where a person is charged with an offence listed in s.469 (which includes the most serious offences, such as murder and treason), the hearing must be held before a superior court judge of the province. In these circumstances, the onus is on the accused to "show cause" why a release should be ordered. The onus also shifts to the accused in certain situations, listed in s.515(6), where the hearing is before a justice—for example, where a person is charged with committing an indictable offence while on pre-trial release for another indictable offence.

11. Civil and Criminal Responsibility of Arresting Person

Section 28 of the Criminal Code states that where a person who is authorized to execute an arrest warrant believes, in good faith and on reasonable grounds, that the person arrested is the person named in the warrant, the person is protected from criminal responsibility.

When a police officer or private citizen makes an arrest without a warrant, the arresting individual must have an honest belief based on reasonable grounds that the accused has either committed the offence for which he or she is arrested, or is about to commit an offence. If the accused proves that the arresting person's belief was not based on reasonable grounds, he or she may sue for damages for false imprisonment. See ss. 495(3), 497(3), and 498(3).

12. Rights upon Arrest or Detention

a. Right to Remain Silent

Chapter Two described the right to remain silent during the trial process as a principle of fundamental justice under s.7 of the Charter. This right also applies at the pre-trial stage. This means that the accused has the right not to answer police questions.

Usually, the police inform the accused that he or she does not have to answer questions; however, it is generally thought that there is no obligation to inform the accused of this right.[15] The right to remain silent is based on the principle of the presumption of innocence and on the right not to incriminate oneself.

Once an accused person indicates that he or she does not want to make a statement, the police cannot use deception or trickery to override the person's decision. In *R. v. Hebert*,[16] the accused was arrested and charged with robbery. After talking with his lawyer, he stated that he did not wish to make a statement. The police placed an undercover agent in his cell. The accused made incriminating statements to the officer. The trial judge excluded the statements and acquitted the accused. The appeal court allowed the statements and ordered a new trial. On appeal to the Supreme Court of Canada, the issue was whether the accused's right to remain silent had been violated because the statements were allowed as evidence. The Court held that the right to remain silent in s.7 includes the right to choose whether to make a statement to the authorities. The question was whether the conduct of the authorities had in this case effectively and unfairly deprived the accused of his right to choose. It was found that the police had improperly elicited information that they could not otherwise have obtained. The Court stated that the right applies after detention, so evidence gathered from under-cover operations before detention is not protected. Also, the right to silence does not cover voluntary statements made to cell mates.

Another case, decided shortly after Hebert, had slightly different facts. In *R. v. Broyles*,[17] the accused was charged with murdering his grandmother. While the accused was in custody the police arranged for him to be visited by a friend who was wearing a recording device. During their conversation the friend asked the accused about the killing. He also made negative comments about Broyle's lawyer and suggested that he change counsel. The accused eventually made an incriminating statement. The accused was convicted at his trial, and his appeal to the Alberta Court of Appeal was dismissed. In deciding whether to allow the statement, the Supreme Court of Canada first considered whether the friend was acting as an agent of the state. The test to be applied to determine this was whether the conversation between the accused and the friend would have taken place in the way that it had but for the intervention of the police. Here there was no doubt that the friend was acting as an agent of the state, since the meeting had been set up by the police. However, the Court went on to say that obtaining evidence in this way violates s.7 of the Charter only if the agent elicits the statement. Evidence is elicited if there is a causal link between the conduct of the agent and the making of the statement. The Court looked at the nature of the conversation (e.g., whether the conversation was in fact an interrogation), and at the nature of the relationship (e.g., whether it was based on trust). Here, the agent undermined the accused's confidence in his lawyer (who had told him to remain silent), exploited his relationship as a friend, and actively asked questions about the killing. Therefore, he had elicited the damaging

15 See, for example, *R. v. Van Den Meerssche* (1989), 53 C.C.C. (3d) 449 (B.C.C.A.); but in *R. v. Campbell* (1989), 7 W.C.B. (2d) 301 (P.E.I.S.C.Gen.Div.) the court held otherwise.
16 (1990), 57 C.C.C. (3d) 1 (S.C.C.).
17 (1991), 68 C.C.C. (3d) 308 (S.C.C.).

statement. The Court considered that a serious violation of the accused's s.7 rights had taken place and ordered a new trial, with the damaging statement to be excluded.

There are exceptions to the right to remain silent. *Moore v. The Queen*[18] illustrates one exception. The accused had run a red light on his bicycle. An officer saw him and attempted to give him a ticket for a provincial offence. Moore refused to stop or to give his name to the officer. Because he refused to identify himself, Moore was finally charged with the offence of obstructing a police officer in the performance of his duty. Under the provincial Summary Convictions Act, s.495(2) of the Criminal Code applied, so the officer could not arrest Moore unless, among other reasons, it was necessary to establish his identity. The Supreme Court of Canada held that Moore had obstructed the officer, who was performing his duty when asking Moore his name so that Moore could be charged with the offence. The decision is limited to situations where the officer actually observes the accused committing an offence and where there is no power to arrest unless and until the officer tries to identify the accused so that the accused can be charged with the offence.

The Court distinguished *Moore* from another case where a person was acting in what the police regarded as a suspicious manner. The accused refused to identify himself, saying that the police would have to arrest him. In this case, the court held that the accused did not need to identify himself. The difference was that the police did not observe the accused committing an offence.

Moore was decided before the Charter, so it is not known how the Supreme Court would rule today. However, a decision of the Saskatchewan Queen's Bench in 1990 followed *Moore*. In *R. v. Hudson*,[19] the accused allowed his dogs to run loose, which violated a city by-law. He was observed by a police constable. When asked to identify himself, he refused, saying that he would get a ticket if he did. The court held that he had obstructed a police officer in the performance of his duties. The court stated that even if requiring people found committing offences to identify themselves violated the Charter, it was a reasonable limit under s.1.

Another exception is found under provincial law (such as Ontario's), which requires motorists to produce a driver's licence, vehicle registration, and proof of insurance when requested by an officer.

b. Statement Must Be Voluntary

Any statement that the accused does make to the police must be voluntary if it is to be admitted at trial. The courts have developed rules regarding voluntary statements. One test for whether a statement is voluntary is if the statement was obtained without fear of prejudice or hope of advantage held out by a person in authority. For example, if a person is promised a more

---

18   (1979), 43 C.C.C. (2d) 83 (S.C.C.).
19   (1990), 83 Sask.R. 177 (Sask.Q.B.); affd. (1990), 87 Sask.R. 288 (Sask.C.A.).

lenient sentence, or is threatened with a greater punishment if a statement is not given, the statement is not voluntary. An example of the court's application of this rule is *R. v. Zappone*,[20] a decision of the Alberta Court of Appeal. The accused was involved in a traffic accident in which one person was killed. The accused asked the arresting officer if she would be charged with manslaughter. The officer told her that he was charging her with an offence under the provincial Highway Act and that she would receive a ticket and that the maximum fine was $2,000 under the Act. The accused then gave a statement to the officer which suggested that she had failed to stop for a stop sign. The accused was charged with the provincial offence but also with dangerous driving causing death, an indictable offence under the Code. At her trial, she testified that she had given a statement to the officer because the officer had led her to believe that she would be charged with the less serious offence if she cooperated.

The court of appeal held that the officer had offered her an inducement—in this instance, a lesser charge. Therefore, her statement should not have been admitted. The court ordered her acquittal.

However, this is not the only test for whether a statement has been voluntary. The Supreme Court of Canada, in *R. v. Horvath*,[21] has held that "voluntary" means, among other things, "of free will." So, for example, a statement that was given under oppressive or coercive circumstances may not be considered voluntary. In *Horvath*, the accused, a 17-year-old male, had undergone intensive interrogation that left him in a state of "complete emotional disintegration." His final interview, with a skilled interrogator, put him in a mild hypnotic trance and as a result he made a confession. In this situation, the statement could not be considered voluntary.

The Supreme Court of Canada, in *R. v. Whittle*,[22] considered the mental capacity necessary for a statement to be considered voluntary. Whittle had been panhandling on the streets of Ottawa when he was stopped and questioned by the police. A computer check turned up three committal warrants against the accused for unpaid fines for provincial offence convictions. He was cautioned and arrested. The officer observed that the accused appeared to be mentally unstable. The accused confirmed that he suffered from schizophrenia. Once in custody, the accused began to talk about some "heavy matters" he had been involved in. He eventually confessed to committing robberies and to murdering a man with an axe. He was cautioned again and then charged with the offences. A lawyer was contacted for him. The lawyer told him "to keep his mouth shut." However, the accused continued to talk to the police, stating that he had voices in his head and that he needed to talk to the police to stop the voices. The incriminating statements were excluded at his trial, and he was acquitted. The court of appeal reversed the trial judge's decision on the

20 (1991), 80 Alta.L.R. (2d) 424 (Alta.C.A.).
21 (1980), 44 C.C.C. (2d) 385 (S.C.C.); see also *R. v. Oickle* (2000), 147 C.C.C. (3d) 321 where the confession was held to be voluntary. This case sets out the proper scope of the confessions rule and gives a good overview of the case law.
22 (1994), 92 C.C.C. (3d) 11 (S.C.C.).

admissibility of the statements. The case was then appealed to the Supreme Court. The Supreme Court held that the test for mental capacity to give a voluntary statement is not the same as the test for the defence of mental disorder, but is the same as the test for fitness to stand trial. In fact, the Court noted, many people who are found not guilty by reason of mental disorder are fit to stand trial. The key issue is whether the accused has an "operating mind." The test is whether the accused possesses a limited degree of cognitive ability so that he understands what he is saying and what is said to him. Similarly, the question is whether he can communicate with counsel and understand the function of counsel. The accused in Whittle did understand what he was saying and was fit to instruct counsel; but because of the voices that were telling him to unburden himself, he did not care about the consequences. Therefore, his statements were voluntary and admissible.

c. Fingerprinting and Photographing

A person under arrest for an indictable offence (including a hybrid offence) is required to submit to being photographed and fingerprinted. Mandatory fingerprinting has been challenged under the Charter; however, the Supreme Court of Canada has held that it is not a violation of the right against self-incrimination.[23] This requirement is dictated by the Identification of Criminals Act. Note that if an accused is under arrest for a summary conviction offence, the police have no right to require photographing or fingerprinting. Also, under s.502 a person may be given a date and time to appear for fingerprinting and photographing along with the appearance notice, promise to appear, recognizance, or summons.

d. Arbitrary Detention

Section 9 of the Charter provides:

> **9. Everyone has the right not to be arbitrarily detained or imprisoned.**

In *R. v. Hufsky*,[24] the Supreme Court of Canada considered the meaning of "arbitrary." The issue in this case was whether random spot checks of motorists by the police for the purpose of checking driver's licence, insurance, and sobriety are arbitrary detentions. The Court said that such spot checks are detentions, and are arbitrary because the police can stop any motorist without any criteria. However, even though the legislation allowing for random spot checks violates s.9 of the Charter, the legislation is justified under s.1 as a reasonable limitation, in that the police must be able to prevent and stop impaired drivers.

In a later decision in a similar case, the Court held that routine stops of vehicles can be justified on the basis of the pressing and substantial concern

---

23　*R. v. Beare; R. v. Higgins* (1988), 45 C.C.C. (3d) 57 (S.C.C.).
24　(1988), 40 C.C.C. (3d) 398 (S.C.C.).

for safety on the highway.[25] The stop must be for legal reasons—for example, like those in *Hufsky*—or to check for mechanical safety of the vehicle. Once stopped, the occupant can only be questioned regarding driving offences. More intrusive procedures can be taken only if there are reasonable and probable grounds to suspect an offence has occurred.

These "check stop" cases have established the right of the police to arbitrarily detain persons for the purpose of enforcing laws related to driving. A case that looked at the issue more broadly is *R. v. Simpson*,[26] a decision of the Ontario Court of Appeal. A police officer stopped a car because he had seen it at a suspected crack house. The officer pulled the car over to see "what story" the occupants would give and to see if they would trip themselves up and give him grounds to make an arrest. While questioning the occupants, the officer noticed a bulge in the accused's pocket. He asked the accused (who was a passenger in the car) to remove the object. As the accused was doing so, the officer grabbed the accused's hand and removed a baggy containing cocaine. The accused was charged with possession for the purpose of trafficking. The trial judge held that the officer had a right to stop the car and seize the drugs and convicted the accused. The accused appealed to the Court of Appeal on the grounds that his rights under s.9 of the Charter had been violated. The court, in considering whether the detention was arbitrary, noted that the officer had no authority under any federal or provincial statute to stop the car—for example, the officer was not stopping the car under a Highway Traffic Act law to check for impaired driving. Therefore, the "check stop" cases did not apply here. The court then considered whether there was a general common law right to detain persons. The court held that, under the common law, a police officer may detain persons for "investigatory purposes" where the officer has an "articulable cause"—that is, a reasonable suspicion that the detainee is involved in the criminal activity being investigated. Having an articulable cause may or may not be enough to justify the detention, however; other circumstances must exist that make the detention at that time and place reasonable. For example, Constable Jones is justified in detaining on a public street a man whom she suspects is fleeing from the scene of a violent crime he has just committed. In contrast, the detention of a person in the same circumstances based on a suspicion that the person committed a property offence in the far distant past is not justifiable, even though the articulable cause exists.

Simpson is an interesting case in that it clearly recognizes the right of the police to detain where there are not sufficient grounds to arrest—that is, where they have only a reasonable suspicion that the person is involved in a crime. In this case, however, the judges found that the officer did not have an articulable cause for detaining the accused. The officer's information about the "crack house" was of an unknown age and was from an officer who heard it from someone else. He had no reason to think that the information was reliable. He knew nothing about the occupants of the car, and

---

25 *R. v. Ladouceur* (1990), 56 C.C.C. (3d) 22 (S.C.C.).
26 (1993), 79 C.C.C. (3d) 482 (Ont.C.A.).

they had done nothing to suggest that they were involved in criminal activity. Where the sole factor was attendance at a house where criminal activity may have been going on based on information of unknown age and reliability, no articulable cause exists. "Were it otherwise, the police would have a general warrant to stop anyone who happened to attend at any place which the police had reason to believe could be the site of ongoing criminal activity."[27] Therefore, the search was unlawful and the evidence excluded. The court ordered an acquittal.

e. Section 10 Rights

Section 10 of the Charter contains two specific rights upon arrest or detention.[28]

> **10. Everyone has the right on arrest or detention**
>
> **(a) to be informed promptly of the reasons therefore . . .**

A person who has been arrested or detained has a right to know why he or she has been arrested or detained. Also recall that if a warrant is used, under s.29(2)(a) the officer needs to have the warrant, if feasible, and the accused has a right to examine it.

> **(b) to retain and instruct counsel without delay and to be informed of that right . . .**

The right to counsel does not arise until a person has been arrested or detained. As you have already read, "detention" is a broader term than "arrest"; all arrests involve detentions, but not all detentions involve arrests. Because of the importance of the s.10(b) right, there have been many cases considering the meaning of detention under this section.

(I) MEANING OF DETENTION

There are three ways a person can be detained: by physical restraint; by psychological means (i.e., where a person is made to believe that he or she has no choice but to remain, even though no threat has been made); and by giving a demand or direction (i.e., where there will be legal consequences if the person refuses the demand or direction). An example of the last type of detention is found in *R. v. Therens.*[29] The accused had a car accident. When the police arrived, they asked him to take a breathalyzer test. The police did not inform him of his right to counsel. In deciding whether he had been denied his right to counsel, the issue for the Court was whether the accused

---

27 Ibid. at 504.
28 Section 10 also includes the right to "have the validity of the detention determined by way of habeas corpus and to be released if the detention is not lawful." The right of habeas corpus is one of our oldest rights. It means that a person has a right to a hearing to determine whether the detention is legal and, if it is not, to be released. Although an important right, it is not used generally at the pre-trial stage. It tends to be used to test detention issues that arise once a person is in an institution—for example, where an inmate challenges being placed in solitary confinement or in a special handling unit. It allows a court to examine whether the decision for detention was made fairly and whether the decision maker had the authority to order the detention.
29 (1985), 18 C.C.C. (3d) 481 (S.C.C.).

had in fact been detained. The Court stated that a person is detained when he or she submits or acquiesces to the deprivation of liberty in the reasonable belief that the choice to do otherwise does not exist. Since refusing to take the test is an offence, the accused did not have a reasonable choice not to take the breathalyzer. Therefore, the Court found that he had been detained.

A case that considered the meaning of psychological detention is *R. v. Moran*.[30] The police were investigating the murder of a man Moran had known. Moran was called by the police and asked if he would talk to an officer. He was given a choice of meeting the officer at his home or going to the station. Moran went to the station. A few days later, he was called again and asked to come to the station to add some details to his statement, which he did. He was then questioned in a pressing manner concerning one of his statements. He was allowed to leave the station. Several months later he was charged with the murder. The question before the Ontario Court of Appeal was whether he had voluntarily gone to the station or whether he had been detained. The court stated that in deciding whether a person has been detained, the court should look at such factors as:

- The language used by the police.
- Whether the accused had a choice of being questioned at home rather than at the police station, and whether the accused expressed a preference as to where the interview would be held.
- How the accused arrived at the station—that is, whether he was escorted or alone.
- Whether the accused was arrested at the end of the interview.
- The stage of the investigation—that is, whether the police had concluded that a crime had occurred and that the accused was a suspect, or were still gathering information.
- Whether the police had reasonable and probable grounds to believe that the accused had committed the offence.
- The reasonable belief of the accused as to whether or not he was detained.
- The type of questions put to the person—that is, whether the questions were an attempt to gather information, and whether the accused was confronted with evidence pointing to the accused's guilt.

In this case, the court ruled that the accused was not detained.

A more recent case involving psychological detention is *R. v. Hawkins*.[31] The accused was charged with sexually assaulting a 13-year-old girl who was the daughter of his girlfriend. The victim reported the assaults to her school guidance counsellor, who contacted the police. An officer called Hawkins and requested an interview about the complaint. He stated that the interview could be held at the station or at Hawkin's home or place of business. Hawkins agreed to be interviewed at the station. At the station he was given a standard police caution but not advised of his right to counsel since

30 (1987), 36 C.C.C. (3d) 225 (Ont.C.A.), affd. 44 C.C.C. (3d) 193 (S.C.C.).
31 (1992), 72 C.C.C. (3d) 524 (Nfld.C.A.), revd. (1993), 79 C.C.C. (3d) 576 (S.C.C.).

the officer did not believe that Hawkins was detained. Hawkins gave a statement to the police in which he admitted entering the girl's bedroom and tickling her sometimes. He said that if he had ever touched her breast, he "never meant anything by it. It was all done in fun." At the end of the interview the officer said that he did not know if charges would be laid, because he had to wait for legal advice. The charges were laid, and Hawkins was convicted. The issue for the court of appeal was whether he had been psychologically detained and therefore denied his right to counsel. The court held that Hawkins had been detained and stated that psychological detention can arise even if there are no feelings of compulsion by the person. Detention arises when the officer begins to question the person with a view to charging the person. Here the purpose of the interview was to investigate the accused's involvement in an alleged crime. There was a dissenting opinion in this case, one judge stating that there was no detention. His opinion was that it is not a detention where an officer requests a statement without any sense of compulsion on the part of the accused. *Hawkins* was appealed to the Supreme Court of Canada. Without giving reasons, the Court stated that there was no detention in this case. Presumably, the Court, agreeing with the dissenting opinion, found the lack of compulsion a factor in not finding a detention.

Another type of case in which the meaning of detention has been considered involves people being questioned by customs officials at border crossings. For example, in *R. v. Simmons*,[32] the Supreme Court of Canada said that the routine questions that are asked at border crossings are not a detention, nor are baggage checks or a pat or frisk of outer clothing. However, it is a detention if a person is given a strip or skin search in a private room or is taken to a hospital for a search of body cavities.

(II) RIGHT TO COUNSEL

The right to counsel has two parts: the right to be informed of the right to counsel, and the right to consult counsel. There have been many cases considering both parts to this right.

- *Right to Be Informed*

Court decisions have expanded the right to be informed to more than being told simply, "You have a right to a lawyer." For example, a 1990 decision of the Supreme Court of Canada[33] held that the police must tell the accused of the existence and availability of legal aid and duty counsel (duty counsel is a legal aid lawyer who is available to advise accused persons, usually before the first court appearance). The police must also inform the accused of all services, including free preliminary legal advice, that is available 24 hours a day.[34] However, there is no obligation on the government to provide free preliminary advice or 24-hour-a-day legal advice.[35] The accused also has the

---

32 (1988), 45 C.C.C. (3d) 296 (S.C.C.).
33 *R. v. Brydges* (1990), 53 C.C.C. (3d) 330 (S.C.C.).
34 *R. v. Bartle* (1994), 92 C.C.C. (3d) 289 (S.C.C.).
35 *R. v. Matheson* (1994), 92 C.C.C. (3d) 434 (S.C.C.).

right to be informed about the above at a time he or she is capable of understanding,[36] and in language he or she can understand.[37]

In *R. v. Evans*,[38] the accused, who was mentally handicapped, was charged with first-degree murder. He was arrested for possession of marijuana and told that he had a right to a lawyer. When he was asked if he understood his rights, he said "no." As the police questioned him, they came to believe that he was the prime suspect in two murders. The focus of the interview then changed. However, the police did not restate to him his right to a lawyer. Nor did they formally tell the accused that he was being detained for the murders, although the accused made several statements which indicated that he knew he was suspected of committing the murders. The police then lied to the accused, saying that his fingerprints had been found at the murder scene. At this point he confessed. The Supreme Court of Canada held that his rights had been seriously violated. First, when the accused was advised of his right to counsel and he stated that he did not understand, the police were obligated to take steps to help him understand, particularly since they were aware of his limited mental capacity. Second, the police failed to restate his right to counsel when the investigation shifted to the murders. The police must restate the right whenever there is a fundamental change in the investigation involving a different, unrelated offence or a significantly more serious offence.

- *Right to Consult a Lawyer*

Once a person indicates a desire to speak to a lawyer, the police cannot question that person further until he or she has a reasonable opportunity to consult a lawyer. What a reasonable opportunity is depends on the circumstances. So for example, in jurisdictions where duty counsel is not available, the accused has a longer period to obtain the advice of counsel. The reasonable opportunity might extend to when the legal aid office opens or a lawyer is found who will give free advice.[39] The Supreme Court of Canada said, in *R. v. Burlingham*,[40] that reasonable opportunity includes the means to call a lawyer and privacy when talking to a lawyer. The accused, Burlingham, was charged with first-degree murder. During his interrogation by the police, the accused had spoken to a lawyer, who advised him to say nothing to the police. The police continued questioning him, however, despite his protests that he wanted to follow his lawyer's advice. The police also spoke badly about his lawyer, suggesting that the lawyer did not have his interests at heart whereas the police did. The police also said that if he cooperated, the charge would be second-degree murder instead of first-degree murder, but the deal would only be available for a short time. The questioning took place on a Saturday, and the police knew that the lawyer would not be available until Monday. The Supreme Court held that the accused's right to counsel was violated in three ways. First, the police continued questioning him after he said he would say nothing until he talked to his lawyer (s.10(b) requires

---

36 *R. v. Vanstaceghem* (1987), 36 C.C.C. (3d) 142 (Ont.C.A.).
37 *R. v. Clarkson* (1986), 25 C.C.C. (3d) 207 (S.C.C.).
38 (1991), 63 C.C.C. (3d) 289 (S.C.C.).
39 *R. v. Prosper* (1994), 92 C.C.C. (3d) 353 (S.C.C.).
40 (1995), 97 C.C.C. (3d) 385 (S.C.C.).

the police to stop questioning once the accused asserts the right to speak to a lawyer). Second, s.10(b) prohibits the police from belittling an accused's lawyer for the purpose of undermining their relationship. And third, by unduly pressuring the accused to accept the deal without consulting his lawyer, the police again violated s.10(b).

In *R. v. Black*,[41] the accused was arrested for attempted murder. She called her lawyer from the police station and had a brief conversation. Two hours later the police told her that the victim had died and that the charge was being upgraded to first-degree murder. She again asked to speak to her lawyer, but attempts to reach him were not successful. At this time, she was intoxicated, upset, and physically injured. The police knew that she had limited intelligence and only a grade four education. She asked the police if she would be held over the weekend and was told yes. At that point a police officer asked her where the knife was. She told him it was in the kitchen drawer. He then asked her to tell him the whole story. She responded by giving a long statement to the officer. The Supreme Court of Canada held that she had been denied her right to counsel. The right to counsel can only be exercised meaningfully if the accused is aware of the jeopardy she is in. When she first spoke to her lawyer, the charge was attempted murder, a significantly different offence than first-degree murder. In other words, after the charge became murder, before questioning her the police should have waited until she had an opportunity to speak to her lawyer again.

An accused person can waive the right to consult a lawyer. However, the waiver must be voluntary and with full knowledge of the right being waived. The Supreme Court considered the issue of whether a waiver was valid in *R. v. Smith*.[42] The accused was charged with first-degree murder. He had been drinking with some friends when an argument began. He eventually left his friends but returned with a 12-gauge shotgun. He shot the victim at the distance of 30 metres in the face and body. The victim died immediately. Smith called the police the next morning to surrender. During the arrest, the police had him walk out of his sister's house while three officers trained guns on him; they then ordered him to fall to his knees before they handcuffed him. He was told that he was being arrested for the shooting incident and that he had a right to counsel. The police asked him if he understood what that meant. He said that he didn't want a lawyer and then made a statement to the police. After he made the statement, he was told that the victim had died. The Court held that it is not necessary for the accused to know the exact charge or all of the facts of the case before validly waiving the right to counsel. Here, the accused must have known that he was in serious jeopardy when he chose not to call a lawyer. He saw the shotgun blast, and the fact that three officers had been sent to arrest him indicated the gravity the situation. Although the Crown conceded that the accused's s.10(a) right had been violated, the Court held that the violation was not serious, since the accused probably knew that the victim had died. The Court held that the waiver was valid.

---

41 (1989), 50 C.C.C. (3d) 1 (S.C.C.).
42 (1991), 63 C.C.C. (3d) 313 (S.C.C.).

C. EXCLUSION OF EVIDENCE UNDER THE CHARTER

Where a person's rights under the Charter are violated, the person may attempt to have any evidence that was obtained as a result of the violation excluded from the trial.

Section 24 provides:

> **(2) Where . . . a court concludes that evidence was obtained in a manner that infringed or denied any rights or freedoms guaranteed by this Charter, the evidence shall be excluded if it is established that, having regard to all the circumstances, the admission of it in the proceedings would bring the administration of justice into disrepute.**

Section 24(2) was used successfully in some of the cases discussed above. For example, in *Black*,[43] the accused's confession was excluded. However, there was enough other evidence that her conviction stood. In *Evans*,[44] however, the result of excluding the confession was that the conviction was overturned and an acquittal entered. Similarly, in *Therens*,[45] the results of the breathalyzer test were excluded, and since there was no other evidence to support the conviction, the accused was found not guilty.

The excluding of evidence so that an apparently guilty person goes free is often criticized in the media. To clarify the application of s.24, it is worth looking at a case where the Court examined closely the grounds for excluding evidence. In *R v. Collins*,[46] a case concerning a search that violated the Charter, the Supreme Court of Canada discussed the steps for deciding whether evidence should be excluded when a Charter right has been violated. Not every Charter violation will lead to the exclusion of evidence that has been obtained because of the violation. Generally, it is up to the accused to establish on a balance of probabilities that a violation has occurred.[47] The accused must then show on a balance of probabilities that the admission of the evidence would bring the administration of justice into disrepute. Disrepute may result if the accused would be denied a fair trial, or if the admission would amount to the judiciary condoning improper police conduct. The court must consider the long-term consequences of regular admission or exclusion of this type of evidence. In other words, in not allowing improperly obtained evidence, the court is discouraging the police from violating the rights of individuals. However, the court must also consider whether disrepute will result from excluding the evidence. The notion of disrepute includes the idea of community views—but not the community as presented in opinion polls (i.e., uninformed members of the public). The Supreme Court noted:

---

43 Supra, note 41.
44 Supra, note 38.
45 Supra, note 29.
46 (1987), 33 C.C.C. (3d) 1 (S.C.C.).
47 An exception to this is where a warrantless search takes place. The Supreme Court has said that in this situation it is up to the Crown to show that the search was reasonable (see below for powers to search).

*Members of the public generally become conscious of the importance of pro-
tecting rights only when they are in some way brought closer to the system
either personally or through some experience of friends or family . . . The
Charter is designed to protect the accused from the majority so the enforcement
of the Charter must not be left to the majority . . .*[48]

The Court went on to say that the test is whether admission of the evidence would in the eyes of a reasonable and dispassionate person who is
fully aware of the circumstances bring the administration of justice into disrepute.

To assist in determining whether the evidence should be excluded, the
court suggested placing the factors into three groups:

1. Those Factors Going to the Fairness of the Trial

In deciding whether admitting the evidence will make the trial unfair, the
court should look at a number of factors, including the nature of the right
violated and the type of evidence obtained. The Supreme Court distinguished two types of evidence: self-incriminating and real. Incriminating
evidence is more likely to make the trial unfair than real evidence. For example, if the police obtain a confession after denying a person the right to counsel, using this confession would make the trial unfair because the accused
has been "conscripted against himself"—that is, used to create the evidence.
On the other hand, real evidence, such as a gun or a knife already exists.
Using real evidence that was obtained through a Charter violation may not
make the trial unfair. The more serious the offence, the less likely that real
(i.e., pre-existing) evidence will be excluded.

2. Those Factors Going to the Seriousness of the Violation

Important factors in this category include whether the violation was committed deliberately or inadvertently, and whether the violation was technical or serious. Other questions are: Were the police acting in good faith? Did
the violation occur in circumstances of urgency or necessity? Another question the court should ask is: Would the evidence have been obtained if the
right had not been violated? If the evidence was obtained illegally when it
was possible to have obtained it otherwise, then a blatant and serious violation has occurred.

3. Factors Related to the Effect of Excluding the Evidence

Would admitting or excluding evidence better serve the judicial system's
reputation? Excluding evidence because of a trivial breach of the Charter

---

48 Supra, note 46 at page 17.

would, if an acquittal followed, place the system in disrepute. On the other hand, where there was a serious breach of the Charter, admitting such evidence would have the same effect.

Since the decision in *Collins,* the first group of factors has become the most important. If the court finds that the admission of the evidence would make the trial unfair, the court will exclude the evidence without considering the other two groups of factors.[49] The courts have continued to hold that self-incriminating evidence obtained by violating a right will almost certainly make the trial unfair. However, the courts now distinguish between real evidence that the police would have obtained anyway (pre-existing) and real evidence that could not have been obtained but for the accused's participation. If the evidence was obtained because of the accused's participation, it will tend to make the trial unfair.

For example, in *R. v. Mellenthin,*[50] the police pulled over the accused for a routine spot check. While questioning the accused, the officer spotted an open gym bag in the car. Inside the bag was a small brown bag with a plastic sandwich bag inside it. He asked the accused what was in it. The accused opened the bag and said it was food. The officer thought he saw a reflection from glass in the plastic bag. He became suspicious that there might be drugs in the bag. He asked the accused what was in the brown bag. The accused pulled the bag out, and the officer saw that it contained glass vials of the type commonly used to store cannabis resin. The officer now considered that he had reasonable grounds to believe that drugs were present. He searched the bag and found cannabis resin. He then arrested the accused, searched the car, and found other drugs. At the trial, the physical evidence of the drugs was excluded on the grounds that it was obtained by an illegal search. The court of appeal in turn held that the evidence was admissible. The Supreme Court of Canada later found that the search was illegal. In considering whether the evidence of the drugs should be admitted, the Court held that "the evidence of the marijuana would not have been discovered without the compelled testimony [the search] of the accused." Thus, its use would make the trial unfair. The court added:

> The unreasonable search carried out in this case is the very kind which the court wish[es] to make clear is unacceptable. A check stop does not and cannot constitute a general search warrant for searching every vehicle, driver, and passenger that is pulled over. Unless there are reasonable and probable grounds for conducting the search, or drugs, alcohol, or weapons are in plain view in the interior of the vehicle, the evidence flowing from such a search should not be admitted.[51]

49 *R. v. Mellethin* (1992), 66 C.C.C. (3d) 481 (S.C.C.).
50 Ibid.
51 Ibid. at page 491.

D. POWERS TO SEARCH

1. General Powers and the Charter

Section 8 of the Charter states:

> **8. Everyone has the right to be secure against unreasonable search or seizure.**

The Supreme Court of Canada has said that this section is to prevent unreasonable searches and seizures before they occur.[52] This means that, generally, searches require a prior authorization (i.e., a search warrant). If the police do search without a warrant, the Crown will have the burden of showing that the search was reasonable. The Supreme Court has said that a search is reasonable if it is authorized by law, if the law itself is reasonable, and if the search is carried out in a reasonable manner.[53]

As a general rule, then, the police cannot search a place without first obtaining a search warrant. There are a few exceptions to this rule. Some warrantless searches are authorized by the Criminal Code and under the common law. Others are authorized by such federal acts as the Narcotic Control Act (NCA), the Food and Drugs Act (FDA), and the Customs Act. The authority to search under the NCA and the FDA is discussed in Appendix A. Note that the authority given to the police under these statutes is somewhat broader than the general authority given under the Criminal Code. Also, certain provincial statutes grant search powers to the police. Finally, a warrantless search is legal if the person consents to the search.

A reasonable amount of force may be used in making the search. However, if the searching officers use an excess of force, they may be liable in a civil action for damages, or charged with the offence of assault. Sections 25 and 26 protect any person who is legally authorized to conduct a search from criminal or civil liability if the person acted on reasonable grounds.

If the search violates the Charter, the evidence may be excluded, as discussed earlier.

2. With a Warrant (Form 5)

Section 487 authorizes a justice to issue a search warrant:

> **487. (1) A justice who is satisfied by information on oath in Form 1 that there are reasonable grounds to believe that there is in a building, receptacle or place**
>
> **(a) anything on or in respect of which any offence against this Act or any other Act of Parliament has been or is suspected to have been committed,**
>
> **(b) anything that there are reasonable grounds to believe will afford**

---

52 *Hunter v. Southam Inc.* (1984), 14 C.C.C. (3d) 97 (S.C.C.).
53 Supra, note 46.

evidence with respect to the commission of an offence, or will reveal the whereabouts of a person who is believed to have committed an offence, against this Act or any other Act of Parliament, or

(c) anything that there are reasonable grounds to believe is intended to be used for the purpose of committing any offence against the person for which a person may be arrested without warrant,

(c.1) any offence-related property

may at any time issue a warrant authorizing a peace officer or a public official who has been appointed or designated to administer or enforce a federal or provincial law and whose duties include the enforcement of this Act or any other Act of Parliament and who is named in the warrant

(d) to search the building, receptacle or place for any such thing and to seize it, and

(e) . . . bring the thing seized before, or make a report in respect thereof to, the justice . . .

The courts have consistently held that a search warrant should not be lightly granted. A search warrant cannot authorize what in reality would amount to a "fishing expedition" for evidence. When requesting that a search warrant be issued, the police must convince the justice in writing and under oath that there are reasonable grounds for believing that the conditions set forth in s.487 are satisfied. The evidence that is being sought needs to be described with enough particularity that the searchers can identify the thing to be seized.[54]

The Supreme Court of Canada considered the standard of reasonable grounds for conducting a search in *R. v. Debot*.[55] Although this case involved a warrantless search that was authorized under the Food and Drugs Act, the principles stated by the Court on the standard of reasonable grounds also apply to searches done with a warrant. The accused was searched by the police based on information from an informer that the accused would be completing a drug transaction. Drugs were found on him, and he was charged with possession. At the accused's trial, the judge held that the search was unreasonable and excluded the evidence of the drugs. The appeal court allowed the Crown's appeal and ordered a new trial. The case reached the Supreme Court, which said that in determining whether the standard of reasonableness has been met, courts must consider all the circumstances, including these:

• Was the information predicting an offence compelling?
• When information is based on an informer's tip, was the informer credible?

54 *Purdy v. R.* (1972), 8 C.C.C. (2d) 52 (N.B.C.A.).
55 (1989), 52 C.C.C. (3d) 193 (S.C.C.).

- Was the information corroborated by a police investigation before it was decided to conduct the search?

In *Debot*, the information about the offence was specific: the time and location were named as well as the parties to the transaction. The following circumstances were also noted:

- The informer gave the basis for the allegations.
- The police could take into account the accused's past record of drug offences.
- The informer was known to the police as being reliable.
- Police information had confirmed that the accused and the informer had been seen together.
- Police surveillance confirmed the arrival of the accused's vehicle at the location of the transaction.

Therefore, the police had reasonable grounds to search Debot. The Court noted that if the informer had not been known as reliable, or if fewer details of the transaction had been given, greater police corroboration that the offence had occurred would have been required. In *R. v. Berger*,[56] the Saskatchewan Court of Appeal held that a warrant based on information from unnamed confidential sources, where there was no evidence to support the truth of the sources' information, no information about how the sources obtained their information, and no independent evidence to support the sources' information, was not a sufficient basis for issuing a warrant.

The place of search must be specified in the warrant. "Building, place or receptacle" is given a very wide meaning. It includes, for example, boats, cars, backyards, safety deposit boxes, furniture, household plumbing, dwelling-houses, business offices, and summer cottages. As well, the owner or occupier of the property must be identified, along with the name of the accused. In addition, the warrant must describe the offence for which the evidence is being sought.

Police searchers may seize, in addition to the things mentioned in the warrant, anything that they believe on reasonable grounds has been obtained or used in the commission of an offence (s.489). However, they can only search in areas where the things listed in the search warrant might be located. Also, the police must have reasonable grounds and cannot seize property on the mere suspicion that the goods have been used or obtained through the commission of an offence. In *R. v. Askov*,[57] the police had a warrant to search the accused's home for weapons. While searching the home, they also seized property that they suspected was stolen. The property was taken to the police station for investigation to determine whether it was indeed stolen. The court stated that the police action was a deliberate and flagrant disregard of the accused's right under the Charter to be free from unreasonable seizure. The police had no reasonable or probable grounds to believe that the goods were stolen.

---

56 (1989), 48 C.C.C. (3d) 185 (Sask.C.A.).
57 (1987), 60 C.R. (3d) 261 (Ont.Dist.Ct.).

Section 488 states that the warrant must be executed by day unless it specifically authorizes the officers to use it at night. "Day" is defined in s.2 as "the period between six o'clock in the forenoon and nine o'clock in the afternoon of the same day." The same section defines "night" as "the period between nine o'clock in the afternoon and six o'clock in the forenoon of the following day."

There are other sections in the Criminal Code that grant the right of search to the police if certain specific offences are involved. For example, s.164 authorizes a police officer to apply for a warrant to seize obscene publications. Section 199 allows a police officer to apply for a search warrant for any premises if he or she believes on reasonable grounds that a gaming house (s.201), bookmaking place (ss. 202 and 203), lottery (ss. 206 and 207), or common bawdy house (s.210) exists. Under s.462.32 a warrant can be issued to seize "proceeds of crime." Such a warrant must be applied for by the Attorney General. The Firearms Act, the gun control legislation passed in 1995, provides that under s.117.04 a peace officer can apply for a warrant to search for and seize weapons or other items controlled by the Firearms Act where a justice is satisfied that "there are reasonable grounds to believe that it is not desirable in the interests of the safety of the person, or of any other person, for the person to possess any weapon . . ." (Note: this section had not yet been proclaimed into force as of early 1996.)

When executing the warrant, the police have the same duties as discussed earlier in *Landry*[58] when entering private premises to make an arrest. That is, the police must give notice of their presence, authority, and purpose. Section 29, which requires the person to have the warrant on his or her person where feasible, and to produce it when requested to do so, applies to search warrants as well as to arrest warrants. If entry is refused, the police are entitled to use force. They do not have to announce themselves if, for example, evidence will be destroyed. However, as the Supreme Court of Canada said in *R. v. Genest*,[59] a case that concerned an illegal search:

> *The greater the departure from the standards of behaviour required by the common law and the Charter, the heavier the onus on the police to show why they thought it necessary to use force in the process of an arrest or a search. The evidence to justify such behaviour must be apparent in the record, and must have been available to the police when they chose their course of conduct. The Crown cannot rely on ex post facto justifications.*

3. Searches of the Human Body

In general, a search warrant cannot be obtained to search a human body. In *Laporte v. Laganière*,[60] the police sought a warrant to search in the body of the accused for a bullet that was alleged to have been fired from a police revolver.

---

58   Supra, note 4.
59   (1989), 45 C.C.C. (3d) 385 at 408 (S.C.C.).
60   (1972), 8 C.C.C. (2d) 343 (Que.Q.B.).

To conduct the search, a major operation would have been necessary, because the bullet was deeply embedded in the accused's shoulder. The Quebec court held that for the purposes of s.487, the body is not a "place or receptacle."

There are exceptions, however. In impaired driving cases, it is possible under s.256 to get a warrant to obtain a blood sample (see Chapter Eleven).

A significant exception was created in 1995, when Bill C-104 was enacted by the government. This law allows police to obtain a warrant to collect bodily substances for DNA testing from persons who are suspected of committing certain serious crimes. There are three types of samples that can be taken: hair, blood, and skin cells from a mouth swab. The application for a warrant must be made to a provincial court judge. Section 487.05 states:

> **487.05 (1) A provincial court judge who . . . is satisfied by information on oath that there are reasonable grounds to believe**
>
> **(a) that a designated offence has been committed,**
>
> **(b) that a bodily substance has been found**
>
> **(i) at the place where the offence was committed,**
>
> **(ii) on or within the body of the victim of the offence,**
>
> **(iii) on anything worn or carried by the victim at the time when the offence was committed, or**
>
> **(iv) on or within the body of any person or thing or at any place associated with the commission of the offence,**
>
> **(c) that a person was a party to the offence, and**
>
> **(d) that forensic DNA analysis of a bodily substance from the person will provide evidence about whether the bodily substance referred to in paragraph (b) was from that person**
>
> **and who is satisfied that it is in the best interests of the administration of justice to do so may issue a warrant in Form 5 authorizing a peace officer to obtain . . . a bodily substance from that person . . .**

Section 487.07 requires the peace officer who is executing the warrant to inform the person of the nature of the procedure, its purposes, the possibility of the results being used as evidence, and the authority of the peace officer to use reasonable force to execute the warrant.

Under s.487.09 the bodily substance and test results must be destroyed if the results establish that the bodily substances were not from the person; if the person is finally acquitted of the offence or any related offence (except for a finding of not criminally responsible because of a mental disorder); or if one year after the person is discharged from a preliminary inquiry, the charges are dismissed or withdrawn or proceedings are stayed, unless within the year a new information is laid or indictment preferred charging the person with the same offence or another arising out of the same transaction. However, a provincial court judge can order that the substance and results not be destroyed for a designated period if the judge is satisfied that the substance or results might reasonably be required in an investigation or prosecution of the person for another designated offence or of another person for the offence.

The designated offences include crimes of personal violence such as assault, murder, sexual assault, kidnapping, and robbery, as well as breaking and entering and arson.

Note that this law deals only with collecting the evidence. It will be up to the courts to determine under what circumstances the evidence will be admissible. No doubt there will be court challenges to this law.

4. Telewarrants

In most situations, to obtain a search warrant the police officer must appear before a justice and lay an information. Recent amendments to the Code allow the police in certain circumstances to obtain warrants over the phone or through other methods of telecommunication. Such warrants are called telewarrants. Section 487.1 states:

> **487.1 (1) Where a peace officer believes that an indictable offence has been committed and that it would be impracticable to appear personally before a justice . . . the peace officer may submit an information on oath by telephone or other means of telecommunication to a justice . . .**

The justice will record the information verbatim and must, as soon as practicable, file it with the court.

The information must include:

- A statement of the circumstances that make it impracticable for the officer to appear personally before a judge.
- A statement of the offence alleged, the place to be searched, and the items likely to be seized.
- A statement as to the officer's grounds for believing that the items will be found in the place to be searched.

Once the search warrant has been issued, the officer must file a written report stating when the warrant was executed and what was seized.

A 1994 amendment to the Code allows a justice to receive an information by a telecommunication that produces a writing (e.g., a fax). When the justice receives the written communication, he or she must file it with the clerk of the court as soon as practicable.

A telewarrant must be executed by day, unless the justice authorizes execution of it by night.

5. Search Without a Warrant

a. For Certain Offences

The Code allows the police, in certain limited circumstances, to conduct a search without a search warrant. This power is granted only for specific offences.

The most significant circumstances in the Code relate to the new gun control legislation, the Firearms Act, which received Royal Assent in December 1995 but as of early 1996 had not been proclaimed into force. They concern situations where guns or other weapons are involved. Section 117.02 of the Code provides:

117.02 (1) Where a peace officer believes on reasonable grounds

(a) that a weapon, an imitation firearm, a prohibited device, any ammunition, any prohibited ammunition or an explosive substance was used in the commission of an offence, or

(b) that an offence is being, or has been committed under any provision of this Act that involves, or the subject-matter of which is, a firearm, an imitation firearm, a cross-bow, a prohibited weapon, a restricted weapon, a prohibited device, ammunition, prohibited ammunition or an explosive substance,

and evidence of the offence is likely to be found on a person, in a vehicle, or in any place or premises other than a dwelling-house, the peace officer may where the conditions for obtaining the warrant exist but, by reason of exigent circumstances, it would not be practicable to obtain a warrant, search, without warrant, the person, vehicle, place or premises and seize any thing by means of or in relation to which that peace officer believes on reasonable grounds the offence is being or has been committed.

Section 117.03 permits a peace officer to seize any firearm, or other regulated device where the person in possession fails to produce for inspection a licence or registration certificate.

Under s.117.04(2), an officer can search for and seize firearms or other devices where the officer would have grounds to obtain a warrant under s.117.04 (discussed above) but "by reason of a possible danger to the safety of that person, or any other person, it would not be practicable to obtain a warrant."

b. Incident to Lawful Arrest

Apart from the provisions in the Criminal Code and other federal Acts, such as the Customs Act, Narcotic Control Act, and Food and Drugs Act, the right to search the person exists only as an incident to arrest. This power is not conferred by the Criminal Code; rather, it comes from the common law, which is preserved in such matters by s.8 of the Code. After the police have arrested an accused they are entitled to conduct a search of the accused's person and to seize any thing in his or her possession or immediate surroundings for the purpose of securing evidence, preventing escape, and guaranteeing the safety of the accused and the officer.[61]

---

61 *Clouthier v. Langlois* (1990), 53 C.C.C. (3d) 257 (S.C.C.).

In *Cloutier v. Langlois,*[62] the Supreme Court of Canada recently considered the application of the authority to search incident to arrest. Cloutier had been stopped by the police for making an illegal right-hand turn with his car. A police check showed that he had several unpaid traffic fines. He became highly agitated and verbally abusive. The police had him put his hands on the car roof and spread his legs. They then frisked him (lightly patted him down). He sued the officers for assault. The Court held that reasonable grounds are not necessary for a "frisk" search incident to an arrest: "[A] frisk search incidental to a lawful arrest reconciles the public's interest in the effective and safe enforcement of the law on one hand, and on the other its interest in ensuring the freedom and dignity of individuals."

The Court set out these limits on the common law right to search incident to arrest:

• The police have a discretion as to whether a search is necessary for the effective and safe application of the law.
• The search must be for a valid objective of criminal justice (e.g., to check for weapons or prevent escape).
• The search cannot be used to intimidate, ridicule, or pressure the accused to gain admissions.
• The search must not be conducted in an abusive way.

The Court concluded that the search was justified. Although, in retrospect, the police did not have any real reason to fear physical violence, there was ample evidence that at the time they believed the search was necessary for their safety.

The Supreme Court has also held that before conducting a frisk search, the police must inform the accused of the right to counsel. However, the police do not have to wait until the accused calls a lawyer before conducting the search.[63]

Another recent Supreme Court of Canada case reached a different result. In *R. v. Greffe,*[64] the police had information that the accused would be bringing drugs into Canada from Amsterdam. The accused was detained at the airport by Customs authorities. His luggage was searched. Nothing was found. He was then taken to a room for a strip search. At this point he had not been told of his right to counsel. He was then turned over to the RCMP, who told him that he was being arrested for outstanding traffic warrants, that he had a right to consult counsel, and that he was being taken to a hospital for a rectal search. He was then taken to a hospital for a rectal exam. Two plastic bags containing heroin were recovered from his body.

The Court held that there were two serious violations of Charter rights in this case. First, although the Customs Act authorizes this type of search without an arrest if there are reasonable grounds for the search, the accused was not informed of his right to counsel when he was detained for the strip search at the airport. Second, the intrusive body search that took place at the

62 Ibid.
63 Supra, note 55.
64 (1990), 55 C.C.C. (3d) 161 (S.C.C.).

hospital on the basis of an arrest for traffic violations was a violation of the accused's right to be secure against unreasonable search and seizure. In other words, a rectal search cannot be justified on the basis of an arrest for outstanding traffic warrants. Also, even though the accused was informed of his right to counsel before the rectal search, the notification was "tainted" because he did not know the true reasons for his arrest. The Court also found that the police had not acted "in good faith." In other words, the violation of the accused's rights was not unintentional. The Court concluded that the evidence of the heroin had to be excluded because of the cumulative effect of the denial of the accused's rights: "Therefore, and not without great hesitation given the manifest culpability of the appellant, of a crime I consider heinous, I conclude that the integrity of our criminal justice system and the respect owed to our Charter are more important than the conviction of this offender."[65]

E. WIRETAPPING AND ELECTRONIC SURVEILLANCE

1. Introduction

A police officer may intercept private communications in several situations. The meaning of "intercept" includes listening, recording, or acquiring a communication (see s.183). A private communication is defined in s.183 as "any oral communication or any telecommunication . . . that is made under circumstances in which it is reasonable for the originator to expect that it will not be intercepted by any person other than the person intended by the originator to receive it." The key point is whether it is reasonable to expect the communication to be private. In *Goldman v. The Queen*,[66] the accused had called a police station and made threatening remarks to an officer. The remarks had been recorded. The Supreme Court of Canada held that, in this situation, it was not reasonable to expect that the remarks would not be overheard or recorded by another person. In most but not all situations, interceptions must be authorized by a judge.

2. Authorized Interceptions

There are two situations where authorization can be obtained for interceptions.

a. Section 185

This sections sets out the procedure for applying for authorization to intercept private communications. The application must be made in writing before a superior court judge (or a judge as defined in s.152). It must be signed by the Attorney General of the province, or by the Solicitor General

---

65 Ibid. at page 194.
66 (1979), 51 C.C.C. (2d) 1 (S.C.C.).

of Canada, or by an agent specially designated by the Solicitor General or Attorney General. The application must be accompanied by an affidavit, which may be sworn on the information and belief of a peace or public officer. The affidavit must state:

185. . .

(c) the facts relied upon to justify the belief that the authorization should be given together with the particulars of the offence,

(d) the type of private communication proposed to be intercepted,

(e) the names, addresses and occupations, if known, of all persons, the interception of whose private communications there are reasonable grounds to believe may assist the investigation of the offence, a general description of the nature and location of the place, if known, at which private communications are proposed to be intercepted and a general description of the manner of interception proposed to be used,

(f) the number of instances, if any, on which an application has been made under this section in relation to the offence and a person named in the affidavit pursuant to paragraph (e) and on which the application was withdrawn or no authorization was given, the date on which each application was made and the name of the judge to whom each application was made,

(g) the period for which the authorization is requested, and

(h) whether other investigative procedures have been tried and have failed or why it appears that they are unlikely to succeed or that the urgency of the matter is such that it would be impractical to carry out the investigation of the offence using only other investigative procedures.

Section 186 requires that before authorizing an interception, the judge must be satisfied:

(a) that it would be in the best interests of the administration of justice to do so; and

(b) that other investigative procedures have been tried and have failed, other investigative procedures are unlikely to succeed or the urgency of the matter is such that it would be impractical to carry out the investigation of the offence using only other investigative procedures.

Authorization for an interception under s.186 is only allowed for the offences listed in s.183. This is a long list that includes treason, weapons offences, various fraud offences, offences involving personal violence, drug offences, and any other offence for which an offender may be imprisoned for five years or more.

b. Section 184(2)(a)

This section provides that it is not an offence to intercept a communication if one of the parties to the conversation consents. Until recently, the police used this exception to intercept conversations between police informers and suspects without authorization. A 1990 decision of the Supreme Court of Canada held, however, that the right to be secure against unreasonable searches and seizures applies to interceptions of private communications. This means that where the state (i.e., the police) is recording the conversation, s.8 of the Charter requires that the police get judicial authorization for the interception.[67] This decision is now reflected in s.184.2, which sets out a procedure for obtaining authorization where one party consents to the interception. The authorization can be applied for any offence. The application can be made to a provincial court judge, superior court judge, or judge as defined under s.552.

3. Unauthorized Interceptions

In certain circumstances an interception can be done without court authorization. Under s.184.1 an agent of the state, defined as a peace officer or anyone working under the authority of or in cooperation with an officer, can intercept a private communication with the consent of one of the parties to the communication if the agent of the state reasonably believes that there is a risk of bodily harm to the person who consented to the interception and if the purpose of the interception is to prevent the bodily harm. So, for example, if a woman is being harassed or threatened over the phone, this section can be used to allow the police to intercept the call. Section 184.4 also allows interception without authorization where a peace officer, on reasonable grounds, believes:

- That the urgency of the situation is such that authorization could not with reasonable diligence be obtained.
- That the interception is immediately necessary to prevent an unlawful act that would cause serious harm to any person.
- That either the originator of the communication or the person intended by the originator to receive the communication is the person who is likely to perform the unlawful act or is the intended victim.

Unless the interception is authorized, or falls under the exceptions where authorization is not required, or is required to maintain service or to manage radio frequencies, it is an offence under s.184 of the Code.

4. Warrants Under Section 487.01

Amendments to the Code made in 1993 allow the police to obtain warrants for gathering information in ways that are not covered by s.487 warrants or warrants under any other federal law. Section 487.01 allows an officer to apply to a judge to obtain a warrant to use "any device or investigative technique or procedure or to do any thing described in the warrant that would,

---

67 *R. v. Duarte* (1990), 53 C.C.C. (2d) 1 (S.C.C.).

if not authorized, constitute an unreasonable search or seizure." This section has been used, for example, to authorize video surveillance. Before issuing the warrant, the judge must be satisfied by information under oath that there are reasonable grounds for believing that an offence has been or will be committed, and that information concerning this offence will be obtained through the use of the technique, procedure, or device or through doing the thing. The judge must also be satisfied that it is in the best interests of the administration of justice to issue the warrant, and that there is no other provision in the Code or in any other Act of Parliament that would provide for a warrant for the technique, procedure, or device, or for the doing of the thing. Subsection (2) limits the scope of the search warrants:

> **(2) Nothing in subsection (1) shall be construed as to permit interference with the bodily integrity of any person.**

Where the warrant authorizes videotaping or the use of similar devices in circumstances where a person has a reasonable expectation of privacy, the warrant must contain such conditions as the judge considers advisable to ensure that the person's privacy is respected as much as possible.

Section 492.1(4) allows the police to obtain a warrant to install a "tracking device [defined as] any device that, when installed in or on any thing, may be used to help ascertain the . . . location of any thing or person."

Section 492.2(1) allows a judge to issue a warrant to install a "number recorder [defined as] any device that can be used to record or identify the telephone number or location of the telephone from which a telephone call originates, or at which it is received or is intended to be received."

The Supreme Court recently considered whether the unauthorized use of computerized electricity records was an unreasonable search or seizure. In *R. v. Plant*,[68] the police suspected that marijuana was being grown in a particular house. They were able to gain access, through the police station's computer terminal, to the city of Calgary's utilities mainframe computer and to determine that the dwelling's electrical consumption was four times more than that of similar dwellings. This information formed part of the grounds for obtaining a search warrant. Among other issues, the Supreme Court considered whether accessing the city's utilities computer was a violation of s.8 of the Charter. The Court first noted that the s.8 guarantee against unreasonable searches protects a right of privacy. Section 8 can be used to protect "a biological core of personal information" that individuals in a free and democratic society would wish to shield from the state. However, in this case, the Court found that the computer records could not be said to reveal intimate details of the accused's life. As well, there was no relationship of confidence between the utility company and the accused. Furthermore, because of the place and manner in which the information was retrieved, the accused had no reasonable expectation of privacy. Also, the seriousness of the offence supported the use of the evidence. In sum, using the utility records was not a violation of s.8.

---

68 (1993), 84 C.C.C. (3d) 203 (S.C.C.).

Questions for Review and Discussion

1. Explain the difference between a summons and an appearance notice.
2. When can an appearance notice be used?
3. When can force be used in making an arrest?
4. Summarize the situations in which a police officer can make an arrest without a warrant.
5. Explain the authority of private security guards to make arrests.
6. Outline the pre-trial release procedures that must be followed.
7. What can happen to a police officer who makes an illegal arrest?
8. Briefly list the rights of a person on being arrested.
9. How have the courts defined detention?
10. When is a detention arbitrary?
11. Explain how the Supreme Court of Canada has interpreted the accused's right to retain and consult counsel.
12. What is the usual procedure the police must follow to obtain a search warrant?
13. What can the police seize with a warrant?
14. What is a telewarrant?
15. In what circumstances can the police search without a warrant?
16. What must a judge be satisfied about before authorizing the interception of a private communication?
17. The RCMP were investigating a serious assault on three Americans who had been driving to their homes in Michigan. As they approached the international bridge in Windsor, the Americans were cut off by another vehicle and forced to stop. The Americans were punched and attacked with a knife. The assailants then sped away. The victims identified the car of the assailants as a 1973 or 1975 blue Thunderbird. They picked a photograph from police files of a man who looked like one of the attackers. However, it turned out that this man was not in Ontario at the time of the assault.

    One of the officers, Larkin, reviewed the police files looking for owners of Thunderbirds. He found that a man named Storrey had been stopped numerous times driving a 1973 blue Thunderbird. Larkin discovered that Storrey's police photograph closely resembled the photograph of the man identified by the victims. Also, Storrey had a record of violent crime.

    Did the police have authority to arrest Storrey? Explain. See *Storrey v. The Queen* (1990), 53 C.C.C. (3d) 316 (S.C.C.).
18. **a.** If a police officer finds a person committing an offence under s.553, what must that officer first consider before he or she can lawfully make an arrest?

b. What might the officer do, if he or she doesn't arrest the person, to compel the person's appearance in court?

19. Sam is walking down the street. Behind him he hears a woman shout, "My purse! He's stolen my purse!" Sam turns around. He sees the woman who has had her purse stolen. She is standing still, staring at her empty hands. He can also see the head and shoulders of a man who appears to be running through the crowd on the sidewalk. A lot of people are staring at him but nobody is chasing him.
    a. Explain the authority of a private person to make an arrest.
    b. Should Sam chase the man who is running and make an arrest?

20. Constable Dust has been issued a search warrant in accordance with s.487 of the Criminal Code, empowering him to search Gerry's house. When he arrives at the house, he insists that the warrant also entitles him to search Gerry. Is he right?

21. Constable Armstrong arrests Blaine in a department store for theft. She asks Blaine where his car is and is informed that the car is outside in the parking lot. Constable Armstrong proceeds to the parking lot. She finds Tom and John sitting in the car. She orders them out and then searches them both. Was she legally entitled to search Tom and John?

22. At the beginning of a visit to the supermarket, L. picked up a carton of cigarettes. He subsequently made a trip to his car and returned. When he "checked out," the cigarettes were not among his purchases. The manager of the store called Constable P., and told him that several employees had seen L. pick up the carton of cigarettes and that it had been neither returned nor paid for. The constable came to the store and stopped L.'s car as it was leaving the parking lot. The constable told L., "There appears to be a mix-up in your order. The store believes that you have something for which you have not paid." Constable P. then asked L. to move his car to where the police car was parked. The officer asked L. if he could search the vehicle. L. replied, "Go ahead, I'd like to get this cleared up." The constable proceeded to search the main area of the car, the glove compartment, the trunk, and the back seat.

    The police officer was polite, and almost apologetic for the inconvenience he was causing. L. was cooperative, polite, calm, and not visibly upset. L. made no attempt to leave and made no request to be allowed to leave. However, L. said that he felt he had no alternative but to submit to the search; and that he unlocked the trunk of the car at the request of Constable P. because he felt he would be arrested if he refused to do so.

    Was L. in fact arrested? Explain. See *Lebrun v. High-Low Foods Ltd.* (1970), 70 D.L.R. (2d) 718 (B.C.S.C.).

Part Two
CRIMINAL
CODE
OFFENCES

Chapter Six

JURISDICTION AND PUBLIC ORDER, FIREARMS, AND OTHER OFFENCES
PARTS I, II, III, AND IV OF THE CODE

A. INTRODUCTION: JURISDICTION OVER OFFENCES

In general, Canadian criminal law deals with crimes that are committed in Canada. Section 6(2) provides:

> **(2) Subject to this Act or any other Act of Parliament, no person shall be convicted or discharged . . . of an offence committed outside Canada.**

Section 7 creates some of the exceptions by stating that, if certain acts are committed outside Canada, they will be deemed to have been committed in Canada if certain circumstances exist. For example, acts or omissions that are indictable offences if committed in Canada that are committed on a Canadian aircraft or on any aircraft if the flight is terminated in Canada, are deemed to have been committed in Canada. Other exceptions created by s.7 concern international law. Two of these, discussed below, concern committing an act or omission against an internationally protected person (s.7(3.1)) and hijacking (s.7(2)).

B. OFFENCES AGAINST PUBLIC ORDER

The offences in Part II of the Code have to do with harm to the government or to the government's authority. Offences not discussed below include: committing an act that intimidates Parliament or the legislature (s.51), inciting to mutiny (s.53), and engaging in an unauthorized prize fight (s.83).

1. Treason

There are two types of treason in the Code: high treason under s.46(1), and treason under s.46(2):

46. (1) Every one commits high treason who, in Canada,

(a) kills or attempts to kill Her Majesty, or does her any bodily harm tending to death or destruction, maims or wounds her, or imprisons or restrains her;

(b) levies war against Canada or does any act preparatory thereto;

(c) assists an enemy at war with Canada, or any armed forces against whom Canadian Forces are engaged in hostilities, whether or not a state of war exists between Canada and the country whose forces they are.

(2) Every one commits treason who, in Canada,

(a) uses force or violence for the purpose of overthrowing the government of Canada or a province;

(b) without lawful authority, communicates or makes available to an agent of a state other than Canada, military or scientific information or any sketch, plan, model, article, note or document of a military or scientific character that he knows or ought to know may be used by that state for a purpose prejudicial to the safety or defence of Canada;

(c) conspires with any person to commit high treason or to do anything mentioned in paragraph (a);

(d) forms an intention to do anything that is high treason or that is mentioned in paragraph (a) and manifests that intention by an overt act; or

(e) conspires with any person to do anything mentioned in paragraph (b) or forms an intention to do anything mentioned in paragraph (b) and manifests that intention by an overt act.

Section 46 is a rarely used section of the Code and is largely self-explanatory. Its general purpose is to prohibit acts that threaten the security of Canada.

High treason includes killing or attempting to kill the Queen, levying war against Canada, and assisting an enemy at war with Canada. High treason is a very serious indictable offence, as is indicated by the penalty for its commission: a minimum term of life imprisonment.

Treason, an indictable offence, includes using force or violence to overthrow the government and providing to an agent of another country military or scientific information that might threaten the safety of Canada. Treason also includes conspiring with another person to commit high treason or treason and forming the intention to commit high treason or treason; and demonstrating that intention by some overt act. In *R. v. Bleiler,*[1] the accused wrote letters to the German Emperor during World War I advising him to purchase a certain device or invention that would be of assistance to the German army. Writing those letters was held to be an overt act that demonstrated an intention to commit treason.

Treason is another example of an offence that may be committed outside Canada but lead to criminal liability within Canada. Section 46(3) states:

> **(3) Notwithstanding subsection (1) or (2), a Canadian citizen or a person who owes allegiance to Her Majesty in right of Canada,**

> **(a) commits high treason if, while in or out of Canada, he does anything mentioned in subsection (1); or**

> **(b) commits treason if, while in or out of Canada, he does anything mentioned in subsection (2).**

Thus, if the acts of treason or high treason are committed within Canada, any person, whether or not a citizen of Canada, may be convicted. If the acts of treason or high treason are committed outside Canada, only Canadian citizens and persons owing allegiance to Canada may be convicted.

There have been few cases of treason in Canada. One of them was *Lampel v. Berger,*[2] which involved the meaning of the phrase "assisting an enemy at war with Canada," found in s.46(1)(c). In 1917, during the World War I, Berger agreed to sell to Lampel a piece of property in Sarnia, Ontario. Berger was a Hungarian citizen living in the United States. At the time of this contract, Hungary was at war with Canada and the United States was a neutral country. Therefore, Berger was an alien enemy subject living in neutral territory. Before paying for the property, Lampel (a Canadian citizen) learned that Berger regularly sent money to his wife and children in Hungary. Lampel was in doubt as to whether he could lawfully pay the purchase money to Berger, since this might be construed as assisting an enemy at war with Canada. So he started a civil action to have a court determine the matter. The first issue in the case was whether the contract regarding the property was valid. The court held that it was unlawful for a resident of Canada to trade with "the enemy." However, for the purposes of contract law, Berger was not considered an enemy because he was not residing or carrying on business in an enemy country. Therefore, the contract was valid. The second issue was whether Lampel could pay the purchase money to Berger, knowing that Berger would send some of the money to Hungary. The court said that money sent to Hungary would become part of the financial resources of that enemy country and thus would aid the enemy by contributing to its capacity to prolong the war. Lampel knew of Berger's intention to send the money, and if he enabled Berger to carry out his intention by paying to him the purchase money, he would be assisting an enemy at war with Canada, contrary to

---

1   (1917), 28 C.C.C. 9 (Alta.C.A.).
2   (1917), 38 D.L.R. 47 (Alta.C.A.).

the Criminal Code. The court concluded that it was its duty to intervene by impounding the money and keeping it in court, to the credit of Berger, until after the war.

2. Sedition

In general, the offences of sedition involve advocating the overthrow of the government by the use of force. The offences of sedition are set in in s.61:

> **61. Every one who**
>
> **(a) speaks seditious words,**
>
> **(b) publishes a seditious libel, or**
>
> **(c) is a party to a seditious conspiracy,**
>
> **is guilty of an indictable offence and liable to imprisonment for a term not exceeding fourteen years.**

Section 61 contains three separate crimes of sedition: speaking a seditious libel; publishing such a libel; and being part of a seditious conspiracy. For each offence a seditious intention must be involved—that is, spoken words or a published libel (e.g., written words) are seditious only if they express a seditious intention. Similarly, a seditious conspiracy is an agreement between two or more persons to carry out a seditious intention. The term "seditious intention" is defined in s.59(4):

> **(4) Without limiting the generality of the meaning of the expression "seditious intention," every one shall be presumed to have a seditious intention who**
>
> **(a) teaches or advocates, or**
>
> **(b) publishes or circulates any writing that advocates,**
>
> **the use, without the authority of law, of force as a means of accomplishing a governmental change within Canada.**

It appears that, in general, seditious intention requires an intention to incite violence or to create a public disturbance or disorder against the state. However, s.59(4) is not an exhaustive definition. This is because of the use of the words "without limiting the generality of the meaning of the expression . . ." In a 1950 Supreme Court of Canada decision, *R. v. Boucher*,[3] five of the judges held that a seditious intention always requires an intention to incite violence or public disorder. Four of the judges were of the view that promotion of violence is not a necessary element when the sedition is based on an intention to bring into hatred or contempt the administration of justice. This case concerned a member of the Jehovah's Witnesses who was charged with seditious libel for publishing a pamphlet, which alleged that the courts and the police were persecuting members of the religion.

---

3   (1951), 99 C.C.C. 1 (S.C.C.) at p. 106.

Since this offence is rarely charged, the scope of the offence is not clear, as the decision in *Boucher* indicates. Some legal authorities believe that the offence could be found to violate the Charter because of vagueness.[4] However, some assistance is given by s.60:

> **60. Notwithstanding subsection 59(4), no person shall be deemed to have a seditious intention by reason only that he intends, in good faith,**
>
> **(a) to show that Her Majesty has been misled or mistaken in her measures;**
>
> **(b) to point out errors or defects in**
>
> **(i) the government or constitution of Canada or a province,**
>
> **(ii) Parliament or the legislature of a province, or**
>
> **(iii) the administration of justice in Canada;**
>
> **(c) to procure, by lawful means, the alteration of any matter of government in Canada; or**
>
> **(d) to point out, for the purpose of removal, matters that produce or tend to produce feelings of hostility and ill will between different classes of persons in Canada.**

This provision recognizes that free criticism is a basic element of modern democratic government. The purpose of s.60 is to protect the widest range of public discussion and controversy, so long as it is in good faith and for the purposes mentioned. However, this section does not protect a person from criminal liability if the person intends to incite violence or public disorder.

3. Unlawful Assemblies and Riots

a. Unlawful Assemblies

It is a summary conviction offence for a group of three or more persons who have assembled for a common purpose to conduct themselves in such a way that their neighbours have reasonable fears that the peace will be disturbed.

Section 63(1) defines the term "unlawful assembly":

> **63. (1) An unlawful assembly is an assembly of three or more persons who, with intent to carry out any common purpose, assemble in such a manner or so conduct themselves when they are assembled as to cause persons in the neighbourhood of the assembly to fear, on reasonable grounds, that they**
>
> **(a) will disturb the peace tumultuously; or**
>
> **(b) will by that assembly needlessly and without reasonable cause provoke other persons to disturb the peace tumultuously . . .**

---

4   See *Mewett and Manning on Criminal law*, 3rd edition, Butterworths, Canada, 1994, p.604.

(3) Persons are not unlawfully assembled by reason only that they are assembled to protect the dwelling-house of any one of them against persons who are threatening to break and enter it for the purpose of committing an indictable offence therein.

There are three elements of an unlawful assembly: (1) there is an assembly of three or more persons; (2) those persons have the intent to carry out a common purpose; and (3) their conduct (or manner of assembling) causes the persons in the neighbourhood to fear that there will be a tumultuous disturbance of the peace. The disturbance of the peace can be by the members of the assembly or by others who are needlessly or without reasonable cause provoked to disturb the peace.

Under s.63(2), an assembly that starts out lawful can become unlawful if the conduct of the group creates fear of a disturbance. Also, there may be an unlawful assembly even though the common purpose of the persons involved is lawful. The important point is the manner in which the purpose is, or is likely to be, carried out. If the manner causes persons in the neighbourhood to fear that there will be a disturbance, an offence is committed regardless of the lawfulness of the common purpose. Of course, the fear must be based on reasonable grounds. For example, in *R. v. Kalyn*,[5] the accused set up a stereo system in front of his cottage and organized a party. The party got out of control, and eventually there was a confrontation with the police. The court held that the common intention was to have a party, and that this was not unlawful; therefore, the assembly was at first lawful. However, the assembly became unlawful when the crowd became unruly and violent. The court also held that the conduct of a few members of the assembly could make the assembly unlawful and that all the members would be liable for the offence.

This decision was considered recently in *R. v. Brien*.[6] The defence counsel argued that the offence of unlawful assembly was one of absolute liability and therefore unconstitutional. Their argument, which was based on the definition of unlawful assembly, was that it was possible for persons in the neighbourhood to reasonably, but mistakenly, fear that the assembly would disturb the peace, and that the persons assembled might be unaware of these reasonable fears. In other words, the offence does not require mens rea, or an awareness that the assembly has become unlawful, on the part of the persons assembled. The court disagreed, stating that the reasonable grounds referred to in s.63 would be apparent to persons in the neighbourhood as well as to anyone in the assembly. Therefore, the mens rea required is objective foreseeability that the assembly has become unlawful.

b. Riots

A riot occurs when the unlawful assembly actually begins to disturb the peace. Section 64 states:

---

5   (1980), 52 C.C.C. (2d) 378 (Sask.C.A.).
6   *R. v. Brien* (1993), 86 C.C.C. 550 (N.T.S.C.).

64. A riot is an unlawful assembly that has begun to disturb the peace tumultuously.

The term "tumultuous" is not defined in the Code, but in *R. v. Lockhart*,[7] the Nova Scotia Court of Appeal said that "the word must connote in a general sense some element of violence or force which may be exhibited by menaces or threats." In this case, a person named Keddy was arrested for disturbing the peace. A short while later, a group of 20 or 30 people arrived at the police station demanding his release. One person in the crowd threatened to break Keddy out if he wasn't released. Another person offered to fight the police. The court held that a riot had taken place when the threats were made. The threats, swearing, and yelling created an atmosphere of violence that was "tumultuous."

R. v. Brien, referred to earlier, actually concerned a charge of taking part in a riot. The court held that taking part in a riot is different from being part of an unlawful assembly because s.65 requires that the person actually take part in the rioting—that is, take part in causing the disturbance. In other words, a person who is part of the unlawful assembly that has begun to disturb the peace is not necessarily part of the rioting. In addition, the person must either intend to take part in the riot or be so reckless as to have acted as if he or she intended to take part in the riot.

Under s.67, where a riot of at least 12 persons is taking place, a justice, mayor, or sheriff, or the lawful deputy of a mayor or sheriff, can go to the place and after commanding silence read the following proclamation:

> *Her Majesty the Queen charges and commands all persons being assembled immediately to disperse and peaceably to depart to their habitations or to their lawful business on the pain of being guilty of an offence for which, on conviction, they may be sentenced to imprisonment for life . . .*

It is an indictable offence under s.68 to oppose, hinder, or assault anyone making or beginning to make a proclamation. It is also an offence under this section not to disperse within 30 minutes after the proclamation has been made, or within 30 minutes of when the proclamation would have been made if the person trying to make it had not been opposed, hindered, or assaulted.

4. Explosive Substances

Section 79 states that any person who has explosives in his or her possession is under a duty to use reasonable care to prevent harm to property or persons:

79. Every one who has an explosive substance in his possession or under his care or control is under a legal duty to use reasonable care to prevent bodily harm or death to persons or damage to property by that explosive substance.

---

7   (1976), 15 N.S.R. (2d) 512 (C.A.).

Section 2 defines "explosive substance" as including a bomb, grenade, dynamite, or any other incendiary substance or device. The term also includes anything intended to be used to make an explosive substance, as well as anything used or intended to be used to cause an explosion with an explosive substance.

Section 80 makes it an indictable offence to fail, without lawful excuse, to perform the duty regarding explosives. If an explosion resulted from the breach of the duty and a person was killed, or was likely to have been killed, the punishment is life imprisonment. If the explosion caused or was likely to have caused bodily harm or property damage, the punishment is imprisonment for 14 years. In other words, it is not necessary that harm or damage actually took place—only that death, harm, or damage was likely. On the other hand, when a person fails to perform the duty but no explosion takes place, no offence under this section has occurred.

Under s.81, it is an indictable offence to do anything with the intent to cause an explosion that is likely to cause serious bodily harm, death, or serious property damage; to cause an explosion with the intent to do bodily harm; to throw or place an explosive anywhere with the intent to damage property without lawful excuse; and to make or possess an explosive with the intent to endanger life or cause serious property damage. These and other offences in s.81 require proof of the specific intents mentioned, unlike s.80 offences, which simply require proof of a failure to exercise reasonable care.

A separate offence of making, or having in possession or under care and control, an explosive without lawful excuse is contained in s.82. The section puts the onus on the accused to show the "lawful excuse." This section is open to challenge under the Charter because it sets up a reverse onus clause. (See Chapter Two for a discussion of these clauses.)

C. FIREARMS AND WEAPONS

In December 1995, Canada's new gun control legislation, the Firearms Act, was enacted after much hot debate over the central core of the law, which requires gun owners to be licensed and to register their firearms in a central registry. Although mainly concerned with guns, the Act also regulates other weapons and devices such as knives, crossbows, and ammunition. The Act also increases penalties for gun-related offences, and expands the categories of restricted and prohibited weapons and devices.

Under the Firearms Act, everyone, with a few exceptions, must have a licence to possess a firearm. Persons such as police officers and members of the Canadian Forces do not need licences. Gun owners had until 2001 to obtain a licence and until 2003 to register their firearms. There are also transitional provisions to recognize firearms acquisition certificates (FACs) as licences. FACs were required before the Firearms Act was passed to purchase guns. Until the Act is fully in force, people will continue to apply for FACs, which will be valid until they expire or the year 2001, at which point a licence under the Firearms Act will have to be obtained.[8]

Generally speaking, to be licensed to possess a firearm, or other device, a person must be at least 18 and pass a firearms safety test. There are exceptions to these rules. For example, Jacques, even though under 18, may be licensed if he hunts and traps to sustain himself and/or his family. When a person applies for a licence, the chief firearms officer will determine whether the person is eligible. A person is not eligible if "it is desirable, in the interests of the safety of that or any other person, that the person not possess a firearm, a cross-bow, a prohibited weapon, a restricted weapon, a prohibited device, ammunition or prohibited ammunition" (s.5). In determining whether a person is eligible, the officer will consider such circumstances as whether the person has been convicted of an offence involving violence against other persons or a weapons offence in the last five years, has been treated for a mental illness associated with violence, or has a history of violent behaviour.

A person can be licensed to have a restricted firearm for special purposes, such as target shooting, or if requiring a restricted firearm for his or her lawful occupation (for example, being a Brinks guard). A licence to possess a prohibited firearm will only be issued to the person who owned the firearm before it was declared prohibited. Allowing persons to keep firearms that are now prohibited was an amendment to the bill in response to criticism that it would not be fair to make people give up the guns they already have. For the sake of further controlling prohibited firearms, a person can only transfer or sell the prohibited firearm to a person who already is licensed to possess a prohibited firearm.

Before the enactment of the Firearms Act, Part III of the Criminal Code contained the regulatory provisions related to gun control (such as the procedure for obtaining FACs and permits for transporting restricted weapons). The Firearms Act takes over this regulatory function, leaving in the Code most of the offences and penalties related to firearms and weapons.

Although Part III of the Code has been extensively amended by the Firearms Act, some sections have merely been reorganized. Therefore, some of the case law decided under the old Part III is still relevant. The following discusses Part III of the Criminal Code as it has been changed by the Firearms Act. Cases under the previous Part III that are still relevant are included.

1. Definitions

Section 84 defines many of the terms used in Part III. Some of the important definitions are:

> **"prohibited firearm" means**
>
> **(a) a handgun that**

---

8   Although the Firearms Act has been brought into force, there is a phasing in of some sections, readers should always check the most recent Criminal Code amendments to determine the current state of the law.

(i) has a barrel equal to or less than 105 mm in length, or

(ii) is designed or adapted to discharge a 25 or 32 calibre cartridge

but does not include any such handgun that is prescribed, where the handgun is for use in international sporting competition governed by the rules of the International Shooting Union

(b) a firearm that is adapted from a rifle or shotgun whether by sawing, cutting or any other alteration and that, as so adapted,

(i) is less than 660 mm in length or

(ii) is 660 mm or greater in length and has a barrel less than 457 mm in length,

(c) an automatic firearm, whether or not it has been altered to discharge only one projectile with one pressure of the trigger, or

(d) any firearm that is prescribed to be a prohibited firearm

"prohibited weapon" means

(a) a knife that has a blade that opens automatically by gravity or centrifugal force or by hand pressure applied to a button, spring or other device in or attached to the handle of the knife, or

(b) any weapon other than a firearm that is prescribed to be a prohibited weapon;

The New Brunswick Court of Appeal considered the meaning of (b), "a knife that has a blade that opens automatically by gravity or centrifugal force." The court stated that a knife can fall within this definition even if it was not designed to open as such if, because of wear or alteration, it can be opened through gravity or centrifugal force.[9] In *R. v. Vaughn*,[10] the Supreme Court of Canada held that even though an additional manual operation that required some skill had to be performed before the knife would open automatically by centrifugal force, the knife fell within the definition of a prohibited weapon.

restricted firearm means

(a) a handgun that is not a prohibited firearm,

(b) a firearm that

(i) is not a prohibited firearm

(ii) has a barrel less than 470 mm in length

(ii) is capable of discharging centre-fire ammunition in a semi-automatic manner,

9 *R. v. Richard and Walker* (1981), 63 C.C.C. (2d) 333 (N.B.C.A.).
10 (1991), 69 C.C.C. (3d) 576 (S.C.C.).

(c) a firearm that is designed or adapted to be fired when reduced to a length of less than 660 mm by folding, telescoping or otherwise, or

(d) a firearm of any other kind that is prescribed to be a restricted weapon;

The definition of "weapon" for Part III is in s.2 of the Code. It includes firearms as well as anything used or intended to be used to cause death or injury to persons, and anything used or intended for use for the purpose of threatening or intimidating any person.

Two provincial courts of appeal have held that it is the subjective intent of the user that determines whether a thing is a weapon and not the objective intent of the manufacturer.[11] For example, a rifle is designed to be used as a weapon. A beer bottle is not designed to be used as a weapon; it is designed to be used as a container for beer. However, it could be a weapon if a person used it or intended to use it to assault another person. In other words, almost any object can be a weapon.

"Firearm" is defined under s.2 of the Code as "any barrelled weapon from which any shot, bullet, or other projectile can be discharged and that is capable of causing serious bodily injury or death to a person, and includes any frame or receiver of such a barrelled weapon and anything that can be adapted for use as a firearm."

However, s.84 states that certain types of weapons are not considered firearms in certain situations. These include antique firearms, devices used for such purposes as signalling distress or firing blanks, and devices used for slaughtering or tranquillizing animals.

In *R. v. Covin and Covin,*[12] the Supreme Court of Canada considered the last part of the definition of firearm (i.e., "anything that can be adapted for use as a firearm"). The Court noted that most pieces of wood, pipe, and metal could, given time and expertise, be adaptable for use as firearms. The Court held that the exact meaning of this part of the definition depends on the offence for which it is being used. The accused were charged with robbery and with using a firearm while committing an indictable offence. Their conviction for robbery was not appealed. However, their conviction for the second offence was appealed on the grounds that the weapon they used was not a "firearm." The gun they had used in the robbery was a damaged airgun with several missing pieces, some of which were necessary for the gun's operation.

The Court looked at the purpose of the offence and stated that it is to protect the victim of an offence (e.g., robbery) from serious injury or death by discouraging the use of firearms during the commission of offences. The Court concluded:

> *Therefore, whatever is used at the scene of the crime must . . . be proven by the Crown as capable, either at the outset or through adaptation or assembly, of being loaded, fired and thereby having the potential of causing serious bodily*

---

11 *R. v. Murray* (1991), 65 C.C.C. (3d) 507 (Ont.C.A.); *R. v. Roberts* (1990), 60 C.C.C. (3d) 509 (N.S.C.A.).
12 (1983), 8 C.C.C. (3d) 240 (S.C.C.).

harm during the commission of the offence, or during the flight after the commission of the main offence . . .[13]

In this case, it would have taken an experienced person 10 to 15 minutes to replace the missing parts. The Court concluded that there were not the necessary "ingredients" to make the gun operable.

2. Use Offences

The penalties for certain offences—including s.220, criminal negligence causing death; s.236, manslaughter; s.239, attempted murder; s.244, causing bodily harm with intent; s.272, sexual assault with a weapon; s.273, aggravated sexual assault; s.279, kidnapping; s.279.1, hostage taking; s.344, robbery; and s.346(1.1), extortion—were changed in 1996 so that when a weapon is involved, the minimum term of imprisonment is four years.

For other offences, s.85 makes it a separate indictable offence to use a firearm while committing or attempting to commit an indictable offence or while in flight after committing or attempting to commit an indictable offence. It is also an offence to use an imitation weapon while committing or attempting to commit an indictable offence or while in flight after committing or attempting to commit an indictable offence. The penalties for these offences are, for a first offence, one to fourteen years' imprisonment, and for subsequent offences, three to fourteen years.

Section 86(1) makes it a hybrid offence for anyone without lawful excuse to use, carry, handle, ship, transport, or store a firearm, a prohibited or restricted weapon, a prohibited device, or ammunition in a careless manner or without reasonable precautions for the safety of others.

Two Supreme Court of Canada decisions considered the mens rea required for this offence, which is the same as the previous offence under Part III. Both cases involved careless use of firearms. In *R. v. Gossett*,[14] a police officer was charged with unlawful manslaughter when he shot a fleeing suspect. The unlawful act was the careless handling of a firearm. In *R. v. Finlay*,[15] the accused was charged with the careless storage of firearms and ammunition. In both cases, the Court held that the proper test to be applied for liability is objective: Was the behaviour of the accused a marked departure from the behaviour of a reasonable person? Would a reasonable person be aware of the risk?

It is also an offence under s.86 to contravene regulations under the Firearms Act respecting the storage, handling, transportation, shipping, displaying, advertising and mail-order sales of firearms and restricted weapons.

Section 86 offences are hybrid. If they are treated as indictable, the penalties are up to two years' imprisonment for first offences and up to five years' imprisonment for subsequent offences.

---

13 Ibid. at page 243.
14 (1993), 83 C.C.C. (3d) 494 (S.C.C.).
15 (1993), 83 C.C.C. (3d) 513 (S.C.C.).

Section 87(1) makes it a hybrid offence to without lawful excuse point a firearm at another person, whether the firearm is loaded or not. If treated as an indictable offence, the penalty is a maximum of five years' imprisonment.

3. Possession Offences

Under s.88, it is an indictable offence to possess a weapon or an imitation of a weapon for a purpose dangerous to the public peace or for the purpose of committing an offence. To gain a conviction under this section, the prosecution must prove both possession and intention.

The fact that a person is carrying a weapon for a defensive purpose does not necessarily mean that the weapon is not possessed for a purpose dangerous to the public. In *R. v. Nelson*,[16] the accused feared being attacked by two men, the Bougie brothers, with whom he had had some previous trouble. Before going to a club where he expected that they would be, he armed himself with a homemade knife with a double-edged, 18-inch blade. After drinking some beer at the club, the accused got into a fight with one of the Bougies and the two of them were required to leave the club. Outside the club, the Bougie brothers confronted the accused, who began swinging his knife at them, injuring both of them. The accused was convicted of carrying a weapon for a purpose dangerous to the public peace. The court noted that even though the weapon was intended for defence, other factors, such as the nature of the weapon, how it was acquired, the manner of its use, the time, the place, and relevant statements or actions of the accused, had to be considered. The court concluded:

> In this instance the character of the weapon and the reasons for its acquisition as well as the clear intention of the [accused] to make use of what was, under the circumstances, a clearly illegal method of defence make it clear that the weapon was being carried for a purpose dangerous to the public peace.[17]

In *R. v. Proverbs*,[18] the Ontario Court of Appeal considered the meaning of the phrase "having possession for a purpose dangerous to the public peace." It stated that the purpose must be determined as at the instant of time that preceded the use of the weapon. Here the police had a warrant to search Proverbs's apartment. When they arrived at the apartment, they knocked on the door and announced that they were the police. There was no response, but they believed that someone was inside. They eventually had the caretaker open the door. They found the accused crouched over a loaded shotgun. He claimed that he had only heard the knocking and thought someone was breaking in, and that he did not know the visitors were police. He was convicted of an offence under the former s.87. On appeal, on the issue of whether the trial judge properly instructed the jury, the court stated:

---

16 (1972), 8 C.C.C. (2d) 29 (Ont.C.A.).
17 Ibid. at page 35.
18 (1983), 9 C.C.C. (3d) 249 (Ont.C.A.).

> *If the jury were satisfied that prior to the entry of the police into his premises, Proverbs did not have the weapon for a purpose dangerous to the public peace, and he only loaded it on the sudden . . . unaware that it was the police seeking entry, because he was in fear of harm to himself and only intended to use it if necessary to defend himself . . . then the Crown would not have proved [the elements of the offence] . . .*[19]

The court ordered a new trial.

It is a summary conviction offence under s.89 to, without lawful excuse, have possession of a weapon while attending or on the way to attending a public meeting.

Section 90 makes it a hybrid offence, punishable on indictment by a maximum of five years' imprisonment, to carry a concealed weapon, a prohibited device, or any prohibited ammunition unless authorized to do so under the Firearms Control Act. The meaning of "concealed weapon" was considered by the Supreme Court of Canada in *R. v. Felawka.*[20] The Court held that to prove the weapon was concealed, the Crown must establish that the accused took steps to hide an object that he knew to be a weapon so that it would not be observed or come to the attention of others.

Sections 91 to 95 create various offences for possessing a firearm or weapon without a licence or without registering the firearm or weapon. Section 96 makes it an offence to possess a firearm or other regulated device that was obtained by the commission in Canada of an offence. Section 97 makes it an offence to give, sell, or barter a crossbow to another person who is not licensed to possess a crossbow.

Sections 99 to 101 create "trafficking" offences for the unauthorized transfer of firearms and weapons. Section 102 makes it an offence to alter a firearm so that it is capable of rapid fire of projectiles by one pressure of the trigger (i.e., automatic firearms). Section 103 deals with offences for importing and exporting firearms. It is an offence under s.105 to not report the loss of a firearm, or licence, or registration certificate transferring firearms.

D. BRIBERY, OBSTRUCTING A POLICE OFFICER, PERJURY, AND OBSTRUCTING JUSTICE

1. Bribery

In general terms, bribery is the accepting or offering of an undue reward or "payoff," in relation to influencing the conduct of public officials. There are several Code sections involving bribery. These sections mention various types of rewards, public officials, and behaviours.

An example of a Code section involving bribery is s.119:

119. (1) Every one who

---

19 Ibid. at page 261.
20 (1993), 85 C.C.C. (3d) 248 (S.C.C.).

(a) being the holder of a judicial office, or being a member of Parliament or of the legislature of a province, corruptly

(i) accepts or obtains,

(ii) agrees to accept, or

(iii) attempts to obtain,

any money, valuable consideration, office, place or employment for himself or another person in respect of anything done or omitted or to be done or omitted by him in his official capacity, or

(b) gives or offers, corruptly, to a person mentioned in paragraph (a) any money, valuable consideration, office, place or employment in respect of anything done or omitted or to be done or omitted by him in his official capacity for himself or another person,

is guilty of an indictable offence and liable to imprisonment for a term of imprisonment not exceeding fourteen years.

In this bribery offence, it is clear that the public official could be a judge, a member of Parliament, or a member of a provincial legislature. The reward could be money, a job, or practically anything of value. The behaviour involved could be any act or omission by the official in carrying out his or her public duties.

Section 119(2) protects judges from spurious charges by requiring the consent of the Attorney General of Canada before proceedings can be instituted.

Bribery involves two parties: the public official and any other person. Offences may be committed by one or both of them. Paragraph (a) refers to three separate offences that may be committed by the public official: actually accepting a bribe; simply agreeing to accept a bribe; and soliciting or trying to obtain a bribe. Paragraph (b) refers to two offences that may be committed by the other person: actually giving a bribe to the official; and simply offering a bribe to the official.

When a person offers a bribe to an official, it is no defence that the official refused it. In other words, the offence is complete when the offer is made.

It is also necessary that the offering, giving, or accepting be done "corruptly." The word "corruptly" has been interpreted as meaning with the intention to accomplish the purpose forbidden by the Code.[21] Thus, under s.119 it must be shown that the offering, accepting, and so on, was done with the intention of having the official do or omit to do some act in his or her official capacity.

In *R. v. Bruneau*,[22] the accused was charged with agreeing to accept $10,000 for the use of his influence in his official capacity as a member of Parliament. Bruneau had agreed to accept the money from B., one of his constituents, in return for using his influence to have the federal government buy B.'s property as the site for a post office. The usual practice, which was followed in

---

21 *R. v. Gross* (1946), 86 C.C.C. 68 (Ont.C.A.).
22 (1964), 1 C.C.C. 97 (Ont.C.A.).

this case, was that after a number of possible sites were examined by federal officials, the local MP was consulted for a recommendation. B.'s property was purchased, and Bruneau accepted $10,000 from B. Bruneau's lawyer argued that Bruneau had not been acting "in his official capacity" because that phrase refers to an MP's power to take part in legislation and matters directly related to it in the House of Commons. The court rejected this argument and found Bruneau guilty. The court felt that since the accused had been consulted because of his membership in Parliament, any action taken by him was "in his official capacity."

2. Other Bribery Offences

Section 120(a) makes it an offence for a justice, police commissioner, peace officer, public officer, or officer of juvenile court, or other person employed in the administration of criminal law, to accept, obtain, agree to accept, or attempt to obtain a bribe with intent:

(iv) to interfere with the administration of justice,

(v) to procure or facilitate the commission of an offence, or

(vi) to protect from detection or punishment a person who has committed or who intends to commit an offence, or

(b) [to give or offer], corruptly, to a person mentioned [above] any money, valuable consideration, office, place or employment with intent that the person should do anything mentioned in . . . (a) (iv), (v) or (vi) . . .

Section 120(b) prohibits the offering of a bribe to any of the officials listed in s.120(a) with any of the intents set out in s.120(a).

A person cannot be convicted under s.120 of offering a bribe to a peace officer with intent to interfere with the administration of justice unless he or she knew that the person to whom the offer was made was a police officer.[23]

The meaning of "administration of justice" was discussed in *R. v. Kalick*.[24] The accused gave a bribe of $1,000 to a police officer in order to persuade him not to charge him with an offence he had committed. Kalick argued that there could be no intent to interfere with the administration of justice until after some proceeding, such as the formal charging of the accused, had taken place. The Supreme Court of Canada decided that "administration of justice" must be given a wider meaning that "includes the taking of necessary steps to have a person who has committed an offence brought before the proper tribunal and punished for his offence. It is a very wide term covering the detection, prosecution and punishment of offenders." Kalick was convicted under this broad definition. The Court also held that this section applies to provincial offences as well as federal crimes. In this case, it was immaterial whether the officer actually intended to lay a charge.

23 *R. v. Smith* (1921), 38 C.C.C. 21 (Ont.C.A.).
24 (1920), 35 C.C.C. 159 (S.C.C.).

Section 121 makes it an offence to bribe government officials. "Official" is broadly defined in s.118 as "a person who (a) holds an office, or (b) is appointed to discharge a public duty."

Section 123 makes it an offence to bribe a "municipal official." This refers to a member of a municipal council or a person who holds an office under a municipal government. The term includes persons such as the chief building inspector for a city.[25]

3. Obstructing a Peace Officer

129. Every one who

(a) resists or wilfully obstructs a public officer or peace officer in the execution of his duty or any person lawfully acting in aid of such an officer,

(b) omits, without reasonable excuse, to assist a public officer or peace officer in the execution of his duty in arresting a person or in preserving the peace, after having reasonable notice that he is required to do so, or

(c) resists or wilfully obstructs any person in the lawful execution of a process against lands or goods or in making a lawful distress or seizure, is guilty of

(d) an indictable offence and liable to imprisonment for a term not exceeding two years, or

(e) an offence punishable on summary conviction.

The essential elements of a charge under s.129(a) are that the accused obstructed; that the obstruction was wilful; that the person obstructed was a public officer or peace officer; and that the officer was in the lawful execution of his or her duty.

a. Obstruction

The ordinary meaning of the term "obstruct" is to hinder, block, or stop up.[26] The obstruction may involve physical force, such as assaulting a police officer.[27] The obstruction may occur without the use of physical force where the accused does an act that leads the officer to believe that there will be violence if the officer proceeds.[28] However, it is not obstruction to not do anything. In *R. v. Lavin,*[29] a police officer observed the accused driving a car with an illegal radar detector. When the accused saw the officer, he put the detector in his pocket. The officer then stopped the accused, told him he had seen the detector, and asked him to hand it over. The accused refused to do so and

25 *R. v. Belzberg* (1962), 131 C.C.C. 281 (S.C.C.).
26 *R. v. Matheson* (1913), 21 C.C.C. 312 (N.B.C.A.).
27 *Bain* (1955), 111 C.C.C. 281 (Man.C.A.).
28 Supra, note 26.
29 (1992), 76 C.C.C. (3d) 279 (Que.C.A.).

was charged with obstruction. The Court of Appeal held that a person cannot be found guilty of obstruction for not doing something unless there is a duty to act. In this case, the court could not find any duty prior to arrest for the accused to hand over the device. The court distinguished this case from others where (a) the accused was found guilty after he denied possession of a detector, and (b) the accused hid a weapon and then lied about its existence. In *Lavin*, the accused was not charged because he hid the detector or lied about it but because he refused to hand it over.

It is obstruction to mislead the police. For example, in *R. v. Johnson*[30] the driver of a car was stopped for speeding. He gave the officer a false name and was given a ticket under that name. The Saskatchewan Court of Appeal held that the accused's intent was to mislead the officer and thereby obstruct the officer in the execution of his duty. This case referred to *R. v. Moore*, discussed in Chapter Five.[31] In that case, the Supreme Court of Canada said that the accused had obstructed an officer in the execution of his duty by not providing his name where the officer had no authority to make an arrest except for the purpose of establishing the person's identity. On the other hand, the Alberta Court of Appeal held that an accused was not guilty of obstruction where she refused to give her name where the officer had no evidence that the accused had committed an offence.[32] In *R. v. B*,[33] another case from Alberta, the police were looking for a runaway youth. They spoke to the accused, who gave them false information about her whereabouts. He was convicted of obstruction.

b. Wilfully

The term "wilfully," as used in this section, means deliberately or intentionally. It refers to a deliberate purpose to accomplish something forbidden—a determination to carry out one's own will in defiance of the law.[34]

c. Peace Officer or Public Officer

In general, "peace officer" and "public officer" refer to persons who have the duty of enforcing the law.

A "peace officer" is defined in s.2 and was discussed in Chapter Five. In most situations, it refers to a police officer.

The term "public officer" is also defined in s.2:

"public officer" includes

(a) an officer of customs or excise,

(b) an officer of the Canadian Forces,

(c) an officer of the Royal Canadian Mounted Police, and

30 (1985), 41 Sask.R. 205 (Q.B.).
31 See Chapter Five, note 18.
32 *R. v. Guthrie* (1982), 69 C.C.C. (2d) 216 (Alta.C.A.).
33 (1985), 41 Alta.L.R. (2d) 341 (Prov.Ct.Youth Div.).
34 *R. v. Griffin* (1935), 63 C.C.C. 286 (N.B.C.A.).

(d) any officer while the officer is engaged in enforcing the laws of Canada relating to revenue, customs, excise, trade or navigation.

d. Execution of Duty

The officer must be in the lawful execution of duty when obstructed. This means that the officer must be carrying out some duty or obligation imposed by law. If the officer is not carrying out such a duty, then there is no offence committed under s.129 if the person resists or obstructs the officer.

The courts have recognized that the police have a common law duty to preserve the peace, prevent crime, and protect lives and property.[35] Where there is a charge of obstruction and a question of whether the police were in the execution of their duty, courts have said that it must first be determined whether the specific conduct of the police fell within the scope of a general duty. A case that considered the question of whether the officer's conduct was within a general duty is *R. v. Westlie*.[36] Two plain-clothes police officers were working in the skid row area of Vancouver. The accused knew that they were police officers and starting shouting: "Undercover Pigs! Undercover Fuzz! Watch out for the pigs!" Many people in the area were attracted by the shouting. One of the officers told the accused that he was on duty in the area and warned him to stop. At that point, the accused began stopping people on the street, pointing at the two police officers, and referring to them as "undercover pigs" and "undercover fuzz." The accused was charged with wilfully obstructing a peace officer in the execution of his duty. There were three main issues in the case: At the time of the incident, were the police officers in the execution of their duty? Was there obstruction of the police officers? And was the obstruction wilful? The court held that the officers were in the execution of their general duty, which was to take all steps necessary to ensure that the public peace was kept, to prevent and detect crime, to bring offenders to justice, and to protect property from criminal damage. Also, that the accused did all he could to identify them to the public and thus completely frustrate them in the execution of their duty. This amounted to obstruction. Also, that there was no question that the conduct of the accused was intentional and deliberate. Clearly, the accused was trying to warn law violators in the area that the two men were police officers and that they should stop breaking the law until the officers had left the area. The accused was convicted.

Another case that involved the general duty of police officers is *Knowlton v. R.*[37] In 1971, Premier Alexei Kosygin of the Soviet Union was to visit Edmonton as part of his official visit to Canada. He was going to make a short stop at the Chateau Lacombe Hotel. A few days before the visit, Kosygin had been assaulted in Ottawa by a man who grabbed him and tried to drag him to the ground. To prevent another such incident, 26 police officers cordoned off an area in front of the entrance to the hotel. The accused wanted to enter the cordoned-off area to take pictures. A police officer told him that he could not enter the area and warned him that if he did, he would

---

35 *R. v. Dedman* (1985), 20 C.C.C. (3d) 97 (S.C.C.).
36 (1971), 2 C.C.C. (2d) 315 (B.C.C.A.).
37 (1973), 10 C.C.C. (2d) 377 (S.C.C.).

be arrested. The accused ignored the warning. He began to enter the restricted area, pushing his way through two constables. He was arrested and charged with wilfully obstructing a peace officer in the execution of his duty. The incident took place at about the time Kosygin was scheduled to arrive. The Supreme Court of Canada said that the police had interfered with Knowlton's right to move freely on a public street. Such an interference could only be justified if the police were carrying out some duty imposed on them by law. The Court held that the police acted in the execution of their general duty to preserve peace, order, and public safety. They had a duty to prevent another criminal assault on Kosygin, and the accused obstructed them in carrying out that duty.

One type of case where a conflict arises between the police officer's general duty and an individual's rights is where the police trespass on private property while executing their duty and the occupier resists. As noted in Chapter Five, the police can trespass on private property to make an arrest or when in hot pursuit of a suspect.[38] There are a few other situations under common law and statute law where they may be authorized to enter private property. A case that discussed some of these situations is *R. v. Custer*.[39] The police received a report of a stabbing and went to investigate. When they arrived at the house where the stabbing was reported to have taken place, the man who answered the door stated that his wife had been stabbed but that she was all right. The accused told the officers to leave, but they insisted on entering the house to investigate the stabbing. A fight ensued, and the accused was charged with obstruction. The court held that although the police were exercising their general duty under statute to investigate crime, in this case, entering the house was not justified under the statute law duty. The police cannot enter a private home against the owner's will to investigate a possible offence with a view to apprehending the offender. However, under the common law the police have the right to enter private property to prevent death or serious injury. The police would have been justified in entering the home if they had had reasonable grounds to believe that an emergency situation existed involving the preservation of life or the prevention of serious injury.[40]

Another case that considered whether the police were justified in trespassing is *R. v. Thomas*.[41] The police were called to investigate complaints of a noisy party. When the police arrived at the house, they were taken by one of the guests to the accused's bedroom. After being asked some questions, the accused ordered the police to leave the house. A fight erupted between the police, a guest, and the accused. The accused was found not guilty on the grounds that the guest did not have the authority to invite the police in, and even if there was an implied permission to enter the house, once the police were asked to leave, they became trespassers. Therefore, the accused could not be charged with obstruction.

38 See Chapter Five, page 101.
39 (1984), 12 C.C.C. (3d) 372 (Sask.C.A.).
40 The accused was acquitted, however, because this argument was not made at the trial and therefore could not be considered at the appeal.
41 (1991), 67 C.C.C. (3d) 81 (Nfld.C.A.).

Where the police make a warrantless arrest under s.495(b) (which allows them to arrest where they find a person committing any offence), and where the accused is later found not guilty of the offence, a charge for resisting arrest can still stand. This decision was made in *R. v. Biron*.[42] The accused was charged with causing a disturbance and resisting arrest. He was acquitted of the disturbance charge. He then argued that since he had not committed an offence, the arrest was unlawful and the obstruction charge should be dismissed. The Supreme Court disagreed, holding that for an arrest to be lawful, the officer need only find a person apparently committing an offence. In such situations, a charge of resisting arrest can be laid.

There will be a different result where the police misapply the law. In *R. v. Potvin*,[43] the accused was charged with resisting a peace officer. The accused and a friend had gone to a park in Montreal. He had placed his kayak on a lake in the park when a police officer told him that boating was not permitted on the lake and warned him that he would be arrested if he did go boating. The accused went for a boat ride and was arrested. He resisted the arrest, and two police officers had to push him into a patrol car. The Crown argued that the accused had violated a city by-law that prohibited, among other things, throwing anything in city lakes and playing unauthorized games. The Crown also argued that the arrest was lawful. The court disagreed, saying that the accused had the right to resist the arrest because he had not violated the by-law and, even if he had, it was not an offence that allows an arrest without a warrant. The police officers were acting without authority and thus were not in the execution of their duty. Therefore, the accused had a lawful excuse for resisting the arrest and was not guilty under s.129(a).

The police will not be acting in the execution of duty where the law is not in force. In *R. v. Houle*,[44] a police officer attempted to give the accused a ticket for an offence that no longer existed. The regulation creating the offence had been repealed two days earlier, unknown to the officer. The accused's conviction for obstruction was overturned on appeal because the officer was not in the execution of his duty. A similar case is *R. v. Sharma*,[45] a decision of the Supreme Court of Canada. Sharma was a street vendor who was given a ticket for not having a street vending licence and told to move on. When the officer returned, the accused was still selling goods on the street. He was charged with obstruction for failing to obey the officer's instructions. The Supreme Court held that the by-law the accused was charged with violating was ultra vires. Since the by-law was invalid, Sharma could not be convicted of obstruction for disobeying the officer's order to comply with it.

e. Failure to Assist

Section 129(b) makes it an offence to fail to help a peace officer or public officer to arrest a person or to keep the peace, unless there is a reasonable excuse

---

42 (1975), 23 C.C.C. (2d) 513 (S.C.C.); see discussion of this case in Chapter Five at page 107.
43 (1973), 15 C.C.C. (2d) 85 (Que.C.A.).
44 (1985), 24 C.C.C. (3d) 57 (Alta.C.A.).
45 (1993), 79 C.C.C. (3d) 142 (S.C.C.).

for not helping. In *R. v. Foster*,[46] a police officer observed a car being driven in a dangerous manner. He stopped the vehicle. The driver got out and started running away. The officer caught up with him in a place where several people were camping. The driver struggled with the officer. The officer asked Foster, who was watching, to help him get the man back to his police car. Foster told the man to go with the officer. The officer again requested his help. Foster said "no way" and walked away. It turned out that the driver was Foster's son. The court held that the fact that the driver was Foster's son was no excuse for Foster not to help the police officer.

f. Obstructing a Person Executing a Process

Section 129(c) prohibits interfering with a person who has the legal authority to seize or hold land or goods. For example, if a sheriff's bailiff is acting under a court order to take possession of a house, a person living in the house who refuses to allow the bailiff to take possession is violating s.129(c).

4. Perjury

Perjury involves knowingly making a false statement under oath. Section 131 states:

> **131. Subject to subsection (3), every one commits perjury who, with intent to mislead, makes before a person who is authorized by law to permit it to be made before him, a false statement under oath or solemn affirmation, by affidavit, solemn declaration or deposition or orally, knowing that the statement is false.**
>
> **(1.1) Subject to subsection (3), every person who gives evidence under subsection 46(2) of the Canada Evidence Act, or gives evidence or a statement pursuant to an order made under section 22.2 of the Mutual Legal Assistance in Criminal Matters Act, commits perjury who, with intent to mislead, makes a false statement knowing that it is false, whether or not the false statement was made under oath or solemn affirmation in accordance with subsection (1), so long as the false statement was made in accordance with any formalities required by the law of the place outside Canada in which the person is virtually present or heard.**
>
> **(2) Subsection (1) applies whether or not a statement referred to in that subsection is made in a judicial proceeding.**
>
> **(3) Subsection (1) and (1.1) do not apply to a statement referred to in that subsection that is made by a person who is not specially permitted, authorized or required by law to make that statement.**

The offence of perjury can be committed at a judicial proceeding, which is defined in s.118 as including proceedings before a court, the House of

---

46   (1981), 65 C.C.C. (2d) 388 (Alta.C.A.).

Commons, the Senate, or any other body or person authorized to make an inquiry and to take evidence under oath. Perjury can also be committed during extra-judicial proceedings.

For a witness to be convicted of perjury, the following must be proved beyond a reasonable doubt: that evidence given by the witness was false; that the witness knew when giving the evidence that it was false; and that the false evidence was given with the intent to mislead. These requirements were considered by the Supreme Court of Canada in *Calder v. R.*[47] The accused was a witness in a divorce case. He made a false statement at the divorce trial regarding the length of time a woman had been living in a trailer on his business premises. At the perjury trial, he claimed that his evidence had been an honest statement of what he could remember. The Court held that he was not guilty of perjury because, even though he had made a false statement, there was no proof that he knew the evidence was false or that he intended to mislead the court. In short, an honest error made by a witness is not perjury.

In *R. v. Regnier,*[48] the Ontario Court of Appeal held that to constitute perjury, it is not necessary that the false statement mislead the court. It is enough that the witness knew the statement was false and that the intent was to mislead.

In *R. v. Hayford,*[49] the Saskatchewan Court of Appeal held that if a witness makes a statement that is true in one sense and false in another, the Crown must prove that the statement was false in the sense that the witness used it. The accused had been a witness at a preliminary hearing on a charge of assault. He stated at the hearing that he had not agreed to sell to R. certain furniture. A month before, he had told a police officer that he had made an agreement with R. to sell the furniture. It was decided at the assault trial that the agreement was void (i.e., it had no legal effect). At the perjury trial, the court said that there was an agreement in the sense that the accused and R. had gone through the form of an agreement. However, there was no agreement in the sense that it was not legally binding. The Crown failed to prove in which sense the accused had stated that there was no agreement. Thus, the accused could not be convicted of perjury.

5. Obstructing Justice

a. Professional Bondspersons

139. (1) Every one who wilfully attempts in any manner to obstruct, pervert or defeat the course of justice in a judicial proceeding,

(a) by indemnifying or agreeing to indemnify a surety, in any way and either in whole or in part, or

47 (1960), 129 C.C.C. 220 (S.C.C.).
48 (1955), 112 C.C.C. 79 (Ont.C.A.).
49 (1921), 35 C.C.C. 293 (Sask.C.A.).

(b) where he is a surety, by accepting or agreeing to accept a fee or any form of indemnity whether in whole or in part from or in respect of a person who is released or is to be released from custody,

is guilty of

(c) an indictable offence and is liable to imprisonment for a term not exceeding two years, or

(d) an offence punishable on summary conviction.

This section outlaws the business of providing bond money. For example, assume that Jean-Luc acts as a surety for Konrad by posting bond or giving money to the court to release Konrad from custody on the understanding that Konrad will appear for trial. The idea behind allowing Jean-Luc to post bond for Konrad is that Jean-Luc will have a real interest in seeing that Konrad appears for trial. If Konrad appears, then Jean-Luc gets the money back. If he does not appear, then Jean-Luc does not get the money back. Under s.139(l), it is an offence for Jean-Luc to attempt to defeat the course of justice by making an agreement with Konrad that when released from custody, Konrad will pay him back ("indemnify") the amount of the bond or the amount of the bond plus a fee. Under such an agreement, Jean-Luc would have no interest in seeing that Konrad appeared for trial because he would get the money back whether Konrad appeared for trial or not.

b. Obstructing the Course of Justice

139. . . . (2) Every one who wilfully attempts in any manner other than a manner described in subsection (1) to obstruct, pervert or defeat the course of justice is guilty of an indictable offence. . .

The phrase "course of justice" has been given a broad meaning and is not limited to proceedings that follow the laying of a charge. In *R. v. Morin*,[50] the Quebec Court of Appeal held that "course of justice" should be given the same meaning as "administration of justice," which has been interpreted by the Supreme Court of Canada as a very wide term covering the detection, prosecution, and punishment of offenders.[51] Morin was charged with attempting to obstruct the course of justice by offering a bribe to a peace officer. While being driven to the police station, he had offered money to the officers in the hope of avoiding arrest. He was convicted. Note that Morin could have been charged with offering a bribe to a peace officer, contrary to s.109, instead of attempting to obstruct justice.

In *R. v. Zeck*,[52] a police officer observed the accused destroying parking tickets that he had placed on cars. The Ontario Court of Appeal held that he was properly convicted of obstructing the course of justice. The offence applies to wilful attempts to obstruct the enforcement by the police of a municipal parking by-law.

---

50   (1968), 5 C.R.N.S. 297 (Que.C.A.).
51   *R. v. Kalick*; see note 24.
52   (1980), 53 C.C.C. (2d) 551 (Ont.C.A.).

In *R. v. Balaram*,[53] the accused sent a threatening letter to a judge and made two threatening phone calls. The accused was unhappy about a sentence he had received from the judge. He was convicted of obstruction for making the threats, even though there was little chance that he could follow them through.

If something is said or done that obstructs justice, but the person did not have the mens rea to obstruct justice, then no offence is committed. In *R. v. Savinkoff*,[54] the accused was charged with attempting to obstruct justice after he had tried to induce two men to give false evidence at their trial. The Crown failed to prove that the accused knew that the evidence was false. Without this guilty knowledge, the accused had no mens rea. He was acquitted.

c. Bribes and Threats

The use of bribes and threats is mentioned in s.139(3) as a specific way of obstructing the course of justice in a judicial proceeding:

> **(3) Without restricting the generality of subsection (2), every one shall be deemed wilfully to attempt to obstruct, pervert or defeat the course of justice who in a judicial proceeding, existing or proposed,**
>
> **(a) dissuades or attempts to dissuade a person by threats, bribes or other corrupt means from giving evidence;**
>
> **(b) influences or attempts to influence by threats, bribes or other corrupt means, a person in his conduct as a juror; or**
>
> **(c) accepts or obtains, agrees to accept or attempts to obtain a bribe or other corrupt consideration to abstain from giving evidence, or to do or to refrain from doing anything as a juror.**

In short, it is obstruction of justice to use bribes or threats to try to corrupt witnesses and jurors. It is also obstruction of justice for a witness or juror to accept a bribe. Note that the section refers to judicial proceedings that are already in progress and to those that are not yet in progress but are proposed.

Under paragraph (a), it is no defence that the accused believed that the evidence to be given by a witness was false. In *R. v. Silverman*,[55] the accused offered a bribe to a witness to persuade him not to give certain evidence at a trial. His purpose was to get the witness to tell what the accused believed was a true version of the facts. The court found him guilty because the offence was complete when he made the offer of a bribe not to give evidence. It made no difference that the accused honestly believed that the witness was going to give an untrue version of the facts.

---

53 (1991), 13 W.C.B. (2d) 346; Reported in the Toronto Star, February 15, 1991, and in the Lawyer's Weekly, February 22, 1991.
54 (1963), 3 C.C.C. 163 (B.C.C.A.).
55 (1908), 14 C.C.C. 79 (Ont.C.A.).

Questions for Review and Discussion

1. Does an offence have to be committed in Canada for a person to be tried in Canada? Explain.

2. Explain the difference between treason and sedition.

3. **a.** What are the essential elements of an unlawful assembly?
   b. How is a riot different from an unlawful assembly?

4. What is a lawful excuse for being in possession of an explosive substance? Would this lawful excuse protect the possessor from criminal liability for an injury caused by the explosion of the explosive substance? Explain.

5. What is the main object of the Firearms Act?

6. What is the mens rea requirement for the offence of carelessly using a firearm?

7. What did the Supreme Court of Canada decide in *R. v. Covin* and *Covin*?

8. What is the offence of bribery? Give an example.

9. How have the courts defined the term "administration of justice" in the offence of bribery?

10. Give an example of a police officer not acting in the execution of duty.

11. What are the essential elements of the offence of perjury?

12. Why doesn't the law allow the business of providing bond money?

13. Mrs. C. called the police to report damage to her car. The police came to her house to talk to her about the incident. Mrs. C. suggested that her son D. might know something about the damage. When the officer started questioning D., he became upset and ordered them out of the house. He then ran and got a gun. The police left the house. D. was charged with possession of a weapon for a purpose dangerous to the public. Should he be convicted? Explain. See *R. v. Cassidy* (1989), 50 C.C.C. (3d) 193 (S.C.C.).

14. Frank sent a letter to his brother asking that he intimidate a witness at his upcoming trial. The letter was intercepted by the prison authorities and never received by the brother. Has Frank committed an offence? Explain. See *R. v. Graham* (1985), 20 C.C.C. (3d) 210 (Ont.C.A.).

15. R. was a lawyer representing clients who were charged with theft. It was alleged that R. offered to pay a certain amount of money to the investigating police officer if the charges were withdrawn. What can R. be charged with, and what must be proved to convict R.? See *Rousseau v. The Queen* (1985), 21 C.C.C. (3d) 1 (S.C.C.).

16. K.'s friend was charged with shoplifting. K. approached the owner of the store and offered to make a $20,000 donation to a charity on behalf of the store if they would withdraw the charge. He also suggested that the donation could be used as a promotion. K. had spoken to a lawyer before talking to the manager, and was told that his offer would not be

a bribe as long as there was no benefit going to the store. K. did not tell the lawyer about making the donation on behalf of the store, or about the promotion. What can K. be charged with? Should he be convicted? Explain. See *R. v. Kotch* (1990), 61 C.C.C. (3d) 132 (Alta.C.A.).

Chapter Seven

SEXUAL OFFENCES, PUBLIC MORALS, AND DISORDERLY CONDUCT

PART V OF THE CODE

A. INTRODUCTION

At one time, Part V of the Criminal Code contained the offence of rape and various offences involving intercourse with female minors. In 1985, most of these offences were repealed. "Rape" is now defined as a type of assault and is contained in Part VII of the Code, which deals with offences against the person. Part V now deals mainly with public morality offences, offences involving disorderly conduct, and sexual offences against children.

B. SEXUAL OFFENCES

With a few exceptions, which are noted below, the Part V sexual offences relate to sexual activity with children and young persons.

1. Sexual Interference

151. Every person who, for a sexual purpose, touches, directly or indirectly, with a part of the body or with an object, any part of the body of a person under the age of fourteen years is guilty of an indictable offence and is liable to imprisonment for a term not exceeding 10 years or is guilty of an offence punishable on summary conviction.

2. Invitation to Sexual Touching

152. Every person who, for a sexual purpose, invites, counsels or incites a person under the age of fourteen years to touch, directly or indirectly, with a part of the body or with an object, the body of any person . . . is guilty of an indictable offence and is liable to impris-

onment for a term not exceeding ten years or is guilty of an offence punishable on summary conviction.

Sections 151 and 152 are distinct offences. Section 151 makes it an offence to touch, directly or indirectly, for a sexual purpose, a child under 14. Section 152 makes it an offence to encourage a child under 14 to touch, directly or indirectly, for a sexual purpose, the body of any person. For an offence under s.152 there may or may not be a sexual touching by the child. The offence only requires an invitation to touch. The person to be touched can be either the accused or a third person. The term "sexual purpose" is not defined, but presumably it refers to any contact for the purpose of sexual gratification.[1]

In *R. v. Sears*,[2] the Manitoba Court of Appeal considered a case where a 12-year-old girl offered to perform a sexual act in return for money. The accused agreed to it, and the child performed an act of fellatio on him. He was charged with sexual assault and sexual interference. He was acquitted of assault but convicted of sexual interference. On appeal, he argued that since he did not initiate the act and was a passive participant, an offence under s.151 was not committed. The court disagreed, stating that a person who intends sexual interaction of any kind with a child and who with that intent makes contact with the body of the child, "touches" the child regardless of who initiated the contact and who is the active participant.

The meaning of "touches" was considered in *R. v. Fong*,[3] a decision of the Alberta Court of Appeal. The accused was charged under s.152 when he invited a seven-year-old girl to hold a tissue onto which he had ejaculated. He argued that there had been no physical contact either directly or indirectly, since the semen was no longer part of his body once it left his body. The court did not accept this argument. It held that the objective of s.152 is to prevent the sexual exploitation of children and that the section must be interpreted in a way that is consistent with its purpose. The court stated, "in the terms of s.152, the appellant invited the child complainant to indirectly touch his body—through his semen—with the use of an object, the tissue."[4]

3. Sexual Exploitation

153. (1) Every person who is in a position of trust or authority towards a young person or is a person with whom the young person is in a relationship of dependency and who

(a) for a sexual purpose, touches, directly or indirectly, with a part of the body or with an object, any part of the body of the young person, or

---

1   See, for example, *R. v. Sears* (1990), 58 C.C.C. (3d) 62 (Man.C.A.).
2   Ibid.
3   (1994), 92 C.C.C. (3d) 171 (Alta.C.A.).
4   Ibid. at page 175.

(b) for a sexual purpose, invites, counsels or incites a young person to touch, directly or indirectly, with a part of the body or with an object, the body of any person . . .

is guilty of an indictable offence and liable to imprisonment for a term not exceeding five years or is guilty of an offence punishable on summary conviction.

(2) In this section, "young person" means a person fourteen years of age or more but under the age of eighteen years.

Notice that s.153 combines elements of the offences of sexual interference and invitation to sexual touching where the complainant is 14 to 18 years old and the accused is in a position of trust or authority or the complainant is in a relationship of dependency. The Code does not define "position of trust or authority" or "relationship of dependency." Presumably these terms refer to persons such as parents, teachers, babysitters, and employers. However, court decisions have generally held that the question of whether a special relationship exists depends on the facts of each given case; such a relationship cannot be presumed just because the accused and the complainant are parent and child, or employer and employee, for instance.[5] In *R. v. Galbraith*,[6] the meaning of "relationship of dependency" was considered. The accused was a 27-year-old male who had been living with and supporting a 14-year-old girl. He was convicted of sexual exploitation. The appeal court held that the trial judge erred in interpreting "relationship of dependency" as meaning one where a person relies on another for economic support. The court pointed out that a sexual relationship with a person between 14 and 18 is an offence only if there is a relationship of trust, authority, or dependency. The judge held that the term "relationship of dependency" must be given a meaning similar to relationships of trust or authority. All of these relationships under s.153 refer to ones in which there is a reliance by a young person on a figure who has assumed a position of power, such as one based on trust or authority, over the young person. Sexual relations are prohibited in these situations because the nature of the relationship makes the young person particularly vulnerable to the influence of the other person. The circumstances of this case did not establish a relationship of dependency. The relationship was described as boyfriend/girlfriend. There was no evidence that the relationship was exploitative, or that there was an obvious power imbalance. The accused did not force her to work. He did not take her away from her friends, home, school, or parents. She had the option of living with her mother but chose not to because she did not like the house rules. There was no evidence that the rules at her mother's house were onerous or inappropriate. She had been living with friends before living with the

---

5   For example, see *R. v. J.(R.H.)* (1993), 86 C.C.C. (3d) 354(B.C.C.A.), leave to appeal to S.C.C. refused 87 C.C.C. (3d) vi, where the relationship between a man and his 17-year-old stepdaughter did not automatically give rise to one of authority, trust or dependency. See also *R. v. Casknette* (1993), 80 C.C.C. (3d) 439 (B.C.C.A.) for the same result, where the relationship was between an employer and a teenage boy. However, on May 30, 1996, the Supreme Court of Canada in *R. v. Audet* (1996), 106 C.C.C. (3d) 481 (S.C.C.) held that teachers will almost always be found to be in a position of trust and authority.
6   (1994), 90 C.C.C. (3d) 76 (Ont.C.A.), leave to appeal to S.C.C. refused 92 C.C.C. (3d) vi.

appellant and was living with friends at the time of the trial. The Crown conceded that she liked the appellant and that he was good to her.

4. Incest

Incest is one of the few offences in this section that is not directed at children or young persons only:

> **155. (1) Every one commits incest who, knowing that another person is by blood relationship his or her parent, child, brother, sister, grandparent or grandchild as the case may be, has sexual intercourse with that person.**
>
> **(2) Every one who commits incest is guilty of an indictable offence and liable to imprisonment for a term not exceeding fourteen years.**
>
> **(3) No accused shall be determined by a court guilty of an offence under this section if the accused was under restraint, duress or fear of the person with whom the accused had the sexual intercourse at the time the sexual intercourse occurred.**
>
> **(4) In this section "brother" and "sister", respectively, include half-brother and half-sister.**

Sexual intercourse is defined in s.4(5):

> **4. . . . (5) For the purposes of this Act, sexual intercourse is complete on penetration to even the slightest degree, notwithstanding that seed is not emitted.**

5. Anal Intercourse

> **159. (1) Every person who engages in an act of anal intercourse is guilty of an indictable offence and liable to imprisonment for a term not exceeding ten years or is guilty of an offence punishable on summary conviction.**
>
> **(2) Subsection (1) does not apply to any act engaged in, in private, between**
>
> **(a) a husband and wife, or**
>
> **(b) any two persons, each of whom is eighteen years of age or more, both of whom consent to the act.**
>
> **(3) For the purposes of subsection (2),**
>
> **(a) an act shall be deemed not to have been engaged in in private if it is engaged in in a public place or if more than two persons take part or are present; and**

(b) a person shall be deemed not to consent to an act

(i) if the consent is extorted by force, threats or fear of bodily harm or is obtained by false and fraudulent misrepresentations respecting the nature and quality of the act, or

(ii) if the court is satisfied beyond a reasonable doubt that the person could not have consented to the act by reason of mental disability.

"Public place" is defined in s.150 as including "any place to which the public has access as of right or by invitation, express or implied." For example, private property to which the public has access with no objection from the owner may be considered a public place.[7] Likewise, a cubicle in a public washroom where the public can see.[8]

An Ontario Court of Appeal decision has held that s.159 violates the equality provisions under s.15 of the Charter by discriminating on the basis of age. One of the three judges hearing the case also stated that denying homosexual persons under 18 a choice of sexual expression that is open to heterosexual persons at the age of 14 also violates s.15. The court considered whether s.159 could be justified as a reasonable limitation under s.1 of the Charter. All of the judges agreed that s.159 is not a reasonable limit. The court rejected the Crown's argument that protecting young persons from engaging in a type of sexual activity that leads to an increased risk of transmitting HIV is a substantial social objective that justifies limiting equality rights under s.15 of the Charter. The court held that sending young persons to jail is not a reasonable way to protect them from the risks associated with consensual anal intercourse.[9]

6. Bestiality

This is another offence that is directed to all persons regardless of age, with a special provision in s.160(3) where a child is involved.

> **160. (1) Every person who commits bestiality is guilty of an indictable offence and is liable to imprisonment for a term not exceeding ten years or is guilty of an offence punishable on summary conviction.**
>
> **(2) Every person who compels another to commit bestiality is guilty of an indictable offence and is liable to imprisonment for a term not exceeding ten years or is guilty of an offence punishable on summary conviction.**
>
> **(3) Notwithstanding subsection (1), every person who, in the presence of a person under the age of fourteen, commits bestiality or who incites a person under the age of fourteen years to commit bestiality is guilty of an indictable offence and is liable to imprisonment for a**

7   *R. v. Lavoie*, [1968] 1 C.C.C 265 (N.B.C.A.).
8   *R. v. Hogg* (1970), 15 C.R.N.S. 106 (Ont.C.A.).
9   *R. v. M.(C.)* (1995), 98 C.C.C. (3d) 481 (Ont.C.A.).

term not exceeding ten years or is guilty of an offence punishable on summary conviction.

The term "bestiality" is not defined in the Code but it generally refers to a human being having sexual intercourse in any way with an animal or bird.

7. Exposing

> 173. . . . Every person who, in any place, for a sexual purpose, exposes his or her genital organs to a person who is under the age of fourteen years is guilty of an offence punishable on summary conviction.

8. Consent and Mistake of Age as Defences

The general rule is that consent is not a defence to these offences. Section 150.1(1) states:

> 150.1. (1) Where an accused is charged with an offence under section 151 or 152 or subsection 153(1), 160(3) or 173(2) . . . it is not a de-fence that the complainant consented to the activity that forms the subject-matter of the charge.

Section 150.1(2) provides exceptions to the general rule. Thus, consent can be a defence if certain circumstances exist:

> (2) Notwithstanding subsection (1) . . . it is not a defence that the complainant consented to the activity that forms the subject-matter of the charge unless the accused
>
> (a) is twelve years of age or more but under the age of sixteen years;
>
> (b) is less than two years older than the complainant; and
>
> (c) is neither in a position of trust or authority towards the complainant nor is a person with whom the complainant is in a relationship of dependency.

In addition, s.150.1(3) provides that:

> (3) no person aged twelve or thirteen years shall be tried for an offence under section 151 or 152 or subsection 173(2) unless the person is in a position of trust or authority towards the complainant or is a person with whom the complainant is in a relationship of dependency.

These exceptions mean that no offence takes place where the victim and the accused are in more or less equal positions.

The general rule in s.150.1(1) has been challenged under the Charter as violating ss. 7 and 15 of the Charter by limiting the defence of consent.

Most court decisions have found that it is not a violation of the Charter, or that it is a reasonable limitation.[10]

Section 150.1(4) provides for the defence of mistake of age:

> **(4) It is not a defence to a charge under section 151 or 152, subsection 160(3) or 173(2) . . . that the accused believed that the complainant was fourteen years of age or more at the time the offence is alleged to have been committed unless the accused took all reasonable steps to ascertain the age of the complainant.**

Section 150.1(4) allows an honest mistake if it was reasonable. However, the accused must show what steps he or she took to determine the age of the victim and that these steps were all that could be reasonably required in the circumstances.[11]

A similar defence is set out in s.150.1(5), where the accused mistakenly believes that the complainant is 18 or over. This relates to offences under ss. 153, 159, 170, 171, and 172.

C. CORRUPTION OF MORALS

1. Pornography

The Criminal Code creates certain offences concerning obscene materials (i.e., pornography). The main section is s.163:

> **163. (1) Every one commits an offence who**
>
> **(a) makes, prints, publishes, distributes, circulates, or has in his possession for the purpose of publication, distribution or circulation any obscene written matter, picture, model, phonograph record or other thing whatever . . .**
>
> **(2) Every one commits an offence who knowingly, without lawful justification or excuse,**
>
> **(a) sells, exposes to public view or has in his possession for such a purpose any obscene written matter, picture, model, phonograph record or other thing whatsoever . . .**

Subsection (1)(a) is directed toward publishers and distributors of obscene material. However, the Supreme Court of Canada has said that this section includes private individuals who make obscene material even if the material is not meant for publication.[12] Courts have held that a person who shows an obscene film in a private home is not "circulating," but a person in the business of renting videos is "circulating or distributing."[13]

---

10 See, for example, *R. v. M.(R.S.)* (1991), 69 C.C.C. (3d) 233 (P.E.I.C.A.); *R. v. Gallant* (1986), 29 C.C.C. (3d) 291 (B.C.C.A.).
11 *R. v. Osborne* (1992), 17 C.R. (4th) 350 (Nfld.C.A.).
12 *Hawkshaw v. The Queen* (1986), 26 C.C.C. (3d) 129 (S.C.C.).
13 *R. v. Rioux*, [1970] 3 C.C.C. 149 (S.C.C.); *R. v. Red Hot Video* (1985), 18 C.C.C. (3d) 1 (B.C.C.A.).

Subsection (2)(a) is directed toward sellers of obscene material (such as the operator of a bookstore) and toward those who expose obscene material (such as the manager of an art gallery).

An important difference between s.163(1) and s.163(2) is that under s.163(2) the Crown must prove that the accused acted knowingly—that is, that the accused knew of the nature of the material. Under s.163(1), the Crown does not have to prove knowledge.

The requirement of "knowingly" under s.163(2) was considered by the Supreme Court of Canada in *R. v. Jorgenson*.[14] The accused, who owned a video store, was convicted of "knowingly" selling obscene videotapes. His conviction was upheld by the Ontario Court of Appeal. The issue on appeal to the Supreme Court of Canada was whether the Crown had to prove that the accused had actual knowledge that the videos sold contained specific scenes that were obscene, or was aware of the qualities that made the video obscene overall. The Court held that the word "knowingly" means that the Crown must prove actual knowledge. The Court acquitted the accused because the Crown only proved that the accused had a general knowledge that the films dealt with the exploitation of sex. The Court noted that a person is not protected from charges because he or she did not know that the material was obscene or was unaware that there are laws against selling obscene materials. For the accused to be convicted, it only has to be proved that he or she knew of the qualities or specific scenes that make the material obscene. The Court also noted that it may not be necessary to prove that the accused actually watched the video. The mens rea could be proved, for example, by showing that the accused was warned of the material or failed to comply with requirements to excise portions of a film. It would also be possible to prove wilful blindness if the retailer suspected material was obscene but refrained from making the necessary inquiries.

a. The Meaning of Obscenity

A major issue in the law concerning pornography has been the definition of obscenity. The present law was enacted in 1959. Since that time, societal values have changed. In the past few years, the government has tried several times to amend the obscenity laws so that they reflect more modern views. Each of these attempts has failed.[15] The problem is how to strike the proper balance between protecting freedom of expression and limiting a type of expression that violates societal values. Parliament has been unable to agree on a definition of obscenity; however, the courts have played a significant role in developing that definition.

The basic definition of obscenity is in s.163(8):

> **(8) For the purposes of this Act, any publication a dominant characteristic of which is the undue exploitation of sex, or of sex and any**

---

14 (1995), 102 C.C.C. (3d) 97 (S.C.C.).
15 See for example, Bill C-54, which died on the order paper in November 1987.

one or more of the following subjects, namely crime, horror, cruelty and violence, shall be deemed to be obscene.

This definition is not limited to print publications but has been applied to films, videos, and sexual devices and articles.[16]

b. What Is "Undue Exploitation of Sex"?

The Supreme Court of Canada considered the meaning of "undue exploitation of sex" most recently in *R. v. Butler*.[17] The accused was the operator of a video store that carried "hard porn" videos. In its extensive decision, the Court surveyed the tests for obscenity that had been developed in previous court decisions. In this landmark decision, the Court pulled together the various tests that lower courts had developed.

(I) COMMUNITY STANDARD OF TOLERANCE TEST

The Court noted that the community's standard of tolerance has become the most important factor in deciding whether material is obscene. The Court quoted a previous judgment which stated that the community standards must be Canadian and in keeping with the times.[18] In a case it had examined earlier, *Towne Cinema Theatres Ltd. v. R.*,[19] the Court had stated that in determining community standards, the test isn't what the average Canadian would want to see but what the average Canadian would tolerate others seeing.

(II) DEGRADATION AND DEHUMANIZATION TEST

The Court noted that many decisions have recognized that material which may be said to exploit sex in a "degrading or dehumanizing" manner will necessarily fail the community standards test, not because it offends against morals but because it is perceived by public opinion to be harmful to society, particularly to women.

(III) INTERNAL NECESSITIES TEST

The third test considered is the "internal necessities test" or artistic defence. The Court stated: "Even material which by itself offends community standards will not be considered 'undue' if it is required for the serious treatment of a theme."[20] The question here is whether the exploitation of sex is justifiable in light of the work's plot or theme; in considering this, it is necessary to consider the work as a whole.

---

16 Supra, note 13.
17 (1992), 70 C.C.C. (3d) 129 (S.C.C.).
18 The court referred to a dissenting judgement in *R. v. Dominion News and Gift*, [1963] 2 C.C.C. 103 (Man.C.A.), which was relied on by the Supreme Court in hearing the appeal of that decision at [1964] 3 C.C.C. 1 (S.C.C.).
19 (1985), 18 C.C.C. (3d) 193 (S.C.C.).
20 Supra, note 17 at page 149.

(IV) APPLYING THE TESTS

The Court, having established these tests, put them together in a working relationship. First, the Court divided pornography into three categories:

- Explicit sex with violence.
- Explicit sex without violence but that subjects people to degrading or dehumanizing treatment.
- Sex without violence that is neither degrading nor dehumanizing.

Next, the Court combined the first two tests, stating:

> [T]he courts must determine as best they can what the community would tolerate others being exposed to on the basis of the degree of harm that might flow from such exposure. Harm in this context means that it predisposes persons to act in an antisocial manner as, for example, the mental or physical mistreatment of women by men . . . The stronger the inference of risk of harm the lesser the likelihood of tolerance."[21]

In applying this standard to the three categories of pornography, the Court stated that sex with violence will almost always be undue exploitation. Sex that is degrading and dehumanizing may be undue exploitation if risk of harm is substantial. The third category, sex without violence or degradation, is generally tolerated in our society unless it employs children.

Only if the material is found to unduly exploit sex is the internal necessities test applied.

The portrayal of sex then must be examined in context to determine the dominant theme of the work as a whole—that is, is undue exploitation of sex the main object of the work? Or is this portrayal of sex essential to a wider artistic, literary, or other similar purpose? Community standards are still important. The question is whether the sexually explicit material, when viewed in the context of the whole work, would be tolerated by the community as a whole.

(V) SUMMARY

The *Butler* decision marks a distinct shift in the definition of obscenity. The basis of deciding whether material offends community standards is whether the material is seen as causing harm to society, not whether it offends present standards of community morality.

c. *Defence of Public Good*

A defence to charges under s.163 is the defence of the public good:

> **(3) No person shall be convicted of an offence under this section if the public good was served by the acts that are alleged to constitute the offence and if the acts alleged did not extend beyond what served the public good.**

---

21 Ibid. at page 150.

There are two parts to this defence: that the public good was served, and that the acts (e.g., publishing or selling obscene books) did not go beyond what served the public good. Material that otherwise would be obscene will not be considered obscene if this defence is established.

Something serves the public good if it is necessary or advantageous to objects of general interest, such as religion, science, literature, or art. In *Delorme v. R.*,[22] the accused, who ran a bookstore, was charged with selling an obscene book. The book was about a woman who was subjected to many cruel and violent sexual acts. Experts testified that the book had value as a psychological study and would be useful to students of literature or psychology. The book had a plain cover that would not attract attention. One expert testified that the book was difficult to read and not within everyone's grasp. The court held that, although the book may have been of benefit to certain students, since it was available in a public bookstore it could not be said that the public good was being served. The defence failed and the accused was convicted.

d. Obscenity and the Charter

Butler dealt with the argument that s.163 violates the Charter. First, with reference to s.1 of the Charter, it was argued that the definition of obscenity in s.163 is too vague to be "a limit prescribed by law" and so imprecise that it is not "a reasonable limit prescribed by law." The Court disagreed, stating that the section plus court decisions—including the one the Court was now making—provide an intelligent and enforceable test.

Next, the Court looked at whether s.163 violates the Charter guarantee to freedom of expression. The Court said that it does but that it is a reasonable limitation under s.1 of the Charter. Using the test set out in *R. v. Oakes*[23] for determining whether a law that violates the Charter is a reasonable limitation, the Court held that the object of the legislation is not to enforce moral standards, which would not be a valid objective. Rather, it is to prevent harm to society. The Court quoted the Report on Pornography (the MacGuigan Report), which stated:

> The clear and unquestionable danger of this type of material is that it rein-forces unhealthy tendencies in Canadian society. [I]t reinforces male-female stereotypes, makes degradation, humiliation, victimization and violence in human relationships appear normal and acceptable. A society which holds that egalitarianism, non-violence, consensualism and mutuality are basic to any human interaction, whether sexual or not, is clearly justified in controlling and prohibiting any medium . . . which violates these principles."[24]

However, is banning obscene materials a pressing and substantial objective? The court said "yes": the harm caused by the proliferation of materials that seriously offend our fundamental values is a substantial concern that justifies the restriction of freedom of expression.

---

22 (1973), 15 C.C.C. (2d) 350; 21 C.R.N.S. 305 (Que.C.A.).
23 See Oakes test in Chapter Two at page 27.
24 Supra, note 17 at page 157, quoting the Report on Pornography by the Standing Committee on Justice and Legal Affairs (the MacGuigan Report, 1978).

The Court also found that s.163's definition of obscenity meets the proportionality test. Even though it may be impossible to prove that pornography directly harms society, it is reasonable to assume that exposure to it affects people's beliefs and attitudes. There is a sufficient rational link between the criminal sanction and the objective, and the law minimally impairs the right to freedom of expression. The section does not prohibit all sexually explicit erotica, but only that material which creates a risk of harm to society.

2. Child Pornography

In 1993, Parliament enacted new offences of child pornography. Section 163.1(1) defines the term "child pornography":

163.1 (1) In this section, "Child Pornography" means

(a) a photographic, film, video or other representation, whether or not it was made by electronic or mechanical means,

(i) that shows a person who is or is depicted as being under the age of eighteen years and is engaged in or is depicted as engaged in explicit sexual activity, or

(ii) the dominant characteristic of which is the depiction, for a sexual purpose, of a sexual organ or the anal region of a person under the age of eighteen years; or

(b) any written material or visual representation that advocates or counsels sexual activity with a person under the age of eighteen years that would be an offence under this Act.

Under s.163.1(2) it is an offence to print, publish, or possess for the purpose of publishing child pornography. Under s.163.1(3) it is an offence to import, distribute, sell, or possess for purposes of distribution or sale child pornography. These offences are hybrid, and if treated by indictment are punishable by a maximum of 10 years' imprisonment. Under s.163(4), it is a hybrid offence to possess child pornography, punishable by five years' imprisonment if treated as indictable.

Section 163.1(5) allows the defence of mistake of age only if all reasonable steps were taken to ascertain the age of the young person. The court is directed to find the accused not guilty under s.163.1(6) where the material alleged to be child pornography has artistic merit or an educational, scientific, or medical purpose.

Section 163(3) to (5) applies to this section as appropriate.

Note that in determinations whether an offence under s.163.1(b) has taken place, reference must be made to ss. 151, 152, 155, 160, 170, 171, 172, and 271 to 273 of the Code (which relate to sexual offences involving children or young persons).

The offences are similar to those under s.163 except that simple possession of child pornography is an offence.

In one of the reported cases under the section, *R. v. Pecchiarich*,[25] the accused was convicted of distributing child pornography by modem on computer bulletin boards. The uploaded files were stories about children having sex with adults, animals, and other children. The accused also created graphic images of children having sex. One case widely reported in Toronto newspapers concerned an artist named Eli Langer.[26] His paintings were seized from an exhibit at a Toronto art gallery, and he and the gallery owner were charged under this section. The paintings represented children having sex with adults. The charges were finally dismissed on the grounds that the works had artistic merit. On the issue of community standards, the judge found that the work did not pose a risk of harm to children. The judge found that the intent and effect of the work was not to condone child sexual abuse but to lament the reality of it.

In the context of artistic merit in the possession of child pornography, in Langer, the court found it must include consideration of contemporary standards of community tolerance. The test for the defence of artistic merit is objective. The defence of artistic merit was discussed in *Sharpe*[27] and the Supreme Court of Canada concluded "that artistic merit should be interpreted as including any expression that may reasonably be viewed as art. Any objectively established artistic value, however small, suffices to support the defence."[28] However, the Supreme Court of Canada did not agree with the court in Langer that a community standard should be incorporated into the defence because Parliament clearly intended that some pornographic material and possibly harmful material would escape prosecution on the basis of section 163.1(6); otherwise, Parliament would not have included the section.

In *Sharpe*, the accused was acquitted at trial and his acquittal was upheld by the British Columbia Court of Appeal and section 163.1(4) was struck down as being unconstitutional. The Supreme Court of Canada found that, while subsections 1(a), (b) and (4) violated section 2 of the Charter, the violation was justified under section 1. The Court stated[29] that "...prohibiting the possession of child pornography restricts the rights protected by s.2(b) and the s.7 liberty guarantee. While the prurient nature of most of the materials defined as "child pornography" may attenuate its constitutional worth, it does not negate it, since the guarantee of free expression extends to even offensive speech." Society's interest in protecting children from the evils associated with child pornography must be balanced with the freedom of expression. The Supreme Court decided that the appropriate remedy was to read in an exclusion of the application of section 163.1 in certain situations. Persons who take pictures of themselves engaged in lawful sexual activity or self-created expressive material, such as a teenager's diary, are examples of

---

25 (1995), 22 O.R. (3d) 748 (Ont.Prov.Ct.); reported in The Lawyer's Weekly, September 29, 1995.
26 *Ontario (Attorney General) v. Langer* (1995), 97 C.C.C. (3d) 290 (Ont.C.A.); leave to appeal refused (1995), 42 C.R. (4th) 410n (S.C.C.).
27 *R. v. Sharpe* (2001), 150 C.C.C. (3d) 321 (S.C.C.).
28 Ibid. at page 355-56.
29 Ibid. 344.

where section 163.1 would not apply. The Court upheld the defence of artistic merit stating that "the various statutory defences (i.e., artistic merit; educational, scientific or medical purpose; and public good) must be interpreted liberally to protect freedom of expression, as well as possession for socially redeeming purposes.[30] The Supreme Court allowed the Crown's appeal, upheld the constitutionality of section 163.1 and sent Sharpe back for trial.

3. Immoral, Indecent, or Obscene Theatrical Performance

> **167. (1) Every one commits an offence who, being the lessee, manager, agent or person in charge of a theatre, presents or gives or allows to be presented or given therein an immoral, indecent or obscene performance, entertainment or representation.**
>
> **(2) Every one commits an offence who takes part or appears as an actor, a performer, or an assistant in any capacity, in an immoral, indecent or obscene performance, entertainment or representation in a theatre.**

Section 167(1) is directed against the person in charge of the theatre in which the immoral, indecent, or obscene performance takes place. Section 167(2) is directed at those who participate in the performance.

a. Indecent Performance

"Indecent" is not defined in the Code, and the courts have not developed a clear test. However, in general, something is indecent if it offends against community standards of decency or good taste. In *R. v. Mara and East*,[31] it was ruled that "lap dancing," which involves nude dancers grinding their bodies against the crotches of male patrons of strip bars while being fondled, offends community standards. In this case, the owner of the bar and the manager were charged with allowing an indecent theatrical performance. They had been acquitted at their trial when the judge found that the practice did not offend community standards. The appeal court, in reversing the trial court decision, and finding the accused guilty, said that such activity degrades and dehumanizes women and publicly portrays them in a servile and humiliating manner.

b. Immoral Performance

"Immoral" is another term not defined in the Code. In general, it refers to behaviour that does not conform with accepted patterns of conduct. The

---

30 Ibid. at page 378.
31 (1996), 105 C.C.C. (3d) 147 (Ont.C.A.), on appeal to the Supreme Court of Canada (1997), 115 C.C.C. (3d) 539 (S.C.C.) the Court reversed Mara's conviction on the grounds Mara did not have the requisite *mens rea*, but the Court upheld East's conviction stating that the performance engendered social harm and exceeded the standard of tolerance in Canadian society.

meaning of the word was clarified somewhat by the Supreme Court of Canada in *Johnson v. R.*[32] In that case, the issue was "whether the performance of a dance in a theatre before a public audience, which would have been unexceptional if performed when fully or partly clad, becomes 'immoral' on the sole ground that it is performed 'in the nude'."[33] The accused woman appeared on stage in a cabaret in front of about 17 people. She danced five dances. In three dances, she was topless, and in another she was completely nude. At the time of the nude dance, she was alone on the stage. She did nothing offensive by way of words or gestures while she danced. The Court held that the performance was not immoral; there was nothing immoral about displaying a naked human body, and there was no evidence that the dance was "immoral" in any other way. The Court noted that the section makes it an offence to be unclothed in a public place. But the simple fact that Parliament makes it an offence does not mean that it is a breach of moral standards. Thus, the dancer was not guilty of an immoral performance. In *R. v. MacLean and MacLean (No.2),*[34] the Ontario Court of Appeal held that the test for whether a performance is immoral is the community standard for tolerance. The judge must consider all of the surrounding circumstances, including the performer's purpose.

c. Obscene Performance

The definition of obscenity in s.163(8) applies to this section. In *Hawkshaw v. The Queen,*[35] the Supreme Court of Canada held that s.163(8) sets out the sole test for obscenity for all offences in the Code, even if they are not based on a publication.

D. DISORDERLY CONDUCT

1. Indecent Acts

173. (1) Every one who wilfully does an indecent act

(a) in a public place in the presence of one or more persons, or

(b) in any place, with intent thereby to insult or offend any person, is guilty of an offence punishable on summary conviction.

The essential elements of this offence are:

a. "Indecent" Defined

As mentioned earlier, indecency is not defined in the Code. Generally, it refers to a violation of community standards of decency or good taste. A common example of an indecent act is when a person exposes his or her

---

32 (1975), 13 C.C.C. (2d) 402 (S.C.C.).
33 Ibid. at page 409.
34 (1982), 1 C.C.C. (3d) 412 (Ont.C.A.); leave to appeal to the Supreme Court of Canada refused, loc.cit.
35 Supra, note 12.

"private parts" (which is indecent exposure). But simply being nude in public, such as lying nude on a public beach, is not an indecent act, although the person could be charged under s.174 (see below). Some courts have held that an indecent act must have an element of "moral turpitude." This is why, for example, a person who for a joke ran naked through a football stadium was acquitted of a charge under this section.[36]

b. Wilfully

The term "wilfully" has the same meaning as in most other sections of the Code: to do an act purposely and with a criminal intention.

c. Place of the Act

The act may occur in a public place. Courts have interpreted "public place" broadly as meaning a place where the public is able to view the indecent act. This position is consistent with the purpose of the section, which is not to prohibit "indecent acts" but to prohibit indecent acts that might be upsetting to the public that is exposed to them. In *R. v. Buhay*,[37] a man while standing in the doorway of his home exposed his genitals to two 13-year-old boys who were outside on the street between 3 and 7 metres away. The accused was convicted. In contrast, in *R. v. Sloane*,[38] a prostitute performed an indecent act on a man in a car that was parked in an empty parking lot in a dark area. The act was seen by an officer who had been following the car and who walked up to the car to look through the windows. The appeal court found that the indecent act had not taken place in public.

d. In the Presence of One of More Persons

Court decisions agree that where there is more than one participant in the act, no one participant counts as being the person in the presence of whom the act is performed. In other words, there must be a third, nonparticipating person before whom the indecent act is performed.[39]

Similarly, a police officer was not considered a "person" in *R. v. Hastings*.[40] The court held that urinating on a public street at night, when there is no exposure to any person other than a police officer, is not an offence.

In *R. v. Follett*,[41] the accused performed an indecent act in a public washroom with another man. The act was captured on a surveillance video. The court held that the act was not performed in the presence of others. The videotape could not substitute for a person.

If the indecent act is done with the specific intent to insult or offend any person, under s.173(1)(b) it makes no difference where the act occurs. In

---

36 *R. v. Springer* (1975), 24 C.C.C. (2d) 56 (Sask.Dist.Ct.).
37 (1986), 30 C.C.C. (3d) 30 (Man.C.A.).
38 (1994), 89 C.C.C. (3d) 97 (Ont.C.A.); leave to appeal to the Supreme Court of Canada refused 91 C.C.C. (3d) vi.
39 See for example, *R. v. Sloane*, ibid.
40 (1947), 90 C.C.C. 150 (N.B.C.A.).
41 (1994), 91 C.C.C. (3d) 435 (Nfld.S.C.).

other words, the indecent act may occur in any place, public or private, but it must be shown that the accused did the act in order to insult or offend someone.

2. Nudity

174. (1) Every one who, without lawful excuse,

(a) is nude in a public place, or

(b) is nude and exposed to public view while on private property, whether or not the property is his own,

is guilty of an offence punishable on summary conviction.

(2) For the purposes of this section, a person is nude who is so clad as to offend against public decency or order.

No act is required for this offence to be committed—simply being nude is enough. Under s.174(2), nudity does not mean completely naked. The Supreme Court of Canada, in *R. v. Verette*,[42] held that complete nudity in a public place does not require that the Crown prove that the nudity offended public decency. Proof that public decency was offended is only required under s.174(2) where the person is not completely nude. So in *R. v. Giambalvo*,[43] the Ontario Court of Appeal held that a dancer who is only partly clad has committed an offence under this section only if she has offended public decency or order. The test for this offence is the standard of community tolerance in the circumstances in which the dance was performed.

A 1990 Ontario Court of Appeal decision suggests that a female nude dancer may have a lawful excuse and therefore not be liable under this section if her performance is legitimate entertainment.[44]

Under s.174(3), to bring a proceeding under this section the consent of the Attorney General is required.

3. Causing a Disturbance

175. (1) Every one who

(a) not being in a dwelling-house, causes a disturbance in or near a public place,

(i) by fighting, screaming, shouting, swearing, singing or using insulting or obscene language,

(ii) by being drunk, or

---

42 (1978), 40 C.C.C. (2d) 273 (S.C.C.).
43 (1982), 70 C.C.C. (2d) 324 (Ont.C.A.).
44 *R. v Zikman* (1990), 56 C.C.C. (3d) 430 (Ont.C.A.).

(iii) by impeding or molesting other persons, . . .

is guilty of an offence punishable on summary conviction.

The essential elements of this offence are: the accused was not in a dwelling-house; he or she caused a disturbance; the disturbance occurred in a public place or near a public place; and the disturbance was caused by conduct such as fighting or screaming, or by the person being drunk, or impeding or molesting other persons.

a. Dwelling-house

Dwelling-house is defined in s.2 as:

. . . the whole or any part of a building or structure that is kept or occupied as a permanent or temporary residence, and includes

(a) a building within the curtilage of a dwelling-house that is connected to it by a doorway or by a covered and enclosed passageway, and

(b) a unit that is designed to be mobile and to be used as a permanent or temporary residence and that is being used as such a residence.

In *R. v. Jones*,[45] an issue was whether the administrative office of a university was a dwelling-house. Students at Simon Fraser University conducted a "sit-in" at the university. They occupied the administrative office and prevented officials and administrators from entering the office. They were charged under s.175(1)(a)(iii) with causing a disturbance by impeding other persons. The lawyer for the students argued that the sit-in occurred in a dwelling-house within the meaning of the definition in s.2 and that, therefore, no offence was committed. First, the lawyer argued that, for legal purposes such as being sued, the "residence" of a university is its administrative office. The court agreed that for certain legal purposes, but not for the purpose of s.175, the administrative office is the residence of the university. Second, the lawyer argued that because the students brought and used sleeping bags and food, they used the premises as their temporary residence within the meaning of the definition in s.2. The court disagreed, stating that trespassers cannot turn university property into a dwelling-house by wrongfully occupying it.

In *R. v. Campbell*,[46] the accused was charged with causing a disturbance in a public place by using insulting or obscene language. He was in the hallway and TV room of a hospital when the incident occurred. The trial court dismissed the charge on the grounds that the TV room and hallway were dwelling places. An appeal court disagreed, holding that although the rooms of the patients were probably dwelling places, a TV room and hallway where the public could come and go were not dwelling places.

---

45   (1970), 1 C.C.C. (2d) 232 (B.C.C.A.).
46   (1980), 22 C.R. (3d) 219 (Alta.Q.B.).

b. Disturbance

The meaning of "disturbance" was discussed by the Supreme Court of Canada in *R. v. Lohnes*.[47] The accused was charged with causing a disturbance because he had on two occasions, while standing on his verandah, shouted obscenities to his neighbour, with whom he had a long-running dispute. The neighbour filed a complaint, and the accused was convicted at trial. The conviction was upheld by the Nova Scotia Court of Appeal. The case was then appealed to the Supreme Court of Canada, which analysed the offence and found that it has two elements: a prohibited act (e.g., swearing, shouting) and a resulting disturbance in a public place. In *Lohnes,* the only issue was whether the prohibited act had caused a disturbance. The Court noted that the word "disturbance" has a wide range of meanings. It can refer to something innocuous, such as a jarring colour, or (at the other end of the range) to incidents of violence or apprehension for physical safety. The Court said that its task was to decide where to draw the line for a disturbance that creates criminal liability. In doing so, the Court had to consider two conflicting values: the individual right to sing, shout, or otherwise express oneself; and the right of the community to peace and tranquility. In looking at previous decisions, the Court noted that "emotional upset" had not been sufficient cause for an act to be considered a "disturbance" for criminal liability. For example, in *R. v. C.D.*,[48] where the accused shouted obscenities and rammed his car into the complainant's car, reducing the latter's wife to tears, the appeal court overturned a conviction for causing a disturbance because the emotional upset experienced by the complainant and his wife was not enough to constitute a disturbance. Similarly, in *R. v. Wolgram*,[49] shouting obscenities in a barroom was not a disturbance, because no one appeared to be disturbed and there was no interference with the ordinary use of a public place. On the other hand, in *R. v. Swinimer*,[50] the accused's fighting, shouting, and obscene language in front of his residence interfered with the usual activities of his neighbours. For example, one neighbour had to return to her children's bedroom to calm them down. In *R. v. Chikoski*,[51] shouting obscenities at an officer caused 200 nearby workers to stop work to watch the dispute.

The Court, in *Lohnes,* concluded that the conduct must cause a disturbance that creates an interference with the ordinary and customary use by the public of the place in question. There must be more than mere mental or emotional annoyance or disruption. "By addressing 'disturbance' in a public context, Parliament signaled that its objective was not the protection of individuals from emotional upset, but protection of the public from disorder calculated to interfere with the public's normal activities."[52] In *Lohnes,* there was no evidence of a disturbance in the use of the premises in question and no evidence that the conduct of the complainant or anyone else in the area

47 (1992), 69 C.C.C. (3d) 289 (S.C.C.).
48 (1973), 13 C.C.C. (2d) 206 (N.B.C.A.).
49 (1976), 29 C.C.C. (2d) 536 (B.C.S.C.).
50 (1978), 40 C.C.C. (2d) 432 (N.S.C.A.).
51 (1973), 14 C.C.C. (2d) 38 (Ont.Prov.Ct.).
52 Supra, note 47 at page 297.

was affected or disturbed by the conduct of the accused. The Court allowed the appeal and quashed the convictions.

4. Trespassing at Night

Trespassing on private property by itself is not a criminal offence, although it may be a provincial offence. Under the criminal law it is, however, an offence to loiter or prowl at night near a dwelling-house. This offence is set out in s.177:

> **177. Every one who, without lawful excuse, the proof of which lies on him, loiters or prowls at night on the property of another person near a dwelling-house situated on that property is guilty of an offence punishable on summary conviction.**

This is sometimes referred to as the "Peeping Tom" section. For the offence to be committed, a person must "loiter or prowl"; the loitering or prowling must occur at "night"; it must be on another person's property; and it must be near a dwelling-house on that property. The section contains a reverse onus clause, in that, if the person has some lawful excuse for his or her actions, it is up to that person to prove it.

a. Night

The term "night" is defined in s.2 as the period between 9 p.m. and 6 a.m. If the loitering or prowling occurs before 9 p.m. or after 6 a.m., even if it is dark outside, the offence is not committed.

b. Loiters or Prowls

This section creates two offences: loitering at night and prowling at night. The meaning of the terms was discussed in *R. v. Cloutier*,[53] a decision of the Quebec Court of Appeal. The accused was discovered in an alcove near the garage door of a condo. The day before, the box containing the electric locking device had been found damaged, and the garage owner had immediately repaired it. The accused was discovered when the owner heard a noise coming from outside the garage that sounded like someone was putting a key in the box or unscrewing it. When he went to investigate he found the accused. He also found that the box was missing a screw and that another had been three-quarters removed.

The accused was charged with loitering. The court distinguished loitering from prowling in this way: Loitering refers to wandering about without a precise destination. A loiterer is one whose movements do not appear to have a purpose or reason. Loitering by itself is not reprehensible if it is not done at night on private property near a dwelling. Prowling, on the other hand, has some element of evil. "The prowler does not act without purpose like the loiterer, his actions lead one to believe that he has something in mind and that this something is not commendable." The evidence in this case sug-

---

53 (1991), 66 C.C.C. (3d) 149 (Que.C.A.).

gested that the accused's purpose was to commit a break and enter. Therefore, he should have been charged with prowling. Since these are not interchangeable offences, he had to be acquitted of the loitering charge.

Questions for Review and Discussion

1. List the offences concerning sexual activity and children. Indicate the age the victim must be for the offence to occur.

2. Give an example of a person in a position of authority or trust under s.153. Make a list of the factors you think put a person in a position of authority or trust, or in a position of dependency.

3. **a.** When is consent not a defence to offences involving sexual conduct and children?
   b. What are the exceptions to situations where consent is not a defence?
   c. Why do these exceptions exist?

4. **a.** What has become the most important test for determining whether material is obscene?
   b. Explain the nature of the test.

5. Explain the elements of the offence involving child pornography.

6. What is the test for deciding whether a theatrical performance is immoral, indecent, or obscene?

7. What are the ways the offence of nudity can be committed?

8. **a.** What are the elements of the offence of causing a disturbance?
   b. How has the Supreme Court of Canada defined the term "disturbance" for this offence?

9. What are the elements of the offence of trespassing at night?

10. L. was charged with sexual touching under s.151 of the Code. The complainant was under 14 at the time of the incident, so even though she consented, her consent was not a defence unless the exception in s.150.1(2) applied. The accused was over 12 and under 16 years of age and less than two years older than the complainant. The only issue for the court was whether he was in a position of authority or trust toward the complainant. Six years earlier, at the age of 10, the accused had been placed in the home of the complainant as a foster child. Sexual activity began between the two about seven months after the accused came to the home. The complainant testified that she said nothing to her parents because the accused was stronger, and because she did not know what the appellant would do and did not think her mother would believe her. The sexual activity progressed and they eventually had intercourse. The final incident that led to the charge occurred when the complainant was 12 and she realized that she might become pregnant. She told the accused that they must stop, but he would not accept this. They were finally discovered when she confided to her best friend, who then told her mother.

The trial judge found that the accused was in a position of trust and that, therefore, the defence of consent was not available to him. He was convicted. The accused has appealed his conviction. Make a decision in this case. Was the accused in a position of trust? See *R. v. L.(D.B.)* (1995), 25 O.R. (3d) 649 (Ont.C.A.).

11. **a.** Cameron was the manager of an art gallery. She was charged with exposing to public view seven obscene drawings in her gallery. She collected the drawings from other galleries and from the artists themselves. She arranged for the display of the drawings in her gallery. She argued that she did not know the drawings were obscene.

    Should Cameron be convicted? See *R. v. Cameron*, [1966] 4 C.C.C. 273 (Ont.C.A.); aff'd (1967), 2 C.C.C. (2d) 195 (S.C.C.).

    b. Britnell, the operator of a bookstore, was charged with selling obscene books. The accused carried a stock of nearly 250,000 books in his store. The ordering of the copies of obscene books was done by a clerk, not the accused. The accused stated that he was unaware of the presence of the books in his store.

    Should Britnell be convicted? See *R. v. Britnell* (1912), 20 C.C.C. 85 (Ont.C.A.).

    c. Are your decisions in the above two cases the same or different? Explain.

12. Do you agree or disagree with the Supreme Court decision in Butler? Do you believe that the types of pornography identified by the Supreme Court of Canada as being harmful to society are harmful? Do you agree that s.163 is a reasonable limitation to freedom of expression? Discuss your position.

Chapter Eight

SOLICITING AND PROCURING, DISORDERLY HOUSES, BETTING, AND LOTTERIES

PART VII OF THE CODE

A. INTRODUCTION

This part of the Code deals with offences involving prostitution and gambling.

B. SOLICITING AND PROCURING

It is not an offence to engage in sex for money. The Code controls prostitution in three other ways. First, to solicit in public is an offence; second, to engage in "pimping"—that is, in procuring a person to be a prostitute—is an offence; third, there are several offences related to keeping a common bawdy-house (house of prostitution). Common bawdy-houses are discussed in the section of this chapter on disorderly houses.

Section 197 states that "prostitute means a person of either sex who engages in prostitution." Until this definition was added, there had been conflicting decisions on whether a man could be a prostitute. Note also that the pronoun "he" in these offences, and in all parts of the Code, refers to male and female persons (Interpretation Act, R.S.C. 1985, c.I-21).

1. Procuring

Section 212 sets out the offences involving procuring:

> **212. (1) Every one who**
>
> **(a) procures, attempts to procure or solicits a person to have illicit sexual intercourse with another person, whether in or out of Canada,**
>
> **(b) inveigles or entices a person who is not a prostitute to a common bawdy-house . . . for the purpose of . . . prostitution,**

(c) knowingly conceals a person in a common bawdy-house . . .

(d) procures or attempts to procure a person to become, whether in or out of Canada, a prostitute, . . .

(g) procures a person to enter or leave Canada, for the purpose of prostitution, . . .

(h) for the purposes of gain, exercises control, direction or influence over the movements of a person in such manner as to show that he is aiding, abetting or compelling that person to engage in or carry on prostitution with any person or generally,

(i) applies or administers to a person or causes that person to take any drug, intoxicating liquor, matter or thing with intent to stupefy or overpower that person in order thereby to enable any person to have illicit sexual intercourse with that person, or

(j) lives wholly or in part on the avails of prostitution of another person, . . .

These offences are indictable, and the maximum penalty is a 10-year prison term. However, if the accused is charged with living on the avails of a prostitute who is under 18, under s.212(2) the penalty is a maximum term of imprisonment of 14 years. Under s.212(2.1), a minimum penalty of 5 years will be imposed if the person charged with living on the avails of a prostitute who is under 18:
(i) for the purposes of profit aids, abets, counsels or compels the person under that age to engage in prostitution, and
(ii) uses, threatens to use or attempts to use violence, intimidation or coercion in relation to the person under that age.

There is an additional offence in this section concerning prostitutes under 18:

(4) Every person who, in any place, obtains for consideration, or communicates with anyone for the purpose of obtaining for consideration, the sexual services of a person who is under the age of eighteen years is guilty of an indictable offence and liable to imprisonment for a term not exceeding five years.

"Consideration" means money or something else of value. The Supreme Court of Canada said, in *Deutsch v. the Queen*,[1] that the term "illicit sexual intercourse" in s.212(1)(a) means sexual intercourse that is not authorized or sanctioned by lawful marriage. The accused was interviewing a prospective employee and told her that if she took the job she might be required to have sexual intercourse with clients. She was also told that she could make a lot of money doing this. The Court held that the offence of procuring was made out where the Crown could prove that the employer intended to induce or persuade the woman to seek employment that would require her to have intercourse with clients; and that during the interview the employer did in fact offer her a large financial reward for having intercourse with clients.

1   (1986), 27 C.C.C. (3d) 385 (S.C.C.).

"Prostitution" is not defined in the Code, but it has been given a wide meaning by the courts. In *R . v. Lantay*,[2] the Ontario Court of Appeal held that prostitution is not limited to sexual intercourse: it also includes a woman offering herself for money as a participant in physical acts of indecency for the sexual gratification of men. This case involved masturbation performed on customers of a massage parlour. The court held that this conduct amounted to prostitution. The Supreme Court of Canada, in a case that challenged ss. 193 and 195 of the Code, stated that there is little dispute as to the basic definition of prostitution: "that being the exchange of sexual services of one person in return for payment by another."[3]

In *R. v. Celebrity Enterprises Ltd.*,[4] the British Columbia Court of Appeal considered s.212(1)(j), which refers to living on the avails of prostitution. The court held that the Crown must prove that the accused received some of the proceeds of the prostitute's earnings or that those proceeds somehow supported the accused's living. The accused were operators of a nightclub that was frequented by prostitutes. Their convictions for living on the avails of prostitution were overturned because indirect benefits, such as admission fees to the club, could not be considered "avails of prostitution."

Section 212(3) creates a mandatory presumption that a person is living on the avails of prostitution when the person is living with or is habitually in the company of a prostitute:

> **(3) Evidence that a person lives with or is habitually in the company of a prostitute or lives in a common bawdy-house, is in the absence of evidence to the contrary, proof that the person lives on the avails of prostitution . . .**

This section was challenged in *R. v. Downey*[5] as a violation of the presumption of innocence under the Charter. The Supreme Court of Canada agreed that the section is an infringement but held that it is justifiable under s.1 of the Charter.[6] The objective of the legislation—to deal with the "social evil" of pimping—is sufficiently important to override the presumption of innocence. The section also meets the proportionality test. There is a rational connection between the fact and the presumption—that is, it is reasonable to presume that persons who have close connections to prostitutes are living on the avails of prostitution. This presumption recognizes the well-documented reluctance of prostitutes to testify against their pimps. As well, all an accused must do to rebut the presumption is raise a reasonable doubt. The Court noted that women who are prostitutes are often abused and exploited by their "pimps." This presumption is an attempt to protect them by eliminating the necessity of having them testify.

A decision of the Ontario Court of Appeal[7] has held that a charge of "living on avails" means that the accused "was living parasitically on the earn-

---

2 [1966] 3 C.C.C. 270 (Ont.C.A.).
3 Ref re Criminal Code ss.193 and 195.1(1)(c) (1990), 56 C.C.C. (3d) 65 (S.C.C.).
4 (1978), 41 C.C.C. (3d) 540 (B.C.C.A).
5 (1992), 72 C.C.C. (3d) 1 (S.C.C.).
6 The Court used the test set out in *R. v. Oakes*, see Chapter Two at page 27.
7 *R. v. Grilo* (1991), 64 C.C.C. (3d) 53 (Ont.C.A.).

ings of the prostitute for his own advantage." So, where the accused and the prostitute are in a legitimate and normal living arrangement as spouses or roommates, and share living expenses, the accused cannot be said to be "living on the avails."

2. Soliciting

Section 213 creates the offences concerning the public solicitation of sex:

> **213. (1) Every person who in a public place or in any place open to public view**
>
> **(a) stops or attempts to stop any motor vehicle,**
>
> **(b) impedes the free flow of pedestrian or vehicular traffic or ingress to or egress from premises adjacent to that place, or**
>
> **(c) stops or attempts to stop any person or in any manner communicates or attempts to communicate with any person**
>
> **for the purpose of engaging in prostitution or of obtaining the sexual services of a prostitute is guilty of an offence punishable on summary conviction.**

This section makes it an offence for both the prostitute and the person seeking the services of a prostitute to communicate in public. In other words, either the "client" or the prostitute can be charged. This section of the Code has been the subject of several challenges under the Charter as a violation of fundamental justice under s.7 and freedom of expression under s.2(b). The Supreme Court of Canada, considered at the same time three cases that were being appealed on this issue.[8] All of the judges held that s.213(c) violates the guarantee of freedom of expression. However, four of the judges—a majority—went on to hold that this section is a reasonable limitation under s.1 of the Charter. The objective of the law, the Court held, is to prevent the nuisance caused by the public purchase of sex. The Court considered the street congestion, noise, and oral harassment of non-participants in urban environments as part of the social nuisance caused by this conduct. A majority of the judges also agreed that the offence does not violate a principle of fundamental justice under s.7. A minority disagreed, stating that where communication is a protected right (i.e., freedom of expression) and prostitution itself is legal, the possibility of imprisonment for this offence is too drastic a response. In other words, a person can be imprisoned (i.e., denied liberty under s.7) without the principle of fundamental justice being followed: that the penalty must be in proportion to the offence.

C. DISORDERLY HOUSES

"Disorderly house" is a general term that refers to a common bawdy-house, a common gaming house, or a common betting house. It is an offence to

---

8   *Supra*, note 3.

"keep" a disorderly house, to be "found in" a disorderly house, or to "knowingly permit" a place to be used as a disorderly house.

The term "keeper" is defined in s.197:

"keeper" includes a person who

(a) is an owner or occupier of a place,

(b) assists or acts on behalf of an owner or occupier of a place,

(c) appears to be, or to assist or act on behalf of an owner or occupier of a place,

(d) has the care or management of a place, or

(e) uses a place permanently or temporarily, with or without the consent of the owner or occupier.

The Supreme Court of Canada has held that a person cannot be convicted of keeping a disorderly house simply because he or she falls within the above description. In general, to be a keeper, a person must participate in the wrongful use of the disorderly house.[9]

If a person is "found in" a disorderly house, then it is up to that person to show some evidence that he or she had a lawful excuse for being there. For example, a furnace repairer would have a lawful excuse if present in the house to repair the furnace.

If the owner or someone else having charge or control of a place is charged with "knowingly permitting" the place to be used as a disorderly house, then that person will be guilty only if he or she had knowledge of how the place was being used. A landlord who does not know that one of her apartments is being used for illegal betting could not be criminally liable.

Discussion of each type of disorderly house follows.

1. Common Bawdy-house

A common bawdy-house is defined in s.197(1):

"common bawdy-house" means a place that is

(a) kept or occupied, or

(b) resorted to by one or more persons

for the purpose of prostitution or the practice of acts of indecency.

Offences regarding bawdy-houses are stated in s.210:

210. (1) Every one who keeps a common bawdy-house is guilty of an indictable offence and liable to imprisonment for a term not exceeding two years . . .

---

9   *R. v. Kerim*, [1963] 1 C.C.C. 233 (S.C.C.).

(2) Every one who

(a) is an inmate of a common bawdy-house,

(b) is found, without lawful excuse, in a common bawdy-house, or

(c) as owner, landlord, lessor, tenant, occupier, agent or otherwise having charge or control of any place, knowingly permits the place or any part thereof to be let or used for the purposes of a common bawdy-house,

is guilty of an offence punishable on summary conviction.

To be convicted of keeping a common bawdy-house, as well as partici-pating in the illegal activity, the accused must have some degree of control over the care and management of the premises. In *R. v. Corbeil*[10] the accused was a masseuse at a massage parlour that offered masturbation to its clients. She would keep half the fee and turn the other half over to the owners of the parlour. Also, it was up to the masseuses to keep a record of the clients. The Supreme Court of Canada held that although she occupied a space and used it, she did not exercise the requisite care and control necessary for the offence.

One isolated act of prostitution is not enough to make a place a bawdy-house. There must be frequent resort to, or habitual use of, the place for pur-poses of prostitution or indecent acts. In *Paterson v. R.*,[11] two women went with three plain-clothes police officers to a suburban home for the purpose of prostitution. On their arrival, the two women went to another part of the house. They later returned wearing nothing but their underwear. At this point, the officers disclosed their identity and charged the two women with keeping a common bawdy-house. The Supreme Court of Canada held that to be convicted of "keeping," a person must frequently or habitually use the premises for the purposes of prostitution. The Court found the women not guilty because there was no evidence that the home had been used for pros-titution on any other occasion.

A similar decision was reached in *R. v. Evans, Lee and Woodhouse*,[12] which involved a house that was being used for a stag party. Three women had sex-ual intercourse with a number of men at the party and were paid for their services. The house had never been used before for prostitution. The issue was whether the large number of acts of intercourse that occurred in one evening were enough to convict the women and two male occupants of keeping a common bawdy-house. The court held that they were not guilty because the use of the house on one evening did not amount to frequent or habitual use of the premises for prostitution. *In R. v. Tardif*,[13] the Quebec Court of Appeal held that where there was evidence that on one day five

---

10   (1991), 64 C.C.C. (3d) 272 (S.C.C.).
11   (1968), 2 C.C.C. 247 (S.C.C.).
12   (1973), 11 C.C.C. 2d) 130 (Ont.C.A.).
13   (1995), 97 C.C.C. (3d) 381 (Que.C.A.).

men attended a massage parlour and were offered sexual services, this was not sufficient to establish frequent or habitual use.

The Ontario Court of Appeal has held that any defined space—even a parking lot—can be a bawdy-house if acts of prostitution take place there. However, persons cannot be convicted of keeping a common bawdy-house where they were present in a parking lot on a number of occasions but exercised no control over the lot and had no interest in the lot as owners, tenants, or licensees.[14]

The meaning of "acts of indecency" was considered most recently by the Supreme Court of Canada, in *R. v. Tremblay et al.*[15] The accused were charged with keeping a common bawdy-house. They operated a place where in exchange for money, a woman would dance nude for the customer in a private room. The customer was permitted to be nude and would usually masturbate. The accused were acquitted at their trial because the trial judge found that the acts performed at the place were not indecent. The Quebec Court of Appeal disagreed and entered convictions. The case was then appealed to the Supreme Court of Canada, which reaffirmed that the test for indecency is similar to the one used for obscenity: the community standard of tolerance test. The Court referred to its decision in *Butler*[16] and stated that the purpose of the community standard of tolerance test is to establish the degree of harm that flows from indecent acts. In determining whether the community standard of tolerance has been breached, courts must look at the context in which the acts were performed, since what a community will tolerate depends on where the acts take place and the audience before whom the acts are performed. In this case, the customers were warned before they entered the building about what activities took place. As well, the acts took place in private, and no physical contact was allowed. The Court also held that the expert evidence considered by the trial judge was very appropriate in determining whether community standards had been breached. The trial court had heard testimony from a sexologist and professor of psychology, who stated that masturbation is a normal and common activity and that the acts performed at the place were nonpathological and harmless. The trial court had also heard testimony from the police that the type of dancing that took place was similar to the nude dancing tolerated in strip bars in the city. In sum, the Court held that the trial judge could properly find that the acts were not indecent. There was no evidence of harm flowing from the acts in question. The Court restored the acquittals of the accused.

The Supreme Court of Canada has upheld the validity of the offences of keeping, being found in, and being an inmate of a common bawdy-house as not being violations of freedom of expression or liberty.[17]

---

14 *R. v. Pierce* (1982), 66 C.C.C. (2d) 388 (Ont.C.A.).
15 (1993), 84 C.C.C. (3d) 97 (S.C.C.).
16 See Chapter Seven, note 17.
17 *Supra*, note 3.

2. Common Gaming House and Common Betting House

a. The Offences

The offences involving common gaming houses are set out in s.201:

> **201. (1) Everyone who keeps a common gaming house or common betting house is guilty of an indictable offence and liable to imprisonment for . . . two years.**
>
> **(2) Everyone who**
>
> **(a) is found, without lawful excuse, in a common gaming house or common betting house, or**
>
> **(b) as owner, landlord, lessor, tenant, occupier or agent, knowingly permits a place to be let or used for the purposes of a common gaming house or common betting house,**
>
> **is guilty of an offence punishable on summary conviction.**

b. Common Gaming House

"Common gaming house" is defined in s.197(1):

> **"common gaming house" means a place that is**
>
> **(a) kept for gain to which persons resort for the purpose of playing games, or**
>
> **(b) kept or used for the purpose of playing games**
>
> **(i) in which a bank is kept by one or more but not all of the players,**
>
> **(ii) in which all or any portion of the bets on or proceeds from a game is paid, directly or indirectly, to the keeper of the place,**
>
> **(iii) in which, directly or indirectly, a fee is charged to or paid by the players for the privilege of playing or participating in a game or using gaming equipment, or**
>
> **(iv) in which the chances of winning are not equally favourable to all persons who play the game, including the person, if any, who conducts the game.**

(I) THE MEANING OF GAMING AND GAMES

Notice that under s.197(1)(a), the definition of common gaming house does not refer to the players making bets or wagering. The Supreme Court of Canada, in *Di Pietro v. The Queen*,[18] held that even though the definition of common gaming house under 197(1)(a) does not appear to require that the

---

18 (1986), 25 C.C.C. (3d) 100 (S.C.C.).

patrons be involved in wagering, under the common law, wagering is part of the meaning of gaming. The Court quoted a 1903 English decision: "To amount to gaming the game played must involve the element of wagering— that is to say, each of the players must have a chance of losing as well as of winning."[19] The Court concluded: "The prosecution must prove, as an element of the offence of gaming, that the participants had the chance of winning and losing money or money's worth. This possible outcome must be a result, direct or indirect, of wagering or hazarding a stake prior to or during the game."[20]

In this case, the "loser" bought drinks for the "winners" and no money was exchanged. This practice was not a game under this section but just a convenient way to take turns paying for the drinks.

In addition to the common law meaning of gaming, the Code in s.197(1)(b) defines "game" as "a game of chance or mixed chance and skill." A game of chance is one in which luck entirely determines the winner. The Supreme Court of Canada has held that the term "mixed chance and skill" does not imply any particular proportion of skill to chance. The Court decided that the card game of bridge is a game of mixed chance and skill. Even though the main ingredients of the game involve the use of skill, the players can only use their skill after the cards have been dealt.[21] In *R. v. Lebansky*,[22] target shooting at a miniature shooting range was considered to be a game of skill and not a game of chance. Although some element of chance was involved, it was too small to justify classifying the game as one of mixed chance and skill. In *R. v. McGee*,[23] the game of bingo was held to be a game of chance.

(II) KEPT FOR GAIN

Under paragraph (a) of the definition of common gaming house, the place must be "kept for gain" (or profit). In *R. v. James*,[24] the accused was the manager of a cigar shop. In the rear of the shop was a room in which poker games were played. Out of the stakes that were bet during the games, a small amount of money was set aside to cover the cigars and refreshments consumed by the players. The court decided that the increased profits of the business derived from the sale of cigars and refreshments were a "gain." Thus, the accused was guilty of keeping a common gaming house. A similar case, *R. v. Forder*,[25] involved the players in a poker game paying a small sum each half-hour to the accused for a new pack of cards. The accused made a large profit in this way, and the court held that he was guilty of keeping a common gaming house. It seems that these two cases would also fit within paragraph (b)(ii) of the definition of a common gaming house because in both, a portion of the bets was paid to the keeper of the place.

---

19 Ibid. at page 107.
20 Ibid. at page 110.
21 *Ross v. The Queen*, [1969] 1 C.C.C. 1 (S.C.C.).
22 (1941), 75 C.C.C. 348 (Man.C.A.).
23 (1942), 77 C.C.C. 302 (Man.C.A.).
24 (1903), 7 C.C.C. 196 (Ont.C.A.).
25 (1930), 54 C.C.C. 388 (Ont.C.A.).

(III) KEPT, USED, OR RESORTED TO

Under paragraphs (a) and (b), a place must be used more than once to be a common gaming house. The Supreme Court of Canada, in *Rockert v. The Queen*,[26] held that the words "kept" and "resort" refer to frequent or habitual use, and that the word "used" in paragraph (b) means more than one use. Section 197(4) allows for a place that is used once to be a common gaming house "if the keeper or any other person acting on behalf of or in concert with the keeper has used another place on another occasion in the manner described in that paragraph." In effect, this section prevents people from creating "moving" gaming houses.

(IV) BANK

A place is also a gaming house if it is kept or used for the purpose of playing games in which a "bank" is kept by one or more but not all of the players. In *R. v. Rubenstein*,[27] the accused was charged with keeping a common gaming house in that he was a banker in a game of blackjack played on a picnic table in a public park. A "bank" was defined by the court as the sum of money that the dealer or banker has as a fund from which to draw the stakes and pay any losses, or as the pile of money that the player who plays against all the other players has before him. The accused claimed that, at the time the police interfered, he was only taking his turn at the bank and so did not come within the terms of the definition of a common gaming house. However, during the time that the police watched, the deal went completely around three times and the bank did not change hands. The court found that the accused was running a bank that was "kept by one or more but not all of the players." The court also held that if the bank had been passed around, the offence would not have been committed.

(V) PLACE

In *Rubenstein*, the accused also argued that he should not be convicted because the "place" where the game was played was a picnic table in a public park. The court held that he should be convicted because the table fell within the definition of "place" in s.197(1). It was not necessary that it be a room or building because the definition includes places that are not "covered or enclosed" and that are used by persons who do not have "an exclusive right of use." The accused also fell within the definition of "keeper" because he was a person using the place "temporarily with or without the consent of the owner or occupier."

(VI) GENUINE SOCIAL CLUB

An exception to the definition of common gaming house is found in s.197(2):

> **(2) A place is not a common gaming house within the meaning of paragraph (a) or subparagraph (b)(ii) or (iii) of the definition "com-**

---

26   (1978), 38 C.C.C. (2d) 438 (S.C.C.).
27   (1960), 126 C.C.C. 312; 32 C.R. 20 (Ont.C.A.).

mon gaming house" in subsection (1) while it is occupied and used by an incorporated genuine social club or branch thereof, if

(a) the whole or any portion of the bets on or proceeds from games played therein is not directly or indirectly paid to the keeper thereof; and

(b) no fee is charged to persons for the right or privilege of participating in the games played therein other than under the authority of and in accordance with the terms of a licence issued by the Attorney General of the province in which the place is situated or by such other person or authority in the province as may be specified by the Attorney General thereof.

In general, a social club is a group of people who get together for a social purpose (such as playing games) rather than for the purpose of making a profit. In *R. v. MacDonald et al.*,[28] a secretary-manager of the Royal Canadian Legion was charged with keeping a common gaming house. The defence was that the Legion was a genuine social club[29] and fell within the exception in s.197(2). Members of the public wishing to play bingo were admitted upon payment of a 50-cent admission fee. To participate in prize money, they paid an additional 50 cents. The Legion kept only the admission fees; the other money was returned as prizes to the winning players. The Supreme Court of Canada decided that admission of the public, for a fee, was not occupation and use by a bona fide social club. The Court went on to say: "It is unnecessary to go into the objects (or purposes) of the Canadian Legion . . . The use of these premises on such a widespread scale contradicts any possible inference of the use as a bona fide social club."

There does not seem to be one single test for determining whether a place is being used by a genuine social club. In *MacDonald*, the admission of the general public for a fee on a widespread scale was an important factor in the Court's decision that the place was not being used by a genuine social club. In *R. v. Tatti*,[30] the Ontario Court of Appeal referred to a genuine social club as a club that is owned and controlled by all members equally. The accused was the manager of a recreation club that was used for playing card games, Ping Pong, and billiards. The court held that the exception for social clubs did not apply because the club was owned and controlled completely by the accused. Other courts have taken into account whether the social objects or purposes of the club are really being carried out, and whether non-members are allowed to play the games. However, in *Re Mow Chong Social Club*,[31] the Ontario Court of Appeal decided that the mere fact that a non-member was able to enter the club, and that only some of the purposes of the club were being carried out, did not necessarily mean that a club was not a social club.

---

28 (1966), 2 C.C.C. 307; 47 C.R. 37 (S.C.C.).
29 Until recent amendments to s.197(2), the Code and court decisions used the Latin term for genuine: "bona fide." For clarity, the term "genuine" will be used even if the court used the term "bona fide".
30 [1965] 2 C.C.C. 331 (Ont.C.A.).
31 (1964), 47 C.R. 295 (Ont.C.A.).

Even if a place is being used by a genuine social club, it may still be considered a common gaming house if there is a payment to the keeper from bets on or proceeds from the games, or if unauthorized fees are charged to the players of the games. On this, see s.197(2)(a) and (b). In *R. v. Karavasilis*,[32] members of a soccer club leased a building from the accused where they played rummy. The accused sold refreshments to the soccer club members during their games. Even though they were a legitimate social club, the fact that the accused made a profit from selling refreshments made the place a common gaming house.

c. *Common Betting House*
Section 197(1) contains the following definitions:

> **"bet"** means a bet that is placed on any contingency or event that is to take place in or out of Canada, and . . . includes a bet that is placed on any contingency relating to a horse-race, fight, match or sporting event that is to take place in or out of Canada . . .

> **"common betting house"** means a place that is opened, kept or used for the purpose of

> **(a)** enabling, encouraging or assisting persons who resort thereto to bet between themselves or with the keeper, or

> **(b)** enabling any person to receive, record, register, transmit or pay bets or to announce the results of betting.

The recording of one bet is not enough in itself to make a place a common betting house. In *R. v. Weidman*,[33] the accused was the operator of a small store that sold newspapers, magazines, and cigarettes. There was proof that one or two bets had been made at the store. The British Columbia Court of Appeal held that there must be proof that the place is opened, kept, or used for the purpose of betting. This can be proved by one bet if there are other surrounding circumstances that show that the place is kept for that purpose. These other circumstances did not exist, so the accused was found not guilty of keeping a common betting house. In *R . v. Woodward and Willcocks*,[34] a newspaper office was held to be a common betting house and the editor and business manager of the paper were convicted of "keeping." The newspaper operated a guessing contest in which the contestants paid a fee and tried to guess the results of football games. Prizes were awarded to the top three contestants. The prize money was taken from the fees paid by the contestants. This type of contest falls within the definition of "bet" because the contestants are betting among themselves "on a contingency relating to a sporting event."

32 (1980), 54 C.C.C. 530 (Ont.C.A.).
33 (1954), 108 C.C.C. 89 (B.C.C.A.).
34 (1922), 38 C.C.C. 154 (Man.C.A.).

d. Presumptions

Section 198 creates certain presumptions in regard to disorderly houses. All of these presumptions may be subject to Charter challenges as violations of the presumption of innocence (see Chapter Two for a discussion of reverse onus clauses and presumptions).

(I) OBSTRUCTION

> **198. (1) In proceedings under this Part,**
>
> **(a) evidence that a peace officer who was authorized to enter a place was wilfully prevented from entering or was wilfully obstructed or delayed in entering is, in the absence of any evidence to the contrary, proof that the place is a disorderly house.**

In *Ewaschuk v. R.*,[35] a police officer came to the door of a house with a search warrant. A woman opened the door slightly and, realizing that it was a police officer, slammed and locked the door. By this action she was wilfully obstructing and delaying the officer, who was authorized to enter the house. Because there was no evidence to show that the place was not a disorderly house, the woman's action was enough for the court to decide that it was such a house.

(II) GAMING EQUIPMENT

> **198. (1) . . . (b) evidence that a place was found to be equipped with gaming equipment or any device for concealing, removing or destroying gaming equipment is, in the absence of any evidence to the contrary, proof that the place is a common gaming house or a common betting house, as the case may be;**
>
> **(c) evidence that gaming equipment was found in a place entered under a warrant issued pursuant to this Part, or on or about the person of anyone found therein, is, in the absence of any evidence to the contrary, proof that the place is a common gaming house and that the persons found therein were playing games, whether or not any person acting under the warrant observed any person playing games therein.**

Gaming equipment refers to anything that may be used for playing games of chance or betting. In *R. v. Achilles*,[36] there was evidence that a place was set up with 48 chairs and 8 card tables and other tables on which were cards, score sheets, and pencils. The court said that these items were gaming equipment and were there for the purpose of playing a game of chance or mixed chance and skill. This was enough evidence for the court to presume that the place was a common gaming house. The accused did not testify, and no evi-

---

35 (1955), 111 C.C.C. 377 (Man.C.A.).
36 (1972), 6 C.C.C. (2d) 274 (Ont.C.A.).

dence was given on their behalf. In other words, the presumption was not rebutted; thus, evidence of the gaming equipment was considered proof that the place was a common gaming house.

(III) EVIDENCE OF CONVICTION

> **198. (1) . . . (d) evidence that a person was convicted of keeping a disorderly house is, for the purpose of proceedings against any one who is alleged to have been an inmate or to have been found in that house at the time the person committed the offence of which he was convicted, in the absence of any evidence to the contrary, proof that the house was, at that time, a disorderly house.**

Here is an example of the application of s.198(1)(d): John is convicted of keeping a common betting house. Jim was found in John's place during the time that John was keeping it as a betting house. Jim is later charged with the offence of being "found in" a common betting house. At Jim's trial, John's conviction will be proof that the place was a common betting house unless there is some evidence at the trial to show that it was not. The Quebec Court of Appeal has found that this section violates the Charter and is not a reasonable limitation.[37]

(IV) SLOT MACHINES

> **198. . . . (2) For the purpose of proceedings under this Part, a place that is found to be equipped with a slot machine shall be conclusively presumed to be a common gaming house.**

In general, a slot machine refers to a machine that provides goods or amusement and that involves some element of chance. However, pinball machines are not considered slot machines if the only prize that can be won is one or more free games. The Ontario Court of Appeal[38] has held that the presumption in s.198(2) violates the presumption of innocence.

e. Other Betting Offences

Section 202 creates several betting offences that do not require the existence of a common gaming house or common betting house, which include: knowingly allowing a place to be used for recording or registering bets or selling a pool; making or keeping a gambling or betting machine; being the custodian of a wager; recording or registering bets; engaging in bookmaking or in the business of betting; printing or providing bookmaking information; importing bookmaking information; advertising an offer to bet on a contest; wilfully and knowingly sending betting or bookmaking information; and aiding or assisting in committing any of the above offences. These offences

---

37   *R. v. Janoff* (1991), 68 C.C.C. (3d) 454 (Que.C.A.).
38   *R. v. Shisler* (1990), 53 C.C.C. (3d) 531 (Ont.C.A.).

are directed at prohibiting the business of betting rather than at prohibiting the keeping of a gaming or betting house.

f. Off-track Betting Shops

Under s.203, off-track betting shops are made illegal:

203. Every one who

(a) places or offers or agrees to place a bet on behalf of another person for a consideration paid or to be paid by or on behalf of that other person,

(b) engages in the business or practice of placing or agreeing to place bets on behalf of other persons, whether for a consideration

or otherwise, or

(c) holds himself out or allows himself to be held out as engaging in the business or practice of placing or agreeing to place bets on behalf of other persons, whether for a consideration or otherwise,

is guilty of an indictable offence and liable

(d) for a first offence, to imprisonment for not more than two years,

(e) for a second offence, to imprisonment for not more than two years and not less than fourteen days, and

(f) for each subsequent offence, to imprisonment for not more than two years and not less than three months.

The offences in s.203 are similar to the offence of engaging in the business of betting. The main difference is that s.203 specifically prohibits off-track betting shops. These shops receive money from customers and, for a fee, wager the money for them at the race-track.

Section 204 creates certain exceptions that allow for betting in certain situations. For example, it states that ss. 201 and 202 do not apply to the following:

204. (1) . . . (a) any person or association by reason of his or their becoming the custodian or depository of any money . . . to be paid to

(i) the winner of a lawful race, sport, game or exercise,

(ii) the owner of a horse engaged in a lawful race, or

(iii) the winner of any bets between not more than ten individuals;

(b) a private bet between individuals not engaged in any way in the business of betting . . .

This section also sets out the rules for allowing betting at approved race-courses.

D. LOTTERIES AND OTHER SCHEMES

1. Lotteries

A lottery is a scheme for giving a prize by some method of chance, such as drawing numbered tickets from a container. Section 206(1) covers several offences involving lotteries, including the following: advertising or publishing a lottery; selling or otherwise disposing of lottery tickets; knowingly sending articles that are intended for use in a lottery; and conducting or managing a lottery.

For a lottery to exist, it is essential that the prize ("property") be disposed of by some method of chance. If any skill is involved, then there is no lottery. Because of this rule, many contests include a "skill-testing question" that must be answered before the prize is awarded. However, some lotteries are permitted. In general, s.207(1) provides that a lottery scheme may be conducted and managed by the government of a province. Also, if licensed by the provincial government, lotteries may be conducted and managed by a charitable or religious organization; an agricultural fair or exhibition; or any person at a public place of amusement.

2. Other Schemes

Section 206(1)(e) covers other schemes and games that are not lotteries because they do not involve giving a prize by some method of chance. Briefly, this section prohibits the conduct or management of any scheme by which a person upon paying an amount of money becomes entitled to receive something of greater monetary value because of the contributions of others to the scheme. In *Dream Home Contests Ltd. v. R.*,[39] the accused were charged with operating such a scheme. They built a house called a "Dream Home" that was put on display to the public. Contestants had to buy a one-dollar ticket and had to estimate the total retail value of the Dream Home. The contestant who most closely estimated the total retail value of the home would win the home. In other words, the winning contestant became entitled to a home that was of much greater value than the amount paid ($1.00). Giving away such a valuable prize was only possible because so many other contestants "contributed to the scheme" (i.e., bought tickets). Therefore, the requirements of the offence were present and the accused were found guilty. The accused were also charged with advertising a lottery contrary to s.206(1)(a). However, the accused were not guilty of this offence because the contest was not a lottery, since it did not involve giving a prize by some method of chance. In other words, estimating the value of the house was considered to involve skill.

Section 206(1)(e) also covers pyramid selling schemes, which operate like chain letters. In *R. v. Cote*,[40] the accused was an officer of the company known as Dare To Be Great of Canada Ltd. The company's operation involved sell-

39 (1960), 33 C.R. 47 (S.C.C.).
40 (1973), 11 C.C.C. (2d) 443 (Que.C.A.).

ing a course to persons at a cost of $1,500. The company claimed that the objectives of the course were to strengthen the personality of the subscriber (or "member"), to improve the subscriber's self-confidence, and to make the subscriber more successful in work. The subscriber received a suitcase containing a tape recorder, cassettes, and other materials that had a total value of $100. After completing the course, the subscriber became a sales agent (or "motivator") and received a commission of $900 for every course he or she sold to a new subscriber. Each of these new subscribers also had to pay $1,500 for the course. In turn, these new subscribers became sales agents after completing the course. The court held that this scheme fell within s.206(1)(e) because a person, on paying $1,500, became entitled to receive from the Dare To Be Great company a larger sum of money than he or she had paid personally by recruiting new members who in turn paid a certain amount of money.

The remaining paragraphs of s.206(1) are reasonably clear:

> **206. (1) Every one is guilty of an indictable offence and is liable to imprisonment for two years who . . .**
>
> **(f) disposes of any goods, wares or merchandise by any game of chance or any game of mixed chance and skill in which the contestant or competitor pays money or other valuable consideration;**
>
> **(g) induces any person to stake or hazard any money or other valuable property or thing on the result of any dice game, three-card monte, punch board, coin table or on the operation of a wheel of fortune;**
>
> **(h) for valuable consideration carries on or plays or offers to carry on or to play, or employs any person to carry on or play in a public place or a place to which the public have access, the game of three-card monte;**
>
> **(i) receives bets of any kind on the outcome of a game of three-card monte; or**
>
> **(j) being the owner of a place, permits any person to play the game of three-card monte therein.**

Three-card monte is a card game in which a person tries to guess the location of one playing card among a total of three. Section 206(2) provides that three-card monte includes any other game that is similar to it, whether or not cards are used and notwithstanding the number of cards or things used.

Questions for Review and Discussion

1. Explain the ways that the Criminal Code controls prostitution.
2. Name the three types of disorderly houses.
3. Name three offences which can be committed in relation to disorderly houses.
4. How has the Supreme Court of Canada defined the term "indecency"?
5. What conduct is required for prostitution?
6. What is a common gaming house?
7. What is the definition of game?
8. What is a genuine social club?
9. What is a common betting house?
10. Give two examples of legal betting.
11. What are the essential elements of a lottery?
12. **a.** Discuss the decision of the Supreme Court of Canada in upholding s.213(c). Do you agree or disagree with the decision?
    b. Some people have suggested prostitution should be legalized and "red light" districts established. Discuss the pros and cons of these ideas.
13. Eugene operates a shooting range and charges a $2 admission fee. The most accurate shooter on any day wins a free admission. Is Eugene guilty of keeping a common gaming house? Explain.
14. Christine is charged with keeping a common gaming house. The only evidence presented at the trial is that a slot machine was found in Christine's basement. Should Christine be convicted? Explain.
15. Leslie, Mehta, Enni, and Sharon enjoy betting on horse races. Because Enni lives near the track, he places bets for himself, Leslie, Mehta, and Sharon each week during the racing season. Is Enni guilty of an offence? Why? Does it matter that Enni received no fee for placing bets? Why?

Chapter Nine

THE OFFENCES OF MURDER, MANSLAUGHTER, AND INFANTICIDE

PART VII OF THE CODE

A. INTRODUCTION

Homicide is the causing of death of a human being. Not all homicides are crimes, however—only those which are culpable. As explained in greater detail below, homicides that are not culpable are either justifiable or excusable.

The Code defines homicide and then sets out the three types of culpable homicide: murder, manslaughter, and infanticide.

B. HOMICIDE

Homicide is defined in s.222 of the Code:

> **222. (1) A person commits homicide when, directly or indirectly, by any means, he causes the death of a human being.**
>
> **(2) Homicide is culpable or not culpable.**
>
> **(3) Homicide that is not culpable is not an offence.**
>
> **(4) Culpable homicide is murder or manslaughter, or infanticide.**

1. Meaning of "Human Being"

Since homicide is the causing of the death of a human being, it is important to know when, in the eyes of the criminal law, a human being comes into existence. Section 223 states:

> **223. (1) A child becomes a human being within the meaning of this Act when it has completely proceeded, in a living state, from the body of its mother whether or not**

(a) it has breathed,

(b) it has an independent circulation, or

(c) the navel string is severed.

Thus, according to the criminal law, a foetus (i.e., an unborn child) is not a human being. Section 223 then goes on to state:

(2) A person commits homicide when he causes injury to a child before or during its birth as a result of which the child dies after becoming a human being.

In other words, under this section it is homicide if the injury is caused to a foetus that dies after being born. If the foetus dies before being born, then the death is not homicide. In *R. v. Prince*,[1] the accused attacked a woman who was obviously pregnant. The child was born premature and died 19 minutes after birth because of the injuries suffered by the mother. The court held that the accused was responsible for the child's death.

2. Causation

The issue of causation was dealt with in Chapter Three. Recall that the Supreme Court of Canada has recognized two tests for causation: 1. the contributing cause outside the *de minimis* range test (which is sufficient for a manslaughter charge); and a substantial cause test (for a murder charge). The Code also provides specific sections dealing with causation when a homicide has occurred. However, these sections do not deal with the issue of whether the homicide is culpable; they only consider whether there is what is sometimes called "factual causation." In other words, a person's conduct may fall within one of these sections so that it can be said that he or she caused the death, but the death may still be justifiable or excusable.

a. Section 224

224. Where a person, by an act or omission, does any thing that results in the death of a human being, he causes the death of that human being notwithstanding that death from that cause might have been prevented by resorting to proper means.

This section would apply to the following type of situation: Whitney inflicts a minor wound on Byron. Byron fails to get proper medical treatment for the injury. The wound becomes infected, causing Byron's death. Whitney has caused the death of Byron even though the death could have been prevented if the wound had been given proper treatment.

b. Section 225

This section deals with a situation similar to the one in s.224:

---

1   (1988), 44 C.C.C. (3d) 510 (Man.C.A.).

225. Where a person causes to a human being a bodily injury that is of itself of a dangerous nature and from which death results, he causes the death of that human being notwithstanding that the immediate cause of death is proper or improper treatment that is applied in good faith.

A case that involved s.225 is *R. v. Emkeit and 12 Others*.[2] Emkeit and the other 12 men were members of a motorcycle gang. During a fight with a rival gang, Emkeit hit one man on the side of the head with a chain. The man died while being driven to the hospital. The victim's injuries consisted of several serious head lacerations. Doctors testified that the causes of death were pulmonary edema caused by the head injuries, and tracheobronchial aspiration, which meant in effect that the victim had drowned in his own vomit. This had resulted from the friends of the injured man laying him on his back without depressing his tongue while they were taking him to the hospital.

Emkeit argued that the jury could have found him not guilty if it had found that the victim's life could have been saved through proper treatment. The court held, however, that the jury did not need to consider this argument. The key issue was whether the original wound was the operating and substantial cause of death. Notice that s.225 requires the treatment to be given in "good faith." Presumably, if Jack is seriously injured by Tom and taken to a doctor, and the doctor decides to kill him by giving him the wrong medication, Tom will no longer be the cause of Jack's death, because the doctor's treatment was not given in good faith.[3]

c. Section 226

226. Where a person causes to a human being a bodily injury that results in death, he causes the death of that human being notwithstanding that the effect of the bodily injury is only to accelerate his death from a disease or disorder arising from some other cause.

This section is very similar to the rule in *Smithers* (see Chapter Three) that an accused takes the victim with whatever disabilities the victim has. Thus, when a person injures another in a way that by itself would not cause the death, if the injury accelerates the death from other causes, then the person has still committed homicide. A case that relied on s.226 is *R. v. Nicholson*.[4] The accused and the deceased argued one evening at a schoolhouse meeting. The accused struck the deceased twice. At that point, both were pushed outside the building. The deceased's body was found some hours later. Medical evidence indicated that the deceased was a man in poor physical condition; his heart was abnormally small, and he suffered from Bright's disease. He had also been indulging freely in alcoholic beverages. The doctor who testified at the trial said that the blows struck by the accused were one cause of

2   (1971), 3 C.C.C. (2d) 309, 14 C.R.N.S. 209 (Alta.C.A.).
3   See for example, *R. v. Markuss* (1864), 176 E.R. 598. Whether the original assailant would be liable would depend on whether the court found that the original injury actually contributed to the death.
4   (1926), 47 C.C.C. 113 (N.S.S.C.).

death, others being the man's bad health and drinking. A jury found the accused guilty of manslaughter since the blows contributed to the death.

d. Section 227

> **227. No person commits culpable homicide or the offence of causing the death of a person by criminal negligence . . . unless the death occurs within one year and one day from the time of the occurrence of the last event by means of which the person caused or contributed to the cause of death.**

This section was repealed in 1999. The repeal provides an example of how the criminal law is sometimes amended to reflect scientific developments. The rule in this section originated during medieval times when it was very difficult, if not impossible, to accurately identify as the cause of death an event that occurred more than a year earlier. In modern times there has been some criticism of this rule, for two reasons: medical science has advanced so far that it is not difficult to trace a cause of death to an event that happened long ago; and with better medical care, persons who would have previously died immediately may now linger for months before dying.[5]

3. Culpable and Non-culpable Homicide

a. Non-culpable Homicide

There are two types of non-culpable homicide: justifiable and excusable. Homicide is justifiable if it is authorized or ordered by the law. Examples of justifiable homicide are a soldier killing an enemy during wartime, the execution of a person sentenced to death, and a police officer shooting a person in the course of duty. In these situations, the law may either require the killing, as when a death penalty is imposed, or permit the killing, as when a police officer finds it necessary to kill someone. (Note that Canadian law no longer allows the death penalty.)

Excusable homicide may occur where there was self-defence, or defence of others under the person's protection, or defence of property. These excuses were discussed in Chapter Four. Recall that to rely on an excuse such as self-defence, the force used must have been no more than was necessary to repel the attack.

Homicide may also be excusable where it is accidental. So, for example, where a person is doing a lawful act and unintentionally and without negligence kills another person, the death is considered accidental and no criminal liability will be attached. However, as is discussed more fully later, where a person is doing an unlawful act and accidentally causes a death, the homicide will be culpable.

---

5   1961 Criminal Law Review, 348.

b. Culpable Homicide

Culpable homicide consists of three offences: murder, manslaughter, and infanticide. Murder is the most serious type of culpable homicide. Generally speaking, the difference between murder and manslaughter is that murder requires a specific intent (e.g., to cause a person's death), while manslaughter is a general intent crime that is usually charged when the accused has recklessly caused a death. So, for example, Alfred is angry with his child Billy and beats the child severely. Billy dies from the beating. If it is clear that Alfred did not specifically intend to cause Billy's death but only had the general intention to do the act of beating, and was reckless about the consequences of the beating, he will probably be charged with manslaughter and not with murder.

Infanticide is a rarely used offence that only applies to certain situations involving newborn children.

Before deciding whether a death involves murder, manslaughter, or infanticide, one must first decide whether the homicide is culpable. Section 222(5) lists the methods by which culpable homicide can be committed:

> **222. . . . (5) A person commits culpable homicide when he causes the death of a human being,**
>
> **(a) by means of an unlawful act,**
>
> **(b) by criminal negligence,**
>
> **(c) by causing that human being, by threats or fear of violence or by deception, to do anything that causes his death, or**
>
> **(d) by wilfully frightening that human being, in the case of a child or sick person.**

(I) BY AN UNLAWFUL ACT

There are many types of unlawful acts, ranging from those which involve serious personal injury to those which are prohibited for the purpose of regulating some activity (e.g., parking by-laws). The latter have no role in protecting people or property. When considering whether an act is "unlawful" for the purposes of s.222, the courts do not treat all unlawful acts the same. In a case that has been quoted with approval by Canadian judges, the English Court of Criminal Appeals stated: "Where the act which a person is engaged in performing is unlawful, then if at the same time it is a dangerous act, that is an act which is likely to injure another person, and quite inadvertently the doer of the act causes the death of that person, then he is guilty of manslaughter."[6] Courts have said that in determining dangerousness, an *objective standard* is to be used—that is, the question is, would a reasonable person realize that the act would subject the person to some risk of harm? The Supreme Court of Canada has considered the requirements for unlaw-

---

6   *R. v. Larkin* (1942), 29 Cr.App.R. 18 at page 23.

ful act manslaughter. In *R. v. Creighton*,[7] the Court agreed with previous case law and stated that the unlawful act must be an objectively dangerous act (i.e., likely to injure someone not in a trivial or transitory way). Unlawful act manslaughter is discussed in detail later in this chapter.

(II) CRIMINAL NEGLIGENCE

Culpable homicide may also occur where a person's death has been caused by criminal negligence. The offences of criminal negligence are discussed in Chapter Ten. The definition of criminal negligence, which is set out in s.219, applies to criminal negligence under s.222(5)(b). The offence of causing death by criminal negligence may apply to the same facts as culpable homicide by criminal negligence (the offence would be manslaughter). In other words, these two sections of the Code overlap so that a person can be charged either with causing death by criminal negligence or with manslaughter. The offences involving criminal negligence have been part of the conflict regarding the requirement of *mens rea*. This issue is discussed fully in Chapter Ten.

(III) THREATS OR FEAR OF VIOLENCE

Another way of committing culpable homicide is by causing a person to do something, through threats, fear of violence, or deception, that results in his or her death. An example of a case where the Supreme Court said that there were facts from which a jury could find that the deceased acted through fear of violence is *R. v. Graves*.[8] The accused, along with others, and while intoxicated, trespassed on the victim's front lawn. The accused and his friends were using grossly offensive language and refused to leave when asked. The victim, his wife, and others who had been sitting on the front porch eventually went into the house. After a time, the victim loaded his gun, went to the front of the house, and asked the accused and his friends to leave. Instead of leaving, they rushed at the victim. The victim used the gun as a club to ward off the attackers. The gun went off, killing the victim. The Court held that the accused was properly charged with manslaughter.

(IV) FRIGHTENING A CHILD OR SICK PERSON

It is also culpable homicide to cause a person's death, where the person is a child or sick person, by wilfully frightening him or her. This provision should be read along with s.228:

> **228. No person commits culpable homicide where he causes the death of a human being:**
>
> **(a) by any influence on the mind alone, or**
>
> **(b) by any disorder or disease resulting from influence on the mind alone,**

---

7   (1993), 83 C.C.C. (3d) 346 (S.C.C.).
8   (1913), 21 C.C.C. 44 (S.C.C.).

but this section does not apply where a person causes the death of a child or sick person by wilfully frightening him.

An example of a case where it was found that the death was caused by influence on the mind is *R. v. Howard*.[9] The accused and the victim were travelling on a streetcar. The accused was trying to get off, and the victim was in his way. The men began to argue, and blows were exchanged. A few moments later, the victim became unconscious and then died. The medical evidence showed that the deceased had been an elderly man in poor physical condition. His arteries were weak, and death was caused by a brain hemorrhage. The Court found that the blows had not caused the hemorrhage; rather, the hemorrhage was a result of anger and excitement, which caused an artery to burst. In this situation, death was actually caused by influence on the mind. The charge of manslaughter against the accused was dismissed, since the victim, although elderly, was not a sick person.

C. OFFENCES OF CULPABLE HOMICIDE

Once it is established that the homicide is culpable, the next step is to determine whether the homicide is murder, manslaughter, or infanticide.

1. Murder

Culpable homicide is murder where certain additional factors, besides the culpable causing of death, are present. Under the common law, murder was defined as unlawful killing with "malice aforethought" (i.e., where the person intended to cause someone's death). Until recently, the offence of murder covered situations not only where death was specifically intended but also where the death was not intended but there were certain surrounding circumstances. However, recent decisions of the Supreme Court of Canada have limited the situations in which murder can be charged.

Sections 229 and 230 set out the situations where culpable homicide is murder.

a. Section 229

229. Culpable homicide is murder

(a) where the person who causes the death of a human being

(i) means to cause his death, or

(ii) means to cause him bodily harm that he knows is likely to cause his death, and is reckless whether death ensues or not;

(b) where a person, meaning to cause death to a human being or meaning to cause him bodily harm that he knows is likely to cause

---

9   [1913] 5 W.W.R. 838 (Man.).

his death, and being reckless whether death ensues or not, by accident or mistake causes death to another human being, notwithstanding that he does not mean to cause death or bodily harm to that human being; or

(c) where a person, for an unlawful object, does anything that he knows or ought to know is likely to cause death, and thereby causes death to a human being, notwithstanding that he desires to effect his object without causing death or bodily harm to any human being.

(I) SECTION 229(A)

Murder under s.229(a)(i) is the simplest form of the offence. All that must be shown is that the accused by a voluntary act caused a person's death and that the accused intended to cause that person's death. Since it may be impossible to produce evidence that shows a person actually had the mental intention to cause another person's death (unless, of course, there is a confession), courts have long taken the position that it may be assumed that a person intends the natural consequences of his or her acts. As one judge stated: "If a man is aware that certain consequences will probably follow the act which the person contemplates doing and yet deliberately proceeds to do that act, the person must be taken to have intended those consequences to follow even though he may have hoped they would not."[10] So if Hannah puts a bomb in Carl's car, knowing that Carl will be driving the car soon, and the bomb goes off, killing Carl, a jury can assume that Hannah intended to kill Carl.

Murder under s.229(a)(ii) differs from murder under s.229(a)(i) in that the specific intent necessary is not to cause death, but to cause bodily harm that the accused knows is likely to cause death. Before convicting a person of murder under s.212(a)(ii), it must also be shown that the accused intentionally inflicted bodily harm and that the accused was reckless as to whether death would result. Thus, intent, knowledge, and recklessness must all be present. This means that the accused, knowing that death was likely, must have intentionally and without justification done the act that caused the death. For example, Kim commits an apparently minor assault on Tanya without meaning to cause serious injury and without realizing that it was likely to cause death. Unknown to Kim, Tanya has a weak heart. The assault causes Tanya to suffer a stroke, from which she dies. Kim would probably not be convicted of murder. Although Kim did intend to cause bodily harm, she did not know that the injury was likely to cause death. Therefore, s.212(a)(ii) would not apply. However, she might be convicted of manslaughter.

(II) SECTION 229(B)

This subsection merely provides that where a person's conduct would fall under s.229(a) but, by accident or mistake, the wrong person dies, the per-

---

10   *R. v. Krafchenko* (1914), 22 C.C.C. 277 (Man.K.B.) at page 297.

son has still committed murder, even though he or she had no intent to harm the person who died. In *R. v. Droste*,[11] the accused planned to murder his wife by staging a car accident. Instead, his wife was only injured, while his two children, who were in the back seat, died. The court held that the accused was properly convicted of murdering his children. The intent he had to kill his wife was "transferred" to the victims of his act.

(III) SECTION 229(c)

This subsection makes homicide murder where a person for an unlawful object does something that he or she knows or ought to know is dangerous to life and that causes the death of a human being.

It is essential that the accused acted for an unlawful object. In other words, the act that caused the death must have been done to further or achieve an unlawful purpose. For example, if Rebecca shoots a gun at Owen for the purpose of robbing him and Owen dies, Rebecca can be charged with murder since she fired the gun for the unlawful object of robbing Owen. The Supreme Court of Canada has said that the unlawful object in this section must be a serious crime that is an indictable offence requiring *mens rea*. The case in which the Court made this statement is *R. v. Vasil*.[12] The accused, Vasil had been living with the mother of the two victims. Vasil and the mother were at a party, where they had an argument. Vasil left the party, went back to their house, and took the babysitter home. He then returned to the house, and spread lighter fluid on various things in the house, and set the house on fire. He testified that his purpose in setting the fire was to damage the mother's things. The two children asleep in the house died. The unlawful object in this case was the wilful destruction of property. The dangerous act (the act that the accused knew could cause death) was setting the fire.

The use of the words "ought to know" in s.229(c) means that an objective test may be used to determine whether the accused is responsible for the death. Unlike s.229(a)(ii), which uses a **subjective test** (i.e., "Did the accused actually know that the harm was likely to cause death?"), this section asks, "Would a reasonable person have known that the thing being done was dangerous to life?" The Supreme Court has said that this standard violates the Charter and is not enforceable.[13] In *R. v. Martineau*,[14] the Court said that all offences of murder require a subjective intent. Therefore, the part of s.229(c) that sets out an objective standard is unconstitutional.

In *R. v. Meiler*,[15] the accused was convicted of second-degree murder in the death of Nick Biuk, and sentenced to jail with no possibility of parole for 12 years. He was also sentenced to 10 years, to be served concurrently, for the attempted murder of his wife and Dan Roach.

The accused and his wife, Dianne Meiler, had two children and were separated. After the separation, Meiler suspected that his wife had been dating

---

11 (1979), 49 C.C.C. (2d) 52 (Ont.C.A.).
12 (1981), 58 C.C.C. (2d) 97 (S.C.C.).
13 The issue of subjective and objective intent is discussed in detail in the next section, on s.230 and the constructive murder rule.
14 (1990), 58 C.C.C. (3d) 353 (S.C.C.).
15 (1999), 136 C.C.C. (3d) 11 (Ont.C.A.).

a man named Nick Biuk, whom the accused had known as a casual friend for three years. Bothered by the prospect that his wife was seeing another man, he made inquires and was eventually satisfied that she was not involved with Biuk. His wife later told him she was involved with a man named Dan Roach whom she had known many years before and that the relationship was casual. The accused believed that the relationship was more serious than his wife let on and became convinced that his wife was continually lying to him about her relationship with Roach. On the day of the shooting, April 21, the accused, who had weekend custody of his two children, arranged to drop them off at his brother-in-law's house. While there, he saw his wife and asked her to stop seeing Roach and she said she could not do that. At trial, his brother-in-law testified that the accused then stated, "I guess I know what I am going to do. I am going to kill Dan [Roach] and Dianne [his wife]".[16] As he was leaving his brother-in-law's house, he noticed Biuk and Roach arrive and go into the house. Meiler drove home and returned with a shotgun he had cut down to size. On arriving at the house he accidentally crashed into the back of his wife's car, which was parked in the driveway. He exited his car, cocked the gun, which was loaded, and put his finger on the trigger. Very shortly afterward the gun discharged and Biuk, who was standing nearby, was fatally shot.

The trial judge had instructed the jury that it could convict the accused on the basis of section 229(c) if it found that the accused, with an unlawful object, did anything knowing it was likely to case someone's death. In his charge to the jury, the trial judge stated that Meiler would be guilty of murder under section 229(c) if the jury found that he:

a) for an unlawful object (killing Roach or his wife);
b) did anything (carrying a loaded, cocked gun with his finger on the trigger);
c) that he knew was likely to cause the death of a human being;
d) caused the death of Biuk;
e) whether or not the gun was accidentally discharged.[17]

The Ontario Court of Appeal confirmed Meiler's conviction in 1999 and pointed out that the case law made it clear that section 229(c) may apply to circumstances in which there had been an unintentional killing. The court stated that section 229(c) does not require an accused to foresee the precise situation or all of the events that result in death. The court found that it was sufficient foresight that the acts done for the unlawful object were likely to cause death, and those acts were sufficiently linked to the death to have caused death within the meaning of the section. The ordinary meaning of the section required nothing more.[18]

It should be noted that some legal scholars feel that the Meiler case resurrects a type of constructive murder the Supreme Court found unconstitutional (see below for the discussion on constructive murder). "Any resort to section 229(c) will also unfortunately return the law of murder to former

16 Ibid. at page 16.
17 Ibid. at page 22.
18 Ibid. at page 26.

common law complexities of trying to identify an unlawful objective distinct from the immediate object accompanying the act of killing.[19]

b. Section 230 and the Constructive Murder Rule

Under this section, culpable homicide is murder where a person causes a person's death whether or not the person knew death was likely and whether or not he or she intended to cause death. This section only applies where the death is caused while one of the offences listed in the section is being attempted or committed. The offences listed in s.230 include serious crimes, such as assaulting a peace officer, sexual assault, kidnapping, robbery, and breaking and entering.

The effect of s.230 is that a person can be found guilty of murder even though the person caused the death accidentally. These offences of murder are referred to as "constructive murder" because actual intent to cause death is not required. A series of Supreme Court decisions have found the constructive murder rule unconstitutional. Although parts of the section still appear in the Code, it is not enforceable. Even though the section is no longer in effect, it is worth looking at the legal reasoning used by the Supreme Court of Canada in finding the section invalid, because the Court used general principles applicable to other offences in the Code.

Legal scholars had long criticized s.230 because it was possible to be convicted of the most serious offence, murder, when there was no intention to cause death. This argument was highlighted in *R. v. Rowe*,[20] in which the accused was found guilty of murder when his gun accidentally went off during a robbery. The bullets went through a door, killing a person who was hiding behind it. The Supreme Court of Canada upheld the validity of the constructive murder law. Rowe was executed, since at the time (1951) Canada still had the death penalty. With the enactment of the Charter, the Court was given the opportunity to re-examine this law.

The first cases under the Charter to challenge the law were *R. v. Vaillancourt*,[21] and *R. v. Laviolette*.[22] The section challenged was s.230(d). Note that this section was repealed in 1991.

> **230. Culpable homicide is murder where a person causes the death of a human being while committing or attempting to commit [listed offences] whether or not the person means to cause death to any human being and whether or not he knows that death is likely to be caused to any human being, if . . .**
>
> **(d) he uses a weapon or has it upon his person**
>
> **(i) during or at the time he commits or attempts to commit the offence, or**

19　D. Stuart, Canadian Criminal Law, 4th ed. (Toronto: Carswell, 2001 at page 199. See also R.J. Delise, "Unlawful Object Murder is Alive and Well" (1995), 25 C.R. (5th) 179.
20　(1951), 100 C.C.C. 97; 12 C.R. 148 (S.C.C.).
21　(1987), 39 C.C.C. (3d) 118 (S.C.C.).
22　(1987), 38 C.C.C. (3d) 476 (S.C.C.).

(ii) during or at the time of his flight after committing or attempting to commit the offence , and death ensues as a consequence.

Section 230(d) provided the widest circumstances in which culpable homicide could be murder. Under it, a person who accidentally caused a death could be convicted of murder if the other elements of the offence were present. In effect, murder under s.230(d) was an absolute liability offence.

In *Vaillancourt,* the accused was charged with murder after his accomplice in a robbery shot and killed a bystander. Vaillancourt was charged with murder because of s.21(2), which made him a party to the offence. He testified that he and the accomplice had planned to use knives for the robbery. When the accomplice showed up with a gun, Vaillancourt asked him to take out the bullets before the robbery. In fact, three bullets were found in the accomplice's glove by the police at the scene of the crime. *Laviolette* also involved the combined operation of s.21(2) and s.230(d). The accused took part in a break and enter. The owner was beaten to death by one of the accused's accomplices.

The Supreme Court of Canada held in both these cases that s.230(d) violated the Charter's guarantees of fundamental justice and the presumption of innocence. The Court found the violation of fundamental justice on two grounds. First, the Court held that for a serious offence, the *mens rea* must reflect the nature of the particular crime. For example, theft requires proof of a mental element of dishonesty. The Court said that murder is distinguished from manslaughter by the type of *mens rea* required (i.e., intention instead of recklessness). However, murder under s.230(d) does not require any type of intention. Second, the Court stated that the mens rea required for an offence must reflect the stigma and sentence attached to the crime. Convicting a person of the serious crime of murder—the penalty for which is life imprisonment—when the person did not subjectively or objectively intend to cause death, offends the Charter. For these two reasons alone the section is unenforceable.

The Court went on to consider whether the section violates the presumption of innocence. This presumption requires that all elements of an offence be proved against an accused before a finding of guilty is made. When an accused can be found guilty of murder without proof of even objective foreseeability, the presumption of innocence is violated. Furthermore, s.1 of the Charter cannot save this section.

Since it was not necessary for the decision, the Court did not rule on whether objective foreseeability was sufficient for murder. However, the judgment did strongly suggest that subjective foreseeability was required.

A few years later, the Court was again asked to consider the requirement of *mens rea* for murder. In question this time was s.230(a):

(a) he means to cause bodily harm for the purpose of

(i) facilitating the commission of the offence, or

(ii) facilitating his flight after committing or attempting to commit the offence,

and death ensues from the bodily harm; . . .

The Court issued concurrent judgements in five cases.[23] In brief, the Court held that the offence of murder requires subjective foreseeability. The decisions repeated the statements in *Vaillancourt* and *Laviolette* that it is a principle of fundamental justice that the punishment for an offence must be in proportion to the seriousness of the offence. Murder is the most serious peacetime crime; therefore, the charge of murder must be reserved for those who either intend to cause death or intend to cause bodily harm that they know will likely cause death. Strictly speaking, the decision of the Court only concerned s.230(a). However, given the strong statement from the Court that murder requires subjective intent, it appeared that the entire section was invalid. This was confirmed a year later, when the Court was asked to consider s.230(c), under which murder is committed if a person:

(c) . . . wilfully stops, by any means, the breath of a human being for a purpose mentioned in paragraph (a), and the death ensues therefrom.

In *R. v. Sit,*[24] the accused was charged with murder under this section for causing death to a victim during an attempted kidnapping. The Court confirmed its previous decisions and held that murder requires subjective foreseeability.

c. Attempted Murder

Attempted crimes were discussed in Chapter Three. Recall that s.24(1) creates the offence of attempting to commit an offence. Murder is the sole offence where there is a specific offence for an attempt.

239. Everyone who attempts by any means to commit murder is guilty of an indictable offence and liable

(a) where a firearm is used in the commission of an offence, to imprisonment for life and to a minimum punishment of imprisonment for a term of four years; and

(b) in any other case to imprisonment for life.

The purpose of s.239 is to create a higher maximum penalty than for other attempts. Section 463(a) provides that unless otherwise provided by law, the maximum term of imprisonment for an attempted offence for which the offence is punishable by life imprisonment is 14 years' imprisonment. With s.239, the maximum penalty for attempted murder is life imprisonment. The 1995 gun control legislation has added a minimum penalty of four years' imprisonment when a firearm is used.

---

23   *R. v. Martineau,* supra, note 14; *R. v. Luxton* (1990), 58 C.C.C. (3d) 449 (S.C.C.); *R. v. Rodney* (1990), 58 C.C.C. (3d) 408 (S.C.C.); *R. v. Arkell* (1990), 59 C.C.C. (3d) 65 (S.C.C.); *R. v. Logan and Johnson* (1990), 58 C.C.C. (3d) 391 (S.C.C.).
24   (1991), 66 C.C.C. (3d) 449 (S.C.C.).

As with other attempted crimes, (see Chapter Three), the *mens rea* for attempted murder is the same as that required for the completed offence of murder.

d. Accessory After the Fact

When the offence is murder, there is also a distinct offence of being an accessory after the fact:

> **240. Every one who is an accessory after the fact to murder is guilty of an indictable offence and liable to imprisonment for life.**

This section, like the attempted murder section, creates a separate offence for the purpose of setting a higher penalty than provided for under s.463 for other offences of being an accessory.

e. Classification of Murder for Sentencing

In 1976, legislation was enacted by Parliament to abolish capital punishment (the death penalty). Before this legislation was brought into effect, murder was punishable either by death or by life imprisonment. Generally, at the time the law was repealed, the only murder cases punishable by death were those in which a police officer, prison guard, or other similar person was killed in the course of duty.

Murder is now classified under s.231 as either first degree or second-degree murder. First-degree murder is planned and deliberate. Murder is also first degree even if not planned and deliberate where the victim is a police officer, prison guard, or person working in a prison or other similar person acting in the course of duty. It is also first-degree murder, whether planned and deliberate or not, to cause a person's death while committing or attempting to commit the following offences: s.76(l) (hijacking aircraft), s.271 (sexual assault), s.272 (sexual assault with a weapon), s.273 (aggravated sexual assault), s.279 (kidnapping and forcible confinement), and s.279.1 (hostage taking). All murder that is not first degree is second degree.

(I) MEANING OF "PLANNED AND DELIBERATE"

Section 231 does not create a substantive offence; its purpose is to determine the punishment for a person who has committed murder. Therefore, before it can be considered whether the death was planned and deliberate, the Crown must prove beyond a reasonable doubt that the accused is guilty of murder.[25]

Having proved the murder, the Crown must then prove that the murder was both planned and deliberate. The terms "planned" and "deliberate" mean different things. It is possible for a murder to be planned but not deliberate. For example, a man might make plans over a period of days to kill his wife but at the moment of the actual killing be acting impulsively and not deliberately. "Planned" refers to a calculated scheme or design that has been

---

25 *R. v. Mitchell* (1965), 1 C.C.C. 155 (S.C.C.) and *R. v. Droste,* supra, note 11.

carefully thought out. The term "deliberate" as used in the Code means more than intentional; it is closer in meaning to "considered, not impulsive."[26] One judge has stated that "deliberation proceeds from the will enlightened by an intelligence which has had time to reflect upon the nature and the quality of the incriminating act."[27] In considering whether a murder was planned and deliberate, the jury is concerned with the accused's "mental processes." It should consider the accused's actions, conduct, statements, and capacity to plan and deliberate.[28]

The Supreme Court of Canada established in *R. v. Nygaard*[29] that it is not necessary for the planning and deliberation to be for causing death. It is possible for "planned and deliberate" to apply to a murder under s.229(a)(ii). In other words, a person can plan and deliberately cause such harm that he or she knows is likely to cause death.

In *R. v. Wallin*,[30] the Supreme Court of Canada considered the issue of the effect of intoxication on the ability to plan and deliberate. The accused was charged with murdering his wife. The accused and his wife had separated. He believed that his wife was having an affair with her employer. On the day of the killing the accused had taken tranquillizers and consumed a large amount of alcohol. He went to his wife's office armed with two guns. He shot his wife and then fired several shots at her employer. The issue on appeal to the Court was whether the trial judge had given proper instructions to the jury on the different effects of intoxication on the intent to kill and on the intent needed for planning and deliberation. The Court stated that the jury must first consider the effect of intoxication on the intent to cause death (murder). If the jury finds that there was sufficient intent for the offence of murder, it must then consider whether the murder was first degree or second degree. At this point, the jury would look at how the intoxication affected the accused's ability to plan and deliberate. The Court stated that it is also essential that the trial judge tell the jury that a lesser degree of intoxication is needed to negate the intent for planning and deliberation than to negate the intent for committing the murder. A person may be intoxicated but still have the intent to kill, even while the intoxication may prevent that person from being able to plan and deliberate. Since first-degree murder is the most serious offence in the Code in terms of penalty, it is important that the jury be clearly instructed on the difference between intent for planning and deliberation and intent to cause death. In this case, the trial judge differentiated the two intents but may have misled the jury regarding the different levels of intoxication required to negate the two intents.

(II) PUNISHMENT FOR FIRST- AND SECOND-DEGREE MURDER

There are special sections of the Code that deal with the penalties for murder. Under s.235 both first- and second-degree murder are punishable by a

---

26 *More v. R.* (1963), 3 C.C.C. 289 (S.C.C.).
27 *Pilon v. R.* (1966), 2 C.C.C. 53 (Que.C.A.).
28 *R. v. Mitchell,* supra, note 25.
29 (1989), 51 C.C.C. (3d) 417 (S.C.C.).
30 (1990), 54 C.C.C. (3d) 383 (S.C.C.).

minimum of life imprisonment. The difference between the two offences with regard to punishment concerns eligibility for parole. Under s.745 a person convicted of first-degree murder cannot be paroled until he or she has served 25 years of the sentence. A person who has been convicted of second-degree murder may be eligible for parole after serving at least 10 years, but no more than 25 years. The trial judge usually sets the number of years to be served before parole eligibility. However, if the person convicted of second-degree murder has a previous conviction for murder, the period to be served before parole eligibility is 25 years.

Under s.745.6, a person who has been convicted of first- or second-degree murder and has served at least 15 years of the sentence can apply to have his or her case reviewed for the purpose of reducing the years to be served before eligibility for parole. The application is considered by a judge and jury. They will look at such factors as the character of the applicant, the conduct of the applicant while serving the sentence, the nature of the offence, and any other factors that the judge believes are relevant. After hearing the evidence, the jury may order that a lesser number of years of imprisonment without eligibility for parole be served, or that the person's ineligibility for parole be terminated.

When the jury does not order a change in eligibility for parole, it must set another time when an application for reduction can be made.

When the jury makes an order that reduces the period for parole eligibility, the applicant must still apply to the federal parole board for parole. It is possible that a person could successfully have the period of eligibility for parole reduced but still be turned down by the parole board. A person who is given a life sentence and then released on parole is not totally free: the person will remain on parole for the rest of his or her life. This involves, among other things, reporting to parole officers as required.

2. Manslaughter

The common law defined murder as unlawful killing with malice aforethought, and manslaughter as unlawful killing without malice aforethought. Today manslaughter is still defined in relation to murder:

> **234. Culpable homicide that is not murder or infanticide is manslaughter.**

The effect of this section is that once a homicide is found to be culpable, the next step is determining whether it is murder or infanticide; if the culpable homicide is neither, then the offence is manslaughter. It is not uncommon, where a person has been charged with murder, for a jury to be instructed that it may bring in a verdict of guilty of manslaughter where it finds that the killing has been unlawful but that the Crown has failed to prove beyond a reasonable doubt the additional element needed for murder. Similarly, when an accused appeals his or her conviction for murder, the appeal court may substitute a verdict of guilty of manslaughter.

Section 236 sets out the penalty for manslaughter:

236. Every person who commits manslaughter is guilty of an indictable offence and liable

(a) where a firearm is used in the commission of the offence, to imprisonment for life and to a minimum punishment of imprisonment for a term of four years; and

(b) in any other case, to imprisonment for life.

a. By an Unlawful Act or Criminal Negligence

Manslaughter most often arises where the death is caused by means of an unlawful act or by criminal negligence.[31]

Unlawful act manslaughter has been the subject of several recent Supreme Court of Canada decisions. The key issue in all of these cases concerned the *mens rea* requirement for this offence. These cases were first discussed in Chapter Three. After the Supreme Court decisions which held that murder requires subjective intent, some legal scholars believed that the Court might come out with a decision requiring all true criminal offences to have subjective intent. This has not happened. In fact, as pointed out in Chapter Three, it appears that only a few offences are required under the Constitution to have subjective *mens rea*. The key cases that settled this issue involved unlawful act manslaughter.

In *R. v. Creighton*,[32] the accused was a drug user who had injected a woman with cocaine. She died from a drug overdose. The Supreme Court held that Creighton had committed manslaughter, in that he had committed an unlawful act that was dangerous and that a reasonable person would have known subjected the victim to a risk of harm that was not trivial or transitory. The Court rejected the argument that the standard should be foreseeability of death, and upheld the lower standard of foreseeability of harm.

The Court stated the test for finding unlawful act manslaughter. First, there must be an unlawful act (which is sometimes called the "predicate offence"). The unlawful act must be dangerous and cause the death. Second, the accused must have the *mens rea* required for the unlawful act. Third, the unlawful act must be a federal or provincial offence and cannot be an absolute liability offence. Fourth, the mens rea for causing the death is objective foreseeability of bodily harm that is neither trivial nor transitory in nature.

Manslaughter may also arise through criminal negligence. In many situations, a person could be convicted of manslaughter based either on an unlawful act or on criminal negligence. For example, in *R. v. Mack*,[33] three men, including the deceased, and the accused were sitting in a mobile home. Each of the men had taken heroin that evening. While still feeling the effects of the drug, the accused found a gun in the bedroom and took it to the

---

31 The offence of manslaughter by criminal negligence overlaps with the offence of causing death by criminal negligence, and either can be charged in a given situation. The offence of causing death by criminal negligence is discussed in detail in Chapter Ten.
32 *Supra*, note 7.
33 (1975), 22 C.C.C. (2d) 257; 29 C.R.N.S. 270 (Alta.C.A.).

kitchen table to examine it. Although he claimed that he did not remember pointing the gun at anyone, at some point in the evening he fired three shots, striking the deceased twice and the other man once. The court held that a jury could find the accused guilty of manslaughter if its members believed beyond a reasonable doubt either that the accused committed the unlawful act of pointing the gun at the deceased or that the accused was criminally negligent in the manner in which he handled the gun.

b. Murder Reduced to Manslaughter

A person who has been charged with murder may be convicted of manslaughter instead by successfully raising either intoxication or provocation as a defence.

(I) INTOXICATION

The defence of intoxication was discussed in detail in Chapter Four. Since murder requires specific intent, an accused can raise the defence of intoxication to reduce the charge to manslaughter. Where the Crown proves that the accused unlawfully caused a death but cannot prove that the accused had the specific intent for the offence of murder, the accused can be convicted of the lesser included offence of manslaughter.

(II) PROVOCATION

The defence of provocation can be used only for the offence of murder. If provocation is proved, the accused will be found guilty of the less serious offence of manslaughter. Section 232 of the Criminal Code provides:

> **232. (1) Culpable homicide that otherwise would be murder may be reduced to manslaughter if the person who committed it did so in the heat of passion caused by sudden provocation.**
>
> **(2) A wrongful act or insult that is of such a nature as to be sufficient to deprive an ordinary person of the power of self-control is provocation for the purposes of this section if the accused acted on it on the sudden and before there was time for his passion to cool.**
>
> **(3) For the purposes of this section, the questions**
>
> **(a) whether a particular wrongful act or insult amounted to provocation, and**
>
> **(b) whether the accused was deprived of the power of self-control by the provocation that he alleges he received,**
>
> **are questions of fact, but no one shall be deemed to have given provocation to another by doing anything that he had a legal right to do, or by doing anything that the accused incited him to do in order to provide the accused with an excuse for causing death or bodily harm to any human being.**

Provocation, as defined in s.232, consists of these elements:

- a wrongful act or insult . . .
- sufficient to deprive an ordinary person of the power of self-control . . .
- that actually provoked the offender, who acted in response to it . . .
- on the sudden, before there was time for his or her passion to cool.

These four elements are used to form the two tests for determining whether provocation existed. The accused must satisfy both tests before a defence of provocation will be successful.

"Wrongful Act or Insult." The first test is whether the wrongful act or insult was of a nature sufficient to deprive an ordinary person of self-control. This is the objective test. The test is not whether the wrongful act or insult deprived the accused of self-control, but whether it was sufficient to deprive any ordinary person of the power of self-control. In *R. v. Carpenter*,[34] the Ontario Court of Appeal clarified this test by stating that the question is not whether an ordinary person would have acted as the accused did, but only whether an ordinary person would have lost control.

A common or casual verbal insult, or act, will not be considered provocation. An "ordinary" person has a normal temperament and level of self-control. In *R. v. Young*,[35] the accused stabbed his girlfriend to death. They had been living together when she told him that their relationship was over. The stabbing took place after they had been arguing for several hours about their separation. The Nova Scotia Court of Appeal held that terminating a relationship is not a wrongful act or insult that is of such a nature as to deprive a person of self-control.

If there are particular characteristics of the accused, such as age, sex, or race, that are relevant to the provocation, they can be ascribed to the ordinary person. For example, if the provocation consists of a racial slur, the jury can think of an ordinary person with that racial background. The Supreme Court of Canada has recently expanded the range of characteristics that can be considered. In *R. v. Thibert*,[36] the accused shot a man who had been having an affair with his wife. The victim and accused met in a parking lot, where the victim held the accused's wife in front of him and, while moving her back and forth, taunted the accused with, "Go ahead and shoot me, big fellow." The Court held that the background and history of the relationship between the victim and the accused can be considered in determining whether an ordinary person would have been deprived of self-control. The Court overturned the accused's conviction and ordered a new trial.

Upon the Sudden. An accused who meets the first test for provocation must still satisfy the second. This second test—the subjective test—is that the accused must have acted upon the sudden and before his or her passion had time to cool. In other words, the accused must have reacted almost instantaneously after the insult. So, for example, where the accused had been insulted

---

34 (1993), 83 C.C.C. (3d) 193 (Ont.C.A.).
35 (1993), 78 C.C.C. (3d) 538 (N.S.C.A.).
36 (1996), 104 C.C.C. (3d) 1 (S.C.C.).

but had waited four or five minutes before shooting the victim, the defence of provocation was not available.[37] In *R. v. Young*,[38] discussed above, the argument between the accused and his girlfriend was interrupted when they left the apartment they shared. He went to his mother's house, and she went with a girlfriend to her apartment. They all met back at the apartment when the accused came back for his medicine and the victim and her friend came back for a bottle of juice. The accused, the victim, and her friend then left the apartment again. They were on the stairs outside the apartment when he stabbed her to death. The court noted that the accused had been hearing that the relationship was over for more than four hours with only one interruption—when everyone left the apartment for the first time. The shock value of anything she might have said would have worn off by then. The court concluded that there was no evidence to suggest that the accused had acted in the heat of passion or on the sudden.

3. Infanticide and Offences Concerning Childbirth

a. Infanticide

> **233. A female person commits infanticide when by a wilful act or omission she causes the death of her newly-born child, if at the time of the act or omission she is not fully recovered from the effects of giving birth to the child and by reason thereof or of the effect of lactation consequent on the birth of the child her mind is then disturbed . . .**
>
> **239. Every female person who commits infanticide is guilty of an indictable offence and liable to imprisonment for a term not exceeding five years.**

Section 2 of the Code defines "newly-born child" as a person under the age of one year.

As mentioned earlier, this offence is rarely used. It was first introduced into the law of Canada in 1948. It is based on the reasoning that a woman may be mentally disturbed from the effects of giving birth or of lactation and thus be less responsible for her actions. In this situation, the law mitigates the severity of punishment for what would otherwise be murder or manslaughter.

In *R. v. Marchello*,[39] the judge listed the elements of the offence that the Crown would have to prove:

- The accused must be a woman.
- She must have caused the death of a child.
- The child must have been "newly born."
- The child must have been the child of the accused.

---

37 *R. v. Olbey* (1979), 50 C.C.C. (2d) 257 (S.C.C.).
38 Supra, note 35.
39 (1951), 100 C.C.C. 137; 12 C.R. 7 (Ont.H.C.).

- The death must have been caused by a wilful act or omission of the accused.
- At the time of the wilful act or omission, the accused must not have fully recovered from the effect of giving birth to the child.
- By reason of giving birth to the child, the accused's balance of mind must have been disturbed.

Since *Marchello*, s.663 has been added to the Code, which states:

> **663. Where a female person is charged with infanticide and the evidence establishes that she caused the death of her child but does not establish that, at the time of the act or omission by which she caused the death of the child,**
>
> **(a) she was not fully recovered from the effects of giving birth to the child or from the effect of lactation consequent on the birth of the child, and**
>
> **(b) the balance of her mind was, at that time, disturbed by reason of the effect of giving birth to the child or of the effect of lactation consequent on the birth of the child,**
>
> **she may be convicted unless the evidence establishes that the act or omission was not wilful.**

The purpose of s.663 is to avoid the problems that arise where the Crown is able to prove all the elements of the offence except those concerning the woman's mental state or where the accused raises as her defence that she was fully recovered or that her mind was not disturbed. The result would be that she would be entitled to be acquitted of infanticide and could not be charged later with murder or manslaughter, since an accused cannot be tried twice for the same homicide.

b. Neglect and Concealing

Two offences somewhat related to infanticide are neglect to obtain assistance in childbirth and concealing the body of a child. They are set out in the Code as follows:

> **242. A female person who, being pregnant and about to be delivered, with intent that the child shall not live or with intent to conceal the birth of the child, fails to make provision for reasonable assistance in respect of her delivery is, if the child is permanently injured as a result thereof or dies immediately before, during or in a short time after birth, as a result thereof, guilty of an indictable offence and is liable to imprisonment for a term not exceeding five years.**
>
> **243. Every one who in any manner disposes of the dead body of a child, with intent to conceal the fact that its mother has been delivered of it, whether the child died before, during or after birth, is guilty of an indictable offence and liable to imprisonment for a term not exceeding two years.**

Neither of these offences is used very often today. They seem to be left over from a time when there was greater stigma attached to bearing a child outside of marriage.

c. Causing Death in the Act of Birth

Section 238 covers certain situations where the child dies before becoming a human being:

> **238. (1) Every one who causes the death, in the act of birth, of any child that has not become a human being, in such a manner that, if the child were a human being, he would be guilty of murder, is guilty of an indictable offence and liable to imprisonment for life.**
>
> **(2) This section does not apply to a person who, by means that, in good faith, he considers necessary to preserve the life of the mother of a child, causes the death of that child.**

Under s.238, it is essential that the death of the child occur during the act of birth, and in such a way that it would be murder if the child had been a human being (as defined in the Code). This means that the causing of the death must fall within either s.229 or s.230. The exception provided in s.238(2) is to allow for situations where it is necessary to cause the death of the unborn child to save the mother.

Questions for Review and Discussion

1. What are the two tests of causation used by the courts?
2. Would the law say that a person who through hypnosis convinced someone to commit suicide caused that person's death?
3. How does the Code define "human being"?
4. Is it homicide to cause the death of a child before it is born? What if the injury is caused before the child is born but the child does not die until after its birth?
5. Alice shoots and wounds Blake. Blake's religion forbids him to have blood transfusions. Blake dies from the wound, although he would probably have survived if he had allowed a transfusion. Has Alice caused Blake's death? Which Code section is relevant?
6. If a person assaults another person and the assaulted person bleeds to death because he suffers from hemophilia, has the person who inflicted the injury caused the death?
7. What is the difference between culpable and non-culpable homicide?
8. When may a homicide be justified? When may it be excused? Make up some examples of justifiable and excusable homicide.
9. List the ways of committing culpable homicide.
10. What questions would a judge ask to decide whether an act is unlawful for the purpose of s.222(5)?

11. Would the following acts be unlawful under s.222(5)? What other information do you need?
    a. Failure of a person to file his income tax return by the deadline.
    b. Failure of a person to provide necessaries of life for his children.
    c. Failure of a person to have his pet dog vaccinated for rabies.
    d. Driving through a stop sign.

12. Why does the Code state that a person has not committed culpable homicide where the death has been caused by influence on the mind alone unless the deceased is a child or sick person? Do you agree with the law on this point? Why does the law make an exception in the case of children and sick persons?

13. Answer these questions about the offences of murder under s.229:
    a. Which subsection deals with "transferred intent," and what does this phrase mean?
    b. Which subsection sets out the simplest form of murder?
    c. Which subsection uses an "objective test," and what does this mean?
    d. What has happened to the subsection that allows objective intent?

14. Discuss the basic elements of murder under s.230. Do you agree with the Supreme Court of Canada's decisions on the validity of s.230?

15. What are the differences between first- and second-degree murder?

16. How have courts interpreted the words "planned and deliberate" as used in the Code?

17. **a.** How did the common law distinguish manslaughter from murder?
    b. How is manslaughter defined today?

18. How does manslaughter most often arise?

19. In what circumstances may a charge of murder be reduced to manslaughter?

20. Why is infanticide a difficult offence to prove?

21. Brown had been drinking in a tavern for most of the evening with Schmidt. At closing time he agreed to drive Schmidt home. However, he first drove to an empty field for the ostensible purpose of drinking some beer. While there, Brown savagely beat Schmidt, inflicting many minor injuries and several facial wounds, not mortal in themselves. Schmidt was abandoned in the field, where he died after some extended but uncertain time. The doctor who performed the autopsy stated that in his opinion the deceased died from loss of blood through the facial wounds, but that the injuries would not have caused death if they had received attention. He said that he did not think death was caused by pneumonia resulting from exposure to the cold night air, but he could not exclude that possibility.
    a. Has Brown caused Schmidt's death? Does it make any difference whether the death resulted from loss of blood or pneumonia?
    b. Does the fact that Brown had been drinking all evening give him any special defence? Explain. See *R. v. Popoff* (1959), 125 C.C.C. 116 (B.C.C.A.).

22. John Silvers had lost his job and was deeply in debt. He decided that the only answer to his problems was to commit suicide. He purchased a gun and went home to shoot himself. Just as he put the gun to his head, his wife walked into the room and, realizing what John was attempting, grabbed his arm to push the gun away from his head. The gun fired and Mrs. Silvers was fatally shot in the heart.

    With what offence, if any, should John be charged? What will the Crown have to prove? See *R. v. Hopwood* (1913), 8 Cr. App. R 143, and *Wexter v. R.* (1939), 72 C.C.C. 1 (S.C.C.).

23. Jane, aged 14, was walking home from school one day when a car pulled beside her. A man, John Doe, rolled down the window and asked Jane for directions to a certain street. When she stopped to answer him, Doe pointed a gun at her and told her to get in the car. Jane, very frightened, obeyed him. Doe drove to a highway and started heading out of town. As the car approached an intersection and slowed down to make a turn, Jane opened the door and jumped out. She hit her head on a rock and died almost instantly. Has Doe caused Jane's death? If yes, with what offence can he be charged? Explain. See *R. v. Valade* (1915), 26 C.C.C. 233 (Que.C.A.).

24. Bertrand and Annie were deeply in love. Annie's young daughter would not accept Bertrand, and Annie grew despondent about her relationship with Bertrand. She began to discuss committing suicide. Bertrand could not accept the thought of going on without Annie, so he planned to die with her. Annie lay on top of Bertrand. He held a gun in such a way that a single bullet would go through both of them. The shot was fatal to Annie and seriously wounded Bertrand. He was charged with murder. What argument would you make on his behalf? Note: It is not illegal to commit suicide, but it is illegal to assist someone to commit suicide. See *R. v. Gagnon* (1993), 84 C.C.C. (3d) 143 (Que.C.A.).

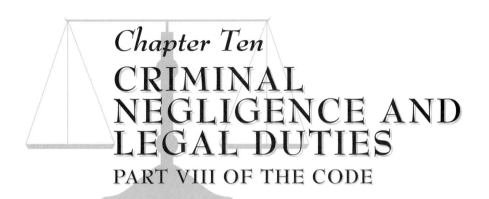

Chapter Ten
CRIMINAL NEGLIGENCE AND LEGAL DUTIES
PART VIII OF THE CODE

A. INTRODUCTION

Part VIII of the Criminal Code contains the offences of criminal negligence and sets out some of the situations where the law imposes a duty to act.

There are two offences of criminal negligence in Part VIII: criminal negligence causing death, and criminal negligence causing bodily harm. Criminal negligence doesn't involve a specific act or omission. It can arise in the doing of any act or in the omitting to do any legal duty, including those discussed in this chapter.

B. CRIMINAL NEGLIGENCE

219 (1) Every one is criminally negligent who

(a) in doing anything, or

(b) in omitting to do anything that it is his duty to do,

shows wanton or reckless disregard for the lives or safety of other persons.

(2) For the purpose of this section, "duty" means a duty imposed by law.

Section 219 of the Code defines criminal negligence. Notice that it does not refer to a specific type of conduct: any act that shows wanton or reckless disregard for the lives or safety of other persons may be a criminally negligent act. Similarly, any omission, or failure to act, where there is a legal duty to act, may be criminally negligent if the omission shows wanton or reckless disregard for the lives and safety of others.

"Duty" is defined as a duty imposed by law. Duties include not only those specified in the Code or other statutes but also those imposed by the common law. For example, under the common law, a person carrying a dangerous weapon, such as a rifle, is under a duty to take proper precautions.[1] An example of a duty imposed by the Code is found in s.263(1), which states that a person who makes an opening in ice that is open to or frequented by the public is under a duty to guard that opening in a manner adequate to prevent accidents.

1. Criminal Negligence Distinguished from Civil Negligence

It is important to distinguish criminal negligence from civil negligence. Generally speaking, the civil law imposes on all persons a duty to act in a manner that does not cause harm to other persons or their property. A person who breaches a duty to take care, and as a result causes harm unintentionally but carelessly, may be found negligent by a civil court and ordered to make compensation to the injured person.[2] A person is civilly negligent who fails to meet the standards of a reasonable person. This is an objective standard or test.

Criminal negligence involves a greater degree of misconduct than civil negligence. All human beings occasionally fail to meet the standard of the reasonable person. When a failure results in a loss to another person, usually the wrongdoer is not punished but is required to compensate the victim for the loss. However, at some point the conduct is such a departure from what society expects that the wrongdoer becomes guilty not only of civil negligence but also of a criminal offence, and liable to punishment. As discussed in previous chapters, our courts have had difficulty in recent years determining where this point lies.[3] The issue concerns the fault element or *mens rea* for criminal offences. As described in Chapter Three, subjective fault is not required for all criminal offences.[4] This holding by the Supreme Court has left the issue of determining the *mens rea* for specific offences open to discussion and legal challenge.

2. Determining the *Mens Rea* for the Offences of Criminal Negligence

As with other offences, the debate is over the issue of whether a subjective or an objective standard should be used to judge a person's mental state. Section 219 defines the *mens rea* for criminal negligence as "wanton and reckless disregard for the lives and safety of others." A subjective standard asks whether the accused knew that the conduct was reckless and wanton, or

---

1   *R. v. Coyne* (1958), 124 C.C.C. 176 (N.B.C.A.).
2   See Chapter Two, pages 15 and 16 for a discussion of some of the differences between criminal and civil law.
3   See Chapter Three at page 46 for a discussion of *mens rea* and penal negligence.
4   Ibid.

turned a blind eye to conduct that was reckless and wanton. An objective standard asks whether a reasonable person would know that the conduct was reckless and wanton.

In 1960, the Supreme Court of Canada, in *O'Grady v. Sparling,*[5] stated that the test for criminal negligence is subjective—that it must be proved that the accused adverted to (actually realized) the risk. In spite of the principle of *stare decisis,* lower courts had difficulty following this decision. Most court decisions after *O'Grady* used a test of gross negligence (conduct that is a marked departure) for a finding of criminal negligence. The position taken by the courts can probably best be understood by considering the kinds of situations often encountered in cases of criminal negligence. Automobile and hunting accidents form a large proportion of these cases. The courts were, perhaps, recognizing that the misuse of guns and cars can result in great suffering, and that society expects persons who cause damage through the careless, even though thoughtless, use of these instruments to be punished. For example, the person who has had one drink too many and ends up driving on the wrong side of the road, and causing a major accident, may not have "adverted to" or thought about the dangerous nature of that conduct. However, courts have found it difficult not to condemn such actions through the use of criminal penalties.

In *R. v. Tutton* and *R. v. Waite,* the Supreme Court of Canada again reviewed the *mens rea* required for criminal negligence. Unfortunately, the Court was unable to agree on the test for criminal negligence. The first decision released was *Tutton.*[6] The accused were Carol and Arthur Tutton, parents of a child who had died. The parents belonged to a religious group that believed in faith healing. Their child was diagnosed as having diabetes. The mother received instruction on how to treat the child's condition. However, both parents believed that the child would be cured through faith. At one point the parents stopped administering the insulin the child needed. The child became ill, and they were warned of the importance of continuing the insulin injections. They again stopped giving him the insulin, and he died three days later. The parents were charged with causing the boy's death by criminal negligence in that they had failed in their duty to provide necessary medical treatment. The evidence was that they were loving and responsible parents. Their defence was that they honestly believed that their son had been cured by divine intervention. The Ontario Court of Appeal stated that a subjective test must be used to determine whether the Tuttons had been reckless and wanton. The case was appealed to the Supreme Court and heard by six justices. There were three opinions written in the case. Two justices stated that an objective standard should be used. One justice agreed that an objective standard should be used but added that, when applying an objective norm, "a generous allowance" must be made for factors that are particular to the accused, such as youth, mental development, and education. The other three justices, in one opinion, stated that a subjective test should be used, and re-affirmed the test set out in *O'Grady.*

5   (1960), 128 C.C.C. 1; 33 C.R. 293 (S.C.C.).
6   (1989), 48 C.C.C. (3d) 129 (S.C.C.).

The decision of the two justices who were in favour of the objective test stated:

> *Our concept of criminal culpability relies, primarily upon a consideration of the mental state which accompanies or initiates the wrongful act, and the attribution of criminal liability without proof of such blameworthy mental state raises serious concerns. Nonetheless, negligence has become accepted as a factor which may lead to criminal liability and strong arguments can be made in its favour. Section 202 [now 219] affords an example of its adoption. . . . Negligence connotes the opposite of thought-directed action. In other words, its existence precludes the element of positive intent to achieve a given result . . . What is punished . . . is not a state of mind but the consequences of mindless action. This is apparent . . . from the words of the section which make criminal conduct which shows wanton and reckless disregard . . .*[7]

The two justices added that in applying this standard to the facts of this case, it would be up to the jury to decide whether the Tuttons' belief was reasonable and honest. They would have to consider the whole background of the case, including the experience of the Tuttons with the child's illness, that they had seen the effect of the withdrawal of insulin on one occasion, that they had been informed of the necessity of the insulin, and that Mrs. Tutton had received some formal instruction in providing care for the child. As well, they would have to consider whether the belief in a miraculous cure, although honest, was reasonable.

All six justices did agree that the case had to be tried again because the judges' instructions to the jury were wrong.

In *Waite,*[8] which was released at the same time as *Tutton,* the same judges took the same positions. Waite was found not guilty at trial of four counts of causing death by criminal negligence and one count of causing bodily harm by criminal negligence. The facts were that after drinking several cans of beer, the accused with two friends got in his car and followed a hayride made up of several tractors pulling wagons. The accused passed the hayride, turned his car around, and drove back toward the wagons. There was evidence that he said to his companions, "Let's see how close we can get," or "Let's play chicken." He then drove down the left side of the road, without his headlights on. When he was within 50 metres of the wagons, he swerved to the right to go around the wagons and struck five people who were running alongside the wagons. Four died and one was injured. The trial judge instructed the jury that they needed to use a subjective standard to find Waite guilty of criminal negligence—that is, to find that he deliberately assumed the risk of his conduct. He was found not guilty of criminal negligence but guilty of dangerous driving. The case was appealed to the Ontario Court of Appeal, which disagreed with the trial judge's directions and stated that an objective standard should be used and that the *mens rea* can be objectively determined from the accused's conduct. A new trial was ordered.

---

7   Ibid. at page 139.
8   (1989), 38 C.C.C. (3d) 1 (S.C.C.).

The Supreme Court agreed with the Court of Appeal that a new trial was necessary because of errors in the judge's directions to the jury, but took the same inconclusive positions on whether an objective or a subjective standard should be used.

There are usually a total of nine Supreme Court justices. At the time these cases were heard, two were ill and one had resigned. There has not yet been a decision of the full court on this issue.

An Ontario Court of Appeal decision that came after these decisions stated that, until the Supreme Court of Canada rules otherwise, the law in Ontario is that criminal negligence requires an objective standard—that is, a marked departure from the standard of a reasonable person.[9] A person will be liable if a reasonable person would have been aware of the risks. Presumably, other provinces will also continue to apply the standards that their own appeal courts have set.

Although there has not been another Supreme court decision on the *mens rea* required for criminal negligence, the decisions in *Creighton* and the companion cases make it clear that for criminal offences, an objective standard is permissible under the Charter. In *Creighton*,[10] which involved unlawful act manslaughter, Justice McLachlin, who wrote the majority's decision, refused to make a ruling on the *mens rea* requirement for criminal negligence because it was not necessary in order to decide the case. However, at one point the justice did comment that the *actus reus* for manslaughter by criminal negligence requires a marked departure from the standards of a reasonable person and that the *mens rea* is the objective standard of a reasonable person. Some legal scholars believe that the Supreme Court will eventually rule that criminal negligence requires only a **marked departure test.**[11] If the marked departure test does become the standard for criminal negligence, there will still be some dispute as to how strictly the objective standard should be applied. Recall that another issue in *Creighton* was whether personal factors such as age, education, and psychological condition should be considered in applying the reasonable person standard.[12] The Supreme Court split 5 to 4 on this issue, with the slim majority holding that personal characteristics short of incapacity to understand the risk should not be considered. Some legal scholars believe that this standard is too rigid and predict that lower courts will have trouble enforcing it.[13]

One court of appeal case since *Creighton* that considered the mens rea for criminal negligence and the place of personal characteristics is *R. v. Ubhi*.[14] The accused was the driver of a dump truck loaded with hot asphalt. While Ubhi was driving down a steep incline, the brakes on the truck failed. The truck hit a recreational vehicle and killed two persons. It was discovered that the truck's brakes were faulty and had not been adjusted for quite

---

9   *R. v. Nelson* (1990), 54 C.C.C. (3d) 285 (Ont.C.A.).
10   (1993), 83 C.C.C. (3d) 346 (S.C.C.).
11   D. Stuart, Canadian Criminal Law, 4th ed. (Toronto: Carswell, 2001 at page 255).
12   See Chapter Nine.
13   See *Stuart*, note 11 at page 260.
14   (1994), 27 C.R. 4th 332 (B.C.C.A.); leave to appeal to S.C.C. refused, 31 C.R. (4th) 405.

some time. The trial court held that the standard to be used in a case of criminal negligence is objective and that the driver's conduct in not maintaining the brakes amounted to a marked and substantial departure from the standard of a reasonable person. The accused was convicted. On appeal, new evidence was produced which indicated that the driver had the mental age of a six- or seven-year-old child. The British Columbia Court of Appeal used an objective standard and, relying on Creighton, held that personal characteristics are irrelevant except as they affect capacity. Here the fresh evidence of the accused's mental deficiency did go to the issue of capacity. Had it been admitted, it could have altered the result of the trial, in that a jury might have concluded that the accused lacked the capacity to understand the necessity of ensuring that the brakes of the truck were maintained in proper working order. The court ordered a new trial for the accused.

Compare *Ubhi* with *Canhoto*. In *R. v. Canhoto*,[15] a grandmother believed she could communicate directly with angels and spirits as well as detect evil spirits in people. She also believed that she could expel those spirits through prayer and forcing them to drink water until they vomited. The grandmother believed that her two-year-old granddaughter, Kiera, was possessed by evil spirits and decided to expel the evil spirits from her. She took Kiera into the kitchen and began to pray and force water down her throat. Kiera resisted and a neighbour who was visiting held her legs. Kiera eventually fell silent and was placed onto the kitchen floor where she died. The mother who was also present was charged with manslaughter on the basis of criminally negligent conduct contributing to the death of her daughter. She was convicted and appealed. The appeal was dismissed and the conviction upheld on appeal.

Fault is determined by considering whether the conduct constitutes a marked departure from that expected of a reasonable person and applies to both acts and omissions. Citing *Creighton,* the court stated ". . . criminal negligence is determined by an application of a uniform legal standard of care. In some situations it may be that a failure to act where there is a duty to do so, will not fall below the requisite standards whereas actions which actually create a risk will fall below the standard."[16] In this case the mother's . . . . "liability did not rest solely on her failure to act. . . . [She] participated to some degree in the activity that caused Kira's death. . . . [Her] liability arose out of a course of conduct that included but was not limited to her failure to come to Kira's assistance."[17] The court found that the mother appreciated the risk to her child despite her religious beliefs. Her religious beliefs did not negate her ability to appreciate the risk to the child. Relying on *Creighton*, the court found that it was not a case of incapacity, but a case of subjugating awareness of risk to religious beliefs.

15 (1999), 140 C.C.C. (3d) 321 (Ont.C.A.).
16 Supra, note 15 at 331.
17 Supra, note 15 at 328.

3. The Offences of Criminal Negligence

220. Every person who by criminal negligence causes death to another person is guilty of an indictable offence and liable

(a) where a firearm is used in the commission of the offence, to imprisonment for life and to a minimum punishment of imprisonment for a term of four years; and

(b) in any other case, to imprisonment for life.

221. Every one who by criminal negligence causes bodily harm to another person is guilty of an indictable offence and liable to imprisonment for a term not exceeding ten years.

The Code also provides in s.222(5)(b) that culpable homicide (i.e., homicide that is a criminal offence) can be caused by criminal negligence. In brief, any person who recklessly causes death or bodily harm has committed the offence of criminal negligence. Although many cases of criminal negligence involve the use of cars, any act can give rise to a charge of criminal negligence. The following are a few examples:

In *R. v. Petzoldt*,[18] the accused was an unemployed animal trainer and performer. He owned two chimpanzees, which he kept in the basement of his house. The female chimp was 150 centimetres tall and weighed 91 kilograms. While he was walking her on a busy street, she reached out and grabbed an eight-year-old girl and bit her on the head and shoulder. The animal had demonstrated its aggressive and dangerous character several times before. The animal trainer was found guilty of criminal negligence causing bodily harm. The judge said that since the accused knew the animal was dangerous, in taking it for a walk on a main street he showed wanton and reckless disregard for the safety of others.

In *R. v. Popen*,[19] the accused's wife was convicted of physically abusing their 19-month-old daughter, causing her death. There was no evidence that the accused had abused the child, but he was aware of his wife's actions. The Ontario Court of Appeal held that a parent has a legal duty under the common law to protect his or her child from abuse by the other parent. Therefore, Popen could be properly charged with criminal negligence.

R. v. Rogers[20] involved criminal negligence caused by breach of a duty imposed by s.198. This section states that a person who undertakes to provide medical or surgical treatment is under a duty to have and use reasonable knowledge, skill, and care. Rogers was an unlicensed physician. At the time of the events leading to the charge, he was registered as a naturopathic physician. The practice of naturopathy is defined as the art of healing by natural methods or therapies. Rogers prescribed a low-calorie, low-protein diet for a young child who was suffering from a skin disease. The child followed the diet from April 22 to June 11, at which time his condition became so

---

18 (1973), 11 C.C.C. (2d) 320 (Ont.Co.Ct.).
19 (1981), 60 C.C.C. (2d) 232 (Ont.C.A.).
20 *R. v. Rogers* (1968), 4 C.C.C. 278 (B.C.C.A.), leave to appeal refused [1968] S.C.R. ix (S.C.C.).

severe that he was hospitalized. The day after he entered the hospital, he died. The testimony of medical doctors at Rogers's trial indicated that the child died from gross malnutrition. The appeal court upheld Rogers' conviction for criminal negligence causing death, stating that in judging whether the conduct is wanton or reckless, the court must look at the standards of reasonable people, not the standards of the accused.

In *R. v. Gagnon*,[21] the accused, with three others, was riding in a car travelling at between 95 and 110 kilometres an hour. After the four drank a number of bottles of beer, the accused threw the empty bottles out on the roadside. One bottle smashed against a rock, and its fragments hit and seriously injured a woman sitting nearby. The court considered that the road was heavily travelled at that time of year and that it was well known that many travellers stopped by the wayside to go walking or to sit and rest. The accused, the court found, had thrown the bottles at random with no concern for the consequences of his act. The accused was found guilty of criminal negligence causing bodily harm.

C. DUTIES TENDING TO PRESERVATION OF LIFE

We now discuss sections of the Code that impose certain duties to act. Most criminal offences require active misconduct; in contrast, these sections make it possible for a person to be found guilty of *not* doing something. As discussed earlier, a breach of one of these duties may be the basis for a charge of criminal negligence if the failure to act shows wanton and reckless disregard for the lives and safety of others. The charge can also be brought under the section imposing the duty.

1. Duty of Persons to Provide Necessaries

215. (1) Every one is under a legal duty

(a) as a parent, foster parent, guardian or head of a family, to provide necessaries of life for a child under the age of sixteen years;

(b) to provide necessaries of life to their spouse or common-law partner; and

(c) to provide necessaries of life to a person under his charge if that person

(i) is unable, by reason of detention, age, illness, mental disorder or other cause, to withdraw himself from that charge, and

(ii) is unable to provide himself with necessaries of life.

(2) Every one commits an offence who, being under a legal duty within the meaning of subsection (1), fails without lawful excuse, the proof of which lies on him, to perform that duty, if

(a) with respect to a duty imposed by paragraph (1)(a) or (b),

21 (1956), 115 C.C.C. 82 (Que.Ct.of Sessions of the Peace).

(i) the person to whom the duty is owed is in destitute or necessitous circumstances, or

(ii) the failure to perform the duty endangers the life of the person to whom the duty is owed, or causes or is likely to cause the health of that person to be endangered permanently; or

(b) with respect to a duty imposed by paragraph (1)(c), the failure to perform the duty endangers the life of the person to whom the duty is owed or causes or is likely to cause the health of that person to be injured permanently.

(3) Every one who commits an offence under subsection (2) is guilty of

(a) an indictable offence and is liable to imprisonment for a term not exceeding two years; or

(b) an offence punishable on summary conviction.

This section places on parents, spouses, and persons in charge of other persons the duty to provide the necessaries of life for their children, spouses, or charges. Notice that for an offence to have been committed, it is not enough that there has been a failure to provide without lawful excuse. Under paragraph (1)(a) or (b), the person to whom the duty is owed must also, because of the failure to provide, be in either destitute or necessitous circumstances, or that person's health or life must be endangered. So a wife who fails to support her husband cannot be convicted of this offence if her husband has sufficient means of his own. If, however, the person to whom the duty is owed falls under paragraph (1)(c), the offence is only committed if his or her health or life is endangered.

"Child" is defined in s.214:

214. In this Part . . . "child" includes an adopted child and an illegitimate child . . .

Since s.214 defines "child" as including an illegitimate or adopted child, parents of these children are included in s.215. Section 215(4)(b) further provides that evidence that a person has in any way recognized a child as being his or her child, is, in the absence of any evidence to the contrary, proof that the child is the person's child. So, for example, when a man supports a child who is not biologically his, this would be evidence that he has recognized the child as his own. Unless evidence is presented that provides another explanation for his actions, the child will be presumed to be his.

The definition of "guardian" is very broad. It would cover a situation where, for example, David has left the child in the care of Jenny. Jenny then has, in fact, the custody and control of the child.

Until 1975, husbands had a duty to support their wives but wives had no duty to support their husbands. In that year the Status of Women Amendment Act was passed. This Act amended certain sections of several statutes, including the Criminal Code, so that the law would treat men and women more equally. Because of this Act, the duty to provide necessaries is now placed on both spouses.

Where a person has another person under his or her charge, the duty to provide is only imposed if the person under charge is unable, for a reason listed in s.215(l)(c)(i), to withdraw from the charge and if the person under charge is unable to provide for himself or herself. In an English case from 1893, *R. v. Instan*,[22] the accused was living with her elderly aunt. The aunt became ill with gangrene and was confined to bed. Only the accused was aware of the aunt's condition. The accused did not provide or attempt to obtain any medical assistance for her aunt. She also neglected to provide food for her, although the accused accepted food that was brought to the house by tradespeople. Although the aunt died from the gangrene, the court found that the aunt's death was substantially accelerated by neglect—that is, by want of food and nursing and medical attention. The accused was found guilty of manslaughter.

a. Necessaries of Life

"Necessaries" in this section of the Code are those things necessary for the preservation of life. Ordinarily, this includes food, shelter, clothing, and medical treatment. However, this is probably not a complete list, especially since what is considered a necessary will depend on the particular circumstances of the case.[23]

b. Lawful Excuses

The failure to provide necessaries must be without "lawful excuse." The Code has not clearly defined lawful excuse. However, courts have stated that inability to provide because of lack of money—where, for example, the parents are unable to find employment—is a lawful excuse.[24] Also, the person must be aware that the necessaries are required before he or she can be found guilty of failing to provide them.[25] Also, when the spouse or child has adequate means of his or her own, the accused has a lawful excuse, since the spouse or child is not in destitute or necessitous circumstances.

c. Destitute and Necessitous Circumstances

The fact that a spouse or child is on welfare or receiving charity from friends or relatives does not mean that he or she is not in destitute or necessitous circumstances. As one judge aptly pointed out, families receive relief because they are in destitute or necessitous circumstances. They do not cease to be in such circumstances because they have received relief to keep them from famishing or suffering.[26]

Furthermore, s.215(4)(d) states that the fact that a spouse or child is receiving or has received necessaries from a person who is not under a legal duty to provide them cannot be used as a defence by an accused. Say that a wife has been deserted by her husband and is forced to live with her parents because she has no means of her own. Even if the parents support her at a

---

22 [1893] 1 Q.B. 450; 17 Cox's C.C. 602.
23 See, for example, *R. v. Sidney* (1912), 20 C.C.C. 376 (Sask.C.A.).
24 See, for example, *R. v. Bunting* (1926), 45 C.C.C. 135 (Ont.C.A.).
25 *R. v. Steele* (1952), 102 C.C.C. 273 (Ont.C.A.).
26 *R. v. Wilson* (1933), 60 C.C.C. 309 (Alta.C.A.).

very high standard of living, her husband cannot defend himself on the grounds that she is not destitute or in necessitous circumstances.

d. Danger to Life or Health

The offence may be committed where the failure to provide necessaries either endangers the life of the person to whom the duty is owed; or causes or is likely to cause the health of that person to be permanently endangered. Whether a person's life has been endangered, or health permanently endangered, depends on the particular facts of each case. It has been said that the words have no special technical meaning.[27]

The Supreme Court of Canada considered a charge under this section in *R. v. Naglik.*[28] Naglik and her husband were charged with aggravated assault and failure to provide necessaries to their 11-week-old son. Only Naglik appealed her conviction. One of the issues on which the appeal was based was whether s.215 imposes an objective or a subjective standard for the mental element of the offence. This decision was one of the companion cases that came out with the Supreme Court of Canada's decision in *Creighton.* It was held that this is an offence of "penal negligence" and that it requires the objective standard of a marked departure from the standard of a reasonable parent. The question was, in brief, whether a reasonable parent would have foreseen the risk of harm to the child. The majority also restated that the personal characteristics of the accused, except for those characteristics which deprive him or her of the capacity to appreciate the risk, should not affect the objective standard.

2. Duties of Persons Undertaking Dangerous Acts

a. Where Medical or Surgical Treatment Is Administered

> **216. Every one who undertakes to administer surgical or medical treatment to another person or to do any other lawful act that may endanger the life of another person is, except in cases of necessity, under a legal duty to have and to use reasonable knowledge, skill and care in so doing.**

This section does not create an offence but merely defines the duty that persons who administer medical or surgical treatment are under. Section 216 would most often be used in conjunction with the offence of criminal negligence. Thus, a person who breaches a duty under s.216 has not committed an offence unless the breach of the duty is criminally negligent. Notice the exception: no duty is imposed "in cases of necessity." Presumably, this would apply in an emergency situation to protect those who attempted to give aid but failed to have or use reasonable knowledge, skill, or care.

An example of a case where an offence other than criminal negligence was the charge is *R. v. Thornton.*[29] The accused was charged with committing a common nuisance under s.180:

---

27 *R. v. Bowman* (1898), 3 C.C.C. 410 (N.S.C.A.).
28 (1993), 83 C.C.C. (3d) 526 (S.C.C.).
29 (1993), 82 C.C.C. (3d) 530 (S.C.C.).

> **180. (1) Every one who commits a common nuisance and thereby**
>
> **(a) endangers the lives, safety or health of the public, or**
>
> **(b) causes physical injury to any person,**
>
> **is guilty of an indictable offence . . .**
>
> **(2) For the purposes of this section, every one commits a common nuisance who does an unlawful act or fails to discharge a legal duty and thereby**
>
> **(a) endangers the lives, safety or health of the public . . .**

The accused had tested positive twice for the HIV virus, which he knew could lead to AIDS. He also knew that the virus was transmitted through blood. He then proceeded to donate blood to the Red Cross, knowing also that the Red Cross would not knowingly accept donations of blood from persons who had tested positive for the HIV virus. The screening process caught his blood, and he was charged with committing a common nuisance. His defence was that it is not an offence to donate contaminated blood. On appeal, the Supreme Court of Canada held that s.216 imposed a duty of care on him when he donated blood to the Red Cross. He failed his duty of care under s.216 by not disclosing to the Red Cross that his blood contained HIV antibodies.

b. Where Omission Is Dangerous to Life

> **217. Every one who undertakes to do an act is under a legal duty to do it if an omission to do the act is or may be dangerous to life.**

This section provides that where a person begins to do an act, he or she is under a legal duty to complete it if the omission of the act is or may be dangerous to life. So, for example, Alex sees Ivan drowning. Alex is under no legal obligation to save Ivan. But if Alex throws Ivan a rope and, before Ivan can grab it, pulls it back in, Alex has breached a legal duty to act. Alex undertook to act, and Ivan's life has been endangered by the omission. Like s.216, this section does not create an offence but could be used as the grounds for a charge of criminal negligence.

3. Child Abandonment

> **218. Every one who unlawfully abandons or exposes a child who is under the age of ten years, so that its life is or is likely to be endangered or its health is or is likely to be permanently injured, is guilty of an indictable offence and liable to imprisonment for a term not exceeding two years.**

> **214. In this Part,**
>
> **"abandon" or "expose" includes**
>
> **(a) a wilful omission to take charge of a child by a person who is under a legal duty to do so, and**
>
> **(b) dealing with a child in a manner that is likely to leave that child exposed to risk without protection . . .**

This section makes it an indictable offence to abandon a child under the age of 10. Notice that the offence can be committed by either a failure to act (i.e., a "wilful omission") or by positive misconduct (i.e., dealing with the child in a manner that exposes the child to risk). "Abandon" has also been defined by the courts as "leaving children to their fate."[30]

An example of a case of child abandonment is *R. v. Motuz and Motuz*.[31] The parents left their two children, aged four and five, alone and locked in a farmhouse while they went out drinking. The farmhouse was about 1.2 kilometres from the nearest neighbour. After the parents had been gone for three hours, the house caught fire and burned down. Both children died. In finding the parents guilty, the judge described the parents' conduct as a total abandonment of parental responsibility.

A similar case of child abandonment is *R. v. Holzer*.[32] The mother of a 15-month-old boy left the child in an unlocked pickup truck in the unheated parking lot of a shopping mall in March. The temperature in the lot was -14°. She had meant to drop off a bill payment but ended up playing bingo. The child was found by a security guard. The court found the mother guilty of child abandonment. The child had no protection from the risk of abduction and only limited protection from freezing.

Questions for Review and Discussion

1. What kinds of acts can lead to liability for criminal negligence?
2. What essential elements must be present before an omission to act can be criminally negligent?
3. What are the main differences between civil negligence and criminal negligence?
4. Discuss the two main approaches used by the courts to determine whether a person's conduct has been criminally negligent. Which approach do you prefer? Explain?
5. List the offences of criminal negligence.
6. Describe the following:
   a. The persons who are under a duty to provide necessaries.
   b. The persons to whom the duty is owed.

---

30 *Re Drummond Infants Adoption* (1968), D.L.R. (3d) 309 (B.C.Sup.Ct.Chambers).
31 *R. v. Motuz* (1965), 2 C.C.C. 162 (Man.C.A.).
32 (1988), 63 C.R. (3d) 301 (Alta.Q.B.).

c. The circumstances in which a breach of duty is an offence.

7. What are "necessaries of life"?

8. In what circumstances may a person who is under a duty to provide necessaries of life have a lawful excuse for not providing them?

9. Why does the law in "cases of necessity" where medical or surgical treatment is administered not impose a duty to have and use reasonable knowledge, skill, and care?

10. Does the law always impose a duty to act if the failure to act will endanger a person's life? If not, in what circumstances does a person have a duty to act? Do you agree with the present law? Explain.

11. Do you think the offence of child abandonment should only apply to children under ten? Explain.

12. LeMay and Sullivan were midwives who helped women who wished to have their babies at home. They had no formal medical training. They attended at the birth of a child of J.V. at her request. The child was partially born but LeMay and Sullivan were unable to complete the delivery. The woman was taken to the hospital by ambulance, where the delivery was completed using "a basic delivery technique." However, the child was dead. Lemay and Sullivan were charged with criminal negligence causing death.

    What do you think were the issues in this case? How would you resolve them? (Note: You may need to refer to some of the sections covered in Chapter Nine.) See *R. v. Sullivan* (1991), 63 C.C.C. (3d) 97 (S.C.C.).

13. Mr. and Mrs. Simon and their seven children lived in a two-room house on a farm in Saskatchewan. For the past two months, Mrs. Simon's 20-year-old brother, Rodney, had been living with them. Because of the limited space, Mrs. Simon did not want her brother staying in the house. She had complained about this to Mr. Simon on several occasions. One night after Mr. Simon and Rodney had returned from work, Mr. and Mrs. Simon argued about whether Rodney should continue living with them. Mrs. Simon finally said there wasn't room for everyone and that she was leaving. She then put on a jacket and hat. She had, however, nothing on her feet except house slippers and stockings and was otherwise thinly clad. Before she left, she told her ten-year-old son, Jimmy, to put on his coat and come with her. A few minutes after, Mrs. Simon and Jimmy left, Rodney asked Mr. Simon if they should go after them. The temperature that night was -40°C. Mr. Simon said no, that they had probably gone to a neighbour's for the night. The neighbour lived one-and-a-half miles to the south. The next day, Rodney went to the neighbour's to see if Mrs. Simon and Jimmy were there. On the way, he found their bodies frozen stiff. Apparently they had taken a wrong turn and lost their way.

With what offence or offences, if any, could Mr. Simon or Rodney be charged? What would the Crown have to show? What other information would be relevant? See *R. v. Sidney* (1912), 20 C.C.C. 376 (Sask.C.A.).

Chapter Eleven

OFFENCES INVOLVING MOTOR VEHICLES
PART VIII OF THE CODE

A. INTRODUCTION

We don't usually think of car drivers as potential criminals. Yet the careless use of motor vehicles is a major cause of death and injury today. Society has had to resort to the criminal law to prevent and control the dangerous use of automobiles.

The Criminal Code contains a number of offences relating to the operation of motor vehicles. Some of these are similar to provincial highway-traffic offences. For example, the Criminal Code includes an offence for failing to stop at the scene of an accident. Most provincial highway-traffic statutes contain similar offences. The provinces create traffic offences as part of their authority to regulate the use of roads and highways. For example, to control the flow of traffic, the provinces set speed limits and make rules regarding turns. Where the use of motor vehicles creates a risk of injury or death, the federal government uses its authority to make criminal law. Remember that however similar a provincial offence may seem to a federal one, the Code offence is more serious, and a crime.

"Motor vehicle" is defined in s.2 of the Code as a vehicle, other than railway equipment, "that is drawn, propelled or driven by any means other than muscular power." This definition would cover, besides cars, such vehicles as farm tractors, snowmobiles, and motorcycles. For some offences, other methods of transportation (e.g., boats, aircraft, railway equipment) are specifically included.

B. CRIMINAL NEGLIGENCE AND MOTOR VEHICLE OFFENCES

Until recently, the Code contained the offence of criminal negligence in the operation of a motor vehicle. In 1985, driving offences were reorganized.

Penalties were increased, new offences were created, and the offence of criminal negligence in the operation of a motor vehicle was repealed. Today, a person who causes death or injury by criminally negligent driving will be charged with either the offence of criminal negligence causing death or the offence of causing bodily harm. When it is being judged whether driving is criminally negligent, the same questions arise as in any other case of criminal negligence. Recall from Chapter Ten that the Supreme Court of Canada has been unable to reach an agreement on whether an objective or a subjective test should be used for determining whether conduct is criminally negligent. As also discussed in Chapter Ten, decisions concerning the *mens rea* required for other offences suggest that eventually the Supreme Court will accept the marked departure test as the standard in cases of criminal negligence.[1]

C. DANGEROUS OPERATION OF A MOTOR VEHICLE

1. Elements of the Offence

The key element of this offence is driving that is dangerous to the public. There need not be actual danger to the public, but only driving that was dangerous to anyone who might reasonably have been expected to be in the vicinity of the dangerous driving.[2] Furthermore, any passengers in the car that is being dangerously driven and the officer in the police cruiser stopping the car are part of the public.[3]

> **249. (1) Every one commits an offence who operates**
>
> **(a) a motor vehicle in a manner that is dangerous to the public, having regard to all the circumstances, including the nature, condition and use of the place at which the motor vehicle is being operated and the amount of traffic that at the time is or might reasonably be expected to be at that place;**
>
> **(b) a vessel or any water skis, surf-board, water sled or other towed object on or over any of the internal waters of Canada or the territorial sea of Canada, in a manner that is dangerous to the public . . .**
>
> **(c) an aircraft in a manner that is dangerous to the public . . .**
>
> **(d) railway equipment in a manner that is dangerous to the public . . .**
>
> **(2) Every one who commits an offence under subsection (1)**
>
> **(a) is guilty of an indictable offence and liable to imprisonment for a term not exceeding five years; or**
>
> **(b) is guilty of an offence punishable on summary conviction.**

---

1 See Chapter Ten, page 236 for discussion.
2 *R. v. Mueller* (1975), 29 C.C.C. (2d) 243 (Ont.C.A.).
3 *R. v. Edlund* (1990), 23 M.V.R. (2d) 31 (Alta.C.A.).

(3) Every one who commits an offence under subsection (1) and thereby causes bodily harm to any person is guilty of an indictable offence and liable to imprisonment for a term not exceeding ten years.

(4) Every one who commits an offence under subsection (1) and thereby causes the death of any other person is guilty of an indictable offence and liable to imprisonment for a term not exceeding fourteen years.

Note that this offence applies to operators of vessels and other water vehicles, and to railway equipment, as well as to motor vehicles.

2. The *Mens Rea* for Dangerous Driving

The Supreme Court of Canada, in *R. v. Hundal*,[4] considered the *mens rea* requirement for the offence of dangerous driving. The accident occurred during the afternoon in heavy traffic on a wet street in downtown Vancouver. The accused was driving an overloaded dump truck when he ran a red light. His truck hit a car, killing the driver. The issue on appeal was whether the offence of dangerous driving is based on objective or subjective *mens rea*. The Court held that the offence requires a modified objective test. It noted that since driving is a licensed activity, it can be assumed that all drivers are mentally and physically capable of driving and are aware of the rules of the road. Furthermore, licensed drivers choose to drive and therefore place themselves in a responsible position to other people who use the roads. The Court concluded: "As a result, it is unnecessary for a court to establish that the particular accused intended or was aware of the consequences of his or her driving . . . As a general rule, a consideration of personal factors, so essential in determining subjective intent, is simply not necessary in light of the fixed standards that must be met by licensed drivers."[5] The Court also noted that driving is an automatic and routine activity: it is almost impossible to determine the state of mind of a driver at any particular moment. "It would be a denial of common sense for a driver whose conduct was objectively dangerous, to be acquitted on the ground that he was not thinking of his manner of driving at the time of the accident."[6] The question to be asked, the Court stated, is whether the accused's conduct was a marked departure from the conduct of a reasonable person. Normally the mental element will be inferred from the conduct. Thus, it can be assumed that a reasonable person would be aware of the risks arising from the dangerous driving. To avoid criminal liability, a person who is accused of dangerous driving is entitled to offer an explanation, such as the sudden onset of an illness. In sum, the *mens rea* should be assessed objectively but in the context of all the surrounding circumstances.

Applying its reasoning to the facts of this case, the Court considered that the trial judge carefully examined the circumstances of the accident: the busy

---

4   (1993), 79 C.C.C. (3d) 97 (S.C.C.).
5   Ibid. at page 105.
6   Ibid. at page 105.

downtown traffic, the weather conditions, the condition of the accused's vehicle, and so on. The Court found that the accused's manner of driving represented a gross (marked) departure from the standard of a reasonable prudent driver, and that the accused offered no excuse for his conduct. The accused's appeal was dismissed.

In *MacGillivray,*[7] the Supreme Court again looked at the offence of dangerous driving. This time a motorboat was the vehicle. It confirmed its decision in *Hundal* that the test for dangerous driving is whether the conduct of the accused was a marked departure from the conduct of a reasonable person.

D. FAILING TO STOP WHEN INVOLVED IN AN ACCIDENT

Section 252 provides that:

> **252. (1) Every person who has the care, charge or control of a vehicle, vessel or aircraft that is involved in an accident with**
>
> **(a) another person,**
>
> **(b) a vehicle, vessel or aircraft, or**
>
> **(c) in the case of a vehicle, cattle in the charge of another person,**
>
> **and with intent to escape civil or criminal liability fails to stop the vehicle, vessel or, where possible, the aircraft, give his or her name and address and, where any person has been injured or appears to require assistance, offer assistance.**
>
> **(1.1) Every person who commits an offence under subsection (1) in a case not referred to in subsection (1.2) or (1.3) is guilty of an indictable offence and liable to imprisonment for a term not exceeding five years or is guilty of an offence punishable on summary conviction.**
>
> **(1.2) Every person who commits an offence under subsection (1) knowing that bodily harm has been caused to another person involved in the accident is guilty of an indictable offence and liable to imprisonment for a term not exceeding ten years.**
>
> **(1.3) Every person who commits an offence under subsection (1) is guilty of an indictable offence and liable to imprisonment for life if**
>
> **(a) the person knows that another person involved in the accident is dead; or**
>
> **(b) the person knows that bodily harm has been caused to another person involved in the accident and is reckless as to whether death of the other person results from that bodily harm, and the death of that other person so results.**

---

7   (1995), 97 C.C.C. (3d) 13 (S.C.C.).

The elements of this offence are (a) having the care, charge, or control of a vehicle that (b) is involved in an accident with a person, another vehicle, or cattle; and (c) failing to stop, to give assistance or name and address (d) with the intent of escaping civil or criminal liability. Note that this offence creates three legal duties: the driver must stop, give assistance, and give his or her name and address.

1. Care, Charge, or Control

To commit this offence a person must have care, charge, or control of the vehicle. Ordinarily this person is the driver. However, when the owner of the car is a passenger, he or she could have care, charge, or control. For example, in *R. v. Slessor*,[8] one of the judges hearing the case on appeal stated that a passenger *could* have care, charge, or control where, for example, the car was being driven by a chauffeur or by an employee of the passenger. However, where a person allows another person to drive his or her car, in a social or business situation, it will usually be the driver who has the care, charge, or control of the vehicle.

2. Involved in an Accident

It is immaterial whether damage actually occurs as a result of the accident. The accused's vehicle need not have actually collided with another car or person. For instance, a driver who caused an accident, or helped to cause it, and witnessed the accident occurring, would be "involved" in the accident. For example, a person who changed lanes abruptly in such a way that a car travelling behind braked suddenly, went out of control, hit the curb, and rolled off the highway, has been involved in the accident. However, a person who did not see the accident and was unaware that it had occurred, even though causing it, would not be involved in the accident.

3. Failure to Render Assistance

Giving assistance does not mean applying first aid. It means taking the necessary steps to ensure that medical assistance or first aid help reaches the scene of the accident as quickly as possible.

4. Failure to Stop with Intent to Escape Criminal or Civil Liability

Courts have held that the intent required for this element of the offence is intent to escape liability *arising from the accident* and not from another cause. So, if a person fails to stop to avoid liability for unpaid parking tickets, the intent for the offence has not been proved.[9]

The offence creates a mandatory presumption, which is set out in s.252(2):

---

8 [1970] 2 C.C.C. 247 (Ont.C.A.).
9 *R. v. Hofer* (1982), 2 C.C.C. (3d) 236 (Sask.C.A.).

(2) In proceedings under subsection (1), evidence that an accused failed to stop his vehicle, vessel or, where possible, his aircraft, as the case may be, offer assistance where any person has been injured or appears to require assistance and give his name and address is, in the absence of evidence to the contrary, proof of an intent to escape civil and criminal liability.

In other words, once it has been demonstrated that the accused was involved in an accident, he or she is required to give an explanation for not stopping. This section was applied in *R. v. Gosselin*.[10] The accused was the driver of a car that hit two pedestrians who were walking on the shoulder of the road. He drove a brief distance past the accident and then stopped his car and walked back. There was conflicting evidence regarding whether he offered any assistance. By the time he arrived at the scene, another car had stopped and some of the occupants had already gone to a farmhouse for help. The accused then went back to his car and drove 2.1 kilometres to a restaurant, where he called the police to report the accident. The police told him that an ambulance and police car were already on the scene. The accused did not give his name to the police or state that he was the driver. He called the police back 22 minutes later and gave his name and stated that he was the driver of the vehicle. The police told him to remain at the restaurant until they arrived, which he did. His statement to the police was that he left the accident to get help. At his trial, he was convicted of failing to remain. The trial judge relied on s.252(2) to convict him. On appeal, the Ontario Court of Appeal held that the judge made an error in applying this section. There was "evidence to the contrary" that the accused did not leave the scene to escape liability. Where a judge does not either reject this evidence or disbelieve it, the presumption in this section cannot be applied and the Crown must prove beyond a reasonable doubt that the accused left the scene to escape liability. The trial judge, although he doubted the accused's evidence, did not reject it. In fact, the Court of Appeal stated that the two phone calls to the police and the fact that the accused stayed at the restaurant were evidence to the contrary that would be difficult to reject (the phone calls were recorded). Once it is established that the Crown cannot rely on s.252(2), the judge must consider all the evidence to determine whether the Crown has proved beyond a reasonable doubt that the accused left the scene of the accident with the intent to escape liability. The trial judge did not do this, so the case was sent back for a new trial.

This type of clause is open to challenge under the Charter for offending the presumption of innocence. The Court of Appeal in Gosselin considered this issue as well. It concluded that although the clause does offend the presumption of innocence, it is a reasonable limitation under s.1 of the Charter. The court used the test set out by the Supreme Court of Canada in *R. v. Oakes*.[11] It held that the objective of the law, which is to curb injuries to persons and damage to property, is sufficiently important to override

---

10 (1988), 45 C.C.C. (3d) 568 (Ont.C.A.).
11 See Chapter Two at page 27 for a discussion of the test in *Oakes*.

the Charter right; and that the duties imposed by the section are reasonable and not out of proportion to the objective of the law. The Court of Appeal in Nova Scotia has also upheld this section as not being an unjustifiable infringement of the Charter.[12]

E. IMPAIRED OPERATION AND HAVING OVER 80 mg OF ALCOHOL IN 100 ml OF BLOOD

1. The Offences

There are two offences that involve driving "under the influence": driving while impaired, and driving with more than 80 mg of alcohol in 100 ml of blood ("driving over 80"). For the offence of impaired driving, the impairment can be caused by drugs or alcohol.

Section 253 sets out these offences:

> **253. Every one commits an offence who operates a motor vehicle or vessel or operates or assists in the operation of an aircraft or of railway equipment or has the care or control of a motor vehicle, vessel, aircraft or railway equipment, whether it is in motion or not,**
>
> **(a) while the person's ability to operate the vehicle, vessel, aircraft or railway equipment is impaired by alcohol or a drug; or**
>
> **(b) having consumed alcohol in such a quantity that the concentration in the person's blood exceeds eighty milligrams of alcohol in one hundred milliliters of blood.**

2. Elements of the Offences

The *mens rea* for these offences is voluntarily becoming intoxicated; the *actus reus* is assuming care and control while voluntarily intoxicated. In *R. v. Penno,*[13] the accused attempted to use the defence of drunkenness to a charge of impaired driving. He argued that he was so intoxicated that he did not know he was driving. The Supreme Court of Canada held that an accused person cannot use the defence of drunkenness where an element of the offence is voluntary intoxication. It would be illogical and contradictory to allow drunkenness as a defence when impairment is an essential element of the offence.

Whether or not a motor vehicle can move under its own power at the time of the offence is not material. In *Saunders v. R.,*[14] even though the motor vehicle in question was wedged into a ditch so that it could not move under its own power (it was eventually moved by a tow truck), the accused, who was in the car and impaired at the time, was found guilty of impaired driving. A similar result was reached in *R. v. Lloyd,*[15] where the car was out of gas.

---

12 *R. v. T.*(S.D.) (1985), 18 C.C.C. (3d) 125 (N.S.C.A.).
13 (1990), 59 C.C.C. (3d) 344 (S.C.C.).
14 [1967] 3 C.C.C. 278 (S.C.C.).
15 [1988] 3 W.W.R. 423 (Sask.C.A.).

Offences under s.253 do not require that the vehicle be on a highway or road or other "public place." In *R. v. Murray*,[16] a Prince Edward Island case, the accused was convicted of impaired driving while the car was in the private driveway beside his house.

There are two ways these offences can be committed: a person can be actually operating (i.e., driving) a vehicle, or a person can have care or control of the vehicle. A person does not have to be operating a vehicle to have care and control of it, and the vehicle need not be in motion. This means, for example, that if the police see an obviously impaired person enter the driver's side of a car and put the key in the ignition, they can charge that person with having care and control, even before the vehicle is set in motion.

3. The Presumption of Having Care or Control

When a person is found in the driver's seat, s.258(1)(a) creates the following presumption:

> **(a) where it is proved that the accused occupied the seat or position ordinarily occupied by [the driver of] a motor vehicle . . . the accused shall be deemed to have had the care or control of the vehicle . . . unless the accused establishes that the accused did not occupy that seat or position for the purpose of setting [the vehicle] in motion . . .**

Thus, if a person is in the driver's seat of a car, it will be presumed that the person had the care or control of the car unless the person can show that he or she did not intend to put it in motion. Until *R. v. Ford*,[17] discussed below, some courts had held that this presumption meant that an accused could avoid a conviction by showing that he or she did not intend to set the car in motion. For example, in *R. v. McPhee*,[18] the accused, a taxi driver, realized that he was impaired. He attempted to call his supervisor to request that someone take his taxi off the road. The line was busy, so he went to his cab and turned on the ignition so that he could use the car radio to call the dispatcher, who could relay the message to his supervisor. Before anyone arrived, he was found by the police asleep in the car. He was acquitted of having care and control while impaired because he did not enter the vehicle for the purpose of setting it in motion.

This interpretation of the presumption was changed by the decision of the Supreme Court of Canada in *Ford*. The accused had been attending a party on a cold winter night. During the evening he started the car to warm the engine so that it would start when he was ready to go home. He did not intend to drive home, however; he had arranged for someone else to drive, since he knew he was impaired. The police found him behind the wheel with the motor running. The Supreme Court affirmed the decision of the Court of Appeal, which held that intent to drive the vehicle is not necessary for the offence. The Court stated that care and control can be shown where the

---

16 (1973), 11 C.C.C. (2d) 296 (P.E.I.S.C.).
17 (1982), 65 C.C.C. (2d) 412 (S.C.C.).
18 (1976), 25 C.C.C. (2d) 412 (Ont.C.A.).

accused does anything involving use of the car where the car could be unintentionally set in motion, "creating the danger that the section is designed to prevent." If the accused rebuts the presumption by showing that he or she did not enter the vehicle for the purpose of putting it in motion, it is still open to the Crown to prove that the accused had care or control by proving that the accused performed an act or series of acts that might put the vehicle in motion.

In *R. v. Diotte*,[19] the New Brunswick Court of Appeal held that an overt act is not necessary to establish care and control. The police found the accused sleeping in his car, which was parked sideways on a street so that it completely blocked one lane of the road. The engine was not running and the lights were off, but the keys were in the ignition. The accused failed a breath test and was charged with having care and control while having over 80 mg of alcohol in 100 ml of blood. The trial judge acquitted the accused because the Crown failed to prove that the accused performed an overt action that involved him with the car in a way that created a danger to the public. The Court of Appeal rejected this position, stating that the position of the car on the roadway created a hazard to the public and that the accused had the immediate capacity and means of operating the vehicle.

4. The Charter and Section 258

The presumption under s.258 has been challenged under the Charter as a violation of the presumption of innocence. The Supreme Court of Canada has held that even though the presumption violates the right to be presumed innocent, the provision is a reasonable limitation under s.1 of the Charter. The Court held that the objective of protecting the public from drunk drivers is "sufficiently important to warrant over-riding a constitutionally protected right."[20]

5. The Meaning of Impaired

In general, an accused is impaired within the meaning of s.253 if, as a result of consuming alcohol or drugs, he or she is no longer in complete control of the motor vehicle. The proof of impairment can be based on a number of factors, including actual driving behaviour, a breathalyzer test, and the appearance and behaviour (e.g., slurred speech, smell of alcohol on the breath) of the accused when examined by the police.

In *R. v. McKenzie*,[21] the court made the following statement about proof of impairment:

> *There appears to be no single test or observation of impairment of control of faculties, standing alone, which is sufficiently conclusive. There should be consideration of a combination of several tests and observations such as general conduct, smell of the breath, character of the speech, manner of walking,*

---

19 (1991), 64 C.C.C. (3d) 209 (N.B.C.A.).
20 *R. v. Whyte* (1988), 42 C.C.C. (3d) 123 (S.C.C.).
21 (1955), 111 C.C.C. 317 (Alta.Dis.Ct.).

turning sharply, sitting down and rising, picking up objects, reaction of the pupils of the eyes, character of the breathing.[22]

In *R. v. Stellato*,[23] the Ontario Court of Appeal held that any degree of impairment, from slight to great, is sufficient for the offence. This decision, which was later approved by the Supreme Court of Canada, rejected the need for proof of driving that was a marked departure from the driving of a reasonable person for the offence of impaired driving.

In *R. v. Graat*,[24] the Supreme Court of Canada affirmed a decision of the Ontario Court of Appeal which held that non-expert opinion is admissible evidence in determining whether a person is impaired. Medical expertise is not necessary to identify whether a person is impaired, since most people can express an opinion on impairment from their own experience.

As mentioned, impairment can be from alcohol or drugs. One court has said that the term "drug" should be given a broad meaning to include any substance which, if consumed, will bring about impairment.[25] Also, it has been held that it is not necessary to prove whether the impairment is from alcohol or drugs.[26]

6. Voluntariness

The question of voluntariness often arises when the accused claims that he or she was unaware of the effects of the drug or alcohol. For example, a person may claim that he or she unwittingly became impaired after taking a prescription drug. In general, a person who can establish that he or she was not aware and should not have reasonably been aware that the medication would cause impairment, will avoid conviction for impairment. On the other hand, a mistaken belief as to how much one can drink before becoming impaired will not be a defence. Nor will overestimating the time it will take for medication to take effect.[27]

Whether an accused's impairment was voluntary or involuntary was discussed in *McLeod v. A.G. Sask.*[28] The accused was charged with impaired driving. He testified that he had two drinks of whisky; then, intending to take two "222" pills, he mistakenly took two pills prescribed for his diabetes. A doctor testified that the diabetes medication could cause symptoms of impairment, and that the accused would be unaware of such symptoms. The court held that through no act of his own will, the accused became incapable of appreciating that he was, or might become, impaired. In such circumstances, the accused could not be convicted of impaired driving.

In *R. v. Honish*,[29] the accused was charged with impaired driving causing bodily harm. At the time of the accident he was depressed about problems

22 Ibid. at page 319.
23 (1993), 78 C.C.C. (3d) 380 (Ont.C.A.); appeal dismissed 90 C.C.C. (3d) 160n (S.C.C.).
24 (1982), 2 C.C.C. (3d) 365 (S.C.C.).
25 *R. v. Marionchuk* (1978), 42 C.C.C. (2d) 573 (Sask.C.A.).
26 *R. v. MacAuley* (1975), 25 C.C.C. (2d) 1 (N.B.C.A.).
27 *R. v. Penner* (1974), 16 C.C.C. (2d) 334 (Man.C.A.); *R. v. Murray* (1985), 22 C.C.C. (3d) 502 (Ont.C.A.).
28 (1972), 6 C.C.C. (2d) 81 (Sask.D.C.).
29 (1991), 68 C.C.C. (3d) 329 (Alta.C.A.).

with his marriage. He had several drinks and then, intending to commit suicide, took a large quantity of pills. He testified that he then lay down on his bed. The next thing he remembered was waking up in the hospital. He had, within an hour of taking the pills, driven his car and collided with another car. At his trial he argued that his intoxication was involuntary. He appealed his conviction to the Alberta Court of Appeal. The court dismissed his appeal, holding that his intoxication was voluntary in the sense that he voluntarily consumed the drugs and alcohol, and also in the sense that he knew that the combination would have an impairing effect. The fact that he was depressed and may have felt compelled to commit suicide did not prevent his acts from being voluntary.

7. Having More Than 80 mg of Alcohol in 100 ml of Blood

The development of machines capable of measuring blood alcohol levels has greatly simplified the task of controlling impaired driving. The offence of driving with more than 80 mg of alcohol in 100 ml of blood does not require any proof of bad driving, or any other evidence of impairment.

There are two types of tests in use today. The first involves a screening device that is usually administered on the spot when the driver is stopped. This practice is sometimes called "roadside testing," although the test is not necessarily administered on the roadside; anyone operating a vessel, aircraft, or railway equipment may be required to take the test. A person who "fails" this test will be asked to take a breathalyzer test at the police station. The result of the second test shows the exact amount of alcohol in the person's blood and is the basis upon which the charge is laid.

a. Screening for Alcohol

The authority for giving screening tests is set out as follows:

> **254. . . . (2) Where a peace officer reasonably suspects that a person who is operating a motor vehicle or vessel or operating or assisting in the operation of an aircraft or of railway equipment or who has the care or control of a motor vehicle, vessel, aircraft or railway equipment, whether it is in motion or not, has alcohol in the person's body, the peace officer may, by demand made to that person, require the person to provide forthwith such a sample of breath as in the opinion of the peace officer is necessary to enable a proper analysis of the breath to be made by means of an approved screening device and, where necessary, to accompany the peace officer for the purpose of enabling such a sample of breath to be taken.**

An "approved screening device" is an instrument that can evaluate a person's blood alcohol level immediately. Approved devices are listed in the Code in s.254. The technology is constantly changing; most commonly, however, a person breathes into the device, which then flashes a red, yellow, or green light. A red flash indicates that the driver's blood alcohol level is over the 80 mg limit. If the device signals red, the driver is taken to the police station for a breathalyzer test, which is more precise.

Notice that an officer can demand that a person take a screening test based on a reasonable suspicion that the person has alcohol in his or her blood. This is a lower standard than for a breathalyzer test, which requires "reasonable grounds." The results of the screening device provide the officer with the reasonable grounds for demanding the breathalyzer test.

b. The Meaning of "Forthwith"

The demand must be made "forthwith." Several cases have concerned the meaning of the term "forthwith." In *R. v. Grant*,[30] an officer pulled the accused driver over because he suspected him of driving while disqualified. While talking to him, he smelled alcohol on his breath. The officer then made a breathalyzer demand. However, the officer did not have the equipment in his car and had to call another officer to deliver it to him. The equipment did not arrive until half an hour later. The Supreme Court of Canada held that the term "forthwith" suggests that the test should be given immediately. In this case, the demand was not authorized by s.254 because it was not a demand to provide a sample "forthwith" but a demand for the accused to give a breath sample when the equipment arrived, which it did a half-hour later. Therefore, the accused could not be found guilty of the offence of refusing to comply with a demand made under s.254. Subsequent provincial court of appeal cases have held that generally, the officer should be equipped with the device; but where, for example, there is a five-minute lapse while the equipment is being obtained, the officer can make a valid demand for the breath sample.[31] The Newfoundland Court of Appeal has stated that whether the time lapse is reasonable depends on the circumstances. In general, a delay of half an hour or more is not acceptable; if the delay was under half an hour, the court must look at the circumstances in deciding if such delay was valid.[32]

The validity of a delay was considered in *R. v. Pierman*,[33] a decision of the Ontario Court of Appeal. The officer in this case waited 15 minutes before administering the test, as recommended by the manufacturer of the device. Otherwise, if the accused had had a drink within the previous 15 minutes, the machine might have registered a "false fail" because of the residual alcohol in his mouth. Since the accused was observed leaving a tavern and admitted to having a couple beers, the court considered that it was reasonable to assume that he had consumed alcohol within the last 15 minutes. The court said that the police could take a flexible approach to administering the test "forthwith." Usually the test must be administered immediately, but where the officer is of the opinion that the test will be contaminated because of mouth alcohol, the officer may wait 15 minutes.

---

30 (1991), 67 C.C.C. (3d) 268 (S.C.C.).
31 See, for example, *R. v. Misai* (1993), 79 C.C.C. (3d) 339 (Ont.C.A.); *R. v. Higgins* (1994), 88 C.C.C. (3d) (Man.C.A.).
32 *R. v. Payne* (1994), 91 C.C.C. (3d) 144 (Nfld.C.A.).
33 (1994), 92 C.C.C. (3d) 160 (Ont.C.A.).

This issue was considered again by the Supreme Court of Canada in *R. v. Bernshaw*.[34] The accused had been stopped by a police officer because of his erratic driving. The officer observed that the accused's eyes were red and that his breath smelled of alcohol. He asked the accused if he had been drinking and the accused replied "yes." Based on this information, the officer demanded a breath sample. The officer did not inquire as to when the accused had last had a drink, nor did he wait 15 minutes to administer the test. The accused failed the screening test, and the officer demanded a breathalyzer test. On appeal, the accused argued that the officer did not have reasonable grounds for demanding the breathalyzer test because the officer did not know when the accused had last consumed alcohol and therefore did not know if the screening test was accurate. The Court considered the decision in Pierman and decided to adopt the "flexible approach." The Court stated that in general, the screening test should be administered immediately. However, an officer who has a factual basis for believing that an immediate test will provide an inaccurate reading can wait up to 15 minutes before administering the test. In *Bernshaw,* there was no evidence to indicate when the accused had his last drink; therefore, the officer was acting properly when he asked for the breath sample immediately and when he used the "fail" on the screening test as the basis for demanding a breathalyzer test. A related issue considered by the Court was whether the police are obligated, before taking a sample, either to wait 15 minutes or to find out when the driver had last consumed alcohol. The Court held that the police are not required to ask the driver when he or she last consumed alcohol. The suspect may volunteer such information, or the officer may inquire, but there is no obligation for one to ask or for the other to answer such a question. If the officer has no grounds for believing that the screening test results will be unreliable, he or she can demand a sample and use those results as the basis for demanding a breathalyzer test.

c. Breathalyzer Tests

Section 254(3) provides:

> **254. . . . (3) Where a peace officer believes on reasonable and probable grounds that a person is committing, or at any time within the preceding three hours has committed, as a result of the consumption of alcohol, an offence under section 253, the peace officer may, by demand made to that person forthwith or as soon as practicable, require that person to provide then or as soon thereafter as practicable**
>
> **(a) such samples of the person's breath. . .**
>
> **as are necessary to enable proper analysis to be made in order to determine the concentration, if any, of alcohol in the person's blood, and to accompany the peace officer for the purpose of enabling such samples to be taken.**

---

34 (1995), 95 C.C.C. (3d) 193 (S.C.C.).

d. Applying the Reasonable Suspicion and Reasonable Grounds Tests

At one time, the breathalyzer test provided for under s.254(3) was the only test available for determining whether a person had committed the offence of driving "over 80." The section requires there to be reasonable grounds for demanding the test. The existence of reasonable grounds has two elements: the officer must have an honest belief that the accused has committed the offence, and the officer must have reasonable objective grounds for this belief. Before there were screening devices, an officer had to have obvious evidence of impairment, such as careless and erratic driving, and physical signs of impairment before demanding a breathalyzer test. The development of screening devices has made the offence of driving over 80 much easier to enforce. Under s.254(2), the police can demand that a person take a screening test on reasonable suspicion that he or she has ingested alcohol. The reasonable suspicion test is satisfied when the officer believes that it is possible that the accused has alcohol in his or her body. So, for example, if a person is stopped for a spot check and the officer observes that the person's eyes are red and that the person's breath smells of alcohol, the officer has grounds for demanding a screening test. If that person fails the screening test, the officer then has reasonable grounds for demanding a breathalyzer test.

e. The Presumption Under Section 258 and Evidence to the Contrary

Since the breathalyzer test is usually taken at the police station, there will be some delay between the time of the alleged offence (driving over 80) and the testing. Section 258(1)(c) (ii) provides that where the test is taken within two hours of the alleged offence, there is a presumption that the results of the breathalyzer test indicate the level of alcohol at the time the offence was committed unless "evidence to the contrary" is raised. The meaning of "evidence to the contrary" was considered by the Supreme Court of Canada in *R. v. St. Pierre.*[35] The accused was stopped by the police because of her erratic driving. She failed a screening test and was taken to the station for a breathalyzer test. The machine was in use, so she had to wait about an hour. During that hour she made several trips to the washroom, where she consumed two small bottles of vodka. After taking the breathalyzer test, which showed that she had 180 mg of alcohol in 100 ml of blood, she told the officers that she was an alcoholic and that she had drunk the vodka in the washroom. She gave the empty bottles to the officer. At her trial, her counsel argued that evidence that she had consumed alcohol at the station was evidence to the contrary. The trial judge agreed, and she was acquitted. The Court of Appeal disagreed and entered a conviction. The case finally reached the Supreme Court on the issue of whether "evidence to the contrary" means evidence that an accused person's blood alcohol was lower at the time of the

---

35   (1995), 96 C.C.C. (3d) 385 (S.C.C.).

offence or just evidence that it was different. The Court held that the plain meaning of the term is that evidence to the contrary is evidence that an accused person's blood alcohol was different at the two points of time: the time of the alleged offence and the time of the testing. (However, evidence of the normal biological processes of absorption and elimination of alcohol is not evidence to the contrary. It can be assumed that Parliament knew that blood alcohol levels change constantly but enacted the presumption anyway.) In *St. Pierre*, there was evidence to the contrary that the accused's blood alcohol was different. Thus, the presumption was rebutted. However, this did not mean that the breathalyzer certificate showing the test results could not be used. An accused can still be convicted if, on the basis of all the evidence, the judge is satisfied beyond a reasonable doubt that the offence was committed. In this case, however, there was no other evidence establishing the accused's blood alcohol level; therefore, the Court restored her acquittal.

f. Random Stopping and the Charter

Most provinces today have legislation that allows for random stopping of vehicles, or "spot checks." When a driver is stopped, the police usually ask to see the person's driver's licence, car registration, and proof of insurance. At the time the car is stopped, the police are able to observe the driver for signs of impairment to determine whether there are grounds to demand a breath sample. There have been several Charter challenges concerning random stops. One issue has been whether a person is detained when stopped. Under the Charter, a person who is detained has a right to consult counsel and must be informed of that right. The Supreme Court of Canada has held that a person is detained during a random spot check or when stopped and required to give a breath sample. However, it is a reasonable limitation on the right to counsel to limit this right to situations where the more serious breathalyzer test is used.[36] Similarly, random spot checks have been challenged as an arbitrary detention that infringes the Charter. Again, the Supreme Court has said that random spot checks are a reasonable limitation on the right not to be arbitrarily detained. The objective of controlling the social evil of drunk driving is of sufficient importance that the infringement is justified.[37] Finally, the Supreme Court has held that requiring a driver to show a driver's licence, car registration, and proof of insurance does not violate a person's right to be free from unreasonable search and seizure. The Court has held that such a demand does not constitute a search within s.8 of the Charter because it is not an intrusion on a reasonable expectation of privacy. There is no intrusion where a person is required to produce a licence, permit, or other documentation which indicates that the person has complied with the law that is a condition for exercising the right.[38]

---

36 *R. v. Thomsen* (1988), 40 C.C.C. (3d) 411 (S.C.C.), and *R. v. Therens* (1985), 18 C.C.C. (3d) 481.
37 *R. v. Hufsky* (1988), 40 C.C.C. (3d) 398 (S.C.C.); *R. v. Ladouceur* (1990), 56 C.C.C. (3d) 22.
38 *Hufsky*, ibid.

g. The Right to Counsel and the Breathalyzer Test

Once a demand for a breathalyzer test has been made, the police must inform the suspect of the right to counsel. Chapter Five on pre-trial procedure discussed the right to counsel generally in any case where there is a detention or arrest. In brief, the right to counsel includes the right to be informed about whatever legal services are available. In most provinces these include free, 24-hour, preliminary legal advice from a "duty counsel," as well as legal aid for those who meet the financial criteria. The officer, as part of the duty to inform, must also tell the detained person how to contact the available legal services (e.g., by providing an 800 number or the phone numbers of lawyers acting as duty counsels).

These rules regarding the right to counsel have a special significance in "over 80" cases. When a detained person expresses a desire to speak to a lawyer, the police cannot administer the test until the person has had a reasonable opportunity to do so. In *R. v. Prosper*,[39] a Nova Scotia case, the accused was pulled over after he was observed driving in an erratic manner on a Saturday afternoon in Halifax. He was told that he had a right to call any lawyer he wished and that he could apply for legal aid. When he got to the station, he told the police that he would take the test but that he wanted to speak to a lawyer first. He was unable to contact any lawyer on the legal aid list. Nova Scotia did not have a free duty counsel system in place at this time, and legal aid lawyers were not taking calls outside of business hours. Eventually, the accused agreed to take the test. His sample was over 80, and he was charged with the offence. He was acquitted at his trial because the breathalyzer certificate that gave the results of the test was not allowed as evidence. The trial court judge ruled that his right to counsel had been violated. The Nova Scotia Court of Appeal allowed the appeal and entered a conviction. When the case finally reached the Supreme Court of Canada, two of the issues were as follows: Are governments required by the Constitution to ensure that there is free and immediate legal advice available on request? And in the circumstances, were the accused's rights violated? The Supreme Court held that there is no obligation to provide free preliminary legal advice upon detention. However, the majority of the justices held that once a person has asserted his or her desire to speak with a lawyer, the police must "hold off" further questioning or eliciting of incriminating evidence until the accused has had a reasonable opportunity to do so. The justices stated that the police must hold off even if this means that the breathalyzer test cannot be given within the two-hour period so that the presumption in s.258(1)(c)(ii) is lost. Although there might be some situations of urgency where the police do not have to hold off, losing an evidentiary presumption is not one of them. The Chief Justice stated: "While this alternative [holding off] may not be ideal from the Crown's perspective . . . this is a trade-off that governments which persist in refusing to implement a 'Brydges duty counsel' system [free preliminary advice] will have to endure and accept."[40]

---

39 (1994), 92 C.C.C. (3d) 353 (S.C.C.).
40 Ibid. at page 374.

The Court added that the meaning of "reasonable opportunity" will depend on the surrounding circumstances, such as availability of duty counsel.

Future cases will have to set more detailed guidelines as to what is reasonable in the circumstances and what are situations of urgency where police do not have to hold off.

F. REFUSAL TO TAKE A BREATHALYZER TEST

It is an offence under s.254(5) to refuse, without a reasonable excuse, to take either a screening test or a breathalyzer test, once the demand is made.

1. Reasonable Excuse for Failure to Comply

In *R. v. Nadeau*,[41] the judge concluded that a "reasonable excuse" must relate to some circumstance that renders compliance with the demand either extremely difficult, or likely to involve a substantial risk to the health of the person on whom the demand has been made. An example of a case where the court found that the accused had a lawful excuse because of "extreme difficulty" is *R. v. Cordeiro*.[42] The accused's dentures were so poorly fitted that when he tried to give a breath sample, they came loose, making it impossible for him to exhale enough for a proper reading. In *R. v. Phinney*,[43] the Nova Scotia Court of Appeal held that there is not an all-inclusive definition of reasonable excuse. In this case, the court held that the accused had an honest belief based on reasonable grounds that the machine was not functioning properly. This was a reasonable excuse for refusing the test. In *R. v. Iron*,[44] the accused would have been driven over 150 kilometres and left with no place to stay or way to get home for the sake of a breathalyzer test. The court held that he had a reasonable excuse for refusing.

Of course, as the cases above indicate, a person also has a right to refuse to take a test if the demand is not made within s.254—for example, if the demand is not made "forthwith."

In *R. v. Swietorzechi*,[45] the accused was convicted of the offence of failing to comply with a demand to provide a breath sample. The demand was made to the accused when he appeared at the police station. He argued that he had not driven the car to the station and therefore was not obligated to take the test. The court held that this element of the offence (i.e., the driving) must exist in fact before the officer can make the demand; it is not enough that the officer has a reasonable suspicion that the accused operated or had care and control of a motor vehicle. In this case, the officer did not know that the accused had driven to the station; therefore, the accused was justified in refusing to take the test.

41 (1974), 19 C.C.C. (2d) 199 (N.B.C.A.).
42 Reported in The Lawyers Weekly, February 19, 1988.
43 (1979), 49 C.C.C. (2d) 81 (N.S.C.A.).
44 (1977), 35 C.C.C. (2d) 279 (Sask.Q.B.).
45 (1995), 97 C.C.C. (3d) 285 (Ont.C.A.).

2. Unacceptable Excuses

The following excuses for refusing the test were judged not reasonable: the accused had a sincere belief that the results would not be accurate because the accused had consumed alcohol after driving;[46] or the accused was on medication;[47] or the accused was not being permitted to smoke;[48] or the accused would suffer a financial loss if he left his truck and its cargo, which was likely to spoil.[49]

G. BLOOD TESTS

It is not always possible for a person to take a breathalyzer test. If there has been an accident, the driver may be injured or unconscious. In these situations, where the person cannot consent, the police can use s.254(3)(b) to demand a blood sample, or s.256 to obtain a warrant for a blood sample. Section 254(3) states:

> . . . the peace officer may . . . by demand made to that person . . . require that person to provide . . . [blood samples]
>
> (b) where the peace officer has reasonable and probable grounds to believe that, by reason of any physical condition of the person,
>
> (i) the person may be incapable of providing a sample of his breath, or
>
> (ii) it would be impracticable to obtain a sample of his breath . . .

To use s.256 to obtain a warrant for a blood sample, the officer must lay an information before a justice of the peace in person or by telephone to state that there are reasonable grounds to believe that:

> (a) a person has, within the preceding four hours, committed, as a result of the consumption of alcohol, an offence under section 253 and the person was involved in an accident resulting in the death of another person or in bodily harm to himself or herself or to any other person, and
>
> (b) a qualified medical practitioner is of the opinion that
>
> (i) by reason of any physical or mental condition of the person that resulted from the consumption of alcohol, the accident or any other occurrence related to or resulting from the accident, the person is unable to consent to the taking of samples of his blood, and
>
> (ii) the taking of samples of blood from the person would not endanger the life or health of the person . . .

---

46 *R. v. Dunn* (1980), 8 M.V.R. 198 (B.C.C.A.).
47 *R. v. Frohwerk* (1979), 48 C.C.C. (2d) 214 (Man.C.A.).
48 *R. v. Leduc* (1987), 56 C.R. (3d) 270 (Que.C.A.), reversed 1 S.C.R. 1586, 18 M.V.R. (2d) 158 on other grounds.
49 *R. v. Gidney* (1987), 7 M.V.R. (2d) 90 (N.S.C.A.).

H. PENALTIES FOR DRINKING AND DRIVING OFFENCES

The penalties for drinking and driving offences in s.255, which sets out fines and terms of imprisonment, s.259, which deals with court-ordered driving prohibitions and s.787, which deals with penalties for summary conviction offences generally. Offences under ss. 253 (impaired or over 80) and 254 (refusing to provide breath or blood sample) are hybrid offences. There are minimum penalties for these offences, whether they are treated as summary conviction or as indictable, or cause death or bodily harm. These are:

- For a first offence, a fine of not less than 600 dollars, and a prohibition from driving for at least one-year and not more than three years (s.255(1)(a)(i) and 259(1)(a)).
- For a second offence, imprisonment for not less than 14 days, and a prohibition from driving for at least two years and not more than five years (s.255(1)(a)(ii) and s.259(1)(b)).
- For each subsequent offence, imprisonment for not less than 90 days and a prohibition from driving for at least three years and up to a life-time ban (s.255(1)(a)(iii) and s.259(1)(c)).

The maximum penalties for first or subsequent offences that do not cause death or bodily harm are:

- Where the offence is prosecuted by indictment, imprisonment for a term not exceeding five years and three years' driving prohibition (s.255(b) and s.259(a)).
- Where the offence is punishable on summary conviction, imprisonment not exceeding six months, a $2,000 fine, and three years' driving prohibition (s.255(c) and s.787).

If the offence under s.253(a) (driving while impaired) causes bodily harm to any other person, the offence is indictable and punishable by a term of imprisonment of up to 10 years and by a 10-year driving prohibition (s.255(2) and s.259(2)(b)).

If the offence of driving while impaired causes death, it is indictable and punishable by a term of imprisonment of up to 14 years and by a 10-year driving prohibition (s.255(3) and s.259(2)(b)).

When sentencing a person charged under section 255, the sentencing judge will take into consideration section 255.1. The effect of section 255.1 is that if the offence is committed by means of a motor vehicle, vessel or aircraft, evidence that the accused's blood alcohol level exceeded .160 at the time the offence was committed is to be considered an aggravating factor. See also section 718.2 which sets out other statutory factors in sentencing.

A person who has been found guilty of committing an offence under s.253 has one possibility for avoiding a conviction and the imposition of at least these minimum penalties. Section 255(5) of the Code allows, under certain circumstances, for the conditional discharge of people who have committed the offence of impaired driving. A person who receives a discharge avoids having a conviction registered on his or her record and thus avoids some of the problems associated with having a criminal record. Under s.736, discharges are generally allowed for any offence except for those that are punishable by a maximum of 14 years' imprisonment. Discharges are allowed for impaired driving cases because it is believed that many of these offenders are addicted to drugs or alcohol, and that the better recourse is for them to seek treatment so that they will not be charged with impaired driving again. The subsection allowing for a conditional discharge for impaired driving is not in effect in every province. The federal government has left it up to the provinces to decide whether to allow this response to cases of impaired driving. At this time, the subsection has been proclaimed in force in Nova Scotia, New Brunswick, Manitoba, Prince Edward Island, Alberta, Saskatchewan, Yukon, and the Northwest Territories.

Section 255(5) states:

> . . . a court may, instead of convicting a person of an offence committed under section 253, after hearing medical or other evidence, if it considers that the person is in need of curative treatment in relation to his consumption of alcohol or drugs and that it would not be contrary to the public interest, by order direct that the person be discharged under section 736 on the conditions prescribed in a probation order, including a condition respecting the person's attendance for curative treatment in relation to his consumption of alcohol or drugs.

I. DRIVING WHILE DISQUALIFIED

It is an offence for a person to drive while disqualified. A person is disqualified from driving if a court has prohibited the person from driving or if the province has suspended the person's licence because of a conviction for an offence under ss. 253 or 254. In *R. v. Prue*,[50] the Supreme Court of Canada held that knowledge is an element of the offence, so that lack of knowledge of the suspension is a defence to the charge.

Driving while disqualified is a hybrid offence. If treated as a summary conviction offence, the maximum penalty is a $2,000 fine, six months' imprisonment, and a three-year driving prohibition. If treated as indictable, the maximum penalty is two years' imprisonment and a three-year driving prohibition.

Questions for Review and Discussion

1. Explain the differences between the federal and provincial powers to create driving offences.
2. What are the elements of the offence of dangerous driving?

---

50 (1979), 46 C.C.C. (2d) 257 (S.C.C.).

3. Annette is involved in an accident as a driver of a motor vehicle. What are Annette's legal responsibilities under the Criminal Code?

4. What is the difference between the offence of impaired driving and the offence of driving with 80 mg of alcohol in 100 ml of blood?

5. How have the courts defined "care and control" as used in s.253?

6. Explain the offence of driving while disqualified.

7. The accused was charged with having care and control of a motor vehicle while impaired. He was found by the police sleeping in his truck, which was located on private property, roughly three metres from the road. His head was by the passenger side door and his lower body, which extended under the steering wheel, was encased in a sleeping bag. The key was in the ignition, and the stereo was playing loudly. The engine and lights were not on. His evidence was that a friend drove him to a party in the accused's truck. The accused was tired and went to sleep in the truck while waiting for his friend to drive him home. He testified that he had no intention of driving home. It was conceded that he was impaired at the time he was found by the police. The issue for the court was whether he had care and control.

    Should the accused be convicted? Discuss the arguments for and against. See *R. v. Toews* (1985), 21 C.C.C. (3d) 24 (S.C.C.).

8. The accused was charged with dangerous driving. The evidence was that he had had very little sleep over a five-day period. He had worked three days on an afternoon shift and then spent two days helping his father move to a new residence. At the end of the fifth day, he had one or two beers and then got in his car to drive to a restaurant for something to eat. On a busy four-lane highway he fell asleep at the wheel and collided with a car going the opposite way. He testified that he knew he was exhausted but felt that he was driving normally. Should he be convicted? See *R. v. Mason* (1990), 60 C.C.C. (3d) 338 (B.C.C.A.).

9. The accused was a passenger in his own car when the driver hit a pedestrian. The driver stopped about 33 metres from the accident, started to reverse, then got confused and drove about 200 metres. The accused then took over driving, went another 33 metres, turned around, and went back to the accident. The accused was charged with failure to remain. Should he be convicted? See *R. v. Shea* (1982), 17 M.V.R. 40 (Nfld.C.A.).

10. John knew that he was very intoxicated when he left the bar and headed toward his car. He saw Mary, a total stranger, walking down the street. He stopped her and asked her to drive him home. She protested that she didn't have a licence and didn't know how to drive. He finally persuaded her to drive the car. After driving a short distance, she hit another car.

    Can John be charged with a driving offence? Discuss.
    See *R. v. Keen* (1994), 10 M.V.R. (3d) 320 (Alta.C.A.).

11. Leanne was the driver in a high-speed police chase. The police car pursuing her car failed to yield at an intersection and collided with a vehicle going the other way. As a result of the accident, Leanne was charged with impaired driving causing bodily harm. What is the main issue in this case, and how would you resolve it?

Chapter Twelve

ASSAULTS AND RELATED OFFENCES AGAINST THE PERSON
PART VIII OF THE CODE

A. INTRODUCTION

This chapter covers offences involving actual or threatened violence against persons. Part VIII also contains offences against a person's reputation, such as libel, as well as offences against marriage, such as bigamy and the unlawful solemnization of marriage.

B. UTTERING THREATS

> **264.1 (1) Every one commits an offence who, in any manner, knowingly utters, conveys or causes any person to receive a threat**
>
> **(a) to cause death or bodily harm to any person;**
>
> **(b) to burn, destroy or damage real or personal property; or**
>
> **(c) to kill, poison or injure an animal or bird that is the property of any person.**

1. Elements of the Offence

The *actus reus* of this offence is the uttering of threats of death or serious bodily harm. In *Clemente v. The Queen,*[1] the Supreme Court of Canada stated that the *mens rea* for this offence is uttering the words with the intent that they will intimidate or be taken seriously. The accused, Clemente, who was on welfare, was told that his case was being transferred back to his former social worker, J.M. He became very upset and said that he would blow up her office and strangle her if she became his worker again. A few days later he told his worker that there would be a dead body in J.M.'s office if his case

---

1   (1994), 91 C.C.C. (3d) 1 (S.C.C.).

was transferred. He repeated the threat the next day in a telephone conversation. He was charged and convicted of uttering threats. He appealed his conviction to the court of appeal, which upheld the conviction. He then appealed to the Supreme Court of Canada, which held that to determine whether words are a threat, courts must look at whether a reasonable person would have considered that the words were uttered as a threat. The courts must review the words in light of the circumstances in which they were uttered, the manner in which they were spoken, and the person to whom they were addressed. So, for example, words spoken in jest or in such a manner that they could not be taken seriously could not lead a reasonable person to conclude that they conveyed a threat. Finally, the Supreme Court held that it is not necessary to find that the words were spoken with the intent of being conveyed to the potential victim. Applying this reasoning to the facts of the case, the Court found that the offence was committed, and dismissed the appeal.

No other action beyond the threat is necessary for this offence. It is the meaning of the words that is important. In *R. v. Leblanc,*[2] the Supreme Court of Canada established that it does not matter whether the person making the threat intends to carry it out; rather, the criminal sanction is aimed at the fear that the issuer of the threat instills in the victim.

The Quebec Court of Appeal has held that the threat does not need to be made to a specific person but can be made to members of an identifiable group. In *R. v. Remy,*[3] after two black men were killed by the police in Montreal, the accused threatened to kill the next police officer who killed a black person in similar circumstances. The court held that the offence was committed even though the identity of the victim was unknown when the threat was made. The Court noted that the officer's identity would become known when the conditions of the threat (i.e., the killing of a black person in similar circumstances) were met.

The meaning of "serious bodily harm" was examined by the Supreme Court of Canada in *R. v. McCraw.*[4] The accused had been seen at the practices of the Ottawa Roughriders cheerleaders. He phoned some of the cheerleaders and, using an assumed name, asked them to pose for photographs. At the same time, he wrote to three of the cheerleaders. In the letters he described the sexual acts that he intended to perform on them. He concluded the letters with a threat that he would have intercourse with them even if he had to "rape" them. The case reached the Supreme Court on the issue of whether the threat to rape the women was a threat to cause serious bodily harm under s.264.1. To answer this question, the Court looked at three underlying questions: What is serious bodily harm? Can psychological harm cause serious bodily harm? And can a threat to rape be a threat to cause serious bodily harm? After considering the definition of "bodily harm" in s.2 of the Code[5] and the dictionary meaning of "serious," the Court defined serious

---

2   (1989), 50 C.C.C. (3d) 192n (S.C.C.).
3   (1993), 82 C.C.C. (3d) 176 (Que.C.A.).
4   (1991), 66 C.C.C. (3d) 517 (S.C.C.).
5   Section 2 defines bodily harm as "any hurt or injury to a person that interferes with the health or comfort of the person and that is more than merely transient or trifling in nature."

bodily harm as being "any hurt or injury that interferes in a grave or substantial way with the physical integrity or well-being of the complainant . . ." As to the second question, the Court found that serious bodily harm includes psychological harm so long as the psychological harm substantially interferes with the health or well-being of the complainant. To answer the third question, the Court said that it must first look at the threat to rape generally. The Court noted that violence is inherent in the act of rape: "[To] argue that a woman who has been forced to have sexual intercourse has not necessarily suffered grave and serious violence is to ignore the perspective of women . . ."[6] The Court added that rape is the ultimate violation of personal privacy and causes devastating psychological consequences that may last a lifetime. Therefore, no other conclusion can be drawn but that rape can cause serious bodily harm. So also can the threat to rape.

In determining whether the particular words in this case were a threat to cause serious bodily harm, the Court stated that it must look objectively at the context of all the words used, at the person to whom the words were directed, and at the circumstances in which the words were uttered. To any reasonable person, the threat to rape would mean the threat of sexual penetration without consent, achieved by means of violence or threatened violence. Here, the threat was made to young women, and included graphic descriptions of various sexual acts that the accused would perform on them. The clear inference was that the three women would be forced to submit to sexual penetration without consent by the use of violence. The complainants testified that they had to carry out their activities knowing that they were being stalked, and that this resulted in restrictions on their movements and actions. The Court concluded that the threat was a threat to cause serious bodily harm. The accused's appeal of his conviction was dismissed.

C. ASSAULT

1. Defined

Section 265 sets out the definition of assault. Notice that the section defines three different sets of circumstances in which an assault may occur:

> **265. (1) A person commits an assault when**
>
> **(a) without the consent of another person, he applies force intentionally to that other person, directly or indirectly;**
>
> **(b) he attempts or threatens, by an act or a gesture, to apply force to another person, if he has, or causes that other person to believe on reasonable grounds that he has, present ability to effect his purpose; or**
>
> **(c) while openly wearing or carrying a weapon or an imitation thereof, he accosts or impedes another person or begs.**

---

6   Supra, note 4 at page 526.

(2) This section applies to all forms of assault, including sexual assault, sexual assault with a weapon, threats to a third party or causing bodily harm and aggravated sexual assault.

In general, assault involves the intentional or threatened application of force without consent. For example, in *R. v. Vandergraaf*,[7] the accused tried to throw a small glass bottle on the ice at a hockey game. His aim was off, and he hit a person who was standing in the front row at ice level. The accused was charged with assault but acquitted on appeal because there was no evidence that he intended to apply force to the victim.

Under subs.(1)(a), force must be actually used and lack of valid consent is an essential element. Where the use of force is only threatened or attempted, subs.(1)(b) requires that the person who was threatening or attempting the assault was able to carry out the assault, or caused the victim to believe on reasonable grounds that he or she was able to carry out the assault. Subsection (1)(c) defines a specific situation in which it may be implied that the use of force is being threatened. Note that subs.(2) provides that the definitions in this section apply to all forms of assault, including sexual assault.

2. Assault: Section 265(1)(a)

a. Elements

The British Columbia Court of Appeal has held that an assault can be committed even when no degree of strength or power is exerted. In *R. v. Burden*,[8] the victim was sitting on a bus when the accused sat next to her. The accused stared at the victim for a short time and then put his hand on her thigh for between 5 and 10 seconds. There were two other people on the bus at the time. In convicting the accused, the court quoted with approval the following passage from an eighteenth-century English authority:

> "Battery [assault] seemth to be, when an injury whatsoever, be it ever so small, is actually done to a person of a man in an angry or revengeful, or rude, or insolent manner . . . For the law can not draw the line between different degrees of violence and therefore totally prohibits the first and lowest stage of it, every man's person being sacred . . . "[9]

b. Consent

Part of the *actus reus* of assault under s.265(1)(a) is lack of consent. Any touching of a person may be an assault if it is done without that person's consent. What in one situation might be a gesture of love and affection, in another situation might be a criminal assault.

Before a person can give consent to an act, he or she must understand the nature of that act and actively consent to it. The law draws a distinction between mere submission and positive consent. As one court stated:

7   (1994), 93 C.C.C. (3d) 286 (Man.C.A.).
8   (1981), 64 C.C.C. (2d) 68 (B.C.C.A.).
9   Ibid. at page 70.

"Consent means an active will in the mind of the [victim] to permit the doing of the act complained of; and that knowledge of what is to be done, or of the nature of the act that is being done, is essential to a consent to the act."[10] So, for example, to obtain valid consent, doctors must inform patients of procedures they intend to perform. Some persons, such as the mentally disabled and young children, are incapable of giving consent. Thus, before a child receives medical treatment, unless emergency conditions exist, a doctor will obtain the consent of the child's parents or guardian.

A case concerning the validity of consent is *R. v. Ssenyonga.*[11] The accused, knowing that he had AIDS, had unprotected sex with several women who subsequently contracted the HIV virus. He was charged with three counts of aggravated sexual assault. He was acquitted at his trial, the judge holding that the victims consented to the application of force involved in sexual intercourse, and that the presence of the virus was irrelevant. The victims were not misled as to the nature of the act of intercourse.

But in a later case, *R. v. Cuerrier* (1998), 127 C.C.C. (3d) 1, the Supreme Court held that an accused who knows he is HIV positive and fails to disclose that fact, has obtained consent by fraud and this may vitiate consent to sexual intercourse with him. The Court, disagreeing with the court in Ssenyonga, found that fraud was not limited to the nature and quality of the act. The Court stated that ". . . it is no longer necessary when examining whether consent in assault or sexual assault cases was vitiated by fraud to consider whether the fraud related to the nature and quality of the act."[12] The Court continued " The deadly consequences that non-disclosure of the risk of HIV infection can have on an unknowing victim make it imperative that as a policy the broader view of fraud vitiating consent . . . should be adopted. . . . In my view, it should now be taken that for the accused to conceal or fail to disclose that he is HIV positive can constitute fraud which may vitiate consent to sexual intercourse."[13] Therefore, the Court determined that ". . . an individual who knows he is HIV positive and has unprotected sexual intercourse without disclosing this condition to his partner may be found guilty of contravening the provisions of s.265 of the Criminal Code".[14]

For consent to be valid, it must be freely given. Section 265(3) lists some of the situations where there is no consent because it is not given voluntarily:

(3) For the purposes of this section, no consent is obtained where the complainant submits or does not resist by reason of

(a) the application of force to the complainant or to a person other than the complainant;

(b) threats or fear of the application of force to the complainant or to a person other than the complainant;

---

10 *R. v. Lock* (1872), 12 Cox C.C. 244 at page 245.
11 (1993), 81 C.C.C. (3d) 257 (Ont.Ct.Gen.Div.).
12 *Cuerrier* at page 45.
13 Ibid. at page 47.
14 Ibid. at page 56-57.

(c) fraud; or

(d) the exercise of authority.

In *R. v. Saint-Laurent*,[15] the Quebec Court of Appeal held that exercise of authority is not limited to situations where there is a right to give orders and enforce obedience. It also refers to situations where there is an imbalance of power, such as between psychiatrist and patient.

c. *The Limited Scope of Consent*

Certain sports, such as hockey, involve physical contact. Courts have held that the players give implied consent to the use of force in these games. However, the force used may exceed that to which the consent was given. One judge has said that "there is a question of degree involved, and no athlete should be presumed to accept malicious unprovoked or overly violent attack."[16] An example of a case where the force used was held to exceed the consent given is *R. v. Cey*,[17] where a fight broke out during a hockey game. One of the players involved in the fight walked over to a player who was standing off to the side and hit him in an unprotected part of the head. The victim suffered a serious eye injury, and the attacker was found guilty of assault. A different result was arrived at in *R. v. Leclerc*,[18] which also involved an incident during a hockey game. The accused was pursuing the complainant down the ice, and they collided as the accused hit the complainant in the back with his stick. The complainant's head hit the boards. A penalty was called against the accused for a deliberate attempt to injure. It was later determined that the complainant had suffered a dislocation of a portion of his spine and was permanently paralyzed from the neck down. The trial judge accepted evidence that even though this game took place within a non-contact hockey league, in practice all players expected and accepted the contacts inherent in the game. He also accepted evidence that the accused had lost his balance and shoved the complainant in the back to push him off in order to avoid more violent contact. The accused was acquitted at his trial, and the Crown appealed. The court of appeal stated that to determine whether consent to conduct can be implied, the court should look at such factors as the setting of the game, the nature of the league, the age of the players, the conditions under which the game is played, the extent of the force used, the degree of risk or injury, and the probability of serious harm. However, the court continued, deliberate infliction of injury will generally be outside the immunity provided by implied consent. In this case, the trial court judge found that the push or shove was part of an "instinctive reflex action." While the no-contact rule was relevant in determining the scope of the implied consent, the trial judge also found that the rule was often breached. Having regard to the facts as found by the trial judge, the appeal court dismissed the appeal of the acquittal.

---

15 (1993), 90 C.C.C. (3d) 291 (Que.C.A.); leave to appeal refused 175 N.R. 240n.
16 *R. v. Maki* (1970), 1 C.C.C. (2d) 333 (Ont.Prov.Ct.).
17 (1989), 48 C.C.C. (3d) 480 (Sask.C.A.).
18 (1991), 67 C.C.C. (3d) 563 (Ont.C.A.).

Another type of case where consent is limited is where two people agree to fight. Until recently, the law was not clear on whether the fact that the parties consented to fight could be a defence where one person was injured. Some courts had allowed the defence of consent even when one person suffered bodily harm;[19] other courts had followed the English common law, which says that a person cannot give valid consent to physical force used in anger or where it is likely to cause or does cause bodily harm. For example, in *R. v. Squire*,[20] the court said: "Where two persons engage in a fight in anger by mutual consent, the blows struck by each constitute an assault on the other unless justifiable in self defence."

The case that finally settled the law was *R. v. Jobidon*,[21] a decision of the Supreme Court of Canada. Jobidon and a man named Haggart were drinking in a bar. Haggart walked over to Jobidon and punched him in the face because he believed that a week earlier Jobidon had punched a friend of his. They started fighting. It appeared that Haggart was winning the fight, but the owner of the bar broke up the fight and told Jobidon to leave. Jobidon waited outside the bar, and when Haggart came out they exchanged mutual invitations to fight. Jobidon rushed at Haggart and hit him in the head, knocking him unconscious and onto the hood of a car. He struck Haggart several more times in the head. Haggart was taken to the hospital. He never regained consciousness and died the next day. Jobidon was charged with manslaughter (causing death by an unlawful act, assault). The trial judge found Jobidon not guilty. He found that the two had consented to fight, that it was a fight in anger, and that physical injury was intended. However, the judge also found that Jobidon did not intentionally exceed the consent that Haggart gave, and that he struck the final blows in the reasonable but mistaken apprehension that Haggart was still capable of returning to the fight. The decision of the trial judge was appealed. The appeal court reviewed the law on the issue of consent and held that the common law limitations on the defence of consent should apply to the offence of assault:

> *The so-called consents to fight are often more apparent than real and are obtained in an atmosphere where reason, good sense and even sobriety are absent. In a case such as the one at hand it seems scarcely necessary to mention that often the results are very serious. To interpret the Criminal Code otherwise would continue to legitimize . . . uncivilized brawling.*[22]

The court granted the appeal, set aside the acquittal, and entered a verdict of guilty in its place.

The case finally reached the Supreme Court of Canada, which dismissed the accused's appeal. The Court held that the common law rules which determine when consent is not legally effective still apply in Canada. Section 8 of the Code preserves common law rules that are not inconsistent with the

---

19 *R. v. Bergner* (1987), 36 C.C.C. (3d) 25 (Alta.C.A.).
20 (1975), 26 C.C.C. (2d) 219; 31 C.R.N.S. 314 (Ont.C.A.).
21 (1991), 66 C.C.C. (3d) 454 (S.C.C.).
22 (1988), 45 C.C.C. (3d) 176 (Ont.C.A.) at page 184.

Code or other federal legislation.[23] The common law rule is based on public policy that it is not in the public interest to allow adults to hurt each other without a good reason. Thus, the rule does not apply to sporting activities where the force used is within the customary rules of the game, to medical treatment or surgery, or even to stuntmen who agree in advance to perform risky or daredevil activities. The judgment also created an exception, where consent can be a defence, for what the court described as "schoolyard scuffles where boys and girls immaturely seek to resolve differences through fighting." However, the Court left open the possibility of a charge of assault in situations where boys or girls under the age of 18 truly intend to harm one another and cause more than trivial bodily harm.

Since the decision in *Jobidon*, the situation of schoolyard fights has been before the courts.

In *R. v. W.(G.)*,[24] two 16-year-old boys were involved in a consensual fist fight. The students attended the same high school. They knew of each other but had not met. Two days before the fight, someone told the accused that the victim wanted to fight him. On the day of the fight, the accused received another message that the victim wanted to fight him. They met in the smoking area outside the school. They exchanged words, then pushes, and finally blows. The accused hit the victim three times in the face. The fight ended when the victim's nose began bleeding heavily. The victim received serious injuries: his nose was broken and he lost his vision in one eye for several hours. The accused was not hurt. His defence of consent was rejected at trial and a conviction was entered. He appealed to the Ontario Court of Appeal. The court found that the "co-existence of an intention to cause serious harm, the use of force clearly capable of causing that result and the actual occasioning of bodily harm made this fight much more serious than an ordinary schoolyard scuffle." The court concluded that the case clearly involved the type of situation described in *Jobidon*, where consent should not be a defence. The accused's appeal was dismissed. A later decision of the Ontario Court of Appeal reached the opposite conclusion. In *R. v. S.M.*,[25] two 16-year-old girls argued in a restaurant and eventually came to blows outside the restaurant. The accused hit the complainant in the face, causing a cut on her nose that did not require stitches. The accused was found guilty of assault, the trial judge holding that consent was not available as a defence. On appeal, the court distinguished this case from *R. v. W.(G.)*. The court considered the intent of the accused, the nature of the assault, and the harm caused. The court found that neither girl intended to hurt the other, and that the injuries were far less serious than in *R. v. W.(G.)*. Therefore, this case fell within the exception of the ordinary "schoolyard scuffle" as set out in *Jobidon*. The court allowed the appeal and entered an acquittal.

---

23 Section 8(3) of the Code states: "Every rule and principle of the common law that renders any circumstance a justification or excuse for an act or a defence to a charge continues in force and applies in respect of proceedings for an offence . . . except in so far as they are altered by or are inconsistent with this Act . . . " See Chapter Four, for discussion.
24 (1994), 90 C.C.C. (3d) 139 (Ont.C.A.).
25 (1996), 97 C.C.C. (3d) 281 (Ont.C.A.).

3. Assault: Section 265(1)(b)

Actual physical contact is not required for an assault. Subsection (1)(b) defines an attempted or threatened use of force as an assault. An example of this type of assault is found in *R. v. Judge*.[26] The accused, accompanied by other men, approached the victim, who was inside a locked car, and while using words and gestures which indicated that he had a weapon, threatened to "burn" the victim. A court of appeal upheld the accused's conviction. Similarly, pointing a gun at a person without a lawful excuse such as self-defence would be an assault.[27] Even where the accused does not intend to carry out the threat, if the victim reasonably believes that the accused has the ability to carry out the threat, the offence will have been committed. This point is illustrated by a New Brunswick case, *R. v. Horncastle*,[28] where an argument between a husband and wife led to the husband taking up a gun and threatening to shoot his wife. It was argued that the husband was not guilty of assault because he did not intend to actually shoot his wife. The court of appeal disagreed, and entered a verdict of guilty of assault. The court ruled that the making of the threat, coupled with the ability to carry it out, constituted the offence of assault.

Interestingly, the courts have held that words alone, no matter how threatening, do not constitute an assault. In *R. v. Byrne*,[29] the accused was charged with robbery, which in one form is assault with the intent to steal. The accused had walked up to the box office of a movie theatre and said to the cashier, "I've got a gun, give me all your money or I'll shoot." Although he had a coat draped over his arm, no gun was visible. Then, while the cashier was gathering the money, the accused fled. The court held that the accused had not committed an assault, since there were no acts or gestures accompanying his verbal threats; therefore, he could not be found guilty of robbery as charged.

4. The Permissible Use of Force

Previous chapters have discussed how in certain circumstances the law allows persons to apply physical force to other persons. For example, a peace officer, or a person assisting a peace officer, can use as much force as reasonably necessary to make an arrest.[30] Similarly, a person can use a reasonable amount of force in self-defence or to defend his or her family or property.[31] Section 43 creates another situation where force may be used:

> **43. Every schoolteacher, parent or person standing in the place of a parent is justified in using force by way of correction toward a pupil or child, as the case may be, who is under his care, if the force does not exceed what is reasonable under the circumstances.**

26 (1957), 118 C.C.C. 410 (Ont.C.A.).
27 *Kwaku Mensah v. R.* (1946), 2 C.R. 113.
28 (1972), 8 C.C.C. (2d) 253 (N.B.C.A.).
29 [1968] 3 C.C.C. 179 (B.C.C.A.).
30 See Chapter Five, Pre-trial Criminal Procedure.
31 See Chapter Four.

This section allows a parent or a person standing in the place of a parent, such as a teacher,[32] to use a reasonable amount of force for the correction of a child. In all the situations where the use of force is allowed, once the amount of force exceeds what is reasonable and necessary in the circumstances, an assault is committed.

The Supreme Court of Canada, in *Ogg-Moss v. The Queen*,[33] said that s.43 only allows force to be used for correction (i.e., for the education of the child) and is not a general authorization for the use of force. So where the child is mentally disabled and will not remember the "correction" within minutes of it being applied, this section cannot be used to justify the force.

It is not always clear what is a reasonable amount of force. In *R. v. LaFramboise*,[34] a father was convicted of assault for hitting his 13-year-old son on the buttocks and legs repeatedly with a piece of wood. The accused had slapped his son for being disruptive and the boy had slammed out of the house, which the accused took as an act of defiance. The father then took the boy to a woodshed, where he hit him with the wood. However, the accused's conviction was overturned on appeal.

In *R. v. P.(D.)*,[35] the accused and his wife and two children, aged five and two, were visiting Canada from the United States. The family was at a restaurant when the father and children went to the car to get a birthday present for the mother. The five-year-old girl began fighting with her brother and pushed him out of the car. When he tried to get back into the car, she slammed the door, catching his fingers in the door. After tending to his son, the father took the girl out of the car, placed her across the trunk, and spanked her on her bare bottom. A witness called the police, and the father was charged with assault. He used s.43 as a defence. The trial judge found that this spanking was for corrective purposes. The father, although angry, was not out of control. When the girl was examined at a hospital shortly after the incident, it was found that the spanking had left no marks. The parents testified as to when they used this form of discipline for their children. The judge found that their discipline routines were reasonable and designed to properly correct and educate their children. In deciding whether the correction exceeded what was reasonable, the judge considered the nature of the offence calling for correction, the age and character of the child, the likely (and actual) effect of the punishment on the child, the degree of gravity of the punishment, the circumstances in which it was inflicted, and the injuries (if any) inflicted. Applying these criteria, the court found that the force used by the accused in spanking his daughter did not exceed what was reasonable in the circumstances.

In *R. v. Graham*,[36] a teacher who spanked a student and was charged with assault relied on s.43. The child was eight or nine years old at the time of the

---

32   As a matter of policy, many school boards no longer allow teachers to use corporal punishment. See Canadian Foundation for Children, Youth and the Law v. Canada (Attorney General) (2000), 146 C.C.C. (3d) 362 (Ont. S.C.J.) which held that section 43 does not violate sections 7, 12 or 15 of the Charter of Rights and Freedoms.
33   (1984), 14 C.C.C. (3d) 116 (S.C.C.).
34   Reported in The Lawyers Weekly, January 25, 1991.
35   (1995), 98 C.C.C. (3d) 319; 39 C.R. (4th) 329 (Ont.Ct. of J. (Prov.Div.)).
36   (1995), 39 C.R. (4th) 339 (N.B.Q.B.).

incident and was known to be a disruptive student. The accused was the school principal and her homeroom teacher. During math class the girl refused to do her work and was bothering other students. The accused finally lifted her up and struck her on the bottom with an open hand.

Among the factors the court considered were these:

- The way the physical punishment was inflicted.
- The part of the body where force was applied.
- Whether the force was reasonable and not excessive.
- The conduct of the child and the nature of the offence.
- Whether the child was capable of appreciating correction.
- The age and character of the child.
- Whether the punishment was arbitrary, or capricious, or carried out in anger.

The court also bore in mind that ensuring respect for authority is part of the duty of the teacher as an educator. In this case the child was spanked for very undisciplined behaviour. She was bright and capable of understanding the correction. The force was reasonable and not excessive. A red mark remained on her buttocks for some 24 hours. There was no evidence that the teacher acted in anger. The accused had taught for 24 years. By all accounts he was a good teacher and was well liked and respected. Interestingly, the court held that two policy documents on discipline from the school district were not admissible as evidence of community standards of tolerance with respect to the physical punishment of students. The court held that such documents are not applicable to a criminal trial where s.43 is concerned: the policy of a school board cannot affect criminal law. The accused was acquitted at his trial, and the Crown's appeal was dismissed.

D. THE OFFENCES OF ASSAULT

Once it is established that an assault as defined in s.265 has taken place, the person who has committed the assault will be charged under one of the other Code sections that define the several different offences of assault. The offence actually charged will depend on the nature and seriousness of the assault and on the surrounding circumstances. For example, it is a more serious offence to commit an assault with a weapon than without one.

1. Assault Under Section 266

> **266. Every one who commits an assault is guilty of**
>
> **(a) an indictable offence and liable to imprisonment for a term not exceeding five years; or**
>
> **(b) an offence punishable on summary conviction.**

Assault under s.266 is the least serious type of assault. It may be used when the assault consists only of threats or attempts, or when the victim has not suffered any bodily harm. It was formerly called "common assault" and is sometimes today referred to as level 1 assault or simple assault.

2. Assault Under Section 267

> **267. Every one who, in committing an assault,**
>
> **(a) carries, uses or threatens to use a weapon or an imitation thereof, or**
>
> **(b) causes bodily harm to the complainant,**
>
> **is guilty of an indictable offence and liable to imprisonment for a term not exceeding ten years or an offence punishable on summary conviction and liable to imprisonment for a term not exceeding eighteen months.**

Bodily harm is defined in s.2 of the Code as "any hurt or injury to a person that interferes with the health or comfort of the person and that is more than merely transient or trifling in nature."

The application of this definition of bodily harm was discussed in *R. v. Dixon*,[37] a decision of the Court of Appeal of the Yukon Territory. The victim had been assaulted by the accused. Her injuries included small bruises on her face and shoulder and a laceration to the back of her head. She testified that she was "all better" within the month. The trial judge held that her injuries did not amount to bodily harm; there was no evidence that the injuries affected her health or comfort, and the injuries, which lasted no longer than a month, were trifling and transient. The court of appeal disagreed and ordered that a conviction of assault causing bodily harm be entered against the accused. The court of appeal held that "transient and trifling in nature" refers to a very short period of time, and to injury of a very minor degree. While the decision did not state exactly what a transient period of time is, one judge stated that it is simply insupportable to describe as transient an injury that lasts a month. Also, the court noted, it was clear that from the time of the injury until the time treatment was completed, the victim had been deprived of a sense of comfort. The judge stated that in this case, the trial judge's decision demonstrated an absence of any reasonable regard for the ordinary meaning of the words.

The British Columbia Court of Appeal in *R. v. Brooks*[38] held that for the offence of assault causing bodily harm, it is not required that the accused be able to foresee that bodily harm would result. In this case the victim and his family were returning from a vacation in their motor home at around midnight. The accused was driving his jeep on the same road. The jeep was behind the motor home, and the accused passed it. For some reason the accused became enraged at the way the motor home was being driven and forced it to the side of the road. The accused walked over to the motor home, reached in the window, and pulled the victim from the vehicle. Both were

---

37 (1988), 42 C.C.C. (3d) 318 (B.S.C.A.).
38 (1988), 41 C.C.C. (3d) 157 (B.C.C.A.).

immediately hit by a passing car, and the victim was seriously injured. In this situation it was irrelevant that the accused did not foresee the harm that resulted.

This ruling was followed in *R. v. Swenson*,[39] where a bouncer in a bar threw a patron out after he became involved in a fight. The victim landed on his head and suffered serious injuries. The court held that the *mens rea* for the offence is the intent to apply force—it is not necessary that the bodily harm be foreseeable. However, the Supreme Court of Canada held in another case[40] that for the offence of aggravated assault, the *mens rea* is foreseeabilty of harm. Thus, it is possible that the Supreme Court may hold that this offence also requires objective foreseeability of harm.

Section 2 defines "weapon" thus:

> **"weapon" means any thing used, designed to be used or intended for use**
>
> **(a) in causing death or injury to any person, or**
>
> **(b) for the purpose of threatening or intimidating any person;**
>
> **and, without restricting the generality of the foregoing, includes a firearm**

In *R. v. McLeod*,[41] the court held that a weapon does not need to be an inanimate object. A dog can be a weapon. The accused had ordered her dog to attack the victim, which it did. The court of appeal entered a conviction against the accused for assault with a weapon.

3. Assault Under Section 268

> **268. (1) Every one commits an aggravated assault who wounds, maims, disfigures or endangers the life of the complainant.**
>
> **(2) Every one who commits an aggravated assault is guilty of an indictable offence and liable to imprisonment for a term not exceeding fourteen years.**

Courts have held that "maiming" means disabling a person so that he or she is less capable of self-defence. Maims include injuries such as a broken leg and damaged eyesight. "Wounding" involves breaking the skin (which includes perforating an eardrum), while "disfiguring" seems to mean harming a person so that he or she is less physically attractive.[42]

In *R. v. Godin*,[43] the Supreme Court of Canada held that an intent to wound, maim, disfigure, or endanger life is not necessary for this offence. The *mens rea* is objective foresight of bodily harm.

---

39 (1994), 91 C.C.C. (3d) 541 (Sask.C.A.).
40 *R. v. Godin* (1994), 89 C.C.C. (3d) 574n; 31 C.R. (4th) 33 (S.C.C.).
41 (1993), 84 C.C.C. (3d) 336 (Y.T.C.A.).
42 See, for example, *R. v. Schultz* (1962), 133 C.C.C. (Alta.C.A.) on maiming; and *R. v. Littletent* (1985), 17 C.C.C. (3d) 520 (Alta.C.A.) where a perforated eardrum was considered a wounding.
43 Supra, note 40.

4. Assault Under Section 270

270. (1) Every one commits an offence who

(a) assaults a public officer or peace officer engaged in the execution of his duty or a person acting in aid of such an officer;

(b) assaults a person with intent to resist or prevent the lawful arrest or detention of himself or another person; or

(c) assaults a person

(i) who is engaged in the lawful execution of a process against lands or goods or in making a lawful distress or seizure, or

(ii) with intent to rescue anything taken under lawful process, distress or seizure.

(2) Every one who commits an offence under subsection (1) is guilty of

(a) an indictable offence and is liable to imprisonment for a term not exceeding five years; or

(b) an offence punishable on summary conviction.

The offences listed under s.270 have the common element of an assault of a person who is engaged in an act of law enforcement, such as a police officer making an arrest or a person seizing property under lawful process (e.g., a court order). A question that often arises under this section is whether the person assaulted was acting within his or her scope of authority at the time of the assault. For example, a person who assaults a police officer who is making an illegal arrest cannot be charged under s.270, although another type of assault may be charged. An interesting case that illustrates this point is *Corrier v. R.*[44] The police were investigating the theft of two wheels from a car. After searching the accused's trunk and finding nothing, the accused was told his car was being seized "to check it out." Apparently, the police wanted to take the car to the station to examine its wheels. On being told that his car was being seized, the accused rolled up his window, catching the police officer's arm between the glass and the car frame, and drove off. After the officer succeeded in freeing his arm, the accused attempted to run him over. The court found that the police officer, by attempting to seize the car over the owner's objections and without arresting him, had exceeded the powers given to him. The accused, therefore, could not be convicted of assaulting an officer in the execution of duty. However, the court substituted a conviction of common assault (this is now assault under s.266), since the accused had used more force than necessary to resist the seizure of his car.

The extent of the police officer's authority is not always easy to deter-

---

44 (1972), 7 C.C.C. (2d) 461; 19 C.R.N.S. 308 (N.B.C.A.).

mine. The Supreme Court of Canada considered this issue in *R. v. Stenning.*[45] The case involved police constables who were investigating a disturbance outside a building. Seeing a suspicious movement inside, they entered the building through an open window. They found two men in the building who refused to identify themselves. One of the men struck one of the constables in the face. It turned out that this man was the son of the owner of the building and was not involved in the outside disturbance. The Court found the accused guilty of assaulting an officer in the execution of duty. The Court stated:

> *Assuming that Wilkinson [the constable] did technically trespass on the premises, the fact remains that he was there to investigate an occurrence which had happened earlier in the evening, which involved the firing of a rifle. He was charged under s.47 of the Police Act, R.S.O. 1960, c.298, with the duty of preserving the peace, preventing robberies and other crimes, and apprehending offenders. He was in the course of making an investigation, in carrying out that duty, when he was assaulted by the respondent.*[46]

Both *Stenning* and the following case, *R. v. Tunbridge,*[47] which had the opposite result, demonstrate how difficult it is to decide whether police are engaged in the execution of their duty.[48] In *Tunbridge,* the police were called to investigate a domestic quarrel. The husband appeared to be intoxicated, and the wife said she wished to take the children and leave the home. While the wife was dressing one child, the father took the other child onto his lap. When the wife was ready to leave, the man refused to let the child go. The police scuffled with the accused in an attempt to take the child from him. The man was charged with assault under s.246(2) (now s.270). The Court directed that the accused be acquitted, stating: "In the absence of reasonable apprehension of injury to the child or of some breach of the peace I think the constables exceeded their duty when they purported to decide that the child should be taken from the father and then proceeded with their attempt physically to take it."[49]

E. THE OFFENCES OF SEXUAL ASSAULT

In 1983, the offences of rape and indecent assault were repealed and replaced by the new offences of sexual assault. With the changes in the law, the victim can be either a man or a woman, and the attacker can be of the same sex as the victim. A spouse can be charged with sexual assault. The old offence of rape was in Part V of the Code, with the offences involving public morals and disorderly conduct. The new offences have been placed with other

---

45 (1970), 3 C.C.C. 145 (S.C.C.). See also *R. v. Landry* (1986), 25 C.C.C. (3d) 1 (S.C.C.) in which the Court upheld an assault conviction where the police entered an apartment without a warrant to make an arrest. The accused resisted and was charged under what is now s.270. The Court held that the police officer was in the execution of his duty when he had reasonable grounds for believing that the person he was seeking was within the premises.
46 Ibid. at page 148.
47 (1971), 3 C.C.C. (2d) 303 (B.C.C.A.).
48 See discussion of the meaning of "execution of duty" in Chapter Six.
49 Supra, note 47, at page 305.

offences against the person. This emphasizes that they involve physical violence to another person.

Remember that the definitions of assault in s.265 apply to sexual assault. The *actus reus* of the offence is a sexual touching without consent. The *mens rea* is the intention to touch in a manner that is sexual where the accused knows or is wilfully blind or reckless to the fact that the accused is not consenting.

Below we discuss the different offences of sexual assault. As with other assaults, the type of assault that is charged will depend on the circumstances surrounding the offence and the nature of the sexual assault.

1. Sexual Assault Under Section 271

This is the least serious offence of sexual assault. It is a general intent offence: an assault as defined by s.265 that is committed in circumstances of a sexual nature.

> **271. (1) Every one who commits a sexual assault is guilty of**
>
> **(a) an indictable offence and is liable to imprisonment for a term not exceeding ten years; or**
>
> **(b) an offence punishable on summary conviction and liable to imprisonment for a term not exceeding eighteen months**

a. The Meaning of "Sexual"

The Code does not define the term "sexual," leaving this task to the courts. The Supreme Court of Canada considered this issue in *R. v. Chase*.[50] The accused, a neighbour, entered the home of the victim, a 15-year-old girl. Her brother was the only other person in the house. The accused seized the girl by the shoulders and grabbed her breasts. He was unable to touch her anywhere else because she fought back. The accused left the house when her brother called another neighbour. The trial court convicted the accused of sexual assault. The court of appeal overturned the conviction and substituted a conviction for assault on the grounds that "sexual" requires involvement of the genitalia. The Supreme Court of Canada disagreed and overturned the court of appeal's decision. The Court said that sexual assault does not depend solely on contact with any specific part of the human anatomy; rather, it is an assault of a sexual nature that violates the sexual integrity of the victim. The test for deciding whether the conduct has the required sexual nature is objective. The question asked is this: "Viewed in the light of all the circumstances, is the sexual nature or carnal context of the assault visible to a reasonable observer?"[51] Relevant factors are the nature of the conduct, the situation in which it occurred, the words and gestures accompanying the act, and all other surrounding circumstances, including threats, which may or may not be accompanied by the use of force.

---

50 (1987), 37 C.C.C. (3d) 97 (S.C.C.).
51 Ibid. at page 103.

In *R. v. V.(K.B.)*,[52] the Ontario Court of Appeal applied the decision in *Chase* to confirm a conviction of sexual assault against a man who grabbed his three-year-old son's genitals as a punishment for grabbing his. The decision stated that "a sexual assault does not require sexuality and indeed may not even involve sexuality. It is an act of power, aggression and control. In general sexual gratification if present is at best a footnote."[53]

In *R. v. Kindellan*,[54] the accused was a male stripper. As part of his act, he pulled a female patron to the stage, handcuffed her and pulled her hands back and forth between his legs. He had performed this part of his act on more than 50 occasions with no complaint. However, this time the woman complained and the accused was charged with sexual assault. The trial judge convicted him, and the conviction was upheld on appeal. It was not relevant that the act was not done for sexual gratification but as part of a performance. The victim had suffered an affront to her sexual dignity.

b. The Meaning of "Consent"

The principles concerning consent that apply to sexual assault are the same as those for any assault. The consent to a sexual touching must be freely given, with knowledge of the nature of the act being consented to. A sexual assault case[55] applied the rule in *R. v. Jobidon*[56] that a person cannot consent to having serious bodily harm inflicted on himself or herself. The accused had tied the complainant's arms and legs to a bed, beat her repeatedly with a belt, and inserted an object into her rectum. He was charged with sexual assault causing bodily harm. He claimed that she consented to this treatment. She said that she had not consented. The trial judge refused to let the defence of consent go to the jury on the grounds that consent was not a defence. The accused was convicted, and appealed. The court of appeal dismissed his appeal. It stated that regardless of whether one accepted his or her version of the events, it was clear that he applied force to her that, viewed objectively, would cause serious bodily harm and that the decision in *Jobidon* therefore applied.

The provisions of s.265(3) regarding consent also apply to sexual assault. In addition, in 1992 Parliament enacted what became known as the "no means no" law, which added a definition of consent and a list of circumstances where there is no consent. The preamble to the Act states that the purpose of the legislation is to protect the constitutional rights of women and children. Part of the legislation is now s.273.1 of the Criminal Code:

> **273.1 (1) Subject to subsection (2) and subsection 265(3), "consent" means, for the purposes of sections 271, 272 and 273, the voluntary agreement of the complainant to engage in the sexual activity in question.**

---

52 (1992), 71 C.C.C. 65 (Ont.C.A.), affd. (1993), 82 C.C.C. (3d) 382 (S.C.C.).
53 Ibid. at page 70.
54 [1988] B.C.W.L.D. 3041 (B.C.Co.Ct.).
55 *R. v. Welch* (1995), 101 C.C.C. (3d) 216; 25 O.R. (3d) 665 (Ont.C.A.).
56 Supra, note 21.

(2) No consent is obtained, for the purposes of sections 271, 272 and 273, where

(a) the agreement is expressed by the words or conduct of a person other than the complainant;

(b) the complainant is incapable of consenting to the activity;

(c) the accused induces the complainant to engage in the activity by abusing a position of trust, power or authority;

(d) the complainant expresses, by words or conduct, a lack of agreement to engage in the activity; or

(e) the complainant, having consented to engage in sexual activity, expresses, by words or conduct, a lack of agreement to continue to engage in the activity.

(3) Nothing in subsection (2) shall be construed as limiting the circumstances in which no consent is obtained.

Subsection (a) applies to situations where, for example, pimps are involved. It makes it clear that only the people involved can consent to sexual activity. Subsection (b) could apply to situations where the victim is intoxicated or mentally disabled. Subsection (c) applies to situations such as between doctors and patients, employers and employees, and students and teachers. The subsection does not mean that there cannot be sexual activity between people in such relationships, but only that there is no consent where there is an abuse of the position of trust, power, or authority. Note that under (e), a complainant can withdraw consent to continue in sexual activity.

Note that subs.(3) states that these are not the only situations where there is no consent. In *R. v. M.(L.M)*,[57] the Supreme Court of Canada held that in a sexual assault case, it is not necessary that the victim offer some minimal word or gesture of objection for there to be no consent, and that lack of resistance cannot be equated with consent. The victim was a 16-year-old girl. The accused was her stepfather. The victim was in bed when she and her younger sister began to argue. She called to her mother and stepfather for help. He came into her room and, while the younger sister was hiding under the bed, touched her genitals. The next night a similar incident occurred. On both occasions the victim pretended to be asleep. She explained her behaviour by saying that she was afraid of her stepfather. Several days later she told her social worker what had happened. The court of appeal dismissed the accused's conviction, holding that lack of resistance must be equated with consent. A dissenting judge disagreed, stating:

> *every consent involves a submission or lack of resistance, but it does not follow that every submission or lack of resistance means consent. The lack of maturity and vulnerability of the complainant and the extent to which the*

---

57 (1994), 89 C.C.C. (3d) 96 (S.C.C.).

accused must be taken to be aware of these traits are all elements which must be considered.[58]

The Supreme Court of Canada, in a very brief judgment, supported the dissenting judge and restored the conviction.

c. Honest Mistake of Consent

The defence of mistaken belief in consent may be an issue in any assault case; however, the defence arises most often in cases of sexual assault. Mistaken belief in consent is a mistake-of-fact defence that goes to the *mens rea* of the offence—that is, the accused is arguing that he or she did not know that the victim was not consenting.

A number of Supreme Court of Canada cases have looked closely at the use of this defence in sexual assault cases. In *Pappajohn v. The Queen*,[59] the Court held that an honest but mistaken belief that the victim consented is a defence even if the belief is not based on reasonable grounds. However, reasonableness is a factor in deciding whether the belief was honest. The defence requires that there be some supporting evidence beyond the mere assertion of belief in consent. The Court referred to this supporting evidence as giving an "air of reality" to the defence. In *Pappajohn*, the victim was a real estate agent who was showing a house to the accused. Once they were in the house, he attacked her. He was charged with rape (this case took place before the offence of rape was repealed). He claimed that she had consented. She claimed that she had not, and there was evidence that she had attempted to fight back. Despite his claim of honest mistake, the accused was convicted because the court found that there was insufficient evidence to place the defence of honest mistake before the jury.

After the decision in *Pappajohn,* the following was added to the Code:

> **265. . . . (4) Where an accused alleges that he believed that the complainant consented to the conduct that is the subject-matter of the charge, a judge, if satisfied that there is sufficient evidence and that if believed by the jury, the evidence would constitute a defence, shall instruct the jury, when reviewing all the evidence relating to the determination of the honesty of the accused's belief, to consider the presence or absence of reasonable grounds for that belief.**

This section supports the decision in *Pappajohn* and restates the common law developed by the courts. First, it confirms the common law rule that a judge can only put a defence before a jury if there is sufficient evidence on which the accused could be acquitted if the evidence is believed by a reasonable jury.

Second, it states that when there is evidence of mistaken belief in consent, the jury should consider the reasonableness of the belief in deciding if the belief was an honest mistake. However the jury is not required to find that the belief was reasonable for the defence to succeed.

---

58 (1992), 78 C.C.C. (3d) 318 (N.S.C.A.) at page 327.
59 (1980), 52 C.C.C. (2d) 481 (S.C.C.).

The constitutionality of s.265(4) was challenged in *R. v. Osolin.*[60] The accused argued that requiring a judge to only allow the jury to consider defences if there is "sufficient evidence" violates the presumption of innocence and denies the right to a trial by jury (one of the duties of the jury being to decide the facts of the case). The Supreme Court of Canada held that the section does not violate the presumption of innocence. The section is consistent with the rule of evidence, applicable to all defences, that a judge cannot put a defence before a jury unless there is some evidence that, if believed by a jury, would lead to an acquittal. The section, which only restates the "air of reality" test, does not violate the right to a jury trial, because it is a question of law whether there is enough evidence for a defence to be considered by a jury. The Court continued:

> *One of the reasons that the jury has been able to function so very well is that the trial judges have been able to direct the mind of the jurors to the essential elements of the offence and to those defences which are applicable . . . Speculative defences that are unfounded should not be presented to the jury. To do so would be wrong, confusing and unnecessarily lengthen jury trials.*[61]

In *Osolin*, the victim was dragged naked from her friend's place to a car. She was driven to another place, where she was tied to a bed and subjected to sexual intercourse. A medical examiner shortly afterwards found that her condition was consistent with being sexually assaulted. The accused said that she had consented, the victim said that she had not. The Supreme Court held that the judge was correct in not allowing the defence to go to the jury. The mere assertion of consent is not enough; there must be some other evidence that supports mistaken belief.

The Supreme Court considered the defence in *R. v. Park.*[62] The victim had met the accused in a parking lot, where he helped her move her car from an icy spot. She gave him her phone number. About a week later they went out on a date, where some sexual activity short of intercourse took place—the testimony of the accused and the victim differed as to what exactly occurred. Two weeks later, the accused called the victim at 6 a.m. after driving all night from Winnipeg. He asked if he could stop by. She agreed. A few minutes later, she met him at her door in her bathrobe and greeted him with a kiss on the cheek. At this point their stories diverged. He claimed that she willingly participated in sexual activity but that there was no intercourse. She claimed that he forced her to have intercourse and that she actively resisted. After the incident, he left and she went to her counsellor. A hospital examination indicated that her condition was consistent with consensual or non-consensual intercourse. The trial judge refused to allow the defence of honest but mistaken belief in consent. The accused was convicted. His appeal to the court of appeal was allowed. The court of appeal held that the trial judge should have allowed the defence because there were factors that gave the defence an "air of reality"—for example, the telephone conversation at 6 a.m., her greeting him in a bathrobe, the kiss, and their prior sexual relationship. The Supreme Court of Canada disagreed. All of these factors were indications that she *might* consent to sex but not that she did consent. Here, there was no evidence that would give an "air of reality" to the defence of mistaken belief.

The Court reaffirmed its decision in *Osolin* and clarified the "air of reality" test by stating that it is not the trial judge's job to weigh the evidence or to decide whether the evidence is believable—this is the jury's job. However, it is the trial judge's job to determine whether there is any evidence that could support the accused's assertion of consent. This supporting evidence might be independent "real evidence" but does not need to be. The evidence may come from the detailed testimony of the accused or of the complainant. The totality of the evidence for the accused must reasonably and realistically be capable of supporting the defence. The Court concluded:

> To summarize, when the complainant and the accused give similar versions of the facts and the only material contradiction is in their interpretation of what happened, then the defence of honest but mistaken belief in consent should generally be put to the jury, except in cases where the accused's conduct demonstrates recklessness or wilful blindness to the absence of consent. On the other hand judges have generally refused to put the defence of honest but mistaken belief in consent to the juries when the accused clearly bases his defence on voluntary consent, and he also testifies that the complainant was an active, eager partner, whereas the complainant testifies that she vigorously resisted. In such cases, the question is generally simply one of credibility, of consent or no consent.[63]

Osolin and *Park* demonstrate how the Supreme Court has limited the defence of mistaken belief in consent by requiring that it at least have an air of reality. In 1992, Parliament went even further by enacting s.273.2 as part of the "no means no" law:

The defence of mistake is simply a denial of *mens rea*. The defence of honest but mistaken belief requires that an accused believe that the complainant affirmatively communicated her consent by words or conduct her agreement to engage in sexual activity with the accused.[64] The defence does not impose any burden of proof on an accused and may arise on any evidence, including in the Crown case-in-chief. It has been held that honest but mistaken belief can be raised if it is established that accused believed that the complainant communicated consent through words or actions. But it is not a defence to argue that the complainant did not resist or was silent as this ambiguous behaviour does not constitute a defence that the complainant consented.

63 Ibid. at page 17.
64 *R. v. Ewanchuk* (1999), 131 C.C.C. (3d) 481 (S.C.C.) at 499-500.

See also *R. v. Darrach*,[65] where the accused was charged with sexual assault of a woman he had been seeing. His defence was that the complainant consented and alternately his belief in that consent. He also sought to introduce evidence of the complainant's prior sexual activity with him. He argued that his right to make full answer and defence to a charge of sexual assault would be impeded if he could not lead this evidence. He also argued that the principle against self-incrimination would be hindered if he were forced to testify. He submitted a detailed affidavit but refused to be cross-examined on it, asserting his right not to have to testify against himself. The trial judge found that it was impossible to assess the probative value and prejudicial effect of the evidence and refused to admit the evidence of prior sexual activity. The Supreme Court of Canada held that section 265(4) may result in placing a tactical or evidential burden on the accused to adduce some evidence capable of raising a reasonable doubt, but it did not infringe the accused's right not to testify against himself and therefore did not infringe the Charter of Rights and Freedoms.

On the issue of mistaken belief in consent, the Ontario Court of Appeal decided the issue on the "basis that the offence of sexual assault carries with it a sufficient social stigma as to require a subjective fault requirement on the part of the accused person. . . .notwithstanding section 273.2(b), the offence is still largely one based on subjective fault—at least to a level that would satisfy constitutional requirements. . . .No doubt, the provision can be regarded as introducing an objective component into the mental element of the offences but it is one which, in itself, is a modified one. It is personalized according to the subjective awareness of the accused at the time. The accused is to take "reasonable steps" in the circumstances known to the accused at the time, to ascertain that the complainant is consenting". . . . the accused it not under an obligation to determine all relevant circumstances—the issue is what he actually knew, not what he ought to have known. . . . The provision does not require that a mistaken belief in consent must be reasonable in order to exculpate. The provision merely requires that a person about to engage in sexual activity take "reasonable steps. . .to ascertain that the complainant was consenting". The accused was convicted and the Supreme Court of Canada upheld the conviction.[66]

> **273.2. It is not a defence to a charge under section 271, 272 or 273 that the accused believed that the complainant consented to the activity that forms the subject-matter of the charge, where**
>
> **(a) the accused's belief arose from the accused's**
>
> **(i) self-induced intoxication, or**
>
> **(ii) recklessness or wilful blindness; or**

---

65 (1998), 122 C.C.C. (3d) 225 (Ont.C.A.); (2000), 148 C.C.C. (3d) 97 (S.C.C.), cited to (1998), 122 C.C.C. (3d) 225 (Ont.C.A.). See also *Darrach* (1994), 17 O.R. (3d) 481 (Prov.Div.) for a discussion of the question as to whether or not *Darrach*, properly attentive to the issue of consent (i.e., not wilfully blind), could have, in light of the ambiguity, honestly concluded that the complainant had the capacity and was consenting to the sexual activity.

66 Ibid. cited to 122 C.C.C. (3d) 225 (Ont.C.A.) at 252.

(b) the accused did not take reasonable steps, in the circumstances known to the accused at the time, to ascertain that the complainant was consenting.

The principle of wilful blindness was discussed by the Supreme Court of Canada in *Sansregret v. The Queen.*[67] The accused was charged with rape on the grounds that the victim's consent had been exhorted by threats or fear of bodily harm. The accused and the victim had been living together, but the latter had broken off the relationship because of the former's violence toward her. A few days later, the accused broke into the victim's home at 4:30 a.m. armed with a file-like weapon. To calm him down, the victim told him there was a chance of reconciliation and consented to having intercourse with him. After he left her home, she called the police and claimed to have been raped. The police investigated but no charges were laid. However, the accused's probation officer had become involved, and there was evidence that he had asked her not to press charges. Three weeks later, the accused again broke into her house. She seized the phone to call the police but he ripped the phone out of the jack. He was armed with a butcher knife. He was furious and violent. The victim testified that she was in fear of her life and sanity. She again pretended that there was hope of reconciliation and consented to have intercourse with him. In the morning she drove the accused to the location he requested. She then went to her mother's and called the police.

At his trial, the accused was found guilty of breaking and entering and unlawful confinement but not guilty of rape, even though the trial judge found that there was no real consent. The judge stated that the accused "saw what he wanted to see, heard what he wanted to hear, believed what he wanted to believe." However, the judge acquitted him of the rape charge because of his honest belief in her consent. The Supreme Court of Canada disagreed and held that the defence of mistake of fact was not available to the accused because of his "wilful blindness." The Court defined wilful blindness as follows: "[W]ilful blindness arises where a person who has become aware of the need for some inquiry [in this case, whether the victim was giving true consent] declines to make the inquiry because he does not wish to know the truth. He would prefer to remain ignorant."[68] The Court concluded that because of the earlier episode and the rape complaint, for the accused to proceed with intercourse constituted "self-deception to the point of wilful blindness."

One of the more controversial aspects of the "no means no" law was the requirement that the accused take "all" reasonable steps in the circumstances to ensure that there is consent. This has been altered from the first version (Bill 49) which removed "all" and replaced it with "reasonable steps."

Pappajohn must now be read in light of section 273.2 as this section imposes the additional requirement of reasonable steps. Citing the dissenting reasons of McLachlin J. in *R. v. Esau* (1997), 116 C.C.C. (3d) 289 (S.C.C.)

---

67 (1985), 18 C.C.C. (3d) 223 (S.C.C.).
68 Ibid. at page 235.

at page 314, the Ontario Court of Appeal stated, in *Darrach*,[69] that "A person is not entitled to take ambiguity as the equivalent of consent. If a person, acting honestly, and without wilful blindness, perceives his companion's conduct as ambiguous or unclear, his duty is to abstain or obtain clarification on the issue of consent. This appears to be the rule at common law. In this situation, to use the words of Lord Cross of Chelsea in Morgan, [supra,] [[1976] A.C. 182] at page 203, "it is only fair to the woman and not in the least unfair to the man that he should be under a duty to take reasonable care to ascertain that she is consenting to the intercourse and be at risk of prosecution if he fails to take such care". As Glanville Williams, Textbook of Criminal Law (London: Stevens & Sons, 1978), at page 101 put it: "the defendant is guilty if he realized the woman might not be consenting and took no steps to find out."

d. Consent No Defence Where Complainant Under 14

Recall from Chapter Seven that there are certain sexual offences involving children where consent is no defence. With regard to sexual assault under ss. 271, 272, or 273, s.150.1 provides that consent is no defence where the complainant is under the age of 14. However, s.150.1(2) creates an exception to this rule. It provides that consent can be a defence to a charge under s.271 where the complainant is between the ages of 12 and 14 and the accused:

(a) is twelve years of age or more but under the age of sixteen years;

(b) is less than two years older than the complainant; and

(c) is neither in a position of trust or authority towards the complainant nor is a person with whom the complainant is in a relationship of dependency.

e. Where Mistake Made as to Age

Where the complainant's age is relevant to whether consent is valid, the accused may want to raise the defence of mistake of fact as to the complainant's age. Section 150.1(4) limits this defence:

(4) It is not a defence to a charge under section . . . 271, 272 or 273 that the accused believed that the complainant was fourteen years of age or more at the time the offence is alleged to have been committed unless the accused took all reasonable steps to ascertain the age of the complainant.

In other words, the accused can raise the defence of reasonable mistake of fact.

Both the general rule under s.150.1(1) regarding consent not being a defence, and the rule under s.150.1(4) regarding mistake as to age, are open to challenge under the Charter as violating a principle of fundamental justice (s.7), and as denying equality under the law (s.15).

---

69 Supra, at page 253.

2. Sexual Assault Under Section 272

Sexual assault under s.272 is more serious than s.271 assault. It involves either a weapon, or actual or threatened bodily harm, or more than one assailant:

> **272. (1) Every person commits an offence who, in committing a sexual assault,**
>
> **(a) carries, uses or threatens to use a weapon or an imitation of a weapon;**
>
> **(b) threatens to cause bodily harm to a person other than the complainant;**
>
> **(c) causes bodily harm to the complainant; or**
>
> **(d) is a party to the offence with any other person,**
>
> **(2) Every person who commits an offence under subsection (1) is guilty of an indictable offence and liable**
>
> **(a) where a firearm is used in the commission of the offence, to imprisonment for a term not exceeding fourteen years and to a minimum punishment of imprisonment for a term of four years; and**
>
> **(b) in any other case, to imprisonment for a term not exceeding fourteen years.**

3. Sexual Assault Under Section 273

The most serious offence of sexual assault is aggravated sexual assault, which involves serious bodily harm to the complainant:

> **273. (1) Every one commits an aggravated sexual assault who, in committing a sexual assault, wounds, maims, disfigures or endangers the life of the complainant.**
>
> **(2) Every person who commits an aggravated sexual assault is guilty of an indictable offence and liable**
>
> **(a) where a firearm was used in the commission of the offence, to imprisonment for life and to a minimum punishment of imprisonment for a term of four years; and**
>
> **(b) in any other case, to imprisonment for life.**

F. OTHER OFFENCES AGAINST THE PERSON

1. Criminal Harassment

> **264. (1) No person shall, without lawful authority and knowing that another person is harassed or recklessly as to whether the other per-**

son is harassed, engage in conduct referred to in subsection (2) that causes the other person reasonably, in all the circumstances, to fear for their safety or the safety of anyone known to them.

(2) The conduct mentioned in subsection (1) consists of

(a) repeatedly following from place to place the other person or anyone known to them;

(b) repeatedly communicating with, either directly or indirectly, the other person or anyone known to them;

(c) besetting or watching the dwelling-house, or place where the other person, or anyone known to them, resides, works, carries on business or happens to be; or

(d) engaging in threatening conduct directed at the other person or any member of their family.

The *mens rea* for this offence is to knowingly or recklessly harass a person by engaging in the conduct stated in s.264(2), thereby causing a person to fear for his or her safety or another person's safety.

This is sometimes called the anti-stalking law. It is aimed at protecting women in particular who are being harassed by men, such as ex-husbands or ex-boyfriends. It became law in 1993. The section has been challenged as violating s.7 of the Charter for being too vague and for violating the right to freedom of expression under s.2 of the Charter.[70] The decision of a judge of the Alberta Court of Queen's Bench[71] was that although there are a number of terms that need to be defined by the courts, such as "fear for their safety," "repeatedly follow," and so on, they are terms capable of being given a "settled meaning" by the courts. Therefore, the section is not overly vague. As to the issue of freedom of expression, the court stated that the behaviour defined in s.264 is only prohibited when it causes the other person to be harassed or to reasonably fear for his or her safety. This type of conduct is an act of violence that can cause psychological harm and so is not protected under the Charter's freedom of expression provisions. The application by the accused to have the section struck down was dismissed and was upheld on appeal.

The court stated in *Sillip* that a jury should be instructed to find the accused guilty of criminal harassment if they believed beyond a reasonable doubt that:

i. That the accused engaged in the conduct set out in section 264(2)(a), (b), (c), or (d) of the Criminal Code;
ii. The complainant was harassed;
iii. The accused knew or was reckless or wilfully blind as to whether the complainant was harassed;

---

70 See Chapter One regarding vague laws violating the principles of fundamental justice under the Charter at page 10.
71 *R. v. Sillip* (1995), 99 C.C.C. (3d) 394 (Alta.Ct.Q.B.); (1997), 120 C.C.C. (3d) 384 (Alta.C.A.), leave to appeal to the Supreme Court of Canada refused (1998), 142 C.C.C. (3d) 195n.

iv. The conduct caused the complainant to fear for her safety or the safety of anyone known to her;

v. The complainant's fear, in all the circumstances was reasonable.[72]

2. Unlawfully Causing Bodily Harm

269. Every one who unlawfully causes bodily harm to any person is guilty of

(a) an indictable offence . . .

(b) an offence punishable on summary conviction. . .

This offence covers any unlawful act that causes bodily harm. In *R. v. DeSousa*,[73] the offence was extensively analysed by the Supreme Court of Canada. The accused had been at a party on New Year's Eve. The victim was standing about 2.5 metres from a group of men when a fight broke out. The men started throwing bottles. One crashed on the wall near her. A glass fragment struck her arm, seriously gashing it. The accused was charged with unlawfully causing bodily harm. At the start of the trial the accused challenged the validity of the offence under the Charter. He argued that the unlawful act could include absolute liability offences, which would offend s.7 of the Charter by allowing criminal liability where there is no moral fault. He also questioned whether the offence requires an intentional causing of bodily harm as part of the *mens rea* of the offence. The Supreme Court of Canada held that it would offend s.7 of the Charter to base criminal liability on an absolute liability offence. However, the unlawful act in s.269 can be interpreted as referring to provincial or federal offences only and as excluding absolute liability offences. This is consistent with general rules of criminal law interpretation. Furthermore, in light of previous court decisions, the meaning of "unlawful" in the context of s.269 is that the unlawful act must be at least objectively dangerous; that is, a reasonable person would realize that the unlawful act would create a risk of bodily harm. The bodily harm must be more than merely trivial or transitory in nature and will, the Court stated, usually involve an act of violence done deliberately to another person. On the second issue, the Court held that there was no requirement that the accused intend to cause bodily harm. Unlawfully causing bodily harm is one of the offences that does not require subjective intent.[74] Section 269 requires only objective foresight of bodily harm. In conclusion, the Court found that s.269 is not unconstitutional. The case was sent back for trial.

3. Kidnapping

279. (1) Every person commits an offence who kidnaps a person with intent

72 Ibid. at page 393.
73 (1992), 76 C.C.C. (3d) 124 (S.C.C.).
74 See Chapter Three, page 47 "*Mens Rea* and the Charter," for a discussion of offences that do not require subjective intent.

(a) to cause the person to be confined or imprisoned against the person's will;

(b) to cause the person to be unlawfully sent or transported out of Canada against the person's will; or

(c) to hold him for ransom or to service against the person's will.

(1.1) Every person who commits an offence under subsection (1) is guilty of an indictable offence and liable

(a) where a firearm is used in the commission of the offence, to imprisonment for life and to a minimum punishment of imprisonment for a term of four years; and

(b) in any other case to imprisonment for life.

(2) Every one who, without lawful authority, confines, imprisons or forcibly seizes another person is guilty of an indictable offence and liable to imprisonment for a term not exceeding ten years.

This section creates the offences of kidnapping, forcible seizure, confinement, and imprisonment. Kidnapping is the most serious offence and requires specific intent to carry out one of the purposes in subs.(1)(a) to (c).

The term "kidnapping" is not defined in the Code. It has, however, long been an offence at common law, being considered a form of aggravated false imprisonment. Many of the older English cases of kidnapping involved sending the victim out of the country.[75] However, an early Canadian case established that kidnapping does not require the stolen person to be taken out of the country.[76] This broader definition is reflected in the present wording of the section. Some help in defining the term is given by the English case of *R. v. Reid*.[77] A husband had been charged with kidnapping his wife. In finding that a man can be convicted of the offence even though the victim is his wife, the court accepted a definition of kidnapping that referred to the stealing, carrying away, or secreting of a person against that person's will. The offence, the court stated, is complete when the victim is seized and carried away.

The kidnapping must be done against the person's will. In *R. v. Brown*,[78] the Ontario Court of Appeal considered this question: If person A willingly goes with person B because of the false statements made by person B, has person A been taken against his or her will? The accused picked up a 10-year-old girl by falsely telling her that her father had asked him to drive her to school. Instead, the accused drove the girl out of the city to an isolated spot. When he approached her, she attempted to get out of the car. The accused then choked her until she was unconscious. Believing her to be dead, he put her body in the car trunk and drove 40 kilometres to a garbage

---

75 See, for example, *Attorney General v. Edge* (1943), I.R. 115; and *R. v. Hale* (1974), 1 All E.R. 1107, where the historical sources of the offence are discussed.
76 *Cornwall v. the Queen* (1872-3), 33 Upper Can. Q.B. 106.
77 (1972), 2 All E.R. 1350 (C.A.).
78 (1972), 8 C.C.C. (2d) 12 (Ont.C.A.).

dump, where he threw the body and covered it with garbage. After the accused drove away, the girl escaped to a farmhouse. For the accused's defence, it was argued that since the child went with the accused willingly, the accused could not be convicted of kidnapping. The court rejected this argument, stating that the kidnapping occurred as soon as the accused's false statements induced the victim to enter the car. The victim did not act willingly when her actions were induced by false statements. Furthermore, the accused's actions of choking her, placing her in the trunk, and driving her 40 kilometres to a garbage dump were "clearly within the kidnapping section." The accused was found guilty of kidnapping.

The offences under s.279 contain a reverse onus clause:

> **(3) In proceedings under this section, the fact that the person in relation to whom the offence is alleged to have been committed did not resist is not a defence unless the accused proves that the failure to resist was not caused by threats, duress, force or exhibition of force.**

The Ontario Court of Appeal, in *R. v. Gough*,[79] held that this clause is an unconstitutional infringement of the Charter and not valid. The accused had known the victim for about five years. At one point they were engaged to be married. The victim had broken off the engagement, however, because of the accused's violence toward her. After breaking the engagement, she went into hiding. She had been hiding for several weeks when she left the house to run errands. She told her friend that if she did not come back or was seen in the presence of the accused, the police should be called. While on her errands, she did encounter the accused and went with him to a restaurant. Over her protests, he insisted on driving her home. They first went to a dental clinic, where she paid a bill. He went into the clinic with her. They then went to a donut shop to continue their conversation. He again insisted on driving her home. Once they were in the car, he said they were going for gas and then for a ride. She testified that when she said she did not want to go for a ride, an angry, blank look came over his face. She thought he was going to hit her, so she remained silent. They then drove for several days to the city where the victim's parents lived. They visited with her parents and spent the night. The next morning the police arrived. The accused was arrested and charged with kidnapping.

At the trial, the judge instructed the jury that to use the defence of consent, the accused was required to prove that the victim's failure to resist was not caused by threats, duress, force, or exhibition of force. The accused was found guilty and convicted. He appealed his conviction, arguing that s.279(3) violates the Charter. The Ontario Court of Appeal, using the *Oakes* test set out by the Supreme Court of Canada,[80] held that the clause does violate the Charter and is not a justifiable limitation. It gave these reasons:

- The clause requires the accused to prove the state of mind of the victim (i.e., that the victim failed to resist because she consented and not because

---

79 (1985), 18 C.C.C. (3d) 453 (Ont.C.A.).
80 (1986), 24 C.C.C. (3d) 321 (S.C.C.). See Chapter Two, page 28 for a discussion of the *Oakes* test.

of threats). Proving the victim's state of mind is an unreasonably heavy burden to put on the accused.

- The proved fact does not rationally tend to prove the presumed fact. In other words, the proved fact that the victim did not resist does not tend to prove that the victim's failure to resist was caused by fear of threats.

The court set aside the accused's conviction and ordered a new trial. A decision of the Alberta Court of Queen's Bench[81] also found the subsection unconstitutional. It will be up to the Supreme Court of Canada to finally decide the constitutionality of s.279(3).

4. Unlawful Confinement

Kidnapping requires moving the victim from one place to another; unlawful confinement or imprisonment involves physically restraining a person from moving from place to place. In *R. v. Gratton*,[82] the accused was charged with unlawfully confining a woman to whom he had been engaged. The victim testified that she was home alone with her two children when at about 1:30 in the morning, she heard a banging on her window. It was the accused. He then went to the back door and pounded on it. She agreed to let him in because she thought he would break the door down. She then asked the accused what he wanted. He rushed out to the porch and returned with a loaded shotgun. He then brought out her two children from their bedroom with the gun pointed at them. He pulled the telephone from the wall. They then talked for a long time. At one point he became very angry and punched a hole through a wall. The police came to the door about 5:45 in the morning. They found the victim hysterical, shaking, and trembling. She did not answer their questions but said, "I can't, he's going to kill me." They found the gun and shells, which he had hidden when the police came to the door. The court held that there was ample evidence for a jury to find that the victim had been unlawfully confined. The confinement did not need to be for the whole period of time the accused was in the house, but only for a "significant period of time." His using the gun, pulling the telephone out of its connection, and displaying the gun in front of the children were all acts that must have had the effect of threatening her and overcoming her resistance.

5. Abduction

a. Distinguished from Kidnapping

There are three basic differences between an abduction offence and kidnapping. First, the mental element or intent required for an abduction offence differs from that required for kidnapping. Second, the victim of the offence of abduction is always a young person (under 14 or under 16, depending on

---

81 *R. v. Grift* (1986), 28 C.C.C. (3d) 120 (Alta.Q.B.). See also *R. v. Pete* (1998), 131 C.C.C. (3d) 233 (B.C.C.A.).
82 (1985), 18 C.C.C. (3d) 462 (Ont.C.A.), leave to appeal to S.C.C. refused, loc. cit.

the offence). Third, kidnapping requires a taking of the victim against the victim's will, whereas abduction is possible in some situations even though the victim consents.

b. Abduction Under Section 280

> **280. (1) Every one who, without lawful authority, takes or causes to be taken an unmarried person under the age of sixteen years out of the possession of and against the will of the parent or guardian of that person or of any other person who has the lawful care or charge of that person is guilty of an indictable offence . . .**
>
> **(2) In this section and sections 281 to 283, "guardian" includes any per-son who has in law or in fact the custody or control of another person.**

Before the changes to the Code in 1983, the offence that is now s.280 only applied to female victims and when the taking was for the purpose of marriage or illicit sexual intercourse. The present offence does not require any specific intent but only that the young unmarried person be taken against the will of the parent or guardian.

Section 286 provides that the consent of the young person is no defence:

> **286. In proceedings in respect of an offence under sections 280 to 283, it is not a defence to any charge that a young person consented to or suggested any conduct of the accused.**

So, for example, in *R. v. Langevin*,[83] the accused was found guilty of abducting two 14-year-old girls even though the court said that the girls had taken a very active if not leading part in the occurrence.

Section 285 does provide a defence, however:

> **285. No one shall be found guilty of an offence under sections 280 to 283 if the court is satisfied that the taking, enticing away, concealing, detaining, receiving or harbouring of any young person was necessary to protect the young person from danger of imminent harm . . .**

This defence was raised in *R. v. Adams*.[84] In *Mendez*, the court found that there had to be a connection between the taking of the child and the escape from the imminent harm. Adams and a man named Dodge began living together with Dodge's young daughter, Sabrina. Adams claimed that their relationship deteriorated because of Dodge's drinking and violence. She thought of leaving but did not want to leave Sabrina, to whom she had become very attached. Adams's mother became concerned about her daughter's condition. She knew that Adams would not leave Dodge without Sabrina. She, her friends, and Adams's sister concocted a plan to take Adams and Sabrina to a women's shelter when Dodge was not home. The plan was

---

83   (1962), 133 C.C.C. 257 (Ont.C.A.).
84   (1993), 79 C.C.C. (3d) 193 (Ont.C.A.). See also *R. v. Mendez* (1997), 113 C.C.C. (3d) 304 (Ont.C.A.), leave to appeal to the Supreme Court of Canada refused 121 C.C.C. (3d) vi.

carried out. While at the women's shelter, Adams and Sabrina were interviewed by a Children's Aid Society worker, who concluded that Sabrina had
not been physically abused. Adams and Sabrina left the shelter to stay with
Adams's aunt because Adams knew that the Children's Aid worker planned
to apprehend Sabrina. A few days later she applied for interim custody of
Sabrina; shortly after that, she surrendered to the police. Sabrina was
returned to her father, and Adams and her mother and friends were charged
with abduction. They were convicted. Their main ground of appeal was that
the judge had not instructed the jury properly on the defence of honest but
mistaken belief that Sabrina was in danger of imminent harm. The appeal
court ruled that to use the defence, the belief must be honest, though it need
not be reasonable. However, the reasonableness of the defence should be
considered in deciding whether the belief was honest. In addition, the
defence was not made out unless the taking of Sabrina was necessary in an
objective sense based on the facts as the accused honestly believed them to
be. The taking must be a response to the perceived danger of imminent
harm. In this case the instructions of the judge adequately directed the jury.
Therefore, the appeal was dismissed.

An element of the offence is that the accused must have taken the person
out of the possession of his or her parents. Thus, if a person leaves home and
later goes with the accused, the accused cannot be found guilty of abduction.
Of course, if the accused aided the young person in leaving home by giving
transportation or other encouragement, the fact that he or she did not physically "take" the young person will not save the accused. *R. v. Cox*[85] considered
whether a girl was taken against the will of her parent when the parent
allowed the girl to be taken based on the accused's fraudulent statements. The
accused told the girl's mother that he needed a baby-sitter for his three children. The mother allowed her 15-year-old daughter to go with the accused in
his car. When the accused did not turn at the street where he said his house
was located, the girl became alarmed and escaped from the car. At his trial, it
was found that the accused had used a false name and address and had lied
about his employment situation. The court of appeal held that a consent
obtained by fraud or trick is not consent; thus, before a person can be said to
do an act willingly, he or she must be consciously consenting to the act.

c. Abduction Under Section 281

> **281. (1) Every one who, not being the parent, guardian or person hav-
> ing the lawful care or charge of a person under the age of fourteen
> years, unlawfully takes, entices away, conceals, detains, receives or
> harbours that person with intent to deprive a parent or guardian, or
> any other person who has the lawful care or charge of that person, of
> the possession of that person is guilty of an indictable offence and
> liable to imprisonment for a term not exceeding ten years.**

---

85   (1969), 4 C.C.C. 321 (Ont.C.A.).

Notice that this offence of abduction is committed even if the accused only "harbours" or "receives" the child. For example, if a 12-year-old runs away from home and is allowed to stay in the home of a person, that person may be convicted of the offence if the necessary intent is proven. It will not matter that the person did not entice or encourage the child to leave home. It is a necessary element of the offence that the detention be for the purpose of depriving a parent or guardian of possession.

The Supreme Court of Canada considered the *mens rea* for this offence in *R. v. Chartrand*.[86] The accused, a 43-year-old man, was hitting golf balls in a schoolyard in Ottawa. An eight-year-old boy, Tyler, and his friends were also in the yard. They asked if they could catch the balls with their gloves. After doing this for a while, some of the boys left to get refreshments. Tyler stayed. The accused began photographing him. When Tyler's friends returned, they found the accused taking pictures of Tyler at the edge of the schoolyard in a wooded area. They began to interfere with the picture taking. Eventually the accused suggested to Tyler that they go somewhere else. Tyler agreed to go in the accused's car, even though his friends told him not to go. The friends returned home and told one of their mothers that Tyler had gone off with a man in a red car. She called Tyler's father. Tyler's father, the boys, and a police officer began to look for him. They found him between 30 and 90 minutes later, at a beach, where the accused was photographing him.

The accused was charged with abduction. The trial judge directed an acquittal on the grounds that there was no evidence on which a jury could conclude that the accused intended to deprive the parents of possession of Tyler. The Crown's appeal was dismissed. The case finally reached the Supreme Court of Canada on the proper interpretation of the section—that is, on the meaning of "unlawfully" and the required *mens rea*. Regarding the meaning of the term "unlawfully," the Court held that the offence does not require an additional unlawful act. "Unlawfully" as it is used in this offence merely means without lawful justification, authority, or excuse. The Court distinguished this offence from unlawfully causing bodily harm, for which an unlawful act (the predicate offence) is required.

To determine the *mens rea* for the offence, the Court first looked at the meaning of "deprive a parent . . . of the possession . . ." The Court explained that possession is not limited to circumstances in which the parent or guardian is actually in physical possession of the child. The concept of possession relates to the ability of the parent to exercise his or her right of control over the child. Therefore, a child playing with a group of other children is still in the possession of his or her parent. The deprivation of possession may only be for a short time and need not be an attempt at permanent removal. So in this case Tyler was in the possession of his parents at the time of the incident.

Regarding the meaning of "with intent to," it is enough that the taker knows or foresees that his or her actions would be certain or substantially

---

86   (1994), 91 C.C.C. (3d) 396 (S.C.C.).

certain to result in the parents being deprived of the ability to exercise control over their child.

The court concluded that there was sufficient evidence on which a jury could convict. The trial judge had erred in directing an acquittal. The appeal was allowed and the case was sent back for trial.

The defence that abduction was necessary to protect the young person from harm (s.285, above) applies to this offence. Section 284 sets out another defence:

> **284. No one shall be found guilty of an offence under sections 281 to 283 if he establishes that the taking, enticing away, concealing, detaining, receiving or harbouring of any young person was done with the consent of the parent, guardian or other person having the lawful possession, care or charge of that young person.**

Before ss. 282 and 283, which deal with abductions by parents, were enacted, the cases reported under s.281 tended to involve separated parents who, in fighting over the custody of their children, engaged in child-stealing. This section proved to be inadequate to deal with the problem of parents abducting their own children. For example, where there was no custody order, it was not clear whether a parent could be guilty of an offence under this section. In *R. v. Kosawan*,[87] a court in Manitoba held that in the absence of a custody order restricting parental rights, each parent has an equal right to custody; therefore, it is not an unlawful act for one parent to take the children. This situation encouraged parents who did not yet have a formal custody order to take the children from the other parent, especially since the parent who has actual possession of the child has a strategic advantage when seeking a custody order. In 1983, two new offences of abduction were added to the Code: one deals with situations where a custody order exists, the other applies whether or not a custody order exists. Thus, under the present scheme, "stranger" abductions are charged under s.281. If a parent is the accused, the charge will be made under s.282 or s.283.

d. Abduction Under Section 282

> **282. (1) Every one who, being the parent, guardian or person having the lawful care or charge of a person under the age of fourteen years, takes, entices away, conceals, detains, receives, or harbours that person, in contravention of the custody provisions of a custody order in relation to that person made by a court anywhere in Canada, with intent to deprive a parent or guardian or any other person who has the lawful care or charge of that person, of the possession of that person is guilty of**
>
> **(a) an indictable offence and is liable to imprisonment for a term not exceeding ten years; or**

87 [1980] 6 W.W.R. 674 (Man.Cty.Ct.).

(b) an offence punishable on summary conviction.

Abduction under this section requires that the parent, guardian or other person having lawful care or charge of a child under 14 take the child in contravention of a custody order with intent to deprive the other parent of possession.

The defences under ss. 284 and 285 are available to the accused. Another defence—that the accused was mistaken about the existence of a custody order—was allowed in *R. v. Ilczysyn*,[88] a decision of the Ontario Court of Appeal. The accused had lived with a man named West in a common law relationship from August 1982 to March 1985. They had a child in September 1984. In March 1985, the accused was sent to a reformatory for an 18-month sentence. While she was in the reformatory, West applied for and obtained a custody order giving him exclusive custody of the child. The accused did not object. When the accused was paroled in August 1985, she resumed living with West. In January or February of 1986, she called her lawyer to find out if the custody order was still valid. Her understanding was that as long as she had resumed cohabiting with West, the order was no longer valid. She lived with West and the child until April, when they had a "falling out." In May, she picked the child up from the baby-sitter and went to another city. About five weeks later she was apprehended and charged with abduction. She was acquitted on the grounds that either the custody order became invalid when she began living with West or that it would be against public policy to enforce it. The court of appeal disagreed with the grounds used by the trial court to acquit her and held that West had legal custody of the child. However, the accused had made a mistake about the validity of the order and could use the defence of mistake of law. The rule that mistake of law is not a defence did not apply in this case because the mistake concerned the civil law. The court dismissed the Crown's appeal from her acquittal.

In *R. v. Hammerbeck*,[89] the court of appeal held that the defence of mistake regarding the validity of the order can be used even if the mistake is not reasonable. In other words, a subjective test is used: Did the accused have an honest, even though unreasonable, belief that the order was invalid?

In 1993, to deal with situations where the defence of honest mistake is raised, s.282(2) was added to the offence:

> **(2) Where a count charges an offence under subsection (1) and the offence is not proven only because the accused did not believe that there was a valid custody order but the evidence does prove an offence under section 283, the accused may be convicted of an offence under section 283.**

The effect of s.282(2) is that where an accused successfully raises the defence of mistake and is found not guilty because there is a reasonable doubt as to whether the accused knew there was a valid custody order, the accused can be convicted under s.283, where it is irrelevant whether a custody order exists.

---

88 (1988), 45 C.C.C. (3d) 91 (Ont.C.A.).
89 (1991), 68 C.C.C. (3d) 161 (B.C.C.A.).

e. Abduction Under Section 283

> **283. (1) Every one who, being the parent, guardian or person having the lawful care or charge of a person under the age of fourteen years, takes, entices away, conceals, detains, receives or harbours that person, whether or not there is a custody order in relation to that person made by a court anywhere in Canada, with intent to deprive a parent or guardian, or any other person who has the lawful care or charge of that person, of the possession of that person, is guilty of**
>
> **(a) an indictable offence and is liable to imprisonment for a term not exceeding ten years; or**
>
> **(b) an offence punishable on summary conviction.**
>
> **(2) No proceedings may be commenced under subsection (1) without the consent of the Attorney General or counsel instructed by him for that purpose.**

An example of the application of this offence is *R. v. Cook*,[90] a decision of the Nova Scotia Court of Appeal. The parents, who were living in Ontario, decided to separate. The mother left their five-year-old child with the father and moved to Nova Scotia. While the child was visiting with her mother, the mother filed an application for custody in Nova Scotia. On the date of the hearing, the father arrived from Ontario and took the child, without the mother's consent, back to Toronto. He was charged with abduction under what is now s.283. The father's argument was that he was only doing what he was legally entitled to do. Their agreement when they separated was that he would have custody of the child. He felt that the custody application by the mother should have been made in Ontario. The court of appeal did not accept his argument, stating that the purpose of the offence is to "force parents to seek the assistance of the courts before taking possession of a child without the consent of the other parent." Here, it was clear that the accused's intention was to deprive the mother of possession. The court of appeal confirmed his conviction.

In *R. v. Dawson*,[91] another decision of the Nova Scotia Court of Appeal, the elements of the offence were considered and upheld by the Supreme Court of Canada. The accused, who was the father of the child, had a common law relationship with the mother. When they separated, the father took custody of their child. No formal custody order was made. After a few years the mother decided to apply for custody. She obtained an order that the child not be removed from the province during the time that the custody issue was being settled. Disregarding the order, the father took the child to the United States, where he was apprehended two years later and charged with abduction. He argued that he had not taken the child from the mother's possession, since at all times the child had been legally in his possession. The court

---

90 (1984), 12 C.C.C. (3d) 471 (N.S.C.A.).
91 (1995), 100 C.C.C. (3d) 123 (N.S.C.A.); application for leave to appeal to the Supreme Court of Canada dismissed (1996), 111 C.C.C. (3d) 1 (S.C.C.).

agreed with his argument, and he was acquitted at his trial. On appeal, the court held that the trial judge was in error. The section is aimed at protecting both the parent's possession of the child and right to possession. Under Nova Scotia law, both parents have an equal right to custody until such time as a custody order is made. Although the mother did not have actual possession, she had a statutory and common law right to possession. The essential element of the offence is the intention of the accused to deprive the other parent of possession or the right to possession. The critical issue in this case was whether the accused had the intent to deprive the mother of her right to possession.

Notice that to bring a charge under this section, the consent of the Attorney General or counsel instructed by the Attorney General is necessary. This requirement indicates that the circumstances are carefully considered before a charge is laid.

6. Inciting Hatred

319. (1) Every one who, by communicating statements in any public place, incites hatred against any identifiable group where such incitement is likely to lead to a breach of the peace is guilty of

(a) an indictable offence and is liable to imprisonment for a term not exceeding two years; or

(b) an offence punishable on summary conviction.

(2) Every one who, by communicating statements, other than in private conversation, wilfully promotes hatred against any identifiable group is guilty of

(a) an indictable offence and is liable to imprisonment for a term not exceeding two years; or

(b) an offence punishable on summary conviction.

(3) No person shall be convicted of an offence under subsection (2)

(a) if he establishes that the statements communicated were true;

(b) if, in good faith, he expressed or attempted to establish by argument an opinion upon a religious subject;

(c) if the statements were relevant to any subject of public interest, the discussion of which was for the public benefit, and if on reasonable grounds he believed them to be true; or

(d) if, in good faith, he intended to point out, for the purpose of removal, matters producing or tending to produce feelings of hatred towards an identifiable group in Canada.

The Attorney General must give consent before proceedings for these offences can be started. "Communicating" includes use of the telephone, broadcasting, or any other audible or visible means. An identifiable group is defined in s.318 as "any section of the public distinguished by colour, race, religion or ethnic origin."

These offences have rarely been used; however, two cases, which were finally heard by the Supreme Court of Canada, are of interest because they considered the application of freedom of expression under the Charter. The cases were *R. v. Keegstra,*[92] and *R. v. Andrews and Smith.*[93] Keegstra was a high school history teacher in Alberta who was charged with an offence under s.319(2). For years he had taught that the Holocaust (the killing of six million Jews during World War II) had never happened and that the story had been started by an international Jewish conspiracy. The charges were laid after a parent discovered what was being taught and complained to the authorities. Andrews and Smith were members of a Toronto-based political party that supported white supremacy. They were charged under s.319(2) for publishing a neo-Nazi magazine which claimed, among other things, that non-white and non-Aryan groups were inferior and responsible for violent crime in Canada.

In both cases, the accused argued that the offences for which they were charged violated their freedom of expression as protected under the Charter. They also argued that s.319(3)(a) creates an unjustifiable reverse onus clause, in that an accused cannot be convicted if he or she can establish (prove on a balance of probabilities) that the statements were true. Thus, a jury could convict an accused if it had even a doubt about the truth of the statements. In other words, the Crown did not have to establish an element of the offence—that statements were not true—beyond a reasonable doubt.

The Alberta Court of Appeal, in *Keegstra,* held that the section was unconstitutional, and acquitted Keegstra. The Ontario Court of Appeal, in *Andrews and Smith,* reached the opposite conclusion and held that the offence does not violate the Charter.

The Supreme Court of Canada released concurrent judgments in the two cases. In a four-to-three split, the majority upheld the validity of the offence. The Court agreed with the Alberta court that the offence violates the right to freedom of expression and that s.319(3)(a) creates a reverse onus clause. However, it also found that both are justifiable limitations. After discussing the importance of freedom of expression in a democratic society, the Court stated:

> *The suppression of hate propaganda undeniably muzzles the participation of a few individuals in the democratic process, and hence detracts somewhat from free expression values, but the degree of this limitation is not substantial . . . expression can work to undermine our commitment to democracy where employed to propagate ideas anathematic to democratic values. Hate propaganda works in just such a way, arguing as it does for a society in which . . . individuals are denied respect and dignity because of racial or religious*

92 (1990), 61 C.C.C. (3d) 1 (S.C.C.).
93 (1990), 61 C.C.C. (3d) 490 (S.C.C.).

characteristics. This brand of expressive activity is wholly inimical to the democratic aspirations of the free expression guarantee.[94]

G. RECOGNIZANCES TO KEEP THE PEACE

810. (1) An information may be laid before a justice by or on behalf of any person who fears on reasonable grounds that another person will cause personal injury to him or her or to his or her spouse or child or will damage his or her property.

(2) A justice who receives an information under subsection (1) shall cause the parties to appear before him or before a summary conviction court having jurisdiction in the same territorial division.

(3) The justice or the summary conviction court before which the parties appear may, if satisfied by the evidence adduced that the person on whose behalf the information was laid has reasonable grounds for his or her fears,

(a) order that the defendant enter into a recognizance, with or without sureties, to keep the peace and be of good behaviour for any period that does not exceed twelve months, and comply with such other reasonable conditions prescribed in the recognizance, including the conditions set out in subsections (3.1) and (3.2), as the court considers desirable for securing the good conduct of the defendant; or

(b) commit the defendant to prison for a term not exceeding twelve months if he or she fails or refuses to enter into the recognizance.

This section gives courts the authority to exercise what is sometimes called "preventative justice." By entering a recognizance, the defendant agrees to keep the peace and to comply with any other conditions prescribed by the court.

The court must consider before making an order whether the recognizance should include as a condition a prohibition from possessing a firearm or other weapon (see s.810(3.1)), or a prohibition from being within a certain distance of a place where the person on whose behalf the information has been laid regularly is, or a prohibition from communicating with that person (see s.810(3.2)).

A surety is a person who is willing to be responsible for ensuring that the defendant keeps the peace. Sometimes a sum of money must be given to the court by the defendant or the surety as additional encouragement for the defendant to keep the peace. The money is forfeited if the defendant does not honour the recognizance. It is not necessary that an assault or any other offence be committed before a justice uses the powers given by this section;

---

94 Supra, note 92 at page 50.

however, those powers can only be exercised upon "reasonable grounds" that a breach of the peace will occur in the future.[95]

In addition to the authority under this section, the justice has a general authority derived from the common law to maintain order and preserve the peace by ordering persons whom he or she thinks may breach the peace to enter a recognizance.[96] The difference between the common law authority and that given under s.747 was explained by a judge of the British Columbia Supreme Court in *R. v. White:*[97]

> *Under s.717 [now s.810] of the Code a defendant cannot be bound over unless the magistrate is satisfied that the informant has reasonable grounds for his fears whereas the prerequisite to the exercise of the common law jurisdiction is that the magistrate (on facts established to his satisfaction) has probable grounds to suspect or be apprehensive that there may be a breach of the peace.*[98]

In other words, under s.810, it is the informant who must have reasonable grounds for fearing future injury, while under the common law, it is the justice who must have reasonable grounds for those fears. So, for example, a justice could require a person to enter a recognizance even though no other person had complained. This was in fact what the magistrate in White had attempted to do. He could not decide whether the informant or the defendant was telling the truth and so ordered them both to enter recognizances. However, the British Columbia Supreme Court found that the magistrate did not have reasonable grounds to exercise his common law authority, since his decision was based on speculation and conjecture as to what the actual facts of the case were.

Questions for Review and Discussion

1. What test is used to determine whether words are a threat under s.264.1?

2. Briefly describe the three sets of circumstances under which an assault may occur.

3. What was the decision of the Supreme Court of Canada in *Jobidon*? Do you agree with the result?

4. Why does the law make an attempted or threatened use of force an offence?

5. Has the offence of assault been committed where the alleged assailant threatens a person with a weapon but does not actually intend to apply force to the victim? What question do you need to ask to answer this?

6. Can threatening words alone constitute the offence of assault? Explain.

7. Discuss the circumstances in which the use of force may be lawful.

---

95 See, for example, *R. v. White* (1969), 1 C.C.C. 19 (B.C.S.C.).
96 See, for example, *MacKenzie v. Martin* (1954), 108 C.C.C. 305 (S.C.C.), where it was established that power exists in Ontario.
97 Supra, note 95.
98 Ibid. at page 29.

8. Why is there more than one offence of assault? What are the different offences?

9. How does the Code define "bodily harm"?

10. Distinguish the following terms: wounding, maiming, disfiguring.

11. What are the elements of the offence of sexual assault?

12. What meaning has been given to the term "sexual"?

13. What is the law regarding an honest mistake regarding consent?

14. What are some of the limits on using the defence of honest mistake in a sexual assault case?

15. What kinds of behaviour do you think would be harassment under s.264? Make up some examples.

16. How is the offence of unlawfully causing bodily harm different from assault?

17. What is the main difference between kidnapping and the offences of forcible seizure, confinement, and imprisonment?

18. Can a parent ever be found guilty of abducting his or her own child? Explain.

19. Do you agree with the Supreme Court of Canada decision in *Keegstra?* Discuss the pros and cons of the decision.

20. What is a recognizance? What is a surety?

21. What is the main difference between the court's common law authority to order persons to enter recognizances and the authority given by the Code?

22. Is it necessary that an offence be committed before a judge can order a person to enter a recognizance? Explain.

23. Bob and Tony are two high school students. One afternoon they were playing basketball in the gym when Bob ran into Tony, knocking him to the floor. Tony got up angrily and punched Bob in the mouth. At that point they began fighting violently until some other students were able to separate them. What charges, if any, could be laid, and against whom? Explain.

24. Paula was involved in a bitterly contested divorce. During one acrimonious court hearing, she burst out, "I am leaving that man and that woman [referring to his girlfriend] better stay out of my way—otherwise they're dead." She was charged with uttering a threat. Should she be convicted? Explain. See *R. v. Payne-Binder* (1991), 7 C.R. (4th) 308 (Yukon Terr. C.A.).

25. The town of Marlboro closed off a downtown street one summer to create a mall. The area became a hangout for teenagers, who sometimes became quite rowdy. One evening Constable Jones observed two young persons, a man and woman, kissing and wrestling in the middle of the sidewalk. Constable Jones told them to get up and stop acting like idiots.

At that point a third person, a young woman named Molly, yelled an obscenity at him. Jones arrested Molly and attempted to take her to his police cruiser. By this time a crowd had developed, which made it difficult for Jones to escort Molly to the cruiser. While all this was happening, Sandra stepped forward and slapped Jones in the face. She was promptly arrested. Sandra was charged with assaulting a peace officer engaged in the execution of his duty. Jones gave evidence at Sandra's trial that he had not arrested Molly for yelling at him; rather, "his authority had been flaunted" and he wanted to have her arrested "to prevent further trouble." Should the court find Sandra guilty of the charge? If not, what other offence could she be charged with? Explain. See *R. v. Allen* (1971), 4 C.C.C. (2d) 194 (Ont.C.A.).

26. Sam, age 19, had been dating Barbara, age 15. Barbara's parents did not like Sam and thought he was a bad influence on their daughter. The previous Wednesday they had forbidden Barbara to see him any longer. On Friday night, Barbara packed a suitcase and slipped out of the house. She went to Sam's apartment and told him she had run away from home. He let her in, and she spent Friday and Saturday night at his apartment. On Sunday night her parents found out where Sam lived. They went to Sam's place and forced her to go home with them.

   Can Sam be charged with abduction? What difference would it make if Sam had picked her up on Friday night and driven her to his apartment? What if Sam had called her and encouraged her to leave home and live with him?

Chapter Thirteen

OFFENCES AGAINST PROPERTY RIGHTS
PART IX OF THE CODE

A. INTRODUCTION

The offences covered in Part IX of the Code concern violations of a person's property rights. A property right includes a right of possession or ownership of a place or a "thing." Owning a car or home and renting an apartment are examples of property rights. Common offences against property rights include theft and "breaking and entering." Except for the offences of robbery and extortion, these crimes do not involve personal violence.

B. THEFT

1. Elements of the Offence

Briefly, theft is the act of a person who dishonestly takes property belonging to another with the intention of depriving the owner of it either permanently or temporarily.

Section 322(1) of the Code defines the offence of theft:

> **322. (1) Every one commits theft who fraudulently and without colour of right takes, or fraudulently and without colour of right converts to his use or to the use of another person, anything, whether animate or inanimate, with intent,**
>
> **(a) to deprive, temporarily or absolutely, the owner of it, or a person who has a special property or interest in it, of the thing or of his property or interest in it;**
>
> **(b) to pledge it or deposit it as security;**
>
> **(c) to part with it under a condition with respect to its return that the person who parts with it may be unable to perform; or**

(d) to deal with it in such a manner that it cannot be restored in the condition in which it was at the time it was taken or converted.

(2) A person commits theft when, with intent to steal anything, he moves it or causes it to move or to be moved, or begins to cause it to become movable.

2. "Converting" Property

A person has converted property to his or her use when the person has legally obtained the property but fails to return it. So, for example, a person who borrows library books and does not return them, and who has the intent of depriving the owner (the library) of them, has committed theft. The taking or converting can be absolute or temporary. In this way, an illegal borrowing can be theft.

The victim of the theft does not need to be the owner of the property. For example, a person who has rented property has a special interest in it. One case has even held that a neighbour taking care of a dwelling-house in the owner's absence has a special property interest in the house.[1]

The Supreme Court of Canada considered theft by conversion in *R. v. Milne*.[2] The accused was the owner of a company that provided goods and services to the Hudson's Bay Company. The Bay paid the accused with a cheque, which the accused deposited in his account. By error, the Bay sent a second cheque. Milne, realizing the error, deposited the cheque and withdrew the money from the account. The trial court convicted Milne of theft by conversion. The judge concluded that the actions of depositing the cheque, knowing that it was sent in error, and then withdrawing the money, constituted a theft by conversion. The court of appeal disagreed, holding that there was not a theft because under property law the ownership of the money passed to Milne, even though the Bay had a right to recover the money in a civil court action. The Crown appealed to the Supreme Court of Canada, which restored the conviction, stating that where a person mistakenly transfers property to a recipient, and the recipient knows of the mistake, ownership of the property does not pass for the purpose of the criminal law if the law of property creates a right of recovery. A recipient who then converts the property to his or her own use, fraudulently and without colour of right, and with the intent to deprive the transferor of the property, is guilty of theft.

Milne was applied in *R. v. Smith*.[3] The accused had purchased a quantity of coffee beans. The terms of the sale were a 20 percent down payment on delivery, with the balance to be paid in three days. The accused wrote a cheque for the down payment, knowing that there were insufficient funds to cover it. He then resold the coffee beans. The cheque for the down payment was never replaced, and the balance was never paid. The accused appealed his conviction for theft to the Ontario Court of Appeal, which dismissed his

1   *R. v. Rodrique* (1987), 61 C.R. (3d) 381 (Que.C.A.).
2   (1992), 70 C.C.C. (3d) 182 (Ont.C.A.).
3   (1992), 77 C.C.C. (3d) 182 (Ont.C.A.).

appeal and upheld his conviction. The court stated that the *mens rea* for this offence is satisfied if the accused knows that the transferor has mistakenly transferred the property and the accused keeps the property. Here, the transfer was induced by the accused's fraud. Since the victim had a right under civil law to recover the beans, the offence was made out. The court, in examining *Milne*, commented that the term "mistake" has a broad meaning. It does not matter whether the mistake was made unilaterally by the transferor or was induced by the recipient's fraud, as in this case. The Supreme Court of Canada affirmed the decision of the majority.[4]

3. Taking or Converting "Anything"

In most but not all situations, it is clear what "anything" means. The Supreme Court of Canada had to consider whether the offence of theft had taken place in an unusual situation. In *R. v. Stewart*,[5] the accused was hired by union organizers to obtain a list of the names and addresses of about 600 employees of a hotel. The union was trying to organize the hotel's employees. Stewart approached a security guard and offered him money to obtain the information. The security guard went to the police instead. The police taped a conversation between the guard and Stewart and eventually charged him with counselling theft. The case was appealed to the Supreme Court of Canada on the issue of whether confidential information was included within the term "anything" in s.322. The Crown and defence agreed that there was no written list or other tangible thing involved. The confidential information was to be copied or memorized. In a unanimous decision, the Court held that confidential information is not property: "[T]o be the object of theft, 'anything' must be property in the sense that to be stolen it has to belong in some way to someone. For instance, no conviction for theft would arise out of a taking or converting of the air that we breathe, because air is not property."[6]

The Court also mentioned that it is in society's interest that there be a free flow of information. In addition, the Court noted that if information were considered property, a person who memorized confidential information, knowing that it was stolen, could be charged with having possession of stolen property for every day that he or she had not forgotten it.

Finally, the Court stated that confidential information should perhaps be protected somehow under the Criminal Code. In this regard, however, it is up to Parliament to enact appropriate legislation; it is not up to the courts to expand the offence of theft.

4. Fraudulently and Without Colour of Right

a. Fraudulently

Some courts have held that fraudulent conduct requires a dishonest or immoral intent. In *Cooper v. R.*,[7] the accused was charged with the theft of an

---

4   (1993), 84 C.C.C. (3d) 160 (S.C.C.).
5   (1988), 41 C.C.C. (3d) 481 (S.C.C.).
6   Ibid. at page 489.
7   (1946), 2 C.R. 408 (N.S.C.A.).

aircraft. The accused went to the grounds of the flying school where he had begun taking flying lessons. Using a canoe, he went out to the aircraft, which was moored at a buoy. Without permission he got in and started the plane, intending to bring it alongside a dock. He missed the dock once and was making a second attempt when he was stopped. The evidence indicated that the accused intended only to show the plane to some friends. The court found the accused innocent of the charge of theft. It was held that he had not taken the aircraft fraudulently. Even though the accused had taken the plane within the meaning of s.322 (he had deprived the owner of it temporarily), he had done so only to show it to his friends; thus, he did not take it with a criminal, or dishonest, intent.

In *Handfield v. R.*,[8] the accused was charged with the theft of an election poster. His defence was lack of criminal intent. He and two of his brothers spent the evening together. On their way home, they passed a residence on which was standing an election poster inviting the electorate to vote for the Progressive Conservatives. The accused removed the poster and placed it on the lawn of a person whom they knew to be a Liberal supporter. One of the accused said that he took the poster to "play a trick" and that he never meant to steal it.

The court held that the accused did not take the election poster fraudulently. The judgment concluded that although the accused should possibly be given a penalty, they should not be subjected to conviction as common thieves and to a criminal record for the future.

In *R. v. Kerr*,[9] the accused was celebrating a victory in a retriever dog championship competition. For some reason, the accused and two companions went to the airport, where a cleaner saw them. All three were staggering and acting in a foolish manner. The accused was carrying one of the ashtrays belonging to the airport. The cleaner saw the ashtray being carried out by the accused. The ashtray was of a floor type and nearly a metre in height. The behaviour of the men made the cleaner think that they were carrying away the ashtray as a prank, and he thought it would be left outside the airport door. Later, two police officers visited the accused's home and saw the ashtray resting on the lawn in front of the house. The accused said that he did not mean to take the ashtray, and that he had intended to return it but the police arrived before he was able to do so. The court decided that the accused did not commit the offence of theft, stating that "the accused's stupid and foolish actions clearly showed the absence of any criminal intent."

Court decisions have not been consistent, so the "prank" defence does not always succeed. In *Bogner v. The Queen*,[10] the accused had taken a rocking chair off the porch of a hotel. The hotel owner's wife chased the accused. She saw a police car and informed the police of what had happened. The accused were later arrested for theft. At their trial, they testified that the taking of the chair was a joke and that they meant to return it later. Their conviction was upheld on appeal. The court stated that the offence was complete when the

8   (1953), 109 C.C.C. 53; 17 C.R. 343 (Que.C.A.).
9   (1965), 4 C.C.C. 37 (Man.C.A.).
10 (1975), 33 C.R.N.S. 349 (Que.C.A.).

chair was taken without any justification. The owner had been deprived of it. It was not necessary to prove a general dishonest state of mind.

In *R. v. Dalzell*,[11] the court considered the meaning of "fraudulently" where there was no prank. The accused, who was earning a master's degree in social work, was working with a group of juvenile delinquents. The youths told her that they shoplifted frequently and were almost never caught; and that when they were caught, they were let go without the police being called. To encourage shopkeepers to support a program she was developing, the accused formulated a plan to prove to them that their anti-shoplifting strategies were not working. She stole several items from some stores in a mall. She had planned to make a list of the items and then return them to the store manager to make a point about how easy it was to steal from them. However, a security guard observed her taking the items and arrested her for theft. She was acquitted at her trial because the trial judge found that she did not have a fraudulent intent. The Crown appealed her acquittal. The appeal court agreed with the trial judge as to the meaning of fraudulently: "Fraudulently in section 283 means a dishonest state of mind, leading to a dishonest intention to 'appropriate' the property taken." The court concluded that there was evidence on which the trial judge could base a decision that there was no fraudulent intent. The court dismissed the appeal.

b. Without Colour of Right

The term "colour of right" with regard to theft refers to a situation where a person asserts a possessory right—that is, a claim of ownership or lawful possession—to the thing that was allegedly stolen. In other words, if a person puts forth what he or she believes to be an honest claim of ownership, that person, even though mistaken, will have a colour of right to the "thing" and cannot be found guilty of the offence of theft.

In *R. v. Wudrick*,[12] the accused, who was a railway employee, believing certain watermelons in a car on the railway tracks had been abandoned, took two. In fact, the melons had not been abandoned. The accused was charged with theft. The accused's defence was that he had a "colour of right"—in other words, a possessory claim to the watermelons. The court concluded that the accused's belief—that the melons were waste and that there was nothing wrong in taking them—was an honest belief. The accused was acquitted.

In *R. v. Howson*,[13] the accused was charged with the theft of a car. The complainant parked his car on a private parking lot without the permission of the owner. The accused, at the request of the superintendent of the lot, towed the complainant's car to his premises, where it remained until the complainant found it there. The complainant demanded the return of his car; the accused refused to release it until he was paid a towing and storage charge. The complainant eventually paid the amount demanded, under

---

11 (1983), 6 C.C.C. (3d) 112 (N.S.C.A.).
12 (1959), 123 C.C.C. 109 (Sask.C.A.).
13 (1966), 3 C.C.C. 348 (Ont.C.A.).

protest. He then recovered his car and laid an information charging the accused with stealing his car.

The accused, in actual fact, could not legally keep the complainant's car. However, the accused stated that he took the car believing that he had a possessory claim to it until such time as he was paid a towing and storage charge. In other words, the accused claimed an honest belief that he had a "colour of right" to the car. The court accepted this argument, and he was acquitted.

5. Doctrine of Recent Possession

The courts have developed through case law the doctrine of recent possession. It states that where it is proved that the accused has possession of recently stolen property, and no explanation is given for that possession, the trier of fact (jury, or judge if no jury) may but not must draw an inference that the accused is guilty of theft or offences incidental to theft (e.g., break and enter, or possession of stolen property), even if there is no other evidence of guilt. The Supreme Court of Canada affirmed the existence of this doctrine in *R. v. Kowlyk*.[14] There had been three break and enters in the Winnipeg area over a short period of time. The police arrested the accused's brother and brought him to the house that he shared with the accused. When they arrived, the brother yelled to the accused, "The police are here!" The accused ran upstairs and started to go out the window, but stopped when he saw the police outside. The police searched the house and found items from the three break and enters in the accused's locked bedroom, in the same containers as when stolen. The accused was charged with break and enter.

The Supreme Court of Canada upheld the accused's conviction, stating that when the presumption applies, the accused may be found guilty even though there is no other evidence of guilt. The presumption does not apply, however, when the accused offers an explanation that might reasonably be true, even if the trier of fact is not satisfied of its truth. In such cases, the Crown must prove all the elements of the offence beyond a reasonable doubt in order to gain a conviction. So, for example, Allen is charged with possession of stolen property, a television set. The TV does not look new, and Allen tells the court that he bought it from a friend who said she did not need it any longer. If Allen's explanation might be true, in order to obtain a conviction the Crown will have to prove beyond a reasonable doubt every element of the offence of possession of property obtained by crime.

In *R. v. Killam*,[15] the British Columbia Court of Appeal had to consider whether goods were "recently" stolen. The accused was found in possession of a shipment of stolen pearls worth between $250,000 and $1,000,000. The pearls had been stolen eight-and-a-half months earlier. One of the judges stated that the question of whether goods have been recently stolen is answered by looking at all the circumstances, such as the nature of the item

---

14 (1988), 43 C.C.C. (3d) 1 (S.C.C.).
15 (1973), 12 C.C.C. (2d) 114 (B.C.C.A.), cited with approval in *Saieva v. The Queen* (1982), 68 C.C.C. (2d) 97 (S.C.C.).

stolen, how rare it is, the ease with which it can be passed from hand to hand, and the ease of its identification. Thus, clothing, household appliances, and jewellery might have a short period to be considered recently stolen, while extraordinary, unique, large, or unusual goods might have a longer period. The volume of the goods might also have a bearing. In *Killam*, the shipment of pearls weighed about 270 kilograms—enough to supply the Canadian market for several years. The judge concluded in the circumstances of this case that possession of the pearls was of recently stolen property.

6. Penalties for Theft

Section 334 sets out the penalties for the various offences of theft:

334. Except where otherwise provided by law, every one who commits theft

(a) is guilty of an indictable offence and liable to imprisonment for a term not exceeding ten years, where the property stolen is a testamentary instrument or the value of what is stolen exceeds five thousand dollars; or

(b) is guilty

(i) of an indictable offence and is liable to imprisonment for a term not exceeding two years, or

(ii) of an offence punishable on summary conviction,

where the value of what is stolen does not exceed five thousand dollars.

C. SPECIFIC THEFT OFFENCES

The Criminal Code contains a number of specific theft offences. Some of these are described in the following paragraphs. If the section that sets out the offence does not contain a penalty, the general penalty in s.334 applies.

1. Theft of Gas, Electricity, or Telecommunications

Section 326 provides:

326. (1) Every one commits theft who fraudulently, maliciously, or without colour of right,

(a) abstracts, consumes or uses electricity or gas or causes it to be wasted or diverted; or

(b) uses any telecommunication facility or obtains any telecommunication service.

(2) In this section and section 327, "telecommunication" means any transmission, emission or reception of signs, signals, writing, images or sounds or intelligence of any nature by wire, radio, visual, or other electro-magnetic system.

Section 326(1)(a) deals with situations in which gas, electricity, or a telecommunication service is stolen. For example, a person who diverts electricity from a public utility commission so that it does not pass through the commission's meter can be charged with the theft of electricity.

In *R. v. Brais*,[16] the accused was convicted of theft for fraudulently obtaining long-distance telephone services. An operator of the telephone company took a call from the accused, who said that she wanted to make a credit card call to Toronto. The accused gave the Toronto number and the credit card number. The call lasted 64 minutes, and the charge for it was $41.60. After 30 minutes, certain checking was done; it was found that the card number was not genuine and that the telephone company could not charge the call to anyone. The court held that the accused placed the telephone call intentionally, without mistake, and with knowledge that she was obtaining the call by using a credit card number that did not exist.

Section 327.1(1) creates the offence of making, owning, or selling any instrument or device that is designed to obtain a telecommunication service without paying for that service. A descrambler for pay TV signals is an example of such a device. So is computer software for making long-distance calls without charge.

2. Theft by a Person Required to Account

Section 330(1) provides:

> **330. (1) Every one commits theft who, having received anything from any person on terms that require him to account for or pay it or the proceeds of it or a part of the proceeds to that person or another person, fraudulently fails to account for or pay it or the proceeds of it or the part of the proceeds of it accordingly.**

Section 330(1) covers situations where an accused has received money, or "anything," from one person and must turn it over to another person. In *R. v. Mckenzie*,[17] a taxi driver was convicted of theft under s.330 because he failed to turn over to the taxi's owner all of the fare money he owed to the owner, his employer. In *Washington State v. Johnston*,[18] the Supreme Court of Canada held that the element of fraud cannot be inferred just because the accused did not return the goods within a reasonable time. In other words, the Crown must prove fraudulent intent.

---

16 (1972), 7 C.C.C. (2d) 30 (B.C.C.A.).
17 (1971), 4 C.C.C. (2d) 296 (S.C.C.).
18 (1988), 40 C.C.C. (3d) 546 (S.C.C.). This case concerned an extradition hearing to have the accused returned to the state of Washington, from which he had fled after being convicted and imprisoned for theft. The Court had to decide, for the purposes of extraditing a fugitive, whether the offence of theft was the same in Washington (where fraudulent intent is not required) as in Canada.

D. OFFENCES RESEMBLING THEFT

1. "Joy-riding"

It is possible to "take" a motor vehicle or vessel without the consent of its owner and not be committing the offence of theft. This offence is loosely referred to as "joy-riding." Section 335 provides:

> **335. Every one who, without the consent of the owner, takes a motor vehicle or vessel with intent to drive, use, navigate or operate it or cause it to be driven, used, navigated or operated is guilty of an offence punishable on summary conviction.**
>
> **(1.1)   Subsection (1) does not apply to an occupant of a motor vehicle or vessel who, on becoming aware that it was taken without the consent of the owner, attempted to leave the motor vehicle or vessel, to the extent that it was feasible to do so, or actually left the motor vehicle or vessel.**

The offence of occupant joyriding created by 335 (1.1) does not violate the Charter of Rights and Freedoms.[19]

Notice that joy-riding is a summary conviction offence. Since most cars are worth more than $5,000, this offence allows a young person who takes a car for a joy ride, intending to return, to be charged with a less serious offence rather than the more serious offence of "theft over." The Supreme Court of Canada has held that joy-riding is not an included offence in theft, but that in certain fact situations either offence could be charged, and that it is up to the Crown to decide which offence to charge.[20]

In *R. v. Wilkins*,[21] the accused, for the purpose of playing a joke, took a policeman's motorcycle while the latter was standing on the sidewalk making out a ticket. He intended to drive it only a short distance. He was charged with theft of the motorcycle under s.283 (now s.322). The court held that the accused should have been charged under s.295 (now s.335) and that he was not guilty of theft. In its judgment, the court stated:

> [T]he facts could not possibly justify a conviction of theft. The accused did not intend to steal the vehicle, that is, to convert the property to his own use, but only to drive it as contemplated by s.295 (s.335). His intention was merely to play a joke on the policeman . . . the intention to perpetrate this joke, stupid though it was, is incompatible with the evil intent which is inherent in the crime of theft.[22]

2. Fraudulent Concealment

Section 341 creates the offence of fraudulent concealment:

---

19 *R. v. H.(P.)* (2000), 143 C.C.C. (3d) 223 (Ont.C.A.).
20 *LaFrance v. The Queen* (1973), 13 C.C.C. (2d) 289 (S.C.C.).
21 [1965] 2 C.C.C. 189; (1964), 44 C.R. 375 (Ont.C.A.).
22 Ibid. at page 380 cited to C.R.

341. Every one who, for a fraudulent purpose, takes, obtains, removes or conceals anything is guilty of an indictable offence and liable to imprisonment for a term not exceeding two years.

Section 341 is designed to cover situations where the thing taken is hidden in the hope that the owner will not be able to find it. For instance, if Mark made two wills, and neglected to destroy the first before he died, and Peter concealed the second because it cut him out of an inheritance that the first will granted, Peter would be guilty of fraudulent concealment under s.341.

3. Taking of a Credit Card

Section 342(1) deals with the theft or forgery of a credit card.

342. (1) Every person who,

(a) steals a credit card,

(b) forges or falsifies a credit card,

(c) possesses, uses or traffics in a credit or a forged or falsified credit card, knowing it was obtained, made or altered

(i) by the commission in Canada of an offence, or

(ii) by an act or omission anywhere that, if it had occurred in Canada, would have constituted an offence, or

(d) uses a credit card that he knows has been revoked or cancelled is guilty of

(e) an indictable offence and is liable to imprisonment for a term not exceeding ten years, or

(f) an offence punishable on summary conviction.

Court decisions have held that where a person innocently finds a credit card but then intends to use it or does use it, that credit card has been "obtained by the commission of an offence." The reasoning is that once the person has the intent to use the credit card, his or her possession of it becomes a theft by conversion.[23]

4. The Unauthorized Use of Computer Facilities

342.1 (1) Every one who, fraudulently and without color of right,

(a) obtains, directly or indirectly, any computer service,

(b) by means of an electro-magnetic, acoustic, mechanical or other device, intercepts or causes to be intercepted, directly or indirectly, any function of a computer system, or

---

23 See, for example, *R. v. Zurowski* (1983), 5 C.C.C. (3d) 285 (Alta.C.A.); *R. v. Elias* (1986), 33 C.C.C. (3d) 476 (Que.C.A.), affd. 46 C.C.C. (3d) 447 (S.C.C.).

(c) uses or causes to be used, directly or indirectly, a computer system with intent to commit an offence under paragraph (a) or (b) or an offence under section 430 in relation to data or a computer system

(d) uses, possesses, traffics in or permits another person to have access to a computer password that would enable a person to commit an offence under paragraph (a), (b) or (c)

is guilty of an indictable offence and is liable to imprisonment for a term not exceeding ten years, or is guilty of an offence punishable on summary conviction.

Notice there are three ways an offence under this section can occur: by obtaining, intercepting, or using a computer service fraudulently and without colour of right.

5. Possession of Device to Obtain Computer Service

342.2(1) Every person who, without lawful justification or excuse, makes, possesses, sells, offers for sale or distributes any instrument or device or any component thereof, the design of which renders it primarily useful for committing an offence under section 342.1, under circumstances that give rise to a reasonable interference that the instrument, device or component has been used or is or was intended to be used to commit an offence contrary to that section,

(a) is guilty of an indictable offence and liable to imprisonment for a term of not exceeding two years; or

(b) is guilty of an offence punishable on summary conviction.

This section makes it an offence to make, possess, sell, offer for sale or distribute any instrument, device or component whose design renders it primarily useful for committing an offence under 342.1. This is a Crown option offence, which means the Crown can use this section to complement section 342.1. The Crown must prove that the accused had the device under circumstances that give rise to a reasonable inference that the device was intended to be used to forge or falsify credit cards. Any device in the possession of a person convicted under this section may be forfeited unless the device belonged to someone who was not a party to the offence.

E. ROBBERY

1. Elements of the Offence

Section 343 of the Code defines the offence of robbery:

343. Every one commits robbery who

(a) steals, and for the purpose of extorting whatever is stolen or to prevent or overcome resistance to the stealing, uses violence or threats of violence to a person or property;

(b) steals from any person and, at the time he steals or immediately before or immediately thereafter, wounds, beats, strikes or uses any personal violence to that person;

(c) assaults any person with intent to steal from him; or

(d) steals from any person while armed with an offensive weapon or imitation thereof.

Section 2 of the Code provides that "steal" means "to commit theft." In general, the difference between theft and robbery is that robbery involves actual violence, or the possibility of violence, to another person. Both theft and assault may be lesser included offences for robbery. Recall from Chapter Three that a lesser included offence is one that has some but not all of the elements of the major offence.

2. Robbery Under Section 343(a)

Section 343(a) sets out the basic definition of the offence of robbery: theft accompanied by actual violence or by threats of violence. The violence need not be severe, nor need it cause an injury to the victim. Generally, any form of physical interference, from a push to a punch, will amount to "violence" for the purposes of s.343. Similarly, a threat of any form of violence will generally bring the accused's actions within the offence of robbery. To "extort" means to compel or to force.

The violence or threat of violence need not be directed at the person being robbed. If the accused struck an innocent bystander at the scene of the theft, he would be guilty of robbery.

The Ontario Court of Appeal, in *R. v. Sayers and McCoy*,[24] held that robbery under this section does not require that the accused be armed: the threat of violence is enough. In *Sayers*, the accused entered a bank at about 12:30 p.m. While one of the accused stood at the door and watched for police, the other jumped on the counter and yelled at the cashiers, "This is a robbery in progress . . . Give me the money . . . I'm not going to hurt anyone." He went up to two tellers and grabbed the cash from their drawers. He then came to the third cashier and tried to open her cash drawer, but found it was locked. He screamed at her, "Unlock the drawer! This is a robbery!" The bank employees testified that they were concerned and afraid. Neither of the accused were armed. After taking the money, the men fled on foot and were apprehended by the police. The appeal court held that the words and gestures of the accused "could only have the effect of causing reasonable apprehension of physical harm unless the tellers complied with the demand." The court held that the conduct of the accused fell within the definition of robbery under s.343(a). It set aside their acquittals and entered convictions for robbery.

---

24 (1983), 8 C.C.C. (3d) 572 (Ont.C.A.).

The courts considered the meaning of "threat of violence" in *R. v. Pelletier*.[25] This case had facts similar to *Sayers* and *McCoy*. The accused was in a bank when he jumped over the counter so that he was standing next to the tellers. He told the manager to get out of his office. The tellers stepped back from their drawers, believing that a holdup was in progress. The accused did not say anything else during the incident. He took the money out of the drawers. He threw one drawer on the floor in anger when it would not open. He was not wearing a mask and was not armed with a weapon. However, witnesses noted that he acted brusquely and did not hesitate to throw the drawer on the floor when he could not open it. He was convicted at trial, and appealed on the grounds that his actions and the words that preceded the theft did not constitute threats of violence to the victims. In reply, the Crown argued that at the very least there was an implied threat of violence in his behaviour. The court, citing the Supreme Court of Canada in *R. v. McCraw*,[26] defined "threat" as a tool of intimidation designed to instill fear. In the context of this case, "a threat of violence is characterized by conduct which reflects an intent to have recourse to violence to carry out the theft or prevent resistance to the theft." The court noted that a threat may be express or implicit and may be made by words, writings, or actions. The determination as to whether a threat was made, the court said, requires an objective test: Would a reasonable person have felt frightened? It is the threat that is assessed, not the strength of the nerves of the person being frightened. The court agreed with the trial court judge that the intimidating actions of the accused were directed toward people who are always susceptible to being victims of this type of crime. His conduct left no doubt as to his intentions should there be resistance. His appeal of the conviction was dismissed.

3. Robbery Under Section 343(b)

Under s.343(b), assault is a lesser included offence for robbery. In other words, the offence of robbery includes the elements of the offence of assault. The Ontario Court of Appeal, in *R. v. Oakley*,[27] held that the words "uses any personal violence" are coloured by the preceding words, "wounds, beats or strikes"; therefore, for robbery under this subsection, there must be more than a "technical assault"—that is, something more than a touching without consent. The accused was a passenger in his sister-in-law's car when he began hallucinating. He thought his sister-in-law was the devil and that she was taking him to the hospital to be killed. He put the car into park while it was moving, causing it to come to an abrupt stop. He then demanded that she give him the keys. When she refused, he took the keys from her and ordered her out of the car. Then he drove off. The court held that no robbery had occurred here under s.343(b) because there was an assault only in the technical sense.

---

25   (1992), 71 C.C.C. (3d) 438 (Que.C.A.).
26   See discussion of *McCraw* in Chapter Twelve, page 273.
27   (1986), 24 C.C.C. (3d) 351 (Ont.C.A.).

4. Robbery Under Section 343(c)

Section 343(c) provides that if the victim was assaulted with the intent to steal, the offence of robbery has been committed whether a theft took place or not. For example, if Carl knocks Peter to the ground with the intent to grab Peter's wallet, and is interrupted by a witness's screams, which cause Carl to flee before he can get Peter's wallet, the offence of robbery has still been committed.

5. Robbery Under Section 343(d)

Section 343(d) provides that robbery is committed if a person steals while he or she is armed with an offensive weapon or with an imitation of an offensive weapon. Section 2 of the Code provides that the definition of "weapon" applies to "offensive weapon." "Weapon" is defined in s.2 thus:

> **. . . any thing used, designed to be used or intended for use**
>
> **(a) in causing death or injury any person, or**
>
> **(b) for the purpose of threatening or intimidating any person**
>
> **and, without restricting the generality of the foregoing, includes a firearm;**

Almost any object can be an offensive weapon. The person must be armed with something, however. In *R. v. Sloan*,[28] the accused was charged with attempted robbery under s.343(d). The accused, whose head and upper body were partially covered with a bedsheet, had come to a hotel in the middle of the night and ordered the night desk man to open the office where the money was kept. The desk man refused. He was prodded backwards in the chest by something protruding from under the sheet. He said to the accused, "Don't push me, I've got a couple of cracked ribs." The accused then said, "If you don't open that door, you'll be in worse shape." The desk man turned, and in so doing hit the protruding object and discovered it was a finger, not a gun barrel. At that point the accused fled.

The court held that the accused did not have an "offensive weapon or an imitation thereof." Part of the judgment states:

> *In this case, all that is shown is that the accused . . . simulated the conduct of a man armed with a weapon. He acted a part or played out a pantomime to give the impression that he had a weapon. While the conduct might have justified a conviction under ss. (a) (theft with threat of violence) or (c) (theft with assault) of s.302 [now s.343] of the Code, . . . it does not meet the requirements of s.302(d). To arm oneself with a weapon means to equip oneself, to acquire, to become possessed of some instrument which is either a weapon or an imitation of a weapon. I am not of the opinion that in these circumstances a man can be armed with his own finger and I am satisfied that the word "imitation"*

---

28 (1974), 19 C.C.C. (2d) 190 (B.C.C.A.).

as used in s.302(d) refers to an imitation of the weapon and cannot be stretched to include a simulation of conduct or actions.[29]

F. EXTORTION

Section 346 defines the offence of extortion:

346. (1) Every one commits extortion who, without reasonable justification or excuse and with intent to obtain anything, by threats, accusations, menaces or violence induces or attempts to induce any person, whether or not he is the person threatened, accused or menaced or to whom violence is shown, to do anything or cause anything to be done.

(1.1) Every one who commits extortion is guilty of an indictable offence and liable

(a) where a firearm is used in the commission of the offence, to imprisonment for life and to a minimum punishment of imprisonment for a term of four years; and

(b) in any other case to imprisonment for life.

(2) A threat to institute civil proceedings is not a threat for the purposes of this section.

Extortion is essentially equivalent to the word "blackmail." An extortion occurs when one person threatens another with some consequence, so that the person is forced to commit an act, or to omit doing something that he or she otherwise would have done.

In *R. v. Natarelli and Volpe*,[30] the accused were convicted of extortion for threatening the life of the victim if he did not deliver to them a large sum of money. The Supreme Court of Canada stated that there were three elements to the offence of extortion: that the accused used threats; that the accused did so with the intention of obtaining something by the use of threats; and that either the use of the threats or the making of the demand for the thing sought to be obtained was without reasonable excuse or justification.

With respect to the last requirement, the Court said that once the threats to cause death, or bodily harm, with intent to obtain the money were proved, the accused were guilty of extortion even though they honestly believed that they had a right to the money. In other words, John cannot threaten William with death, or harm, in an attempt to force William to do something, even if John honestly believes he has a reasonable justification for making the threat. An example of a justified threat is the threat of a creditor to a debtor to turn over an account to a collection agency if payment of the debt is not made. However, if the creditor threatens the person with violence if payment is not made, even though the creditor is owed the money, there will be no reasonable justification for making such a threat.

---

29 Ibid., at page 198.
30 (1967), 1 C.R.N.S. 302 (S.C.C.).

1. Threat or Menace

It is an essential element of the offence that there be a threat, accusation, menace, or violence. In *R. v. Rousseau*,[31] the Supreme Court of Canada found that the offence had not occurred because these elements were not present. The accused was a lawyer who had been representing two men charged with theft. The men were employees of a security company that was under contract to protect the premises from which the goods had been stolen. The accused approached the lawyer for the security company and offered to get the charges dropped in exchange for some money. The accused had already worked out a deal with the police to have some of the charges dropped. Although the accused was guilty of obstructing justice, he was not guilty of extortion.

The threat or menace involved need not amount to a threat to harm or murder the victim. A threat, for example, to damage the victim's property is sufficient for the purposes of s.346.

2. "Anything"

The British Columbia Court of Appeal has held that the word "anything" in this offence has a wide and unrestricted meaning. Thus, an act of sexual intercourse can be the "anything" extorted.[32]

3. Threat to Sue

Section 346(2) provides that a threat to take someone to court in an attempt to force him or her to do something is not a threat for the purpose of committing the offence of extortion. So, when Will threatens to sue Brian in an attempt to get him to pay for damages he caused to Will's property, Will is not committing the offence of extortion.

G. BREAK AND ENTER

Section 348 defines the offence of break and enter:

> **348. (1) Every one who**
>
> **(a) breaks and enters a place with intent to commit an indictable offence therein,**
>
> **(b) breaks and enters a place and commits an indictable offence therein, or**
>
> **(c) breaks out of a place after**
>
> **(i) committing an indictable offence therein, or**

---

31 (1985), 21 C.C.C. (3d) 1 (S.C.C.).
32 *R. v. Bird*, [1970] 3 C.C.C. 340 (B.C.C.A.).

(ii) entering the place with intent to commit an indictable offence therein, is guilty

(d) if the offence is committed in relation to a dwelling-house, of an indictable offence and liable to imprisonment for life, and

(e) if the offence is committed in relation to a place other than a dwelling-house, of an indictable offence and liable to imprisonment for a term not exceeding ten years or of an offence punishable on summary conviction.

Note that the penalty is greater if the place being broken into is a dwelling-house. "Dwelling-house" is defined in s.2 thus:

. . . the whole or any part of a building or structure that is kept or occupied as a permanent or temporary residence, and includes

(a) a building within the curtilage of a dwelling-house that is connected to it by a doorway or by a covered and enclosed passage-way, and

(b) a unit that is designed to be mobile and to be used as a permanent or temporary residence and that is being used as such a residence.

Apartments and motel or hotel rooms are considered dwelling-houses. Even a tent that people intend to sleep in has been considered a dwelling-house. The term "curtilage" refers to buildings close by a dwelling-house that are used for domestic activities—for example, garages and sheds.

1. The Presumptions and the Charter

Chapter Two discussed reverse onus clauses, mandatory presumptions, and the Charter. It explained how many of these clauses are being struck down as violations of the presumption of innocence. Although there are many presumptions and reverse onus clauses in other parts of the Code, they are especially common in the offences involving break and enter. These clauses are all open to challenge under the Charter. Existing case law will be mentioned in the discussion that follows. Some of these decisions are from provincial courts of appeal. As always, it will in the end be up to the Supreme Court of Canada to decide whether any particular clause is invalid for infringing the Charter.

2. Elements of Break and Enter

There are three offences in this section: break and enter with intent to commit an indictable offence; break and enter, committing an indictable offence; and breaking out of a place after intending to commit or committing an indictable offence.

a. Break Defined

"Break" is defined in s.321:

> **321. In this Part,**
>
> **"break" means**
>
> **(a) to break any part, internal or external, or**
>
> **(b) to open any thing that is used or intended to be used to close or to cover an internal or external opening.**

Breaking can involve jimmying a door or window, picking a lock, or breaking a window. However, breaking also includes a number of ways of entering a place that would not normally be associated with the term. Opening a door with a stolen or "found" key, lifting a latch, raising an already open window, and simply opening an unlocked door are all examples of breaking for the purposes of the offence of breaking and entering.

In *R. v. Jewell*,[33] the accused was charged with breaking and entering under s.348. The house he was accused of breaking into had been unoccupied for some time and was in dilapidated condition. He was able to enter the house through the open screen door and inner door. The accused admitted that he entered the house for the purpose of stealing something from the house. The court concluded that because the accused entered through an already open door, it could not be said that he "broke into" the building.

However, in *R. v. Bargiamis*,[34] it was held that further opening an already ajar door does constitute breaking. In *Bargiamis*, the door was open about two centimetres, and the accused pushed it open to allow himself space to enter. The difference between these two cases seems to be that in *Bargiamis*, some minimal force was used to gain entry, while in *Jewell*, no force was needed to enter the building.

b. Entering

Entering is defined by s.350:

> **350. . . . (a) a person enters as soon as any part of his body or any part of an instrument that he uses is within any thing that is being entered; and**
>
> **(b) a person shall be deemed to have broken and entered if**
>
> **(i) he obtained entrance by a threat or artifice or by collusion with a person within, or**
>
> **(ii) he entered without lawful justification or excuse, the proof of which lies on him, by a permanent or temporary opening.**

An entrance is made as soon as any part of the body of the accused, or any part of the instrument used by him, is within any part of the place being

---

33 (1975), 22 C.C.C. (2d) 252 (Ont.C.A.).
34 (1970), 4 C.C.C. 258 (Ont.C.A.).

entered. For example, if the police catch Deborah with a hand inside a window that she opened, she has entered the place for the purposes of s.348.

In *R. v. Marshall*,[35] the accused was charged with breaking and entering. A police officer on patrol noticed a window pane in the premises pushed in about 30 centimetres. The window pane consisted of six glass panels, five of which were broken. One police officer searching in the vicinity of the broken window found the accused lying on his back on the ground, concealed in a trench less than two metres from the building. His hand was cut and his left boot was off. The accused later testified that he had been leaning against the building when he broke the window.

It was acknowledged by all parties, including the accused, that there had been a "breaking." But it was further held that there had been an "entering" as well. The accused had put only his hand through the window in the process of breaking it, but that was enough to constitute an entering. It was therefore established that the accused had broken and entered the building. However, it was not proved that he had done so with the intent to commit an indictable offence, and so he was acquitted.

Section 350(b)(ii) provides that when a person gains entry by threats or with "inside help," he has still broken and entered. The same section also states that a person is presumed to have broken and entered a building if he or she entered through a "permanent or temporary opening." Open doors and windows are not permanent or temporary openings. In *R. v. Sutherland*,[36] the accused entered through a garage that consisted of three walls and an opening at one end for the entrance of a car. He entered for the purpose of stealing gasoline and was charged with breaking and entering. The court held that the opening in the garage was really not an "opening" but was, in fact, an "entrance." An opening in s.350 refers to a hole in a wall, or door, or to an opening where a door or window has not yet been placed. Areas where people usually enter buildings are not openings.

Section 350(b)(ii) also contains a reverse onus clause. The phrase "the proof of which lies on him" means that it is up to the accused to show that the entrance was made with lawful justification. This element has been challenged as a violation of the presumption of innocence. In *R. v. Singh*,[37] the Alberta Court of Appeal stated that the effect of this section is that once it is proved that the accused entered, he or she will be deemed to have broken in unless the accused proves on a balance of probabilities that he or she entered with a lawful justification or excuse. The court held that this provision is not justifiable, since an accused could be convicted of break and enter where a reasonable doubt existed as to whether he or she entered unlawfully. However, to save the section the court held that it could be applied without the phrase "the proof of which lies on him." In other words, the Crown must prove that the accused entered without lawful justification.

An example of lawful justification being applied is found in *R. v. Farbridge*.[38] The accused entered a department store during business hours with the

35 (1970), 1 C.C.C. (2d) 505 (B.C.C.A.).
36 (1967), 2 C.C.C. 84; 50 C.R. 197 (B.C.C.A.).
37 (1987), 41 C.C.C. (3d) 278 (Alta.C.A.).
38 (1984), 15 C.C.C. (3d) 521 (Alta.C.A.).

intent to hide in the store until it was closed and then steal clothing. The Alberta Court of Appeal held that he had not broken and entered under s.350(b) because he had entered with lawful justification—that is, with the lawful justification that any person has to enter a store during business hours.

c. *Place*

Section 348 defines the term "place":

> ... (3) For the purposes of this section ... "place" means
>
> (a) a dwelling-house;
>
> (b) a building or structure or any part thereof, other than a dwelling-house;
>
> (c) a railway vehicle, a vessel, an aircraft or a trailer; or
>
> (d) a pen or enclosure in which fur-bearing animals are kept in captivity for breeding or commercial purposes.

d. *Intent to Commit an Indictable Offence*

Once it is established that the accused broke in or out of a place, it must still be shown that he or she committed an indictable offence, or that he or she entered with the intent to commit an indictable offence.

The most common indictable offence relating to a break-in is theft. However, any other indictable offence—assault, for example—can be the object of a break-in under a breaking and entering charge.

In *Macleod v. R.*,[39] the accused was ordered out of his host's home, where he had been drinking. He later returned and broke into the home to retrieve a bottle of liquor that he had brought to the home earlier. The accused was acquitted on a charge of breaking and entering because he did not break and enter with the intent to commit an indictable offence.

For the same reason, a person who breaks into a cottage only to seek shelter from a storm has not committed an offence under s.348, because there is no intent to commit an indictable offence.

3. Presumption of Intent

Section 348(2) provides:

> 348. . . . (2) For the purposes of proceedings under this section, evidence that an accused
>
> (a) broke and entered a place or attempted to break and enter a place is, in the absence of any evidence to the contrary, proof that he broke and entered the place or attempted to do so, as the case may be, with intent to commit an indictable offence therein; or

---

39 (1968), 2 C.C.C. 365 (P.E.I.S.C.).

(b) broke out of a place is, in the absence of any evidence to the contrary, proof that he broke out after

(i) committing an indictable offence therein, or

(ii) entering with intent to commit an indictable offence therein.

This subsection creates a presumption that requires evidence that the accused did not break into or out of the place for the purpose of committing an indictable offence. Although this evidence would usually come from the accused, it is possible that the evidence could also flow out of the Crown's case. If evidence to the contrary is presented, the Crown must prove every element of the offence beyond a reasonable doubt. The application of this presumption and the meaning of the phrase "evidence to the contrary" was considered by the Supreme Court of Canada in *R. v. Proudlock.*[40] The accused had been drinking at a party in an apartment above a restaurant. He had been living in the apartment with the son of the owner of the restaurant. At some point in the evening, he broke into the restaurant by breaking a window and climbing through. He encountered the restaurant's janitor, who asked him what he was doing. The accused replied that he had been given the key by the owner's son and was looking for some soup. He then left by the back door. Later he was questioned by the police. When asked why he had broken into the restaurant, he said he did not know why but that he had no intention of stealing anything. At his trial, the judge said he didn't believe the accused's testimony that he didn't intend to steal anything, but that his testimony was evidence to the contrary; and therefore, the Crown had to prove the offence beyond a reasonable doubt. The case was appealed on the issue of whether evidence that is disbelieved is "evidence to the contrary." The Supreme Court disagreed with the trial judge, holding that evidence that is disbelieved is not evidence to the contrary. To rebut the presumption, the evidence must be believable and raise a reasonable doubt. The Court ordered that a conviction be entered against the accused.

The decision in *Proudlock* was made before the Charter was enacted, so the Supreme Court did not deal with the issue of whether the section violates the Charter. However, the British Columbia Court of Appeal, in *R. v. Slavens,*[41] found that this section does violate the Charter. The accused was found in a locked parking area of an apartment building by the apartment manager. When confronted, he ran out of the area, where the police were waiting. He was charged with breaking out with intent. The appeal court said that the presumption violates the presumption of innocence under the Charter because:

> *In order to avoid a conviction, the accused . . . has the burden cast upon him to rebut the presumption by ensuring that there is evidence to the contrary before the court . . . And the evidence to the contrary must be sufficient to raise a reasonable doubt that the accused committed an indictable offence . . . or that*

---

40   (1978), 43 C.C.C. (2d) 321 (S.C.C.).
41   (1991), 64 C.C.C. (3d) 29 (B.C.C.A.).

he entered in the first instance with the intent of committing an indictable offence.[42]

However, the court finally held that the presumption is saved by s.1 of the Charter. The court relied on evidence that personal property crimes have reached epidemic proportions in this country and that the presumption only gives the Crown an "evidentiary assist." Therefore, the presumption is a reasonable and justifiable limit under s.1 of the Charter.

H. BEING UNLAWFULLY IN A DWELLING-HOUSE

Section 349 provides:

> **349. (1) Every one who without lawful excuse, the proof of which lies on him, enters or is in a dwelling-house with intent to commit an indictable offence therein is guilty of an indictable offence .. .**
>
> **(2) For the purposes of proceedings under this section, evidence that an accused, without lawful excuse, entered or was in a dwelling-house is, in the absence of any evidence to the contrary, proof that he entered or was in the dwelling-house with intent to commit an indictable offence therein.**

Notice that the place entered must be a dwelling-house. Also, for the purpose of s.349, "enters" has the same meaning as it does under s.348 and as defined under s.350.

To commit an offence under s.349, a person does not have to break in. In other words, a person who walked through an open door into a dwelling-house could not be found guilty of breaking and entering (s.348), but could be found guilty of unlawfully being in a dwelling-house. Also, the person does not need to enter for the purpose of committing an indictable offence— the person can form that intent once in the dwelling-house.

This offence has two elements that have been attacked as violations of the Charter right to be presumed innocent. First, subs.(1) sets out a reverse onus clause, so that the accused must prove that the entry was not unlawful. Second, subs.(2) sets out a mandatory presumption that evidence that the entry was unlawful is, "in the absence of evidence to the contrary," evidence that the accused entered or was in the dwelling-house for the purpose of committing an indictable offence. Both of these elements of the offence were considered by the Ontario Court of Appeal in *R. v. Nagy*.[43] The accused entered M.'s house through an unlocked door at about 3 p.m. M. was sleeping upstairs when he was awakened by someone downstairs saying hello. M. asked the accused, who by this time was on the third stair leading upstairs, what he wanted. The accused said something about being stuck and needing a tow. There was some evidence that he turned his back to M. and took off rubber gloves. The accused then called to a person in a car that

---

42 Ibid., at page 34.
43 (1988), 45 C.C.C. (3d) 350 (Ont.C.A.).

was running in the driveway. The accused's son then entered the house and asked M. if he owned a dog, and said that there was an injured dog on the road. At that point M.'s son walked in and the accused and his son left. M.'s son followed them and could find neither a stuck car nor an injured dog.

The trial judge convicted the accused of being unlawfully in the house. He rejected the accused's explanation as impossible to believe and held that there was no evidence to the contrary for explaining the accused's presence in the house.

The court of appeal stated that the "without lawful excuse" requirement in subs.(1) is an element of the offence and that the accused must prove on a balance of probabilities that he or she had a lawful excuse for being in the dwelling-house. The court did not consider whether the subsection offended the Charter, because it was not necessary: the Crown had proved that the accused's entry was unlawful without relying on the reverse onus clause. With regard to subs.(2), the court found that it contains a mandatory presumption that requires the trier of fact to convict in the absence of evidence to the contrary. This section infringes on the presumption of innocence for two reasons: first, because it is not a necessary inference that a person who enters a dwelling-house without a lawful excuse is doing so with intent to commit an indictable offence; and second, because the subsection may require a person to testify or give evidence to avoid a conviction where the Crown has not proved every element of the offence beyond a reasonable doubt. This violates the accused person's right to remain silent, which is an underlying principle to the presumption of innocence. The court then considered whether the violation could be justified under s.1 of the Charter. The court found that the objective of protecting people and property from the crimes of break and enter is sufficiently pressing to justify an infringement of the Charter. Therefore, the court held, the section is a justifiable limitation. The accused's appeal from conviction was dismissed.

I. OFFENCES INVOLVING POSSESSION

The next two offences to be discussed—possession of break-in instruments, and possession of property obtained through the commission of an indictable offence—share the element of possession as the *actus reus* of the offence.

1. Possession

Possession is defined by s.4(3) of the Code:

> **(3) For the purposes of this Act,**
>
> **(a) a person has anything in possession when he has it in his personal possession or knowingly**
>
> **(i) has it in the actual possession or custody of another person, or**

(ii) has it in any place, whether or not that place belongs to or is occupied by him, for the use or benefit of himself or of another person; and

(b) where one of two or more persons, with the knowledge and consent of the rest, has anything in his custody or possession, it shall be deemed to be in the custody and possession of each and all of them.

There are two types of possession: actual possession under s.4(3)(a), and constructive possession under s.4(3)(a)(i) and (ii) and under s.4.3(b).

All forms of possession require the knowledge of what the "thing" is and a measure or right of control over the thing.

a. Knowledge

This requirement of knowledge for possession was first set out by the Supreme Court of Canada in *Beaver v. The Queen*.[44] The accused was charged with possession of a narcotic and with trafficking in a narcotic. The evidence was that he sold a package of morphine to an undercover police officer. His defence was that he honestly believed that the package contained only powdered milk sugar. The Court held that his honest belief that the package contained milk sugar was a defence to the charge of possession. The Court agreed with a statement made in a 1948 British Columbia Court of Appeal decision, *R. v. Hess:*

> *To constitute possession within the meaning of the criminal law it is my judgment that where as here there is a manual handling of the thing it must be co-existent with knowledge of what that thing is, and both these elements must be co-existent with some act of control (outside of public duty).*[45]

b. Control

Control over the thing does not necessarily mean actual physical control. Control refers to exercising authority over the thing. For example, a person can have control by allowing another person to keep the thing. Also, the control does not need to be absolute; a "measure" of control is sufficient.

c. Constructive Possession and Control

Constructive possession means that the person does not have actual possession of the thing. The case that decided that control was necessary for constructive possession is *R. v. Terrence*.[46] The accused was charged with being in possession of a stolen automobile in which he was a passenger. The evidence was that he was watching television one night when a friend, Hayes, arrived and asked if anyone wanted to go for a ride. The accused said "sure" and went with Hayes. The car that Hayes was driving was stolen and was eventually stopped by the police. The accused was charged with and convicted of possession. He appealed his conviction, arguing that a measure of

44 (1957), 118 C.C.C. 129 (S.C.C.).
45 Ibid., at page 140.
46 (1983), 4 C.C.C. (3d) 193 (S.C.C.).

control is necessary for the charge, regardless of whether the accused knew that the vehicle was stolen. The Supreme Court of Canada agreed with the court of appeal and held that a measure of control is necessary for constructive possession. The conviction was overturned.

d. Consent and Possession

For joint possession under s.4.3(b), consent is required. Consent is really a form of control. If a person can consent or withhold consent to the possession, that person is exercising control over the thing. This type of control was demonstrated in *Re Chambers and The Queen.*[47] The accused was charged with possession of narcotics for the purpose of trafficking. She was living with her boyfriend, whom she knew was importing drugs. When their house was searched, drugs were found in her closet in the bedroom they shared. The case reached the Ontario Court of Appeal on the issue of whether she could properly be charged with possession. The court held that the required element of control was found in the fact that she could either give consent or withhold consent to the drugs being stored in her closet. The court sent the case back for trial.

2. Possession of Breaking-in Instruments

Section 351 makes it an offence for a person to have possession of break-in instruments:

> **351. (1) Every one who, without lawful excuse, the proof of which lies on him, has in his possession any instrument suitable for the purpose of breaking into any place, motor vehicle, vault or safe under circumstances that give rise to a reasonable inference that the instrument has been used or is or was intended to be used for any such purpose is guilty of an indictable offence and liable to imprisonment for a term not exceeding ten years.**

In *Mongeau v. R.*,[48] the accused was arrested along with L. The accused was driving L.'s car when he was stopped by the police and asked for his driver's licence and car registration.

The arresting officer testified that he had no particular suspicion of either of the parties, and that he was merely making a routine spot check. He asked the accused to open the trunk of the car, and the accused did so. The officer observed a packsack and asked what it contained. The accused said that he thought the packsack contained tools, which it in fact did contain.

As the two of them were examining the trunk, the second police officer, who had remained in the police car, watched L., who had stayed in his automobile, open the door and deposit another bag underneath the car. When this was examined, it was found to contain dynamite, caps, and fuse. Both men were then arrested and charged under s.351.

---

47   (1985), 20 C.C.C. (3d) 440 (Ont.C.A.).
48   (1957), 25 C.R. 195 (Que.C.A.).

The accused argued that he did not have possession of the tools and dynamite and had only guessed that the bag in the trunk contained "ordinary tools" because he could see a wooden handle sticking out of the bag. He further explained that he was driving the car, which was L.'s, because L. had an injured foot.

The court acquitted the accused on the charge of possession for these reasons:

- While the accused was in control of the automobile in which the articles were found, his control was merely due to the fact that he was sitting in the driver's seat at the time the police stopped the automobile to check it. The checking of the car was merely routine; the police officer testified that he had no suspicion of either of the parties.
- The mere fact that the accused was driving the car at the time on behalf of the owner, who was also present in the car, did not establish that he had control over, or even knowledge of, the tools or dynamite.
- The explanation offered by the accused was a reasonable one in the circumstances, and he was entitled to the benefit of any doubt that might arise in respect thereof.

a. Instruments Suitable for Breaking In

The term "instrument" is not defined in the Code. In *R. v. Hayes*,[49] the accused was found in possession of certain documents. These documents consisted of elaborate plans or sketches of two villages in Ontario showing the exact location of two banks, and a minute and detailed description of the interior of one of those banks. The documents also contained recipes for making explosives, information about bulletproof vests, and descriptions of other instruments. The sole question in the case was whether the documents, or plans, found in the possession of the accused fell within the category of "instruments for house-breaking, vault-breaking or safe-breaking" (as break-in instruments were previously defined). The court concluded that a "breaking" instrument necessarily implies an object, or article, or tool, that may be used to break something in the sense of the meaning of "break" as it is defined by s.321. Objects such as a crowbar, a jack, a screwdriver, and even a bent coat-hanger, can all be described as "breaking" instruments. Having thus defined "instrument," the court decided that the documents in the possession of the accused could not be classified as "house, vault or safe-breaking" instruments.

Another case that considered whether articles found in the possession of the accused were break-in instruments is *R. v. Benischek*.[50] In the trunk of a motor vehicle owned by the accused, the police seized a briefcase. In the briefcase, the police found bottles containing nitric and sulphuric acid, bicarbonate of soda, a measuring bottle and cup, rubber gloves, and a plastic spatula. The evidence established that the chemicals and implements were all necessary for making nitroglycerine, a powerful explosive used for safe-

---

49 [1958] 29 C.R. 235 (Ont.C.A.).
50 (1963), 3 C.C.C. 286 (Ont.C.A.).

breaking. Glycerine, an essential ingredient for making the explosive, was not found in the possession of the accused. However, glycerine has several legitimate uses and is readily available at any drugstore. The court concluded:

> *Having in mind that the only purpose that could be served by using all the objects found was to make nitroglycerine they are in my opinion substantial things having physical characteristics enabling them to be used to facilitate a breaking and constitute therefore an instrument for safe-breaking.*[51]

b. Reasonable Inference

Once it is shown that a person possessed instruments that could be used for "breaking into any place, motor vehicle, vault or safe," it must then be demonstrated that a reasonable inference can be drawn from the circumstances that the instruments were used or were intended to be used to break into a place, motor vehicle, safe, or vault.

In *R. v. Kozak and Moore*,[52] the accused were found with screwdrivers, a pair of pliers, a metal expandable tool, a wrench, two pallet knives, and two pairs of gloves. The question was whether these "otherwise innocent instruments" were to be used for an intended break-in. The accused were observed using binoculars to study the rear door of an apartment building. One of the accused was found in possession of a card on which was written the licence plate number of the car owned by the occupant of the apartment. The court held that such circumstances were capable of giving rise to a reasonable inference that the instruments in possession of the accused were to be used to break in to the apartment they were studying.

A case that reached the opposite conclusion is *R. v. Sullivan and Godbolt*.[53] The accused was found in possession of possible safe-breaking instruments: a set of pole-climbers, a three-pound hammer, two pieces of soap, steel punches, pieces of wire, a pair of pliers, and a quantity of rubber tape. The court believed the accused's evidence that all of these items could be, and were intended to be, used for a legitimate contracting business.

The Supreme Court of Canada has considered whether this offence contains a reverse onus clause in the phrase "every one who without lawful excuse, the proof of which lies on him." In *R. v. Holmes*,[54] the accused was charged with possession of break-in instruments when he was found with a pair of Vise-Grips and a pair of pliers. Before entering a plea to the charge, the accused applied to have the indictment quashed on the grounds that the section offended the Charter. The Supreme Court agreed with the decision of the Ontario Court of Appeal, which held that this offence does not contain a reverse onus provision. The Crown must prove all three elements of the offence beyond a reasonable doubt: (1) that the accused had possession (2) of break-in instruments (3) under circumstances that gave rise to a reasonable inference that the instruments had been or were intended to be used for the purpose of a break-in. Once these three elements are proved, the onus shifts

---

51 Ibid., at page 288.
52 (1975), 20 C.C.C. (2d) 175 (Ont.C.A.).
53 (1946), 85 C.C.C. 349 (B.C.C.A.).
54 (1985), 41 C.C.C. (3d) 497 (S.C.C.).

to the accused to raise a defence—that is, to present evidence that raises a reasonable doubt. The words of the questioned phrase are superfluous; the accused has the same defences available that would be available even if those words were not contained in the offence. The Supreme Court dismissed the accused's appeal and sent the case back for trial.

3. Possession of Property Obtained by Crime
a. Elements of the Offence
Section 354 provides that it is an offence for a person knowingly to have in his or her possession any "thing" (either in whole or in part) that was obtained, directly or indirectly, by the commission of an indictable offence. It is also an offence under s.354 for a person to have in his or her possession the proceeds of a transaction involving a thing obtained by a crime. Section 354 is often used for possession of stolen property. Section 355 sets out the penalty for an offence under s.354; it is indictable if the subject-matter is a testamentary instrument or worth more than $5,000. In other situations the offence is hybrid.

Section 354(1) states:

> **354. (1) Every one commits an offence who has in his possession any property or thing or any proceeds of any property or thing knowing that all or part of the property or thing or of the proceeds was obtained by or derived directly or indirectly from**
>
> **(a) the commission in Canada of an offence punishable by indictment; or**
>
> **(b) an act or omission anywhere that, if it had occurred in Canada, would have constituted an offence punishable by indictment.**

Paragraph (b) applies to situations where the thing is obtained by a criminal act outside Canada. As long as the act is one that would be an indictable offence if performed in Canada, it will be an offence to have possession of the property or thing.

The elements of an offence under s.354 are that the accused (1) has a thing in his or her possession and (2) knows that the thing was obtained by the commission of an indictable offence in Canada or by an act committed outside of Canada that would have been an indictable crime within Canada.

b. Possession
The definition of possession in s.4(3) was discussed on pages 336 to 338. Section 358 further provides that for the purposes of s.354 (and s.342 regarding theft, and s.356(1)(b) regarding theft from mail), the offence of "having in possession" is complete when a person has, alone or together with another, possession or control over the "thing," or aids in concealing or disposing of it. So, for example, a person who helps someone sell stolen property is considered to have possession.

In *R. v. Kinna,*[55] one of the issues considered was whether the accused had possession of a stolen typewriter. According to the evidence, the accused and W. were in the accused's room in downtown Vancouver. After some time, W. went across to his own room and brought back a typewriter. W. then said it would have to be sold, as they needed money. He spoke of the typewriter in terms indicating that it had been stolen. W. entered a store to sell the typewriter while the accused remained outside. A police officer saw the accused there and questioned him. The accused told the officer a false story. W. was arrested in the store. The accused was not arrested until the next day.

The court held that the accused did not have possession of the typewriter. Mere knowledge that a thing is stolen is insufficient, and a person cannot be said to consent to possession by another (and thereby be in possession) unless that person has some control over the thing. The court concluded that the accused did not have a measure of control over the typewriter.

c. Knowledge

For a person to be convicted under s.354, it must be proved that he or she knew the "goods" were obtained by an indictable crime. A person who has suspicions but deliberately or recklessly omits to make further inquires will be deemed as a matter of law to have "guilty knowledge." That is, it will be assumed that the person was aware that the goods in question were obtained by an indictable offence.

An example of a case of "turning a blind eye" is *R. v. Marabella.*[56] The accused, a scrap or salvage dealer, was charged with having possession of stolen copper. The police seized, in a salvage yard, over a ton of new copper that had been stolen a few nights earlier from a manufacturing company. The accused had delivered the copper to the salvage yard owner after purchasing it from B. The main issue was whether the accused should have known that the copper was stolen, considering the circumstances in which B. had sold it to him.

The court considered these facts: B. was not connected with a business that sold copper. The copper was purchased at a private residence, where copper is not normally found. The accused did not usually deal in new copper, yet this copper was not scrap material. From its size, shape, and appearance, the accused must have known that it was new and unused. There was also the matter of the price paid. The price paid by the accused, according to his own statement, was 25 cents a pound (55 cents a kilogram). This was little more than one-half of the amount normally paid for scrap copper. Even in view of all of the unusual and suspicious circumstances described above, the accused never questioned B. as to the source of the copper.

The court concluded that, in such circumstances, the accused was guilty of having possession of stolen property. To avoid obtaining knowledge that would have been dangerous to him—namely, that the copper was stolen— he had deliberately refrained from asking for further information. A person

---

55 (1951), 98 C.C.C. 378; 11 C.R. 292 (B.C.C.A.).
56 (1957), 177 C.C.C. 78 (Ont.C.A.).

who consciously omits to ask questions because he or she wishes to remain in ignorance is deemed to have "guilty knowledge."

d. Possession of a Stolen Motor Vehicle

Section 354(2) deals with situations where a motor vehicle is the thing in possession. If a person has in his or her possession a motor vehicle with a tampered identification number, the vehicle is presumed to have been stolen, or obtained by another crime.

Section 354(2) states:

> **(2) In proceedings in respect of an offence under subsection (1), evidence that a person has in his possession a motor vehicle the vehicle identification number of which has been wholly or partially removed or obliterated or a part of a motor vehicle being a part bearing a vehicle identification number that has been wholly or partially removed or obliterated is, in the absence of any evidence to the contrary, proof that the motor vehicle or part, as the case may be, was obtained, and that such person had the motor vehicle or part, as the case may be, in his possession knowing that it was obtained,**
>
> **(a) by the commission in Canada of an offence punishable by indictment; or**
>
> **(b) by an act or omission anywhere that, if it had occurred in Canada, would have constituted an offence punishable by indictment.**
>
> **(3) For the purposes of subsection (2), "vehicle identification number" means any number or other mark placed on a motor vehicle for the purpose of distinguishing the motor vehicle from other similar motor vehicles.**

Section 354(2) contains two presumptions: that a vehicle that has had its identification number removed partially or wholly has been obtained through the commission of an indictable offence; and that the person who has possession of the vehicle has knowledge that the vehicle was obtained through the commission of an indictable offence. To rebut these presumptions, the accused need only raise a reasonable doubt. However, if the accused does not do so, the jury (or judge, if no jury) must conclude that the presumed facts are true. Both of these presumptions have been challenged as violations of the Charter presumption of innocence. In *Re Boyle and the Queen*,[57] the Ontario Court of Appeal considered the constitutionality of these presumptions. The court held that the first presumption is constitutionally valid: the fact that the vehicle identification number has been obliterated is cogent evidence that at some time the vehicle was stolen or otherwise obtained through the commission of a crime. The court held, however, that the second presumption is invalid. Guilty knowledge is an element of the offence. It is not reasonable to expect that people other than car dealers

---

57   (1983), 5 C.C.C. (3d) 193 (Ont.C.A.).

would even be aware of the location of vehicle identification numbers. The presumption is not limited to recently stolen vehicles. So upon proof that a person has possession of a vehicle that has its identification number obliterated, that person may be found guilty of possession even though there is no evidence that the person knew the vehicle was stolen. This is not a reasonable limitation on the presumption of innocence; rather, it is arbitrary. However, the offence can still operate with this presumption severed. In other words, the Crown has the burden of proving guilty knowledge like any other element of the offence.

J. LAUNDERING PROCEEDS OF CRIME

Under s.462.31, it is an offence to deal with anything with intent to conceal or convert it knowing that all or part of the property was obtained as a result of an enterprise crime or a designated drug offence. Enterprise crimes are listed in s.462.3 of the Code and include bribery, child pornography, gambling, murder, theft, robbery, and fraud. Designated drug offences are defined under s.462.3 as including most offences under the Narcotic Control Act and the Food and Drugs Act as well as a conspiracy, or an attempt to commit, or being an accessory after the fact, or counselling in relation to, a designated drug offence. Laundering is a hybrid offence punishable on summary conviction by 6 months' imprisonment and/or a fine of $2,000. If treated as an indictable offence, it is punishable by a term of imprisonment not exceeding 10 years.

Questions for Review and Discussion

1. Is a property right the same as ownership? Explain.
2. If a person "takes" a transistor radio on Friday, without the owner's consent, and returns it undamaged on the following Monday, has that person committed the offence of theft? Explain.
3. What is theft by "conversion"?
4. What does "colour of right" mean?
5. Is it possible to steal confidential information? Explain.
6. Explain the "doctrine of recent possession."
7. Explain the elements of the offence of joy-riding. Why is this offence treated differently from theft?
8. What is the offence of fraudulent concealment? Make up an example.
9. How is the offence of theft related to the offence of robbery?
10. What are the elements of the offence of extortion?
11. What constitutes a threat for the purposes of extortion?

12. Define for the purposes of "breaking and entering" the following words:
    a. "break"
    b. "enter"
    c. "place"

13. How have courts dealt with the presumption of intent under s.348(2)?

14. What is the difference between the offence of "breaking and entering" and being unlawfully in a dwelling-house?

15. How does the criminal law define the term "possession"?

16. What are break-in instruments?

17. What are the elements of the offence of possession of property obtained by crime?

18. Does a person have to know for certain that an object is stolen before being convicted of possession of stolen property? Explain.

19. Make up an example of a situation that would lead to a charge of laundering proceeds of crime.

20. Jocelyn grabs at Noreen's purse. Noreen holds tight. Without actually touching her, Jocelyn "wrenches" the purse out of Noreen's hands. Noreen stumbles but does not fall. Is Jocelyn guilty of robbery? Discuss.

21. Johnson opened a bank account and was accidentally given the account number of a person who had not yet used the account. The person then made several deposits in the account. When Johnson discovered the account balance, he immediately withdrew the money. Can he be charged with theft? Explain. See *R. v. Johnson* (1978), 42 C.C.C. (2d) 249.

22. Mr. Miller was having difficulty with his cable TV reception. By hooking up a device he built, he was able to get clearer reception. However, he also started receiving a pay TV station for which he was not paying. Has he committed an offence? Discuss.

23. Albert was entering the unlocked parking lot of an apartment building when he was arrested. At the time of arrest, he was carrying bolt cutters, Vise-Grips, pliers, and broken bicycle locks. He was convicted of possession of break-in instruments under s.351. He appealed his conviction. Consider the elements of the offence under s.351. On what do you think he based his appeal?

24. Alvin and Bernice are husband and wife. Before the marriage, Alvin collected valuable coins. After the marriage, Alvin stopped collecting, but he did keep all of the coins he had collected before the marriage. Bernice took the coins one day, without letting her husband know, and sold them for $500. She spent the money on herself. Alvin did not discover the coins were missing until a month later. His wife pretended that she didn't know what happened to them. Can Bernice be convicted of theft if it is established that she took the coins?

Chapter Fourteen

FALSE PRETENCES, FRAUD, AND FORGERY
PARTS IX AND X OF THE CODE

A. INTRODUCTION

The offences discussed in this chapter are those that might most aptly be described as "crimes of deceit." Like theft, these offences are against property rights and do not usually involve violence. They often concern commercial transactions and contracts.

B. FALSE PRETENCES

1. False Pretences Defined

Section 361 defines the term "false pretence":

> **361. (1) A false pretence is a representation of a matter of fact either present or past, made by words or otherwise, that is known by the person who makes it to be false and that is made with a fraudulent intent to induce the person to whom it is made to act on it.**
>
> **(2) Exaggerated commendation or depreciation of the quality of anything is not a false pretence unless it is carried to such an extent that it amounts to a fraudulent misrepresentation of fact.**

A false pretence is therefore (a) a representation, by words or other means (e.g., an act) (b) about facts, past or present, (c) that the accused knows to be untrue and (d) that is made with dishonest intent to make someone do something. For example, Albert falsely tells Bryce that he has $5,000 in his bank account so that Bryce will accept a cheque as payment for a motorcycle. If Bryce accepts the cheque and gives the bike to Albert, Albert will have obtained the bike by false pretences.

The false pretence must be about an existing or past fact. So, assume that Albert tells Bryce that he will pay for the motorcycle in a week and that

Bryce gives him the motorcycle based on that promise. If Albert changes his mind and does not pay Albert at the end of the week, he will not be guilty of an offence based on a false pretence because he did not make a false representation about a present or past event. His representation was about a future event.

Section 361(2) provides that if a person exaggerates about the quality of an article, this exaggeration will probably not amount to a false pretence. For example, if Charlotte states that her car is in excellent condition when, in fact, she knows it is in only good shape, she probably has not made a false pretence. The exaggeration must be such that it comes close to being an outright lie.

2. The Offences of False Pretences

Section 362 sets out the offences which involve false pretences.

a. False Pretences Under s.362(1)(a)

> 362. (1) Every one commits an offence who
>
> (a) by a false pretence, whether directly or through the medium of a contract obtained by a false pretence, obtains anything in respect of which the offence of theft may be committed or causes it to be delivered to another person . . .
>
> (2) Every one who commits an offence under paragraph (1)(a)
>
> (a) is guilty of an indictable offence . . . where the property obtained is a testamentary instrument or the value of what is obtained exceeds five thousand dollars; or
>
> (b) is guilty
>
> (i) of an indictable offence and is liable for a term of imprisonment not exceeding two years, or
>
> (ii) an offence punishable on summary conviction, where the value of what is obtained does not exceed five thousand dollars.

Section 362(1)(a) covers the general situation in which property is obtained by false pretences. Anything that is capable of being stolen is capable of being obtained by false pretences.

In general, courts have held that to establish an offence under s.362(1)(a), it is necessary to prove that the accused received more than mere possession of the property. Although court decisions have not been consistent, most have held that the owner of the property must intend to transfer ownership or at least some property interest, as distinct from possession. Under the common law, the difference between taking mere possession and obtaining ownership was one of the distinctions between theft and false pretences. Theft involved taking possession but not ownership, while false pretences involved getting ownership of the thing. For example, a person who steals a car has possession but not ownership, while a person who through false representation talks someone into transferring ownership of the car has not committed theft. This point is illustrated in *R. v. Arsenault.*[1] The accused was charged with two counts of false pretences. The false pretence used in both cases was a bad cheque (he lied about the amount of money in his bank account). In the first instance, the accused purchased electric clippers, which were sold and delivered to him on the faith of the cheque. In the second instance, the accused used a cheque as a down payment on a car. However, the vendor refused to deliver the car to the accused until the cheque had cleared and the conditional sale agreement had been accepted and discounted by the finance company. The accused then persuaded the vendor to let him test the car. Instead of returning it, he drove it to Mexico.

The accused was convicted of false pretences in the case of the clippers. However, with respect to the car, he was found not guilty. The court held that the accused acquired only temporary possession of the car because the vendor did not intend to transfer ownership of it; this meant that he had not committed the offence of "false pretences" within the meaning of s.362(l)(a). The court concluded that the charge against the accused should have been theft of a motor vehicle or fraud (discussed below).

b. False Pretences Under Section 362(4)

Writing bad cheques is specifically dealt with under s.362(4), which states:

> **(4) Where, in proceedings under paragraph (1)(a), it is shown that anything was obtained by the accused by means of a cheque that, when presented for payment within a reasonable time, was dishonoured on the ground that no funds or insufficient funds were on deposit to the credit of the accused in the bank or other institution on which the cheque was drawn, it shall be presumed to have been obtained by a false pretence, unless the court is satisfied by evidence that when the accused issued the cheque he believed on reasonable grounds that it would be honoured if presented for payment within a reasonable time after it was issued.**

This subsection creates a presumption that a person who writes a bad cheque did so under false pretences. Like other presumptions, it has been challenged under the Charter. The Alberta Court of Appeal has held that the subsection is of no force or effect because it violates the presumption of innocence.[2] Conversely, the Saskatchewan Court of Queen's Bench has held that the subsection is valid.[3]

1   (1970), 11 C.R.N.S. 366 (B.C.C.A).
2   *R. v. Driscoll* (1987), 38 C.C.C. (3d) 28 (Alta.C.A.).
3   *R. v. Bunka* (1984), 12 C.C.C. (3d) 437 (Sask.Q.B.).

c. *Obtaining Credit by Fraud or False Pretences*

Paragraphs (b), (c), and (d) of s.362(1) read:

> **362. (1) Every one commits an offence who . . .**
>
> **(b) obtains credit by a false pretence or by fraud;**
>
> **(c) knowingly makes or causes to be made, directly or indirectly, a false statement in writing with intent that it should be relied on, with respect to the financial condition or means or ability to pay of himself or any person, firm or corporation that he is interested in or that he acts for, for the purpose of procuring, in any form whatever, whether for his benefit or the benefit of that person, firm or corporation,**
>
> **(i) the delivery of personal property,**
>
> **(ii) the payment of money,**
>
> **(iii) the making of a loan,**
>
> **(iv) the grant or extension of credit,**
>
> **(v) the discount of an account receivable, or**
>
> **(vi) the making, accepting, discounting or endorsing of a bill of exchange, cheque, draft, or promissory note; or**
>
> **(d) knowing that a false statement in writing has been made with respect to the financial condition or means or ability to pay of himself or another person, firm or corporation that he is interested in or that he acts for, procures on the faith of that statement, whether for his benefit or for the benefit of that person, firm or corporation, anything mentioned in subparagraphs (c)(i) to (vi).**

Section 362(3) provides:

> **(3) Every one who commits an offence under paragraph (1)(b), (c) or (d) is guilty of an indictable offence and liable to imprisonment for a term not exceeding ten years.**

Paragraph (b) creates the general offence of obtaining credit by false pretences. Paragraphs (c) and (d) define specific false-pretence situations involving the establishment of a "phony" credit rating. Paragraph (b) would be applicable if, for example, a person deliberately gave false information about his or her assets to a bank officer when negotiating a loan. In *R. v. Winning*,[4] the accused obtained a credit card by giving his correct name and address but lying about his financial worth. It was held that credit was not advanced on the basis of the false information but on the basis of an independent credit investigation; therefore, the offence was not made out. So, in the example of a loan officer being given false information, before the offence of false pre-

---

4 (1973), 12 C.C.C. (2d) 449 (Ont.C.A.).

tences can be made out it must be established that the officer actually relied on the false information to decide whether a loan should be granted.

The false pretences in paragraphs (c) and (d) must be made in writing with the object of procuring one of the benefits listed within the subsection—that is, to obtain delivery of personal property or money, or to obtain a loan, or an extension of credit, and so forth. For example, Naomi owns a company and drafts a letter that falsely describes the company's worth. If Naomi presents this letter to several potential creditors, and they, relying on the letter, loan her money, Naomi will be guilty of an offence under s.362(1)(c).

It was necessary to make the offence of obtaining credit by false pretences a separate offence because "credit" does not fall within the term "anything"—that is, credit cannot be stolen. However, obtaining credit by fraud is included in the general offence of fraud.

C. FRAUD

1. Defined

Fraud is defined by s.380 of the Code:

> **380. (1) Every one who, by deceit, falsehood or other fraudulent means, whether or not it is a false pretence within the meaning of this Act, defrauds the public or any person, whether ascertained or not, of any property, money or valuable security**
>
> **(a) is guilty of an indictable offence and liable to a term of imprisonment not exceeding ten years, where the subject-matter of the offence is a testamentary instrument or the value of the subject-matter of the offence exceeds five thousand dollars; or**
>
> **(b) is guilty**
>
> **(i) of an indictable offence and is liable to imprisonment for a term not exceeding two years, or**
>
> **(ii) of an offence punishable on summary conviction,**
>
> **where the value of the subject-matter of the offence does not exceed five thousand dollars.**

2. Elements of the Offence

The Supreme Court of Canada, in *R. v. Theroux*,[5] considered the *actus reus* and *mens rea* of the offence of fraud. The accused was a businessman involved in residential construction. The company he directed was building two residential projects. The buyers were told that their deposits were insured by the Federation de Construction du Québec. In fact, the deposits were not insured. The company failed, and most of the buyers lost their

---

5   (1993), 79 C.C.C. (3d) 449 (S.C.C.).

deposits. Theroux, as the director of the company, was held responsible for the misrepresentations that the deposits were guaranteed. At his trial, he was convicted of fraud after it was found that the representations were made for the purpose of obtaining the depositors' signatures and deposits. His defence—that he honestly believed that the projects would be built—was rejected. The court of appeal upheld the conviction, holding that all that was required was a dishonest act that had the consequence that someone was deprived of something.

The case was appealed to the Supreme Court of Canada on the issue of whether the accused's honest belief that the housing projects would be completed and that no one would be hurt was a defence. In other words, for the required *mens rea* to exist, must the accused subjectively believe that his or her act is dishonest?

To answer this question, the Court first looked at the *actus reus* for fraud. The Court examined its previous decision in *Olan*,[6] in which the *actus reus* of the offence was analysed extensively. The Court summed up its findings in *Olan:*

- The *actus reus* has two elements: deprivation and dishonesty.
- The dishonest act is established by proof of an act of deceit, falsehood, or other fraudulent means.
- The element of deprivation is established by proof of detriment, prejudice, or risk of prejudice to the economic interests of the victim caused by the dishonest act. Actual economic loss is not essential; placing the interest at risk is enough.

What constitutes a lie or deceitful act is judged on objective grounds: Did the accused represent a situation as of a certain character when it was not? Other fraudulent means are also determined by an objective test: Would a reasonable person consider the dealings dishonest?

The Court noted that *Olan* was an important decision in that it broadened the offence of fraud by finding that deceit and actual economic loss are not necessary for the offence. Any dishonest act and an economic risk of deprivation are enough to establish the *actus reus*.

The Court then considered the *mens rea* of fraud and concluded that it requires the subjective awareness that one is undertaking a prohibited act that could deprive another person of property or put that property at risk. It is no defence that the accused hoped that the deprivation would not take place or believed that there was nothing wrong with what he or she was doing. Recklessness may also be sufficient for the *mens rea* where the accused has knowledge that the prohibited consequences are likely and commits acts being reckless as to whether those consequences will occur.

In conclusion, the Court held that the accused in *Theroux* had committed the *actus reus* of the offence by committing deliberate falsehoods that resulted in deprivation for the depositors, who did not get the insurance protection they believed they were getting and who placed their money at risk. The

---

6   (1978), 41 C.C.C. (2d) 145 (S.C.C.).

mens rea was established because the accused knew that he was depriving the depositors of something they thought they had.

In a case released at the same time, *R. v. Zlatic,*[7] the Supreme Court of Canada again considered the elements of the offence. The accused operated a wholesale clothing company. He had obtained clothing on credit from his suppliers. Instead of paying off his creditors as he sold the clothing, he gambled the money away, eventually going bankrupt. He was charged with fraud. The Court held that the *actus reus* or prohibited act in this case was using the money for gambling rather than for paying off creditors. The Court applied the test of the reasonable person and concluded that the accused's use of the money in which his creditors had an interest was wrongful in that most reasonable people would have found his actions dishonest. This was not just unwise business practice but a wrongful use of money for a purpose that had nothing to do with the business. The *mens rea* consisted of the accused's knowledge that the gambling could place the victims' interest in the money at risk. It was no defense that he believed that he would win and be able to pay off his creditors.

3. Fraud and False Pretences

The offence of fraud is a broader offence than false pretences. In other words, the offence of fraud includes false pretences but also other forms of deceit. In fact, authorities have recommended repealing the offences of false pretences and having one offence of fraud.[8]

4. Examples of Fraud

Fraud can take many forms. The following three cases are examples of some of the ways that fraud can been committed.

- *R. v. Kirkwood.*[9] The accused was the owner of a video store and had been making illegal copies of videotapes and selling or renting them. The trial judge dismissed the charges of fraud against the accused because there was no relationship between the accused and the "victim" of the crime, the holder of the copyright. The trial court said that for the offence of fraud, the accused must cause the victim to act to his or her detriment. The court of appeal disagreed with this narrow interpretation, stating that where fraud is based on deceit or falsehoods, it may be that a relationship between the victim and the accused must exist. However, where the charge is based on "other fraudulent means," it does not matter that the victim was unaware of accused. Deprivation is satisfied by injury to the economic interests of the victim. In this case, intent to injure the economic interests of the victim could be inferred from the accused's willingness to deal in the copied tapes.

7   (1993), 79 C.C.C. (3d) 466 (S.C.C.).
8   Working Paper 19, Criminal Law, Theft and Fraud, Law Reform Commission of Canada (1977).
9   (1983), 5 C.C.C. (3d) 393 (Ont.C.A.).

- *R. v. Gaetz.*[10] The accused was charged with defrauding the bank of a sum of money. The accused operated a car dealership. He borrowed money from the bank to purchase cars for lease. He was to make payments to the bank during the period of the lease but to repay the bank in full when the leases were terminated. The leases terminated earlier than expected. The accused was experiencing financial difficulty, so instead of paying the bank in full he continued to make payments as if the cars were still being leased. The Supreme Court of Canada upheld the decision of the Nova Scotia Court of Appeal that the deceit of continuing the payments led to an extension of credit by the bank. The accused's appeal against his conviction was dismissed.
- *R. v. Wendel and Ballan.*[11] The victim was a 76-year-old woman who had signed a contract for $7,000 worth of renovations to her home. Evidence was that the value of the renovations would reasonably be $800 to $1,300. After obtaining her signature on the contract, the accused had taken the victim to her bank and attempted to have her withdraw $6,000. He told suspicious bank employees that he was her grandson. The bank employees refused to release the money, and the police were called. Here, the fraud was not deceit or misrepresentation but "other fraudulent means." The court applied the test of whether ordinary people would find that the actions of the accused were dishonest, and found the accused guilty.

5. Examples of Specific Fraud Offences

The following crimes concern illegal business practices that tend to cheat the public.

Section 380(2) is a specific type of fraud concerned with the manipulation of the price of stocks or shares or anything else offered for sale to the public. It states:

> **(2) Every one who, by deceit, falsehood or other fraudulent means, whether or not it is a false pretence within the meaning of this Act, with intent to defraud, affects the public market price of stocks, shares, merchandise or anything that is offered for sale to the public, is guilty of an indictable offence and liable to imprisonment for a term not exceeding ten years.**

Section 381 provides that a person who uses the mail to send letters or circulars concerning schemes designed to deceive or defraud the public is guilty of an indictable offence.

Section 382 makes it an indictable offence for a person to manipulate the stock market by creating a misleading or false appearance of active public trading.

Sections 385 and 386 cover any fraudulent behaviour relating to the sale or mortgaging of property—that is, to fraudulent activities on the part of a mortgagor or vendor of property. Specifically, s.385 provides:

10 (1993), 84 C.C.C. (3d) 351 (S.C.C.), affirming (1992), 77 C.C.C. (3d) 445 (N.S.C.A.).
11 (1992), 78 C.C.C. (3d) 279 (Man.C.A.).

385. (1) Every one who . . .

(a) with intent to defraud and for the purpose of inducing the purchaser or mortgagee to accept the title offered or produced to him, conceals from him any settlement, deed, will or other instrument material to the title, or any encumbrance on the title, or

(b) falsifies any pedigree upon which the title depends,

is guilty of an indictable offence and liable to imprisonment for a term not exceeding two years.

Section 386 states:

386. Every one who, as principal or agent, in a proceeding to register title to real property, or in a transaction relating to real property that is or is proposed to be registered, knowingly and with intent to deceive,

(a) makes a material false statement or representation,

(b) suppresses or conceals from a judge or registrar, or any person employed by or assisting the registrar, any material document, fact, matter or information, or

(c) is privy to anything mentioned in paragraph (a) or (b),

is guilty of an indictable offence and liable to imprisonment for a term not exceeding five years.

Section 400 makes it an indictable offence to, among other things, make a false statement about a company to induce persons to become shareholders, or to deceive shareholders, or to induce anyone to put up security or advance money for a company.

D. PERSONATION

A person who passes himself or herself off as another for a criminal purpose has committed an offence under s.403:

403. Every one who fraudulently personates any person, living or dead,

(a) with intent to gain advantage for himself or another person,

(b) with intent to obtain any property or an interest in any property, or

(c) with intent to cause disadvantage to the person whom he personates or another person,

is guilty of an indictable offence and liable to imprisonment for a term not exceeding ten years or an offence punishable on summary conviction.

The intent required for this offence—to gain an advantage or cause a disadvantage—has been given a broad meaning. For example, in *Rozon v. The Queen*,[12] the accused, on being asked to identify himself, handed to the police officers a medical insurance card belonging to another person. He did so in order to avoid being arrested on a warrant issued against him. The accused was convicted of personation because he deliberately and in bad faith sought to gain the "advantage" of avoiding arrest.

In a similar case, *R. v. Dozois*,[13] the accused, whose driver's licence was suspended, was convicted of personation when he used his passenger's licence after being stopped by police for a traffic violation.

In *R. v. Hetsberger*,[14] the accused purchased a plane ticket in another person's name to help N. be admitted to the United States. The court convicted the accused, noting that the advantage obtained need not be an economic one. For this offence, gaining illegal entry into the United States qualifies as an advantage.

E. FORGERY

Section 366(1) defines the offence of forgery:

> **366. (1) Every one commits forgery who makes a false document, knowing it to be false, with intent**
>
> **(a) that it should in any way be used or acted on as genuine, to the prejudice of any one whether within Canada or not, or**
>
> **(b) that a person should be induced, by the belief that it is genuine, to do or to refrain from doing anything, whether within Canada or not.**

Section 366(3) states:

> **(3) Forgery is complete as soon as a document is made with the knowledge and intent referred to in subsection (1), notwithstanding that the person who makes it does not intend that any particular person should use or act on it as genuine or be induced, by the belief that it is genuine, to do or refrain from doing anything.**

Section 367(1) provides:

> **Every one who commits forgery**
>
> **(a) is guilty of an indictable offence and liable to imprisonment for a term not exceeding ten years; or**
>
> **(b) is guilty of an offence punishable on summary conviction.**

Before an accused can be convicted of the offence of forgery, it must be proved that he or she (a) knowingly made a false document with (b) intent

---

12 (1975), 28 C.R.N.S. 232 (Que.C.A.).
13 (1974), R.L. 285 (Que.C.A.).
14 (1980), 51 C.C.C. (2d) 257 (Ont.C.A.).

that it be used (c) as if it were genuine in such a way that someone is prejudiced.

"Document" is defined in s.321 thus:

> **[A]ny paper, parchment or other material on which is recorded or marked anything that is capable of being read or understood by a person, computer system or other device, and includes a credit card, but does not include trade marks on articles of commerce or inscriptions on stone or metal or other like material;**

This revised definition of a document was enacted in 1985. It now includes more than written documents, since information can be stored on various devices such as tapes, computer disks, and so on.

There are two sections that define "false document": s.366(2) and s.321.

1. False Documents Under Section 366(2)

> **366. . . . (2) Making a false document includes**
>
> **(a) altering a genuine document in any material part;**
>
> **(b) making a material addition to a genuine document or adding to it a false date, attestation, seal or other thing that is material; or**
>
> **(c) making a material alteration in a genuine document by erasure, obliteration, removal or in any other way.**

To make a "material addition or alteration," or to change a "material part" of a document, is to change an important part of the document. For example, to change the date on a cheque is to alter a material part of the cheque. In *R. v. O'Hearn*,[15] the accused got an 87-year-old man to subscribe to *Maclean's* for a year. The victim gave the accused a signed cheque with the marginal figures "315" inserted but the amount otherwise blank. The accused gave him a receipt for $3.15, the cost of the subscription. Afterwards he altered the cheque to read $31.50 and filled in the words for that amount in the appropriate space. The court held that the alteration of the figures constituted an alteration of a material part of the cheque.

2. False Documents Under Section 321

The Supreme Court of Canada, in *Gaysek v. The Queen*,[16] held that because of the use of the word "includes" in s.366, the term "false document" also includes the definition in s.321. Section 321 defines a false document thus:

> **"false document" means a document**
>
> **(a) the whole or a material part of which purports to be made by or on behalf of a person**

---

15 (1964), 3 C.C.C. 296 (B.C.C.A.).
16 (1971), 2 C.C.C. (2d) 545 (S.C.C.).

(i) who did not make it or authorize it to be made, or

(ii) who did not in fact exist,

(b) that is made by or on behalf of the person who purports to make it but is false in some material particular,

(c) that is made in the name of an existing person, by him or under his authority, with a fraudulent intention that it should pass as being made by a person, real or fictitious, other than the person who makes it or under whose authority it is made.

Under the common law a false document was described as "one that tells a lie about itself," but not about its contents. Thus, forgery consisted of falsifying the document itself; it did not mean making false statements. If a letter is supposed to have been signed by Paula but was in fact signed in Paula's name by Evelyn, without Paula's permission, and a third party is led to believe that it is Paula's letter, the letter is a false document. It tells a lie about itself, the lie being that Paula signed the letter. If the same letter was actually signed by Paula, even if the contents of the letter are completely untrue, the letter is not a false document. It does not tell a lie about itself; the lie is in the information, not the letter. However, in *Gaysek,* the Supreme Court of Canada gave the term "false document" a broader meaning. The accused prepared false inventory sheets for about 20 Becker Milk stores and certified that the information was correct. The accused was acquitted of forgery at his trial, the trial judge holding that the false inventory sheets were not false documents as required by the Code for the offence of forgery because it was the information the inventory sheets contained that was false, not the documents themselves.

The Supreme Court, after concluding that the definition of false document in s.321 applied, held that any document that is false in some material particular (i.e., in some significant part) is a false document. In this case, a document that was false in reference to the very purpose for which it was created was certainly one that was false in a material particular. The inventory sheets contained false information as to the very matters that they purported to certify and so were false in a number of material particulars; therefore, each was a false document. The Court ordered a new trial.

F. UTTERING

Section 368 states:

(1) Every one who, knowing that a document is forged,

(a) uses, deals with or acts on it, or

(b) causes or attempts to cause any person to use, deal with, or act as if the document were genuine,

(c) is guilty of an indictable offence and liable to imprisonment for a term not exceeding ten years, or

(d) is guilty of an offence punishable on summary conviction.

(2) For the purposes of proceedings under this section, the place where a document was forged is not material.

Section 368 creates the offence of "uttering" a forged document. Generally, uttering means to pass, or to cause to have passed, as if it were genuine, a forged document. If Paul takes to a bank a forged cheque, knowing it to be forged, and attempts to cash it, then he is guilty of an offence under s.368, whether or not he was the one who forged the cheque. Similarly, if Paul, knowing a cheque is forged, gives it to Janet, who has no knowledge of the forgery, with a request that she cash it, Paul is guilty of uttering.

In *R. v. Paquette,*[17] the accused, a notary, was charged with uttering a forged document. He had notarized the signature of a person on a document though that document had not been signed in his presence. (The law requires notaries to actually witness the signature before notarizing any document.) Therefore, the document was a forgery under s.366.(2)(b) (adding a false attestation). However, the accused was charged not with forgery but with uttering. The Supreme Court of Canada agreed with the dissenting judge at the court of appeal in holding that he was guilty of uttering because after making the false document, he affixed it to a mortgage, acting on it.

In a case with similar facts, *R. v. Couture,*[18] the accused was a notary who signed a mortgage falsely attesting that the mortgagor had signed the document in his presence. The accused's appeal of his conviction for forgery was allowed because it was not proven that he intended to cause prejudice to another. He may have been merely incompetent or negligent.

G. OFFENCES RESEMBLING OR RELATED TO FORGERY

There are a number of other offences resembling or related to the offence of forgery. The following paragraphs describe some of these offences.

1. Forgery Equipment

Section 369 provides that it is unlawful, without the proper authorization, to make or possess exchequer bill paper, or revenue paper, or paper that is used to make bank notes, or any paper that is intended to make bank notes, or any paper that is intended to resemble any of the above. Section 369 also states that it is unlawful to make or possess any machinery or instrument that is intended to be used to commit forgery.

An offence under s.369 is indictable and punishable by a maximum of 14 years in prison.

---

17   (1979), 45 C.C.C. (2d) 575 (S.C.C.).
18   (1991), 64 C.C.C. (3d) 227 (Que.C.A.).

2. False Messages

Section 371 states:

> **371. Every one who, with intent to defraud, causes or procures a telegram, cablegram or radio message to be sent or delivered as being sent by the authority of another person, knowing that it is not sent by his authority and with intent that the message should be acted on as being sent by his authority, is guilty of an indictable offence and liable to imprisonment for a term not exceeding five years.**

3. Forging a Trademark

There are a number of offences that deal with trademarks. Generally, a trademark is an identification of a company's product or property. Trademarks are the property of a company. Only that company may use the trademark, unless it grants permission allowing another company to make use of it.

Section 406 states:

> **406. For the purposes of this Part, every one forges a trade-mark who**
>
> **(a) without the consent of the proprietor of the trade-mark, makes or reproduces in any manner that trade-mark or a mark so nearly resembling it as to be calculated to deceive, or**
>
> **(b) falsifies, in any manner, a genuine trade-mark.**

Section 407 then provides:

> **407. Every one commits an offence who, with intent to deceive or defraud the public . . . forges a trade-mark.**

Section 410 has wider application:

> **410. Every one commits an offence who, with intent to deceive or defraud,**
>
> **(a) defaces, conceals or removes a trade-mark or the name of another person from anything without the consent of that other person, or**
>
> **(b) being a manufacturer, dealer, trader or bottler, fills any bottle or siphon that bears the trade-mark or name of another person, without the consent of that other person, with a beverage, milk, by-product of milk or other liquid commodity for the purpose of sale or traffic.**

In *R. v. Irvine*,[19] the accused, a manufacturer, was convicted under s.408 when he filled bottles with his own product and then marked these bottles with another company's name.

---

19 (1905), 9 C.C.C. 407 (Ont.C.A.).

H. COUNTERFEIT MONEY

1. Definition

"Counterfeit money" is defined in s.448:

448. In this Part,

"counterfeit money" includes

(a) false coin or false paper money that resembles or is apparently intended to resemble or pass for a current coin or current paper money,

(b) a forged bank note or forged blank bank note, whether complete or incomplete,

(c) a genuine coin or genuine paper money that is prepared or altered to resemble or pass for a current coin or current paper money of a higher denomination,

(d) a current coin from which the milling is removed by filing or cutting the edges and on which new milling is made to restore its appearance,

(e) a coin cased with gold, silver or nickel, as the case may be, that is intended to resemble or pass for a current gold, silver or nickel coin, and

(f) a coin or a piece of metal or mixed metals washed or coloured by any means with a wash or material capable of producing the appearance of gold, silver or nickel and that is intended to resemble or pass for a current gold, silver or nickel coin.

The word "current" as it is used in the counterfeiting sections usually means that the money counterfeited (copied) must be negotiable, or still in circulation.

In *Robinson v. The Queen,*[20] the accused had in his possession a number of counterfeit U.S. 1941/42 dimes. The peculiarity in their dating, (1941/42) gave them a numismatic value of between $100 and $800. The accused argued that the dimes were not intended to resemble, or pass as "current" coins within the definition of "counterfeit money." They were for the purpose of sale as a numismatic curiosity and not for circulation as legal tender.

The court held that the primary characteristic of the coins was that they were counterfeits of "current" coins and that they were intended to resemble such coins. The Supreme Court of Canada upheld the accused's conviction of having counterfeit money in his possession.

---

20 (1974), 10 C.C.C. (2d) 505 (S.C.C.).

In *R. v. Duane*,[21] the accused was given an envelope of counterfeit money to "hold on to." When the owner left town, she decided to destroy the money. When the police came to see her, she showed them the money that she had torn up. She was convicted of possession even though there was no proof that she intended to use the money. The Supreme Court of Canada held that it is no defence to possession that the accused never intended to use the counterfeit money as currency.

The courts of appeal in both British Columbia and Ontario have held that knowledge that the money is counterfeit is an essential element of the offence of possession, which the Crown must prove beyond a reasonable doubt.[22]

2. Offences Involving Counterfeit Money

It is an offence to make, have possession of, or utter counterfeit money (see ss.449 to 453). It is also an offence to make, repair, buy, sell, or have possession of equipment for making counterfeit money (see s.458).

21 (1985), 22 C.C.C. (3d) 448 (S.C.C.).
22 *R. v. Freng* (1993), 86 C.C.C. (3d) 91 (B.C.C.A.); *R. v. Santeramo* (1976), 32 C.C.C. (2d) 35 (Ont.C.A.).

Questions for Review and Discussion

1. Compare and contrast the offences of theft, false pretences, and fraud.

2. How does the Code define "false document"?

3. Define the elements of the offence of forgery.

4. What is counterfeit money?

5. Alfred is applying to join the Canadian Armed Forces. He never finished high school but provides the recruiting officer with a copy of a high school transcript on which he has put his name. Has Alfred made a false document? What offence or offences could he be charged with?

    What if Alfred had graduated from high school? Alfred lists all of the subjects he studied at high school but he lies about some of the marks he received. Has Alfred made a false document? Explain. What other information might you need? What offence or offences could he be charged with? Explain.

6. Mack worked for Jane, a city councillor. After an election, which Jane won, they had a falling out, in part, Mack testified, because he had witnessed unfair and corrupt practices on the part of Jane. He notified the police but was unhappy with the pace of the investigations. Around this time he altered a cheque he had received for $300 to $30,000, changed the date, and made the cheque payable to Jane's campaign. He photocopied the cheque and photocopied onto the back of the photocopy a cut-out of Jane's signature. He then made several copies of this copy and showed them to several people active in politics. His purpose in fabricating the cheque was to speed up the investigation. This would happen because Jane had declared approximately $27,000 in election donations for the campaign. Mack testified that he knew that the correct amount was over $100,000 and that producing the cheque for $30,000 would show that Jane must have lied.

    He eventually showed the copy to the police, who determined that the cheque was fabricated. What was Mack charged with? What argument would Mack make in his defence? See *R. v. Nuosci* (1991), 69 C.C.C. (3d) 64 (Ont.C.A.).

Chapter Fifteen

MISCHIEF, ARSON, AND CRUELTY TO ANIMALS
PART XI OF THE CODE

Generally, the offences in this part concern interferences with or acts against private property that do not involve taking possession—for example, acts of vandalism can be a type of mischief. Some of the offences, such as arson, may involve danger or harm to persons.

A. MISCHIEF

430. (1) Every one commits mischief who wilfully

(a) destroys or damages property;

(b) renders property dangerous, useless, inoperative or ineffective;

(c) obstructs, interrupts or interferes with the lawful use, enjoyment or operation of property; or

(d) obstructs, interrupts or interferes with any person in the lawful use, enjoyment or operation of property.

(1.1) Every one commits mischief who wilfully

(a) destroys or alters data;

(b) renders data meaningless, useless or ineffective;

(c) obstructs, interrupts or interferes with the lawful use of data; or

(d) obstructs, interrupts or interferes with any person in the lawful use of data or denies access to data to any person who is entitled to access thereto.

The term "property" refers to both real property and personal property. In brief, real property consists of immovable things—for example, land and things attached to the land (e.g., a house or garage). Personal property consists of movable things, such as automobiles and furniture. "Data" is defined in s.342.1 thus:

> **[R]epresentations of information or of concepts that are being prepared or have been prepared in a form suitable for use in a computer system.**

There are many ways of committing the offence of mischief. For example, mischief in regard to a car (which is personal property) includes damaging the car by breaking its radio antenna, or rendering the car dangerous by tampering with its brake system, or obstructing the use of the car by blocking a public highway.

Mischief in regard to a building (which is real property) includes damaging the building by breaking its windows, or rendering the building dangerous by weakening a step in a stairway, or obstructing the use of the building by barricading the entrance so that no one can get in.

An example of mischief in relation to data is altering a computer disk so that the data stored on it cannot be accessed by the owners.

It is usually clear what mischief to property means. A case that considered the meaning of interference with enjoyment of property points out one unclear area. In *R. v. Drapeau*,[1] the accused was charged with mischief under s.430(1)(d). The complainants were his neighbours with whom he had been embroiled in a series of "disagreements, misunderstandings, provocations and reprisals." The evidence at the trial was that over a period of four summers, the accused had stared at his neighbours and made objectionable noises when they were in their backyard. The issue before the Quebec Court of Appeal was the meaning of "enjoyment of property." Two of the appeal judges held that the actions of the accused, while they may have been bizarre and objectionable, did not constitute an interference with the complainants' enjoyment of their property. Enjoyment of property refers to the act of, or entitlement to, possession of the property. The actions of the accused did not interfere with the enjoyment of property in this sense. One dissenting judge stated that enjoyment of property should not be given such a restricted meaning but should include the satisfaction a person derives from his or her property.

The few cases on this issue do conflict; however, the *Drapeau* decision was handed down by one of the highest courts to consider the issue.

The important issue in many mischief cases is whether the damaging, rendering dangerous, or obstructing was done wilfully. "Wilfully" usually means intentionally. As one judge has put it: "Wilfully means not merely to commit an act voluntarily but to commit it purposely with an evil intention, or in other words it means to do so deliberately, intentionally, and corruptly and without any justifiable excuse."[2]

---

1   (1995), 96 C.C.C. (3d) 554 (Que.C.A.).
2   *R. v. Duggan* (1906), 12 C.C.C. 147 (Man.C.A.).

So if a student breaks a window in his school building, it must be shown that the student broke the window deliberately and with a criminal (i.e., evil) intent. The student would not be guilty of mischief if the window was broken accidentally or with a justifiable excuse, such as to escape from a fire.

Section 429(1) extends the meaning of "wilfully" when it is mentioned in Part XI of the Code to include recklessness:

> **429. (1) Every one who causes the occurrence of an event by doing an act or by omitting to do an act that is his duty to do, knowing that the act or omission will probably cause the occurrence of the event and being reckless whether the event occurs or not, shall be deemed, for the purposes of this Part, wilfully to have caused the occurrence of the event.**

In other words, a person may not intend to damage property, but if that person does some act and knows that the damage will probably occur and takes an unjustifiable risk that the damage will not occur, then that person will be considered to have wilfully or intentionally caused the damage if it occurs.

In *R. v. Wendel*,[3] the accused and other youths were charged with breaking and entering with the intent to commit mischief. Early in the evening, they had obtained some beer, which they drank while sitting under a bridge. They then went to an apartment building and found a vacant apartment with a slightly open door. They went in and drank more beer. Later, the caretaker of the building came to the apartment and could not get in because the door had been locked from the inside. There was no question that the youths had broken and entered the apartment. The only question was whether they had intended to wilfully obstruct or interfere with the lawful use of the apartment. The court held that even under the extended meaning of wilfully in s.429(1), the accused was not guilty. He and the others entered the apartment for the purpose of drinking beer, not for the purpose of obstructing or interfering with the use of the property.

The extended meaning of wilfully (i.e., to include reckless) was applied in *R. v. Gotto*.[4] The accused and a group of others ransacked a car. In order to have light so that he could see under the front seat, the accused set fire to a road map that he found in the car. He left the map near the car when he and the others left. The car caught fire and was destroyed. The accused argued that he was not guilty because he had not wilfully set fire to the car. However, the court disagreed and held that his conduct fell within the meaning of "wilfully" as defined under s.429(1). He knew that damage to the car would probably result if he did not take precautions to remove the burning map. He made no attempt to remove it and was reckless about whether or not the damage would occur.

3   (1967), 2 C.C.C. 23 (B.C.C.A.).
4   [1974] 3 W.W.R. 454 (Sask.Dist.Ct.).

A trivial interference with property will not be considered mischief. In *R. v. Chapman*,[5] the accused was charged with wilfully interfering with the lawful use of property. The accused, who was 18 years old, and two younger companions were walking along a street late at night when they saw a small car parked in the street. As a prank, they pushed the car between 3 and 10 metres down the street and left the scene. They did not try to start the car, which was not damaged in any way. The only inconvenience to the owner of the car was that he had to walk a short extra distance the next morning. The court found the accused not guilty. There was no significant interference with the use of the car, nor was there an intention to interfere with the lawful use of the car. Similarly, in *R. v. Quickfall*,[6] the accused was charged under s.430(1)(a) for damaging property by placing a poster on a lamppost. The court of appeal found that his actions did not impair the use or value of the property; therefore, the offence was not committed.

Mischief charges may result during a labour dispute such as a strike. An example of such a case is *R. v. Mammolita*,[7] a decision of the Ontario Court of Appeal. There was a legal strike of employees at a factory in Thunder Bay. Several months after the employer had obtained an injunction limiting pickets to 10, 75 to 100 people formed a picket line and stopped the management and office personnel from entering the building. The police were called and were able to form a wedge to allow the management to pass through. Police photographs were taken of the strikers, and eventually 33 people were charged with mischief for wilfully obstructing or interfering with the lawful use and operation of the property of the company. The accused were acquitted at their trial on the grounds that their mere presence and passive acquiescence at the time did not make them liable for the offence. The court of appeal disagreed and ordered a new trial, stating that:

> *a person may be guilty as a principal of committing mischief . . . if he forms part of a group which constitutes a human barricade or other obstruction. The fact that he stands shoulder to shoulder with other persons even though he neither says anything nor does anything further may be an act which constitutes an obstruction . . . However, criminal liability only results if the act is done wilfully . . . It may not be very difficult to infer that a person standing shoulder to shoulder with other persons in a group so as to block a roadway knows that his act will probably cause the obstruction and is reckless if he does not attempt to extricate himself from the group.*[8]

The right to strike and picket is protected under s.430(6) and (7):

(6) No person commits mischief within the meaning of this section by reason only that

(a) he stops work as a result of the failure of his employer and himself to agree on any matter relating to his employment;

5   [1969] 3 C.C.C. 358 (B.C.Cty.Ct.).
6   (1993), 78 C.C.C. (3d) 563 (Que.C.A.).
7   (1983), 9 C.C.C. (3d) 85 (Ont.C.A.).
8   Ibid., at page 89.

**(b) he stops work as a result of the failure of his employer and a bar-
gaining agent acting on his behalf to agree on any matter relating to
his employment; or**

**(c) he stops work as a result of his taking part in a combination of
workmen or employees for their own reasonable protection as workmen or employees.**

**(7) No person commits mischief within the meaning of this section
by reason only that he attends at or near or approaches a dwelling-
house or place for the purpose only of obtaining or communicating
information.**

Thus, in *R. v. Dooling*,[9] where the accused were participating in a lawful
strike and picketing their employer, the accused were acquitted of mischief.
The court held that for there to be an offence under this section, there must
be some physical act that has the effect of obstructing, interrupting, or interfering with the use of the property. The fact that people were persuaded not
to do business with the employer was an inevitable consequence of the
labour dispute.

B. ARSON

For arson to be committed, there must be a burning of property. In *R. v.
Jorgenson*,[10] the meaning of "burning" was explained:

> *There must be actual combustion, although it is not necessary for the mate-
> rial to blaze openly, so long as it comes to a red heat. Charring, that is, the car-
> bonization of the material by combustion, is evidence of burning, but blacken-
> ing of the material not accompanied by any degree of consumption is not nor
> is mere scorching . . . So long as there is burning in that sense, the extent and
> duration of the fire is immaterial, and the damage may be insignificant.*[11]

In *Jorgenson*, the accused was charged with setting fire to a building. The
only evidence of burning on the building consisted of three blister marks on
a small area of paint on a metal door. The court held that the blistering did
not amount to burning because there had been no consumption of material.

There are several offences involving arson, which is the criminal setting of
fires or explosions.

1. Arson Causing Danger to Human Life

The most serious arson offence is:

**433. Every person who intentionally or recklessly causes damage by
fire or explosion to property, whether or not that person owns the
property, is guilty of an indictable offence and liable to imprisonment for life where**

---

9   (1994), 94 C.C.C. (3d) 525 (Nfld.S.C.).
10 (1954), 111 C.C.C. 30 (B.C.C.A).
11 Ibid., at page 43.

(a) the person knows that or is reckless with respect to whether the property is inhabited or occupied; or

(b) the fire or explosion causes bodily harm to another person.

2. Arson Causing Damage to Property

Where there is no danger to human life, a person who sets a fire can be charged under s.434:

> 434. Every person who intentionally or recklessly causes damage by fire or explosion to property that is not wholly owned by that person is guilty of an indictable offence and liable to imprisonment for a term not exceeding fourteen years.

Where there is a serious threat to the health, safety, or property of another person, a person who causes a fire or explosion can be charged under s.434.1:

> 434.1
>
> Every person who intentionally or recklessly causes damage by fire or explosion to property that is owned, in whole or in part, by that person is guilty of an indictable offence . . . where the fire or explosion seriously threatens the health, safety, or property of another person.

3. The Fraudulent Burning of Property

The offence of fraudulently burning property is contained in s.435:

> 435. (1) Every person who, with intent to defraud any other person, causes damage by fire or explosion to property, whether or not that person owns, in whole or in part, the property, is guilty of an indictable offence and liable to imprisonment for a term not exceeding ten years.
>
> (2) Where a person is charged with an offence under subsection (1), the fact that the person was the holder of or was named as beneficiary under a policy of fire insurance relating to the property in respect of which the offence is alleged to have been committed is a fact from which intent to defraud may be inferred by the court.

This offence applies to situations where, for example, a person burns down a building he or she owns to collect the insurance money. In *R. v. R.N.D.*,[12] a young offender was charged with attempting to defraud the provincial insurance company and with fraudulently burning property. The evidence was that he had been approached by the owner of a car worth approximately $11,000 and asked to get rid of it in exchange for a case of beer and $20. He

---

12 (1994), 89 C.C.C. (3d) 449 (B.C.C.A.).

drove the car to a field and set fire to it. Later, the owner filed an insurance claim that the car had been stolen. The accused was convicted of both offences. His appeal of the conviction for defrauding the insurance company was allowed, since he was unaware that the car was insured against damage by fire. The court dismissed his appeal of the conviction for arson, however. The offence required that the accused wilfully and for a fraudulent purpose set fire to the vehicle. The test for fraudulent purpose is the community's standards for dishonesty. The court held that it was open to the trial judge to infer that the accused knew that the car had a substantial market value and that it was being destroyed for a fraudulent purpose.

4. Arson by Criminal Negligence

436. Every person who owns, in whole or in part, or controls property is guilty of an indictable offence and liable to imprisonment for a term not exceeding five years where, as a result of a marked departure from the standard of care that a reasonably prudent person would use to prevent or control the spread of fires or to prevent explosions, that person is a cause of fire or explosion in that property that causes bodily harm to another person or damage to property.

(2) Where a person is charged with an offence under subsection (1), the fact that the person has failed to comply with any law respecting the prevention or control of fires or explosions in the property is a fact from which a marked departure from the standard of care referred to in that subsection may be inferred by the court.

In *R. v. Harricharan*,[13] the accused woke up one morning in his home, which was located in a rural area, to a loud bang. He discovered that the garage attached to his house was on fire. He ran to find the card with the emergency number written on it. He couldn't find it. Then he ran upstairs, packed a suitcase of clothes, threw them through the window, and jumped out. Then he got a ladder to climb back into the house to get more items out of the house. This time he collected more personal papers and clothing. When the smoke entered the bedroom he climbed out. By this time he was so exhausted that he went to the barn and collapsed. A neighbour driving to work saw the fire and called the fire department. By the time the fire department arrived, only the brick walls were left of the house.

Harricharan was charged with arson by negligence. It was argued that in trying to save his personal belongings instead of going for help, he had behaved in a way that was a marked departure from the standard of care of a reasonable person. He was convicted at trial, and appealed. The appeal court allowed his appeal and entered an acquittal on the grounds that there was no causal connection proved between the accused's failure to get help and the spread of the fire.

---

13   (1995), 98 C.C.C. (3d) 145 (Ont.C.A.).

C. CRUELTY TO ANIMALS

1. General

446. (1) Every one commits an offence who

(a) wilfully causes or, being the owner, wilfully permits to be caused unnecessary pain, suffering or injury to an animal or bird;

(b) by wilful neglect causes damage or injury to animals or birds while they are being driven or conveyed;

(c) being the owner or the person having the custody or control of a domestic animal or bird or an animal or bird wild by nature that is in captivity, abandons it in distress or wilfully neglects or fails to provide suitable and adequate food, water, shelter and care for it;

(d) in any manner encourages, aids or assists at the fighting or baiting of animals or birds;

(e) wilfully, without reasonable excuse, administers a poisonous or injurious drug or substance to a domestic animal or bird or an animal or bird wild by nature that is kept in captivity or, being the owner of such an animal or a bird, wilfully permits a poisonous or injurious drug or substance to be administered to it;

(f) promotes, arranges, conducts, assists in, receives money for or takes part in any meeting, competition, exhibition, pastime, practice, display, or event at or in the course of which captive birds are liberated by hand, trap, contrivance or any other means for the purpose of being shot when they are liberated; or

(g) being the owner, occupier or person in charge of any premises, permits the premises or any part thereof to be used for a purpose mentioned in paragraph (f).

(2) Every one who commits an offence under subsection (1) is guilty of an offence punishable on summary conviction.

The meaning of "unnecessary suffering" in s.446(l)(a) was considered in *R. v. Linder.*[14] The charge of causing unnecessary suffering to a horse was laid by an officer of the Society for the Prevention of Cruelty to Animals. The horse was a bucking horse and was being used in a bucking contest in a rodeo. The prosecution argued that unnecessary suffering was being caused by the use of a "bucking strap." The procedure was to place the horse in a chute with this strap loosely around the back of the horse's belly and in front of its rear legs. When the chute was opened to let the horse out, the strap was drawn tight, which had the effect of making the horse buck more strenuously. The bucking, which lasted for about 10 seconds, loosened the strap. The court held that no offence had been committed. The intent of the section was

---

14 (1950), 97 C.C.C. 174 (B.C.C.A.).

to make it an offence to cause unnecessarily substantial suffering to any animal. The court found that the strap did nothing more than excite or irritate the horse to more strenuous bucking. This did not cause any injury—not even an abrasion of the animal's skin.

A case that reached the opposite result was *R. v. Menard*.[15] The accused operated an animal shelter. Stray animals that were not claimed within a certain period were killed. The animals were placed in a small chamber that was filled with carbon monoxide. The evidence was that the animals died within two minutes but were conscious for 30 seconds, during which time they experienced pain and suffering. There was also evidence that the suffering of the animals could have been lessened by a simple modification of the system that was not expensive, and that the accused had been informed of this possibility. The court of appeal held that the killing of stray dogs was justified but that the accused could have easily modified his system so that the animals would not suffer. The court allowed the appeal and found the accused guilty.

Under s.446(3), a person who fails to exercise reasonable care or supervision of an animal, thereby causing it pain, will be considered to have "wilfully" caused the pain. However, this is only a presumption, which the accused may rebut by producing some evidence that he or she did not wilfully cause the pain, whether or not reasonable care was exercised.

Another presumption is in s.446(4), which states that a person who was present at the fighting or baiting of animals or birds will be considered to have encouraged or assisted at such fighting or baiting, in violation of s.446(l)(d). Again, the accused may rebut this by producing some evidence that, though present, he or she was not encouraging or assisting.

The purpose of s.446(1)(f) was considered in *Prefontaine v. R.*[16] The court held that the paragraph was intended to prevent the use of live captive birds in trap shooting of any kind.

2. Harming Cattle or Other Animals

It is an offence to wilfully kill, maim, wound, poison, or injure animals, or place poison in such a position that it may easily be consumed by animals. A person who does any of these acts in regard to cattle has committed an indictable offence under s.444. In s.2, "cattle" is defined as including a horse, mule, ass, pig, sheep, or goat. A person who does any of the above acts in regard to animals that are not cattle and that are kept for a lawful purpose has committed a summary conviction offence under s.445.

D. LEGAL JUSTIFICATION AND COLOUR OF RIGHT

Section 429(2) provides a defence to any charge of mischief, arson, or cruelty to animals.

---

15   (1978), 43 C.C.C. (2d) 458 (Que.C.A.).
16   (1973), 26 C.R.N.S. 367 (Que.C.A.).

(2) No person shall be convicted of an offence under sections 430 to 446 where he proves that he acted with legal justification or excuse and with colour of right.

A person acts with legal justification or excuse when his or her actions are permitted by law. This legal permission for acts that would otherwise be unlawful can be based on either common law or statutory law. For example, there are provincial statutes that allow the killing of a dog that is found injuring or killing cattle.

Recall that in general, "colour of right" means an honest belief in facts that, if they actually existed, would provide a legal justification or excuse.[17] However, simply having an honest belief is not enough to raise a defence under s.429(2): there must be reasonable grounds for the belief.[18] The accused must prove beyond a reasonable doubt that he or she had the honest belief; however, it is not necessary to prove that the right actually existed.[19]

In the following three cases, colour of right was a defence to a charge of wilfully damaging property.

In *R. v. Pimmett*,[20] the accused was charged with wilfully damaging a telephone pole that was located on his land. Many years earlier, a telephone line to a summer hotel had been erected across his property. The telephone company had never acquired a right to use the land for this purpose. Without deciding whether the accused actually had the right to remove the pole, the court held that the accused was not guilty because he reasonably believed that he had the right to remove the pole, which he considered to be a nuisance.

In *R. v. Adamson*,[21] the accused was charged with wilfully damaging another's land by crossing the land with a load of hay. The accused believed that she had a right to cross the land because the municipality had passed a resolution authorizing her to do so. While the municipality had the authority to open temporary roads across private property, a resolution of the municipal council did not have the effect of opening the road. In short, the resolution was merely a preliminary step before the municipality's decision became law. The court held that the accused had a colour of right for crossing the land because the municipality had the right to open temporary roads and the accused had an honest belief, based on reasonable grounds, that the resolution had that effect.

In *R. v. Johnson*,[22] the accused was charged with wilfully damaging the fence of Mott. There was some confusion as to whether the accused had a right-of-way over Mott's land. The court held that the accused had reasonable grounds for honestly believing that he did have a right of way. Therefore, he had a colour of right for taking down part of a fence that was blocking his use of the right-of-way. In other words, the accused may not

---

17 See defence of mistake of fact and mistake of law in Chapter Four.
18 *R. v. Ninos and Walker*, [1964] 1 C.C.C. 326 (N.S.C.A.).
19 *R. v. Lilly* (1983), 5 C.C.C. (3d) 1 (S.C.C.).
20 (1931), 25 C.C.C. 363 (Ont.C.A.).
21 (1916), 56 C.C.C. 440 (Sask.C.A.).
22 (1904), 8 C.C.C. 123 (Ont.C.A.).

have had a legal right or justification for damaging part of the fence. However, he had an honest belief, based on reasonable grounds, that he had such a right. Therefore, he was not guilty of the offence of wilfully damaging Mott's fence.

Notice that s.429(2) says that the accused must prove "that he acted with legal justification or excuse and with colour of right." This appears to state that both legal justification or excuse and colour of right must be proved in order for the accused to have a defence. However, the courts have interpreted "and" to mean "or." Thus, the accused may prove either legal justification or colour of right as a defence to a charge of mischief, arson, or cruelty to animals.

In general, a person who owns something may legally damage or destroy it. However, s.429(3) clarifies this right:

> **(3) Where it is an offence to destroy or to damage anything,**
>
> **(a) the fact that a person has a partial interest in what is destroyed or damaged does not prevent him from being guilty of the offence if he caused the destruction or damage; and**
>
> **(b) the fact that a person has a total interest in what is destroyed or damaged does not prevent him from being guilty of the offence if he caused the destruction or damage with intent to defraud.**

In *R. v. Surette*,[23] the accused damaged a car that was registered in his wife's name. He was charged with mischief for damaging her property. His defence was colour of right. He had purchased the car from lottery winnings but had put it in her name because he had some outstanding bills. He never intended the car to be a gift to her. The accused and his wife were separated at the time. She testified that her husband had paid for the car and maintained it. The appeal court upheld his acquittal. The fact that a car is registered in a person's name does not mean that person is the owner. Here, the accused had reasonable grounds for believing that he had total interest in the vehicle. A person can damage his or her own property as long as there is no intent to defraud.

Questions for Review and Discussion

1. Make up several examples of conduct that would be covered by the offence of mischief.
2. What is the meaning of "property" in Part XI of the Code?
3. What is the meaning of "wilfully" in Part XI of the Code?
4. In an arson case, which of the following would be sufficient evidence of burning? (a) blackening of the material, (b) scorching of the material, (c) charring of the material, (d) flames on the material, (e) blistering of the material.

---

23 (1993), 82 C.C.C. (3d) 36 (N.S.C.A.).

5. List the offences of arson. Which is the most serious? Why do you think this offence is the most serious?

6. Explain the difference between legal justification and colour of right.

7. Alec operates a slaughterhouse. He slaughters hogs by shackling them by a hind leg, hoisting them to a height of 5 metres, and then slitting their throats. He is charged with causing unnecessary pain and suffering to an animal, contrary to s.446(1)(a). Should he be convicted? What else, if anything, do you need to know? See *R. v. Pacific Meat Co. Ltd.* (1958), 119 C.C.C. 237 (B.C.).

8. Aran is in a music band. The group often practises in his basement late at night. His neighbour, Frank, can hear the music, and it prevents him from sleeping. Frank has called the police. Can Aran be charged with mischief? Explain. See *R. v. Phonix* (1991), 64 C.C.C. (3d) 252 (B.C. Prov.Ct.).

9. Al was the president of a union. He led a demonstration in the lobby of the building where the Ministry of Labour and a number of commercial offices were located. Al instructed the demonstrators that since the police would not let them go up to the ministry offices, no one should be allowed to go upstairs. The demonstrators then linked arms and blocked access to the elevators. Office workers testified that they were stopped from reaching the elevators. What offence has Al committed? Explain. See *R. v. Biggin* (1980), 55 C.C.C. (2d) 408 (Ont.C.A.).

Appendix A
NARCOTIC AND DRUG OFFENCES

The Controlled Drug and Substance Act (CDSA) creates a new scheme for the regulation of dangerous drugs and narcotics. These drugs and narcotics are now known as "controlled substances." The CDSA replaces the Narcotic Control Act and parts III and IV of the Food and Drug Act (FDA). Part III of the FDA concerned controlled substances, such as amphetamines, while part IV concerned restricted drugs such LSD. The CDSA came into force in May 1997.

Although the CDSA is the main piece of legislation controlling illegal drugs, the Criminal Code does have some specific sections aimed at illicit drug use.

Under s.462.2 of the Criminal Code, it is an offence to knowingly import or export, manufacture, promote, or sell instruments or literature for illicit drug use. These are summary conviction offences punishable for a first offence by a fine not exceeding $100,000 and/or a term of imprisonment not exceeding six months. For a subsequent offence, the penalty is a fine not to exceed $300,000 and/or imprisonment for a term not exceeding one year.

One other Code offence that involves drug offences is the laundering of the proceeds of crime under s.462.31, which was mentioned in Chapter Thirteen. There are parallel offences of laundering in the CDSA that are discussed below.

A. THE CONTROLLED DRUG AND SUBSTANCES ACT

A controlled substance is defined as a substance contained in Schedule I-V of the CDSA. The CDSA has included the term "analogue," which is defined as a substance that, in relation to a controlled substance, has a substantially similar chemical structure. The schedules in the CDSA list the substances that are controlled: Schedule I includes the most dangerous drugs and narcotics, such as cocaine and heroine; Schedule II includes cannabis, its preparations, derivatives and similar synthetic preparations; Schedule III includes the more dangerous drugs and narcotics that used to be in Schedule G and H of the FDA, such as LSD and amphetamines; Schedule IV includes drugs from Schedule G of the FDA such as barbiturates and their derivatives; Schedule V CDSA contains substances that were not previously included in the FDA; Schedule VII relates to section 5(4) and 5(6); and Schedule VIII relate to section 4(5) and 4(8) of the CDSA.

1. The Offences

The CDSA specifies the following offences with respect to controlled substances:

- Possession and double doctoring.
- Trafficking.
- Possession for the purpose of trafficking.
- Failure to disclose previous prescriptions.
- Importing and exporting.
- Production of a substance.
- Possession of property obtained by certain offences.
- Laundering proceeds of certain offences.

a. Possession and Double Doctoring

Under s.2 of the CDSA, "possession" means possession as defined in s.4(3) of the Criminal Code. Court decisions on the meaning of possession were discussed in Chapter Thirteen. Recall that there are two types of possession: actual and constructive.

Under s.4 of the CDSA, possession is a hybrid offence. For a summary conviction offence the maximum punishment is a fine of $1,000 and/or imprisonment for a term of six months. For subsequent offences the punishment is a fine not exceeding $2,000 and/or imprisonment for a term not exceeding one year. If the offence is treated as indictable, the maximum penalty is a term of imprisonment not exceeding seven years.

The following cases discuss various situations in which the accused were charged with possession. It should be noted that while most the cases used in this appendix were decided under the NCA, they are still useful under the CDSA.

In *R. v. Brett*,[1] the accused was charged with possession of a cigarette filter containing pentazoine, a prohibited drug under the NCA. When confronted by the police, he admitted that the filter contained the drug. He was convicted at his trial. He appealed, arguing that the Crown failed to prove that the amount of drug in the filter was usable. The appeal court held that the accused admitted that he was in possession of a prohibited drug; therefore, it was not necessary to prove that the amount of the drug was usable.

---

1   (1986), 41 C.C.C. (3d) 190 (B.C.C.A.).

In *R. v. Brady, R. v. Maloney,* and *R. v. McLeod,*[2] the accused were charged with possession of hashish. The accused were present while two others produced hashish and made cigarettes containing the substance. The accused did not smoke the hashish or in any other way handle it. The court held that the accused knew the other two persons present were handling a narcotic. However, since they did not have any measure of control over it, their mere presence while others were smoking hashish was not enough to constitute possession.

In a case decided under the CDSA, *R. v. Malmo-Levine,*[3] the British Columbia Court of Appeal found that the prohibition for marijuana possession was consistent with the principles of fundamental justice set out in section 7 of the Charter of Rights and Freedoms. But the court, in finding Malmo-Levine guilty, stated that although the "harm principle" is a principle of fundamental justice within section 7 of the Charter, there was a reasonable apprehension of harm to other individuals or society from marijuana possession that was neither insignificant nor trivial, therefore the deprivation of Malmo-Levine's liberty interest was in accordance with the harm principle.[4]

In *R. v. Clay,*[5] the accused was charged and convicted of possession of marijuana, possession of marijuana for the purpose of trafficking and trafficking in marijuana. The Ontario Court of Appeal upheld his conviction. He ran a store called "The Great Canadian Hemporium." He sold such items as hemp products, marijuana logos, pipes, and small marijuana plant seedlings. In addition, he was an active advocate for the decriminalization of marijuana. In this case, the Appellant, Christopher Clay, challenged the constitutionality of the cannabis prohibitions in the NCA, arguing that they violated his rights under section 7 of the Canadian Charter of Rights and Freedoms because there was the risk of deprivation of liberty through the possibility of imprisonment. The main issue in the case was the use of criminal law to penalize the possession of marijuana and Clay's main argument was based on the harm principle as a principle of fundamental justice. The court, in *Clay,* agreed with the court in *Malmo-Levine* that the harm principle was a principle of fundamental justice and stated ". . . given the harms identified by the trial judge and the other objective of the legislation, I do not agree that there is no rational basis for the marijuana prohibitions." In other words, there is a rational basis for the marijuana prohibitions.[6]

Courts have also considered the use of marijuana for medical purposes. In *R. v. Parker,*[7] the accused needed marijuana because he suffered a very severe form of epilepsy. Surgery had failed to control his seizures and he found that smoking marijuana substantially reduced his seizures. The court found that the prohibition on the possession of marijuana violated section 7 of the Charter because no provision had been made for a person who

---

2   (1972), 19 C.R.N.S. 328 (Sask.District Ct.).
3   (2000), 145 C.C.C. (3d) 225 (B.C.C.A.).
4   Ibid. at page 274-277.
5   (2000), 146 C.C.C. (3d) 276.
6   Ibid. at page 293. It should be noted that this case and *Malmo-Levine,* have been appealed to the Supreme Court of Canada and were scheduled to be heard in the fall of 2002.
7   (2000), 146 C.C.C. (3d) 193 (Ont.C.A.).

required marihuana for medical purposes. The court found that section 56 of the CDSA, which allows for an exemption by the Minister, was no answer to the deprivation of someone's rights because "Section 56 fails to answer Parker's case because it puts an unfettered discretion in the hands of the Minister to determine what is in the best interests of Parker and other persons like him and leaves it to the Minister to avoid a violation of the patient's security of person."[8] The court found that the violation, in this case could not be saved by section 1 of the Charter. The court struck down the provision on the possession of marijuana in section 4, but suspended the declaration of invalidity for twelve months to allow Parliament to fill the void.

Section 4(2) makes it a hybrid offence for a person to fail to disclose to a practitioner the particulars of previous narcotics or prescriptions for narcotics obtained within the previous 30 days when seeking a narcotic or a prescription for a narcotic. "Practitioner" is defined in s.2 of the Act as "a person who is registered and entitled under the laws of a province to practise in that province the profession of medicine, dentistry or veterinary medicine. . . "

If the offence is treated as indictable, it is punishable by a maximum of seven years' imprisonment, if it is a substance included in Schedule I, five years less a day for substances found in Schedule II, a term not exceeding three years if it is a substance found in Schedule III, and 18 months for Schedule IV substances. If treated as a summary conviction offence, it is punishable on a first offence by a fine not exceeding $1,000 and/or six months' imprisonment. For subsequent offences, it is punishable by a fine of $2,000 and/or one year of imprisonment.

b. Trafficking and Having Possession for the Purpose of Trafficking

Section 5 of the CDSA makes it an indictable offence to traffic in a narcotic or any substance represented or held out to be a narcotic or to have possession of a narcotic for the purpose of trafficking.

Traffic is defined in s.2 of the Act thus:

> **"traffic" means**
>
> **(a) to manufacture, sell, give, administer, transport, send, deliver or distribute, or**
>
> **(b) to offer to do anything referred to in paragraph (a) otherwise than under the authority of this Act or the regulations.**

Trafficking in a narcotic drug includes giving a drug to a person. However, conveying, or carrying, or moving a narcotic from one place to another for one's own use does not constitute trafficking.

The accused does not have to actually handle the drugs to commit the offence of trafficking. He need only exercise control over them. In *R. v. MacFadden*,[9] the accused phoned a delivery service and asked that a parcel be delivered to a garage operator. The parcel contained cannabis. The accused was aware of

8   Ibid. at page 261.
9   (1972), 16 C.R.N.S. 251 (N.B.S.C.App.Div.).

this fact but the garage operator was not. The accused was arrested before he could retrieve the parcel after it had been delivered to the garage. The accused argued that his actions did not amount to trafficking. The court disagreed and concluded that the accused did traffic the cannabis because he exercised control over it.

In *R. v. Rowbottom*,[10] the accused was charged along with others with a conspiracy to traffic in a narcotic. The accused had met with an undercover police officer and agreed to supply him with a quantity of marijuana. However, the accused insisted that the drug be delivered and payment made in Texas. At his trial, the accused was acquitted on the grounds that it was not proved that trafficking was an offence in Texas. This was necessary to establish the conspiracy charge in Canada under the Criminal Code, s.465(3):

> **Every one who, while in Canada, conspires with any one to [commit an indictable offence] in a place outside of Canada that is an offence under the laws of that place shall be deemed to have conspired in Canada to do that thing.**

The Ontario Court of Appeal ordered a new trial, affirmed by the Supreme Court of Canada, on the grounds that it was not necessary to prove that trafficking was an offence in Texas. There was ample evidence that the accused had committed the offence of trafficking in Canada. He had offered to sell drugs to a police agent, and under the definition of trafficking this act constituted the offence. It did not matter that the drugs had not been delivered or payment made.

In *R. v. Young*,[11] the accused was living in Vancouver and his friend, G., lived in Sechelt. The accused and his wife planned to move in with G. in his house in Sechelt. G., with money provided by himself and the accused in equal portions, arranged to buy one kilo of marijuana in Vancouver for $225 and for the accused to transport the drug to Sechelt. The accused was arrested and charged with trafficking while he was delivering the marijuana. G., called as a defence witness, said that it was for "our own personal use." G. also admitted that the drug was "half mine."

The accused contended that he had purchased the marijuana on behalf of himself and G. for their personal use, and that therefore it could not be said he was trafficking when he transported the drug to his friend's house. The court, however, stated that the fact the accused was transporting the marijuana not only for himself, but also for another, and the fact it might be used by others, sufficed to support a conviction of trafficking. The facts demonstrated there was something more extensive than mere conveying, or carrying, or moving of the marijuana incidental to personal use.

In *R. v Rousseau*,[12] the accused, a physician, was charged with trafficking after he sold prescriptions for narcotics. He was acquitted at his trial on the basis that his acts were not trafficking. The court of appeal held that the intention of Parliament was to prohibit all forms of conduct that result in the

---

10 (1992), 85 C.C.C. (3d) 575 (S.C.C.), affirming 76 C.C.C. (3d) 542 (Ont.C.A.).
11 (1971), 2 C.C.C. (2d) 560 (B.C.C.A.).
12 (1991), 70 C.C.C. (3d) 445 (Que.C.A.), refused leave to appeal (1992), 70 C.C.C. (3d) vi (S.C.C.).

circulation of a narcotic. The accused's actions fell under either the term "administer" or the term "sell." The court allowed the Crown's appeal and entered a conviction.

It is an offence to traffic in any scheduled substance. The penalty for trafficking depends on the schedule in which the substance is found. Persons convicted of trafficking in Schedules I and II are guilty of an indictable offences and are liable to life imprisonment, except where the trafficking is for smaller amounts under Schedule II.

Trafficking is a punishable either on summary conviction or by indictment. For example:

Section 5(3):

(a) subject to subsection (4), where the subject matter of the offence is a substance included in Schedule I or II, is guilty an indictable offence and is liable to imprisonment for life;

(b) where the subject matter of the offence is a substance included Schedule III,

a. the person, is guilty of an indictable offence and liable to imprisonment for a term not exceeding ten years, or

b. is guilty of an offence punishable on summary conviction and is liable to imprisonment for a term not exceeding eighteen months; and

(c) where the subject matter of the offence is a substance included in Schedule IV,

a. is guilty of an indictable offence and liable to imprisonment for a term not exceeding three years, or

b. is guilty of an offence punishable on summary conviction and liable to a term not exceeding one year.

c. Importing and Exporting

Section 6 makes it an offence to import or export any scheduled substance to or from Canada. The penalty for trafficking depends on the schedule in which the substance is found. If the offence is treated as indictable, persons convicted of trafficking in Schedules I and II are liable to life imprisonment. Where the subject matter of the offence is a substance included in Schedule III or VI, the person if convicted, is liable to imprisonment for a term not exceeding ten years and in Schedule IV or V, for a term not exceeding three years.

If the offence is treated as a summary conviction offence and the person is convicted of importing or exporting a substance included in Schedule III or VI, they are liable to imprisonment for a term not exceeding 18 months and for a substance found in Schedule IV or V, they are liable to a term of imprisonment of a term not exceeding one year.

Until 1987, there was a minimum penalty of seven years' imprisonment for anyone convicted of importing or exporting narcotics. This offence could be committed regardless of the amount of the drug brought into the country and even if it was brought in for personal use only. In 1987, the Supreme Court of Canada held that the minimum penalty was "cruel and unusual punishment" under the Charter and of no force or effect.[13]

d. Production of a Substance

Section 7 of the CDSA makes it an indictable offence to produce a substance included in Schedules I-IV. The penalty for production of a substance, like the other sections, depends on the schedule in which the substance is found. If the offence is treated as indictable, persons convicted of production in Schedules I and II, other than cannabis (marijuana), are liable to life imprisonment, but if it is cannabis (marijuana), they are liable to imprisonment to a term not exceeding seven years. Where the subject matter of the offence is a substance included in Schedule III, the person if convicted, is liable to imprisonment for a term not exceeding ten years and in Schedule IV, for a term not exceeding three years.

If the offence is treated as a summary conviction offence and the person is convicted of producing a substance included in Schedule III, they are liable to imprisonment for a term not exceeding 18 months, and for a substance found in Schedule IV a term of imprisonment of a term not exceeding one year.

In *R. v. Arnold*,[14] the British Columbia Court of Appeal stated that cultivation starts when the seeds are planted and continues until the plants are harvested. A person who has begun to cultivate does not cease to cultivate during times when the crop is left alone to mature in the environment created by the person. The Ontario Court of Appeal has held that the drying and curing of marijuana plants does not constitute cultivating.[15]

e. Possession of Property Obtained by Drug Offences

Section 8 of the CDSA makes it an offence to possess any property knowing that all or part of the property or proceeds was obtained directly or indirectly as the result of the commission of an offence or an act or omission committed outside of Canada that if it occurred in Canada would be an offence referred to in section 8.

If the value of the property is under $1,000, the offence is hybrid. If treated as a summary conviction offence, the penalty is six months' imprisonment and/or a fine of $2,000. If treated as an indictable offence, where the property is worth less than $1,000, the penalty is a maximum of two years' imprisonment. If the property exceeds $1,000 in value, the offence is indictable and punishable by a term of imprisonment not exceeding ten years.

13 *R. v. Smith* (1987), 34 C.C.C. (3d) 97 (S.C.C.).
14 (1990), 74 C.R. (3d) 394 (B.C.C.A.).
15 *R. v. Gauvreau* (1982), 65 C.C.C. (2d) 316 (Ont.C.A.).

It should be noted that, unlike the NCA, the CDSA has included, under section 8, the offences of conspiracy, attempts, and parties to an offence corresponding to counselling in relation to an offence committed under section 8 and section 9 below.

f. Laundering the Proceeds of Drug Offences

Section 9 creates the offence of dealing with property with intent to conceal or convert the property, knowing that the property was obtained as a result of the commission in Canada of a drug offence or an act or omission anywhere that would have been an offence under section 9 if committed in Canada.

This is a hybrid offence punishable on summary conviction by six months' imprisonment and/or a fine of $2,000. On indictment, the offence is punishable by a term of imprisonment not exceeding ten years.

2. Searches Under the Controlled Drugs and Substances Act

Sections 11-13 set out the powers of search and seizure in the CDSA. Warrantless searches are allowed in exigent circumstances in the CDSA and section 11(7), below, sets out the special provisions for these searches. Changes have also been made in the CDSA to bring the search and seizure section of the legislation into conformity with the Charter.

The authority to search under the CDSA is broader than under the Criminal Code.

a. With a Warrant

Section 11 of the Act reads:

> **11. A justice who, on an ex parte application is satisfied by information . . . that there are reasonable grounds to believe that**
>
> **(a) a controlled substance or precursor in respect of which this Act has been contravened,**
>
> **(b) any thing in which a controlled substance . . . referred to in paragraph (a) is contained or concealed,**
>
> **(c) offence-related property, or**
>
> **(d) any thing that will afford evidence in respect of an offence under this Act**
>
> **is in a place, may, at any time, issue a warrant authorizing a peace officer, at any time, to search the place for any such controlled substance, precursor, property or thing and to seize it.**

Section 11 of the CDSA expands the grounds for searches that were available under the NCA, as well as incorporating telewarrants that are found in the Criminal Code. This section also allows the police to search any person who is found in the dwelling-house (or any other place) at the time of the search. However, the Supreme Court of Canada held in *R. v. Debot*[16] that under the Charter, the officer, before searching a person, must have reasonable grounds to believe that the person searched is in possession of drugs.

The CDSA includes the grounds found in the NCA, but expands the provision for searches. It allows search warrants to be issued even where there is no reason to believe that there are drugs in the place to be searched as long as there are grounds to believe that, for example, there is offence-related property on the premises or "any thing that will afford evidence in respect of an offence under this Act." (See sections 11 (c) and (d) of the CDSA).

Unlike a warrant under s.487 of the Criminal Code, which can only be executed by day unless the justice is satisfied that there are reasonable grounds for it to be executed by night, a warrant under the CDSA can be used at any time of the day or night without the need for a special endorsement to that effect. Section 11 provides that ". . . issue a warrant authorizing a peace office, at any time, to search . . ."

Section 12 of the CDSA allows police, for the purpose of exercising any powers described in section 11 to enlist any assistance the police deems necessary and allows them to use as much force as is necessary in the circumstances.

In *R. v. Gimson,*[17] the Ontario Court of Appeal held that section 14 of the NCA allowed police to make unannounced entries and to break open any door if necessary to gain entry. The decision said that the provisions of the NCA recognize that police need special powers when dealing with drug offences. Here, the police had reliable information that a place was being used to sell cocaine and that the door would be barred. Therefore, the police were justified in forcing entry without announcing themselves. However, the Charter still applies, and when the police use force they must be able to justify its use. Similarly, in *R. v. Genest,*[18] the Supreme Court of Canada recognized that police may need to use force, but added: "The greater the departure from the common law and the Charter, the heavier the onus on the police to show why they thought it necessary to use force in the process of an arrest or a search." For example, the police may need to act quickly to preserve evidence or there may be a real threat that violence will occur. These powers have been continued in the CDSA.

b. Without a Warrant

Section 11(7) the Controlled Drug and Substance Act allows a police officer to, at any time search any place, at any time and seize a controlled substance, precursor, property:

> **. . . without a warrant if the conditions for obtaining a warrant exist but by reason of exigent circumstances it would be impracticable to obtain one.**

---

16 (1989), 52 C.C.C. (3d) 193 (S.C.C.).
17 (1990), 54 C.C.C. (3d) 232 (Ont.C.A.).
18 (1989), 45 C.C.C. (3d) 385 (S.C.C.).

The ability to search without a warrant has been limited by Supreme Court of Canada decisions.[19] The Court has held that a warrantless search of a place is only justified if it is not practical, because of "exigent circumstances," to obtain a warrant. Exigent circumstances generally exist where there is an imminent danger of loss, removal, destruction, or disappearance of the evidence if the search or seizure is delayed. So, for example, vehicles, vessels, and aircraft may in certain circumstances be searched without a warrant, because they move away. However, there must be reasonable grounds for believing that drugs are present. Mere suspicion is not enough.

In *R. v. McCormack*,[20] the accused was charged with possession of cocaine for the purposes of trafficking, as well as possession of cocaine and possession of a restricted weapon. When the police arrived at McCormack's apartment, they entered to ensure no one was present and then they waited outside for the warrant to arrive. The reason for the initial warrantless search was that they believed that McCormack's girlfriend had witnessed his arrest and they were afraid that she might have access to his residence and destroy the evidence.

It was held that the CDSA provided that a peace officer may exercise search powers without a warrant if the conditions of obtaining a warrant existed but it was impracticable to obtain the warrant by reason of exigent circumstances. The court also held that exigent circumstances can exist where a third party observed the arrest of the accused and the third party had access to the accused's residence and had the ability to destroy evidence. In this case, the court found that the police had ample information upon which to obtain a search warrant and the first condition of section 11(7) was satisfied. Given the concern of the police that the woman they believed to be McCormack's girlfriend, witnessed his arrest, exigent circumstances existed.[21]

The Supreme Court of Canada has held that where a warrantless search takes place and there is an allegation of a Charter violation, the onus shifts to the Crown to show on a balance of probabilities that the search was reasonable.[22] Chapter Five discussed the reasoning used by the courts in deciding whether evidence obtained from a search that violates the Charter should be admissible.

19 *R. v. Grant* (1993), 84 C.C.C. (3d) 173 (S.C.C.); *R. v. Wily* (1993), 84 C.C.C. (3d) 161 (S.C.C.); *R. v. Plant* (1993), 84 C.C.C. (3d) 203 (S.C.C.).
20 (2000), 143 C.C.C. (3d) 260 (B.C.C.A.), leave to appeal to S.C.C. refused 147 C.C.C. (3d) vi.
21 Ibid. at page 261-2.
22 *Collins v. The Queen* (1987), 33 C.C.C. (3d) 1 (S.C.C.).

Appendix B
YOUTH CRIMINAL JUSTICE ACT

A. INTRODUCTION

Since the turn of the century, Canada has had special legislation to deal with young people who break the law. A basic principle underlying this legislation has been that young people should be treated differently from adult offenders in the criminal justice system. In practice, this has meant that a separate court system and detention facilities exist for young people, among other things.

In 1982, Canada enacted, the Young Offenders Act (YOA). This legislation replaced the Juvenile Delinquents Act (JDA) and resulted in major changes in how young offenders were handled.

The philosophy of the JDA was that young people who broke the law should be treated as "misguided" and in need of care and protection. It looked at juvenile delinquency as a social welfare problem. So, for example, young people were not charged with specific offences but with "delinquency," which included not only criminal offences but also provincial law violations, such as truancy, as well as a catch-all offence of "sexual immorality and similar forms of vice." Thus, the JDA handled a wide range of youths, from those who committed true criminal offences to those with problems more related to child protection. Since the JDA was seen as helping and not punishing young people, rights and liberties were not emphasized. For example, court hearings often took place without legal representation for the young person.

In contrast to the social welfare approach of the JDA, the YOA set up a more legalistic system, one which acknowledged that the legislation is criminal law. So for example, it only dealt with youths who were charged with criminal offences. The YOA also raised the age for criminal responsibility from 7 to 12 and covered young people up to and including the age of 17. The YOA was amended in 1986, 1992, and 1995. There has been much criticism of the YOA, and much of it was based on misperceptions about youth crime, the legislation, and the operation of the youth justice system. However, statistics support the views of critics that, under the YOA, too many young people were being charged and incarcerated. In addition, despite alternative measure programs being available, these measures were being under-used for the more minor offences committed by youth.

In response to these issues, the government introduced legislation to tackle some of the issues related to the YOA. This legislation is called the Youth Criminal Justice Act and it received Royal Assent on February 19, 2002 and came into force April 1, 2003. The YCJA replaces the YOA.

The YCJA is intended to improve the youth criminal justice system by promoting accountability and responsibility in youth, by providing meaningful consequences for youth who commit offences, and by promoting their rehabilitation and reintegration.

B. MAIN FEATURES OF THE ACT

1. Preamble and Declaration of Principle

The YCJA contains a preamble and a declaration of principle that makes clear the purpose and principles of the youth justice system. Unlike the YOA, the YCJA provides a statement of the goals and principles underlying the Act and the youth justice system. While the Preamble is not legally enforceable, it contains significant statements from Parliament on how the legislation should be interpreted.

The Preamble provides that:

(a) Society shares a responsibility to address the developmental challenges and needs of young persons;

(b) Communities families, parents and others should work in partnership to prevent youth crime by addressing its underlying causes, to respond to the needs of young persons and to provide guidance and support to those at risk of committing crimes;

(c) Accurate information about youth justice, youth crime and the effectiveness of measures taken to address youth crime should be publicly available;

(d) Young persons have rights and freedoms including those in the Canadian Charter of Rights and Freedoms, the Canadian Bill of Rights and the United States Convention on the Rights of the Child;

(e) The youth criminal justice system should command respect, take account of the interests of victims, foster responsibility and ensure accountability through meaningful consequences and effective rehabilitation and reintegration. The most serious responses should be reserved for the most serious offences;

(f) the youth criminal justice system should reserve its most serious intervention for the most serious offences and reduce the over-reliance on incarceration of non-violent young persons.

The Declaration of Principle sets out key principles and provides guidance on the priority that should be given to the key principles in the YCJA.

Declaration of Principle:

Section 3(1): The following principles apply in this Act:

(a) the youth criminal justice system is intended to

(i) prevent crime by addressing the circumstances underlying a young person's offending behaviour,

(ii) rehabilitate young persons who commit offences and reintegrate them into society, and

(iii) ensure that a young person is subject to meaningful consequences for his or her offence

in order to promote the long-term protection of the public;

(b) the criminal justice system for young persons must be separate from that of adults and emphasize the following:

(i) rehabilitation and reintegration,

(ii) fair and proportionate accountability that is consistent with the greater dependency of young persons and their reduced level of maturity,

(iii) enhanced procedural protection to ensure that young persons are treated fairly and that their rights, including their right to privacy, are protected,

(iv) timely intervention that reinforces the link between the offending behaviour and its consequences, and

(v) the promptness and speed with which persons responsible for enforcing this Act must act, given young persons' perception of time;

(c) within the limits of fair and proportionate accountability, the measures taken against young persons who commit offences should

(i) reinforce respect for societal values,

(ii) encourage the repair of harm done to victims and the community,

(iii) be meaningful for the individual young person given his or her needs and level of development and, where appropriate, involve the parents, the extended family, the community and social or other agencies in the young person's rehabilitation and reintegration, and

(iv) respect gender, ethnic, cultural and linguistic differences and respond to the needs of aboriginal young persons and of young persons with special requirements; and

(d) special considerations apply in respect of proceedings against young persons and, in particular,

(i) young persons have rights and freedoms in their own right, such as a right to be heard in the course of and to participate in the processes, other than the decision to prosecute, that lead to decisions that affect them, and young persons have special guarantees of their rights and freedoms,

(ii) victims should be treated with courtesy, compassion and respect for their dignity and privacy and should suffer the minimum degree of inconvenience as a result of their involvement with the youth criminal justice system,

(iii) victims should be provided with information about the proceedings and given an opportunity to participate and be heard, and

(iv) parents should be informed of measures or proceedings involving their children and encouraged to support them in addressing their offending behaviour.

The objectives of the youth criminal justice system are to prevent crime, rehabilitate young persons who have committed offences, and reintegrate them back into society. Providing meaningful consequences for youth when they do commit offences contributes to the long-term protection of society. Young people are to be held accountable through interventions that are fair and proportionate to the offence.

Young people should be treated separately from adults under the criminal law, and a separate youth justice system is in keeping with the dependency, level of development, and maturity of a young person and provides special due process protections for them.

2. Measures Outside the Court Process

Many young people are brought into the court system for minor offences. The YCJA encourages a reduction in the use of the youth court and an increase in the use of non-court measures. The Act refers to these measures as extrajudicial measures.

In addition to the Declaration of Principles above in section 3, the YCJA includes specific principles to guide use of extrajudicial measures and states:

Section 4:

(a) extrajudicial measures are often the most appropriate and effective way to address youth crime;

(b) extrajudicial measures allow for effective and timely interventions focused on correcting offending behaviour;

(c) extrajudicial measures are presumed to be adequate to hold a young person accountable for his or her offending behaviour if the young person has committed a non-violent offence and has not previously been found guilty of an offence; and

(d) extrajudicial measures should be used if they are adequate to hold a young person accountable for his or her offending behaviour and, if the use of extrajudicial measures is consistent with the principles set out in this section, nothing in this Act precludes their use in respect of a young person who

(i) has previously been dealt with by the use of extrajudicial measures, or

(ii) has previously been found guilty of an offence.

Section 5 sets out the objectives of extrajudicial measures and states:

Section 5, extrajudicial measures should be designed to:

(a) provide an effective and timely response to offending behaviour outside the bounds of judicial measures;

(b) encourage young persons to acknowledge and repair the harm caused to the victim and the community;

(c) encourage families of young persons—including extended families where appropriate—and the community to become involved in the design and implementation of those measures;

(d) provide an opportunity for victims to participate in decisions related to the measures selected and to receive reparation; and

(e) respect the rights and freedoms of young persons and be proportionate to the seriousness of the offence.

The range of options for extrajudicial measures include verbal warnings and cautions from police, informal police diversion, such as referrals to community programs or agencies that may help the young person not to commit offences. This may include a wide range of community services including recreational services or counselling.

The YCJA requires police to consider all options, including informal alternatives before turning to the court process and laying charges.

3. Extrajudicial Sanctions Under Section 10

The Act allows provinces to set up what were known under the YOA as alternative measures programs. These programs have also been called diversion programs. These programs allow youths to avoid appearing in court. They are based on the idea that it is sometimes harmful for a young person to go through the formal criminal justice system.

Extrajudicial sanctions, in the YCJA, are the same as Alternative Measures under the YOA and are a more formal type of extrajudicial measures.

Extrajudicial sanctions may only be used if the young person admits responsibility for the offence and the Attorney General must determine that there
is enough evidence to proceed with the prosecution of the young person.
The sanction must also be part of a program designed by the Attorney
General and the young person must agree to the sanction or to participate in
the program. Under the YCJA, extrajudicial sanctions can only be used if the
young person cannot be dealt with adequately under an extrajudicial measure. These programs are an attempt to avoid stigmatizing young offenders.
Often, they require that the young person make restitution to the victim or
perform community service.

It was not clear whether provinces were required to set up alternative
measures programs. In a 1988 decision, the Ontario Court of Appeal held
that it was a violation of the equality rights under the Charter for some but
not all provinces to have these programs. On appeal, the Supreme Court of
Canada[1] held otherwise and stated that the YOA does not make these programs mandatory. These programs now exist in every province and territory and, as noted above, are extrajudicial sanctions programs under the YCJA.

4. Sentencing

Under the YOA, in general, trials of young persons were held in youth
courts. The provinces organized these courts and youths could be transferred to adult court under certain conditions. Under the YCJA all trials are
held in youth court. Once there is a finding of guilt then the sentence is
determined. A young person could receive either a youth sentence or, in very
exceptional circumstances, an adult sentence depending on the charge and
the circumstances surrounding the offence.

The YCJA includes a specific purpose, as well as a set of principles to
guide judges in deciding on a fair and proportionate sentence for a youth.
The purpose of a sentence, under the YCJA, is to hold a youth accountable
though just sanctions that ensure meaningful consequences for them and
promote their rehabilitation and reintegration into society.

Some of the specific sentencing principles include: the sentence that a
youth receives cannot be more severe than the sentence an adult would
receive for the same offence; the sentence must be similar to other youth sentences in similar cases; the sentence must be proportionate to the offence and
degree of responsibility of the young person; and the sentence must be, within the limits of proportionality, the least restrictive alternative. The sentence
option must be one that is most likely to rehabilitate and reintegrate the
young person back into society. It must promote in the young person a sense
of responsibility and acknowledgement of the harm done by the offence.

Under the YCJA, custody is reserved for violent offenders and serious
repeat offenders. This means that a young person cannot be committed to
custody unless he or she: has committed a violent offence; has failed to comply with non-custodial sentences; has committed a serious indictable

---

1   *R. v. S.(S.)* (1990), 57 C.C.C. (3d) 115 (S.C.C.).

offence; and has a history that indicates a pattern of offences; or, in exceptional cases, the young person has committed an indictable offence and the aggravating circumstances of the offences are such that to impose a sentence other than custody would not be consistent with the purpose and principles of sentencing. In these exceptional cases, the judge must give reasons why this is an exceptional case. Before making any custody order, the court must consider all reasonable alternatives to custody and must determine that there is no reasonable alternative that would be capable of holding the young person accountable in accordance with the purpose and principles of sentencing under section 38.

Section 38(1) states:

> **38. (1) The purpose of sentencing under section 42 (youth sentences) is to hold a young person accountable for an offence through the imposition of just sanctions that have meaningful consequences for the young person and that promote his or her rehabilitation and reintegration into society, thereby contributing to the long-term protection of the public.**

The YCJA gives youth court justices the power to impose adult sentences on youth in certain cases. Any youth 14 years or more who is convicted of an offence punishable by more than two years in jail, could receive an adult sentence if the Crown successfully applied to the court for an adult sentence. The test for an adult sentence, section 72, requires the court to determine whether a youth sentence would be of sufficient length to hold a young person accountable. The accountability of the young person must be consistent with the greater level of dependency and their reduced level of maturity. If a youth sentence is of sufficient length to hold the young person accountable, then the court must impose a youth sentence.

Young persons who are convicted of murder, attempted murder, manslaughter, and aggravated sexual assault, or have shown a pattern of convictions for serious violent offences are presumed to be subject to an adult sentence, if they are 14 years or older, unless the youth shows cause why they should receive a youth sentence, or the Crown does not oppose the application. A province may decide to set the age at 15 or 16 instead of 14.

Under the YCJA, every period of custody is to be followed by a period of supervision in the community. This is not parole. The judge, when imposing the sentence, clearly states in open court the amount of time to be served in custody and the amount of time to be serviced in the community. Two-thirds of the sentence will be served in custody and one-third will be served in the community. For example, if a youth is sentenced to nine months, the judge will state that the youth must serve six months in custody and three months in the community. Unlike the YOA, the YCJA requires that a plan for reintegrating the young person back in the community be prepared for each youth in custody to assist them when they are released. But the court can require the youth to serve all nine months in custody if the court, on reasonable grounds, believes that the young person will commit an offence causing death or serious harm before the end of his/her sentence.

5. Age

The JDA applied to children who were at least seven years old. The upper limit was set by provincial law and ranged from 15 to 17 depending on the province. The YOA set a standard age range of 12 to and including 17, which applied across the country. The relevant time for determining a young person's age is when the offence was alleged to have been committed. If the young person becomes an adult during the trial, the case still continues in youth court as if the person were still a young person. Children under 12 who break the criminal law are handled under provincial legislation, usually child welfare laws. These age matters have remained the same under the YCJA.

6. Offences

The YCJA only applies to young people who are charged with criminal offences. Young people who break provincial laws are dealt with under provincial legislation.

7. Pre-trial Procedures and Rights

a. Generally

Young people have the same rights as adults when detained or arrested—for example, the right to remain silent, the right to know the reasons for the detention, and the right to a lawyer. They also have additional rights in recognition of their immaturity. For example, there are special rules regarding the admission of statements made by young persons to the police and others who are persons in authority (see discussion below).

b. Fingerprinting and Photographing

The Identification of Criminals Act applies to young persons who commit offences that would, if committed by an adult, subject the adult to the Act. This Act applies to persons who are charged with committing indictable offences and allows for such persons to be fingerprinted, palmprinted, and photographed.

c. Right to Counsel

The right to counsel is treated very specifically and seriously by the YCJA at all stages, from the first detention through to any hearing to review the sentence or level of custody. A step-by-step process for encouraging young people to be represented is set out in s.25. It states that the youth has a right to personally retain and instruct counsel. This means that the lawyer must take instructions from the youth and not, for example, from the young person's parents. The police must not only inform the youth of the right to counsel but also give the youth the opportunity to consult counsel. A young person who appears in court without a lawyer will be advised of his or her right to a lawyer and will be given reasonable opportunity to obtain a lawyer. Where the young person wishes to obtain a lawyer but is unable to do so, the court must refer the young person to the province's legal assistance plan. If the province does not have a plan, or if the youth is not eligible for legal assistance, the court must direct the Attorney General of the province to appoint a counsel to represent the youth. Where a youth chooses to proceed without a lawyer, on the request of the young person the court can appoint a suitable adult to assist the young person.

In sum, any young person who wishes to have a lawyer is entitled to one even if he or she is not eligible under the province's legal assistance plan.

d. Statements Made to Person in Authority

Section 146 of the Act states that no oral or written statement made by the youth to the police or to any other person in authority at the time the youth is arrested or detained, or in circumstances where the peace officer or other person has reasonable grounds for believing that the young person has committed an offence, is admissible against the young person unless certain conditions are met:

Section 146(2) allows statement to be admitted when:

(a) the statement was voluntary;

(b) the person to whom the statement was made has, before the statement was made, clearly explained to the young person, in language appropriate to his or her age and understanding, that

(i) the young person is under no obligation to make a statement,

(ii) any statement made by the young person may be used as evidence in proceedings against him or her,

(iii) the young person has a right to consult counsel and a parent or other person in accordance with paragraph (c), and

(iv) any statement made by the young person is required to be made in the presence of counsel and any other person consulted in accordance with paragraph (c), if any, unless the young person desires otherwise;

(c) the young person has, before the statement was made, been given a reasonable opportunity to consult

(i) with counsel, and

(ii) a parent, or in the absence of a parent, an adult relative, or in the absence of a parent and an adult relative, any other appropriate adult chosen by the young person; as long as that person is not a co-accused, or under investigation, in respect of the same offence; and

(d) if the young person consults any person in accordance paragraph (c), the young person has been given a reasonable opportunity to make the statement in the presence of that person.

The exception to the above is given in s.146(3), which provides that these requirements do not apply where a young person gives a "spontaneous statement" to a peace officer or other person in authority before the officer or other person can comply with the requirements.

If the young person waives the rights under s.146, the waiver must be in writing or videotaped, or audiotaped, and where it is in writing, it shall contain a statement signed by the young person that the young person has been apprised of the rights being waived.

The YCJA provides under section 146(6) that a judge may admit into evidence a statement when there has been a technical irregularity in complying with section 146 (2)(b) to (d), and the judge determines that admitting the statement would not bring into disrepute the principle in the YCJA that young persons are entitled to greater procedural protections than adults to ensure that they are treated fairly and their rights are protected.

e. Pre-trial Detention and Release

Young people have the same rights as adults to be released while awaiting trial. Where young people are detained, the general rule under s.30(3) is that they are to be held separate and apart from adults unless this is not possible because of the youth's safety or the safety of others, or because there is no youth facility within reasonable distance. However, a young person who is 18 at the time of the detention will be detained with adults, unless the young person applies to the court to be detained in a facility for youth and the youth court is satisfied that, having regard to the best interests of the youth and to the safety of others, the youth should be detained in a facility for young persons.

Section 29 prohibits the use of pre-trial detentions as a substitute for child protection, mental health, or other social measures. It also requires that the judge (or justice of the peace) to presume that detention is not necessary for public safety if the young person could not be sentenced to custody if found guilty of the offence.

Section 31 allows the court to place the young person under the supervision of a responsible person as an alternative to detention.

8. Notice to Parents

Parents have a right to be given notice as soon as possible that their child has been detained pending court appearance under s.26. The notice, either oral or written, must give the place of detention and the reason for the arrest.

The parent must receive written notice where the young person is issued a summons or appearance notice, or is released on a promise to appear, or has entered a recognizance. Where the whereabouts of the parents are unknown or it appears that no parent is available, notice can be given to an adult relative who is known to the young person and seems likely to assist the young person; if no such adult relative is available, that notice can be given to any adult known to the young person who seems likely to assist the young person.

If the parent does not voluntarily attend the court hearing, the court can order the parent to appear. (See section 27)

9. Appearing in Court

a. *First Appearance*

Under section 32(1), when the youth first appears in court the judge shall . . . :

(a) cause the information or indictment to be read to the young person;

(b) if the young person is not represented by counsel, inform the young person of the right to retain and instruct counsel;

(c) if notified under subsection 64(2) (intention to seek adult sentence), or if section 16 (status of accused uncertain) applies, inform the young person that the youth justice court might, if the young person is found guilty, order than an adult sentence be imposed; and

(d) if the young person is charged with having committed an offence set out in paragraph (a) of the definition "presumptive offence" in subsection 2(1), inform the young person. . . . of the consequences of being charged with such an offence.

(3) When a young person is not represented, the youth court, before accepting a plea, shall

(a) satisfy itself that the young person understands the charge;

(b) if the young person is liable to an adult sentence, explain to the young person the consequences of being liable to an adult sentence and the procedure by which the young person may apply for an order that a youth sentence be imposed; and

(c) explain that the young person may plead guilty or not guilty to the charge or, if subsection 67(1) (election of court for trial—adult sentence) . . . applies, explain that the young person may elect to be tried by a youth justice court judge without a jury and without having a preliminary inquiry, or to have a preliminary inquiry and be tried by a judge without a jury, or to have a preliminary inquiry and be tried by a court composed of a judge and jury.

(4) If the youth justice court is not satisfied that the young person understands the charge, the court shall, unless the young person must be put to his election under subsection 67(1) (election of court for trial—adult sentence) . . . enter a plea of not guilty on behalf of the young person and proceed with the trial . . . .

(5) If the youth justice court is not satisfied that a young person understands the matters set out in subsection (3), the court shall direct that the young person be represented by counsel.

b. The Trial

The trial of a young offender in youth court follows the procedures used for trying summary conviction offences. As in any other trial, the Crown has the burden of proving the case beyond a reasonable doubt, and the youth can raise whatever defences apply. Witnesses are examined and cross-examined. The youth will be found guilty or not guilty. The trials are generally open to the public. However, s.132 allows the judge to exclude the public if the judge is of the opinion:

> **(a) that any evidence or information presented to the court . . . would be injurious or seriously prejudicial to**
>
> **(i) the young person who is being dealt with in the proceedings,**
>
> **(ii) a child or young person who is a witness in the proceedings,**
>
> **(iii) a child or young person who is aggrieved by or the victim of the offence charged in the proceedings, or**
>
> **(b) that it would be in the interest of public morals, the maintenance of order or the proper administration of justice to exclude any or all members of the public from the court room.**

10. Rules for Protecting the Youth's Privacy

The concern over burdening a young offender with a criminal reputation has led to strict rules regarding the release of information about young offenders. Under s.110 the name of the youth cannot be reported in the media until a youth court has found the young person guilty and imposed an adult sentence. Publication of identifying information is allowed where a youth sentence is imposed for a presumptive offence unless the court decides that publication is not appropriate after first balancing the public interest against the importance of the rehabilitation of the young person, or the Crown has notified the court that it will not be seeking an adult sentence. Publication is also permitted, on application to a youth court justice by a peace officer, when a youth is at large and is considered by a judge to be dangerous.

The rules strictly limiting the disclosure of information about a young person have been criticized. For example, school officials have complained that they need to know if a young offender, particularly one with a violent history, is in their school system.

Section 125(6) of the YCJA sets out under what circumstances schools and others may receive information about a youth and who may give out that information.

Section 125(6) states:

> **The provincial director, a youth worker, the Attorney General, a peace officer or any other person engaged in the provision of services to young persons may disclose to any professional or other person**

engaged in the supervision or care of a young person—including a representative of any school board or school or any other educational or training institution—any information contained in a records kept under section 114-116 if the disclosure is necessary

(a) to ensure compliance by the young person with an authorization under section 91 (reintegration leave) or an order of a youth justice court;

(b) to ensure the safety of staff, students or other persons; or

(c) to facilitate the rehabilitation of the young person.

11. Youth Sentences Under Section 42

a. Generally

The possible sentences are set out in s.42. They include:

- Reprimand the young person.
- An absolute discharge. This means that although the young person has been found guilty, a conviction is not entered. The young person can then truthfully state (e.g., on a job application) that he or she has never been convicted of a crime.
- A conditional discharge. This has the same effect as an absolute discharge except that the youth must satisfy certain conditions (e.g., attending school, report to and be supervised by the provincial director) before the discharge becomes absolute.
- A fine not exceeding $1,000.
- An order for the young person to make financial compensation to the victim.
- An order for the young person to make restitution of property to the victim.
- A community service order.
- Probation for a period not exceeding two years.
- Require the young person to attend a program at specified times and on conditions set by the judge. This is usually referred to as an attendance order.
- Allow a young person who would otherwise be sentenced to custody to serve the sentence in the community under conditions. If the young person violates the conditions he/she can be sent back to custody. This is called a deferred custody and supervision order.
- Order the young person into an intensive support and supervision program approved by the provincial director.
- A custody and supervision order, ordering that a period be served in custody and that a second period—which is one half as long as the first—be served, with conditions, in the community, the total periods not to exceed two years, or not exceeding three years where the penalty for an adult would be life imprisonment.

b. Sentences for Young Persons Convicted of Murder and other Serious Offences

The penalty for a young person convicted of first-degree murder under the YCJA is ten years, with a maximum of six years in custody, the remainder to be served under conditional supervision. For second-degree murder, the penalty is a sentence of seven years, with four years in custody and the remainder under supervision.

Section 42(2)(q) sets out the sentences for youth convicted of murder:

> **Section 42(2)(q) order the young person to serve a sentence not to exceed:**
>
> **(a) in the case of first degree murder, ten years comprised of**
>
> **(A) a committal to custody, to be served continuously, for a period that must not, subject to subsection 104(1) (continuation of custody), exceed six years from the date of committal, and**
>
> **(B) a placement under conditional supervision to be served in the community in accordance with section 105, and**
>
> **(b) in the case of second degree murder, seven years comprised of**
>
> **(A) a committal to custody, to be served continuously, for a period that must not, subject to subsection 104(1) (continuation of custody), exceed four years from the date of committal, and**
>
> **(B) a placement under conditional supervision to be served in the community in accordance with section 105.**

The YCJA also has an intensive rehabilitative custody and supervision order. It is a special sentence for serious violent offenders. The court can make this order if a young person has been found guilty of murder, attempted murder, manslaughter, aggravated sexual assault or has a pattern of repeated, serious violent offences, is suffering from a mental or psychological disorder, or emotional disturbance. A court can only make this order if an individualized treatment plan has been developed for the young person and an appropriate program is available; and the young person is suitable for admission to the program.

12. Adult Sentences Under the YCJA

As mentioned earlier, under the YCJA all young persons are tried in youth court. Once there is a finding of guilt, the court then determines the sentence. The test for adult sentences is set out in section 72 of the YCJA. If a youth sentence is sufficient to hold a young person accountable then the court must order that the young person is not liable to an adult sentence and impose a youth sentence.

However, if it is the opinion of the youth court justice that a youth sentence would not have sufficient length to hold a young person accountable, the court will impose an adult sentence.

Young persons who are under the age of 18 who receive an adult sentence are placed in youth facilities unless it is not in their best interest or it jeopardizes the safety of others. If the young person is over the age of 18 at the time of sentencing, he or she will be placed in an adult facility.

13. Termination of Sentence and the Use of Records

The philosophy of the YCJA is that a young person should not be unnecessarily burdened with a "record" as a young offender. At the same time, the YCJA recognizes the importance of maintaining records for investigating crime and of having a person's record if that person is again before the courts. The Act tries to balance these two interests.

There are two sections dealing with young persons and their records after the sentence is completed.

a. Termination of Sentence

Section 82 provides that, for many purposes, once the young person has completed the sentence or been given an absolute discharge he or she will be deemed not to have been found guilty of, or convicted of an offence. For example, once a young person completes the terms of probation, he or she is deemed not to have been convicted of any offence. This means that on job application forms, for example, the young person can state that he or she has not been convicted of an offence. This is the general rule. The exceptions are stated in s.82(1):

> **(a) the young person may plead autrefois convict in respect of any subsequent charge relating to the offence [in other words, the young person cannot be charged with the offence again];**
>
> **(b) a youth court may consider the finding of guilt in considering an application under section 63(1) (application for youth sentence) or 64(10) (application for adult sentence);**
>
> **(c) any court or justice may consider the finding of guilt in considering an application for judicial interim release or in considering what sentences to impose for any offence; and**
>
> **(d) the National Parole Board or any provincial parole board may consider the finding of guilt in considering an application for conditional release or pardon.**

Except for (a), which protects the young person, the above circumstances apply to situations where the young person has again become involved in actual or alleged criminal activity. Therefore, if the young person has no further dealings with the criminal justice system, the convictions will be treated as if they do not exist.

b. The Use of Records

Sections 114 to 116 set out the various organizations that can keep records of offences. Records may be kept by the police force responsible for investigating the offence and by the court that deals with the case. Also, certain government agencies and organizations may keep records. Where a young person is charged with an indictable offence, the records concerning the young person can be sent to the central repository maintained by the RCMP.

Section 119 deals with who can have access to these records. In general, disclosure of records is only allowed in certain circumstances—for example, if the youth is again before the courts for a youth or adult sentence, or is reasonably suspected of committing an offence. The records can be disclosed to the young person, to the young person's parents or counsel, to the Attorney General or the Attorney General's agent, to the court, or to any peace officer investigating an offence that the young offender is reasonably suspected of having committed.

Section 128 sets out the rules for non-disclosure and the destruction of records. In brief, the section provides that after certain crime-free qualifying times, records kept under ss. 114 to 116 may not be available for inspection. For example, records cannot be inspected after three years from the time a young offender was found guilty of a summary conviction offence.

GLOSSARY

ABSOLUTE LIABILITY OFFENCE The Crown only has to prove the *actus reus* of the offence to gain a conviction. There is no defence of due diligence.

ACCESSORY AFTER THE FACT A person who receives, assists, or offers comfort to a party to an offence for the purpose of enabling that person to escape.

ACQUITTED An accused who is found not guilty of the offence will be acquitted of the charge by the court.

ACTUS REUS The physical element of a crime. Latin for 'guilty action.'

AIDING AND ABETTING Helping or encouraging a person to commit an offence.

APPELLANT The person (or party) appealing the decision of a court.

ARBITRARY DETENTION A detention that is not based on any criteria; that is, it is random. Section 9 of the Charter guarantees the right not to be arbitrarily detained.

ARRAIGNMENT The stage in a trial when the charge is read to the accused, who then enters a plea of guilty or not guilty.

ARREST Detaining a person who has been charged with an offence for the purpose of bringing the accused before the court.

ATTEMPT Trying to commit but not completing an offence. An offence under s.24 of the Code: requires intent to commit the offence, some act or omission toward completing the crime, and non-completion.

ATTORNEY GENERAL The provincially elected representative and member of the Cabinet responsible for the administration of justice in the province.

BALANCE OF PROBABILITIES The burden of proof in civil cases. The burden is met if it can be said that it is more likely than not that the defendant has committed the wrong. See *defendant.*

BEYOND A REASONABLE DOUBT The burden of proof on the prosecution in a criminal trial. The accused's guilt must be proved beyond a reasonable doubt. See *reasonable doubt.*

BREACH OF PEACE A situation that involves a threat of violence, such as when a group of people are loitering and threatening to become violent.

CANADIAN CHARTER OF RIGHTS AND FREEDOMS Part I of the Constitution Act, 1982, which sets out individual rights and freedoms.

CASE LAW The body of law which consists of the decisions of judges. See *common law.*

CIVIL LAW Another term for private law. Also refers to the legal system used in many European countries and Quebec.

CIVIL WRONG A private wrong that gives the victim a right to sue for compensation in a civil court.

CLAIM OF RIGHT An honest belief in the right to possess property. A person who is in possession of property under a claim of right is protected from criminal liability for defending the possession.

COLOUR OF RIGHT Where the accused honestly but mistakenly believes in a state of facts that if they existed would give the accused a legal justification or excuse for his or her actions.

COMMON LAW The body of laws developed by judges following the rule of precedent when making decisions in cases. See *case law*.

CONSPIRACY An agreement by two or more persons to do an unlawful act.

COUNSEL A term used to describe the lawyer representing an accused.

COUNSELLING To advise, recommend, procure, solicit, or incite the commission of an offence.

CRIMINAL CODE A federal law that is the main source of criminal law in Canada. It sets out offences, penalties, and rules of procedure.

CRIMINAL PROCEDURE The rules that must be followed when enforcing the criminal law, e.g., the rules for making a valid arrest or the steps to be followed in a trial.

CROWN ATTORNEY The lawyer who represents the government in prosecuting criminal cases.

DEFENDANT In a criminal case, the person charged with a crime. In a civil case, the person being sued.

DETENTION A person is detained when he or she submits or acquiesces to the deprivation of liberty when the person believes there is no choice to do otherwise.

DISSENTING OPINION In an appeal that has been heard by more than one judge, the minority opinion.

DUAL PROCEDURE OFFENCE An offence that can be tried by summary conviction procedure or by indictment. Decisions on how to try these offences are made by the Crown attorney. See *hybrid offence*.

DUTY COUNSEL A lawyer "on duty" who is paid by legal aid to assist persons who have been arrested or detained.

FUNDAMENTAL JUSTICE (PRINCIPLE OF) A right under the Charter not to be deprived of life, liberty, or security of the person except in accordance with the principles of fundamental justice. Sections 8–14 of the Charter are specific applications of the principle of fundamental justice, e.g., the right to be secure against arbitrary search and seizure.

GENERAL INTENT OFFENCE An offence that requires an intent to achieve the immediate result. See *specific intent offence*.

(THE) HOLDING IN A CASE The court's decision in a case. The majority opinion in a case where more than one judge hears a case and more than one opinion is given.

HYBRID OFFENCE An offence that can be tried by summary conviction procedure or by indictment. The decision on how to try the offence is made by the Crown attorney. See *dual procedure offence*.

INCLUDED OFFENCE Also, lesser offence or lesser included offence. Refers to an offence that has some but not all of the elements of the major offence.

INDICTABLE OFFENCE The most serious crimes, which are tried by indictment.

INDICTED Where an indictment is brought against a person charging the person with an offence.

LAWFUL JUSTIFICATION Where a person's conduct, which would otherwise be criminal, is allowed by law.

LESSER INCLUDED OFFENCE Refers to an offence that has some but not all of the elements of the major offence, eg., theft is a lesser included offence to robbery. See *included offence*.

MANDATORY PRESUMPTION An element of an offence where a fact is presumed to exist until the accused disproves it. Mandatory presumptions are subject to attack under the Charter as violations of the presumption of innocence. See *rebuttable presumption.*

MARKED DEPARTURE TEST A basis for criminal liability where the accused's conduct is a "marked departure" from the conduct of a reasonable person. The *mens rea* is objective: Would a reasonable person be aware of the risk?

MENS REA The mental element of a crime. Latin for 'guilty mind.'

MISTAKE OF FACT An error as to some circumstance that results in a person committing a crime.

MISTAKE OF LAW An error as to the legal status of a circumstance or fact.

NOTWITHSTANDING/OVERRIDE CLAUSE Refers to s.33 of the Charter, which allows the federal or a provincial government to enact a law that violates certain sections of the Charter in certain circumstances.

OBJECTIVE FORESEEABILITY (or foresight) A description of a mental state where a reasonable person would have foreseen the consequences of the conduct.

OBJECTIVE *MENS REA* A description of a mental state that refers to the standard of a reasonable person in the position of the accused.

OBJECTIVE STANDARD (or test) Refers to the conduct of a reasonable person.

OFFICIALLY INDUCED ERROR A defence to a charge of committing certain offences that the accused broke the law because he or she was misled by an official in charge of enforcing the law.

PARTIES TO A CRIME The people who can be charged with a particular crime.

PERSONAL PROPERTY Tangible property that is not real property. See *real property.*

PRECEDENT (RULE OF) A precedent is a rule to be followed in similar cases. The rule of precedent states that when making a decision a judge

must follow the decisions of (i.e., apply the same rule of law as) higher court judges in cases with the same or similar fact situations. A judge must also attempt to follow decisions of same-level courts.

PRESUMPTION OF INNOCENCE The right to be presumed innocent until proven guilty in a fair and public hearing by an impartial tribunal. This right is guaranteed by the Charter. It means that the burden of proving the charge is on the prosecution.

PRELIMINARY HEARING OR INQUIRY A pre-trial hearing for certain indictable offences; can weed out weak cases and lets the accused see the Crown's case.

PRINCIPAL OFFENDER The party to an offence who actually commits the *actus reus* and has the *mens rea* for the offence.

PROSECUTOR The person, usually a Crown attorney, who presents the case against the defendant.

REAL PROPERTY Land and everything attached to it, e.g., houses and trees. *See personal property.*

REASONABLE DOUBT Real doubt that an honest juror has after considering all the circumstances of the case that results in the juror being unable to say, "I am morally certain of the accused's guilt." See *beyond a reasonable doubt.*

REASONABLE GROUNDS In general, reasonable grounds are grounds that would lead an ordinary, prudent, and cautious person to have a strong and honest belief about the situation at issue.

REASONABLE LIMITATION (or reasonable limits) A term used in s.1 of the Charter. Refers to a law that violates a Charter right but is upheld because it is a justifiable limitation in a free and democratic society.

RECKLESSNESS A type of mental element that may be required for a crime. Where a person does not intend a certain consequence but knows that the consequence is possible and chooses to run the risk that the consequence will not occur.

RECOGNIZANCE An agreement or promise made by an accused to pay a certain amount of money to the court for failing to appear on a particular court date.

RESPONDENT The person (or party) responding to an appeal of a court decision.

REVERSE ONUS CLAUSE An element of an offence that shifts part of the burden of proof to the accused in a criminal trial. Reverse onus clauses are subject to attack under the Charter for offending the presumption of innocence.

RIGHT TO REMAIN SILENT A principle of fundamental justice. A right of an accused person guaranteed by the Charter, which flows from the presumption of innocence, to say nothing pre-trial or at the trial. The right is consistent with the burden of proof being on the prosecution to prove the case against the accused.

SEARCH WARRANT An order issued by a justice of the peace commanding the police to search a particular place for named items.

SPECIFIC INTENT OFFENCE An offence that requires an additional intent beyond the intent to achieve the immediate result. An intent to further an illegal goal. See *general intent offence.*

STANDARD OF REASONABLE CARE The care that is owed to every person. Based on the conduct of a reasonable person.

STARE DECISIS Latin for "to stand by." Refers to the rule that judges must follow the decisions used in earlier cases when the facts are the same or similar. See *rule of precedent.*

STATUTE LAW Law (acts of the legislature) made by our elected representatives.

STRICT LIABILITY OFFENCE An offence for which the Crown only has to prove the *actus reus.* The accused will be convicted unless he or she can establish that he or she acted with due diligence.

SUBJECTIVE FORESEEABILITY (or foresight) A description of a mental state where the accused actually foresaw the consequences of his or her conduct.

SUBJECTIVE INTENT A type of *mens rea* where the accused actually intended the consequences of his or her conduct. Asks whether the accused was aware of certain circumstances or reckless or wilfully blind to certain circumstances.

SUMMARY CONVICTION OFFENCE The least serious criminal offences, which are tried by summary conviction procedure.

SUPREMACY OF PARLIAMENT Refers to the rule that within its areas of authority, Parliament is the supreme law maker. Applies to any law-making body.

SURETY A person who signs a recognizance with an accused and thereby agrees to be responsible for ensuring that the accused appears for his or her court date.

TRIER OF FACT In a trial with a judge and jury, the jury is the trier of fact, i.e., must decide what happened in the case. Where there is no jury, the judge is trier of fact. See *trier of law.*

TRIER OF LAW In a trial, the judge is the trier of law, i.e., must decide what law applies to the case. See *trier of fact.*

ULTRA VIRES Refers to actions that are beyond the authority of a government, e.g., when a government passes a law in an area over which it does not have authority; Latin for "beyond the powers."

WILFUL BLINDNESS A type of mens rea where the accused is aware of the need to make an inquiry but chooses not to, i.e., to remain ignorant.

VOID FOR VAGUENESS Refers to a law that violates the s.7 of the Charter (right to fundamental justice) because it does not give people fair notice of what conduct is prohibited.

INDEX